In Pursuit of Equity in Education

In Pursuit of Equity in Education

Using International Indicators to Compare Equity Policies

Walo Hutmacher

University of Geneva, Switzerland

Douglas Cochrane

*American Institutes for Research/Education Statistics
Services Institute, Washington, DC, U.S.A.*

and

Norberto Bottani

*Service de la Recherche en Éducation,
Département de l'Instruction Publique Genève, Switzerland*

Editors

Published in cooperation with
AIR/Education Statistics Services Institute, Washington, DC
Service de la Recherche en Education-SRED, Geneva
Swiss Federal Statistical Office, Neuchâtel

KLUWER ACADEMIC PUBLISHERS

DORDRECHT / BOSTON / LONDON

LC
213
.I52
2001

Library of Congress Cataloging-in-Publication Data

In pursuit of equity in education : using international indicators to compare equity
policies / edited by Walo Hutmacher, Douglas Cochrane, and Norberto Bottani.
    p. cm.
  Includes bibliographical references and index.
  ISBN 0-7923-6988-2 (alk. paper)
    1. Educational equalization--Cross-cultural studies. 2. Educational
indicators--Cross-cultural studies. I. Hutmacher, Walo. II. Cochrane, Douglas. III.
Bottani, Norberto, 1940-

  LC213 .I52 2001
  379.2'6--dc21

                                                 2001029806

  ISBN 0-7923-6988-2

Published by Kluwer Academic Publishers,
P.O. Box 17, 3300 AA Dordrecht, The Netherlands.

Sold and distributed in North, Central and South America
by Kluwer Academic Publishers,
101 Philip Drive, Norwell, MA 02061, U.S.A.

In all other countries, sold and distributed
by Kluwer Academic Publishers,
P.O. Box 322, 3300 AH Dordrecht, The Netherlands.

Printed on acid-free paper

Printed in the Netherlands.

Contents

Acknowledgement

In Pursuit of Equity in Education: Using international indicators to compare equity policies was authored by members of an Ad Hoc Group focusing on equity issues within the International Education Indicators Project (INES) of the OECD. It is the result of an international effort in terms of participation and of sharing support and resources. Authors come from seven different countries with six different languages and included participants from OECD and UNESCO. Members of the ad hoc group and authors were invited on the basis of their knowledge, expertise and interest and they were sponsored representatives of their respective countries. The editors are very grateful to these countries and the respective organizations and decision-makers for their interest and support for this endeavor.

Equity had been retained as one of the five major priorities for further work in INES at the General Assembly of the Project in 1995. The Steering Group of INES provided the organizational impetus for this effort by mandating an ad hoc group focusing primarily on the development of a coherent and overarching conceptual framework for educational equity indicators. Walo Hutmacher, member of the Steering Group, took the lead of this endeavor. He also presented a summary of the results as the ad hoc groups' report to the OECD/INES General Assembly in Tokyo in September 2000. The Assembly fully acknowledged the progress achieved, especially in the conceptual and methodological field, and approved the main recommendations of the ad hoc group. This book presents these results in their entirety for the first time.

The ad hoc group could not have progressed without the support of the Swiss authorities, through the Swiss Federal Statistical Office and its Deputy Director Heinz Gilomen. The "Unit for Educational Research " (Service de la Recherche en Education - SRED) of the Department of Education of the Canton of Geneva and its director, Norberto Bottani played a paramount role organising the meetings, assisting the members of the ad hoc group and insuring an effective and efficient style of work. Co-chairing the ad hoc group, Norberto Bottani, a former Head of the OECD Unit for Educational Statistics and of the OECD project INES, constantly provided focus and meaning for the participants. He also hosted the four meetings of the ad hoc group between September 1998 and November 1999, mobilizing his gracious and very helpful staff. In particular, Christine Emamzadah provided ongoing secretarial support, communications and travel assistance; Jacques Amos and Hugo Baillon contributed a variety of technical and substantive support throughout the meetings.

The ad hoc group and the editors are deeply indebted to the support of Eugene Owen, director of the International Activities Program (IAP) at the National Center for Education Statistics, U.S. Department of Education. His active interest and participation and the IAP sponsorship greatly helped support the ad hoc group and these successful results.

This book could not have been published without the contribution of translation and editorial support from the American Institutes for Research (AIR), which was made possible by David Goslin, President and CEO of AIR. Douglas Cochrane saw the value and viability of an academic publication, raised the necessary funds and managed the development and production of this book. With first drafts in hand, Valerie Aubrey helped consolidate an outline, so that all efforts could be woven into a coherent product. Carole Ashkinaze both translated from French into English four of the draft chapters and provided editorial support on all chapters. She worked tirelessly with the authors to provide clarity and to meet deadlines.

Final production of the camera-ready proof for the publisher was done by the Publication Group at AIR/Education Statistics Services Institute. Robin Gurley, Cecelia Marsh and Martin Hahn provided the line editing and proofing and Heather Block typeset the book. They all worked under very tight deadlines and over the holiday season to complete the camera ready proof in a timely fashion.

Even with the electronic age of the internet, email and faxes, it is not an easy process to coordinate an international publication. The editors wish to acknowledge all the contributors, who have worked very collaboratively and diligently, meeting numerous expectations and deadlines. We would also like to thank the numerous peer reviewers who provided comments to authors. However, we are responsible for any remaining errors and shortcomings.

The Editors
Geneva and Washington, DC
January, 2001

Introduction

Walo Hutmacher
University of Geneva, Switzerland

Fundamentally, this volume deals with the question of the knowledge base and tools which guide modern education policy debate and decision—particularly the concepts and data that education systems employ to define, describe, analyze, legitimize and monitor themselves. These are all social processes, engaging many stakeholders with unequal resources, opposing interests and diverging perceptions about what is opportune or possible to know and to make known or leave unknown. Dealing with the knowledge base is therefore no neutral endeavor.

As they operate nowadays, schools and education systems are highly evolved and complex social arrangements, aimed at transmitting from one generation to another what are considered to be legitimate and socially valuable knowledge, attitudes and competencies; i.e., in Berger and Luckmann's (1967) terms, the legitimate definition of reality, including educational institutions themselves. The institutionalization of schools and education systems, as they have evolved in Western societies since the 16th century, can be read as a history of conflict and debate over which ideas, representations, values, norms and judgments about childhood and youth, learning and teaching, etc., allow for the delimitation and structure of organizations called schools and education systems, and for legitimate action and decision within them. This knowledge base includes the definition of a legitimate dominant educational authority and of its prerogatives; of the processes for determining the culture (curricula) to be transmitted; of the methods by which that culture is to be transmitted and assessed; of the selection of teachers and learners; of the organizational arrangements (power structure, roles, positions); and of physical assets (for example, buildings and classrooms).

The complex knowledge heritage that guides all these processes, to a large degree, operates as "enacted theory," and represents at the same time a set of action hypotheses, which may become self-fulfilling. Three of its features should be underlined:
- Much of this knowledge is inevitably of a normative and prescriptive nature, because education is a particular kind of "people processing." Deliberate project-driven action of teachers on students in asymmetric power relationships is, by definition, driven by norms, values and standards

of human excellence.
*   Some of the knowledge enacted is formalized in laws, goals, rules,
    curricula, syllabi for teacher training, etc., but much is of a tacit nature,
    operating as self-evident truth reproduced from generation to generation,
    and legitimized through the (increasingly precocious and lengthy)
    experience of children within schools, rather than through formal
    instruction.
*   The processes of knowledge production, management, coordination and
    dissemination are embedded in political and/or bureaucratic power
    structures, where the source of legitimate knowledge ultimately resides in
    the hierarchical structure ("the boss is always right").

Over the last decades, social-science research has increasingly contributed
to this knowledge field, imposing its own methodology. The scientific community
may be divided among conflicting epistemological paradigms and ideological
orientations, but scientific research is controlled by specific principles of
knowledge production. Three of these seem particularly important in our context
because they contrast with those prevailing in the tradition of education systems:
1) Scientific research is primarily geared to descriptive-analytical, as opposed
to normative-prescriptive, knowledge; 2) It strives for explicit formulation of
theoretical concepts and assumptions underlying the research and argument,
and obeys its own rules of valid proof through empirical observation; and 3) It
privileges free examination and critical debate, with respect to theoretical
assumptions, as well as to methods of empirical verification, thus rejecting the
argument of authority. These basic principles may not be respected in every
single piece of research, but they can be invoked and, overall and in the long
run, they control research activity and help to legitimize alternative (though
admittedly provisional), more evidence-based knowledge.

Scientific investigation is increasingly a source of what pedagogical practice
and education policy consider "sound knowledge," on which to base action and
decision. The dominantly positivistic "R&D" (research and development) model,
with its linear sequencing from so-called fundamental research to practical or
political application, has recently come under heavy criticism for being too
simplistic. Alternatives would consider scientific research, policy and pedagogical
practice as partly autonomous social fields with their own goals, stakes and
rules, each characterized by ideological and epistemological plurality. Not all
scientific research is immediately considered relevant by the dominant forces
in the practice or policy fields. The limits of scientific knowledge are also more
frequently recognized, even by researchers. Yet, imperfect scientific knowledge
and data are often considered better than no knowledge at all.

As in other social fields, accumulated scientific evidence thus gradually
combines with existing "theories in action" within schools and education systems,
changing them through selective and oftentimes conflictive processes of

appropriation or, in Piaget's terms, of assimilation and/or accommodation. Results of scientific research are more frequently invoked in policy debate, either by politicians themselves, or more often by other stakeholders, though the trend towards increasingly evidence-based or evidence-driven education practice and policy is sometimes considered too slow. In this respect, a recent report of the Organisation for Economic Co-operation and Development (OECD) argues for instance, that "the knowledge base in education is dangerously small in relation to the volume of educational activity" (OECD, 1996). Highly industrialized countries spend on average nearly 6 percent of their GDP to run their education systems (OECD, 2000a), mobilizing an average of 5 percent of their total work force in education. But systematic investment in scientific research is far less intensive in this field than in others. Countries for which the figure is known spend only one quarter of a percent of their total education expenses on education research (OECD, 1995), as compared with more than 15 percent in such highly dynamic sectors as chemistry, pharmaceuticals, electronics and computer business.

Statistics and indicators typically figure among the tools for evidence-based education policies. And there is a renewed high demand for them as demonstrated by the success of the "Education Indicators Program" (INES) of the OECD. The aim of this volume is precisely, within this framework, to submit to discussion a proposal for a coherent and consistent, internationally comparable system of quantitative indicators focusing on the issues of educational equality and equity.

Such an endeavor raises a number of questions. Indicators are referred to here as statistics with strong policy relevance. They describe attributes of populations or groups, using measures of central tendency and/or variation, or something similar (a mean, a rate, a proportion, a probability or another statistic). The thrust on statistics is by no means a claim for an exclusively quantitative approach to educational issues. Indicators are only a part of the knowledge base of education systems, and many issues cannot yet be approached through statistical methods. But because in education large numbers are involved, statistics are privileged tools for measuring what is variable, what is possible and what is more or less likely, at least at the macro level of systems and policy. Statistics and quantitative indicators on basic dimensions of the society, especially on issues of equality and equity, are of particular importance in large, segmented and pluralistic societies, because they can provide a more balanced overall picture of the variety of experiences, relations and processes than would otherwise be perceived.

Of course, any statistic reflects a view of social reality, which, for the sake of clarity and critical debate, must be made as explicit as possible within a broader theoretical framework grounded in prior scientific work. At the same time however, statistics rest on political judgments and decisions about the relevance and importance of the collected information with respect to major policy issues. The development of statistics and indicators thus lies at the crossroads of scientific research and policy debate and decision. And both fields can be highly controversial, particularly in such sensitive areas as equality and equity in economy, society or education.

The contributions to this volume have been produced by an international group of scholars, researchers and experts[1] within the framework of the above-mentioned Education Indicators Program of OECD. Focusing on the issues of equality and equity in formal education systems, they aim primarily at 1) conceptual discussion and clarification, often on the basis of empirical evidence; and 2) the construction of a comprehensive and coherent system of indicators as part of the knowledge base that informs and guides policy debate and decision on these questions.

Contributions are grouped in four sections. The first deals with the major theoretical approaches and conceptual issues as they emerge from sociology, political philosophy and educational research. The second introduces the framework and rationale for the proposed equity indicator system and presents current perspectives of related work by OECD and UNESCO. A third section presents some international comparisons on equity issues based on recent international data. Finally, the fourth provides examples of the use of equity indicators for education policies within national contexts.

This introduction aims to guide the reader through the volume with some preliminary conceptual clarifications. It will also emphasize the policy relevance of an internationally comparable system of equality and equity indicators by underlining the major stakes for education policy in modern societies with respect to these delicate and controversial questions.

1.   Persistent social inequality in education

In modern societies, all human beings are considered to be free, having equal legal and political rights and equal dignity. This fundamental principle has been embedded in constitutions of Western democracies since the 19th century and is nowadays part of the Universal Declaration of Human Rights, adopted by the United Nations more than 50 years ago. In the meantime, representations, norms and values corresponding to these principles of liberty, equality and dignity have deeply permeated the prevailing visions of human beings and the human condition in modern societies, setting the context for major struggles against segregation and discrimination.

In Chapter 8, Cavicchioni and Motivans describe the gradual convergence of human rights and poverty reduction strategies throughout the world. They recall that the right to education is part of the more recent Convention on the

Rights of the Child, which has gained the status of international law since 1990. Through this most widely ratified international instrument, states of all signatory countries are bound to take responsibility for education provision. Educational disparities have emerged as a key issue in the less developed countries and on the development policy agenda during the 1980s and 1990s, and educational inequality has emerged as a global concern.

The main focus of this volume will be on industrialized countries, i.e., on the developed world. However, it should be remembered that, despite considerable variations and blurred boundaries, a major disparity separates this world from the developing world, where equal access even to primary education is not thoroughly achieved.

Institutional arrangements across industrialized countries differ widely, as do economic, social and political developments and trends. But in all of them, mass public education has been established to give all children and youngsters equal access to and opportunity in education. Formal initial education is organized by the state, i.e., by some form of public authority placed under democratic control. The historical option for a comprehensive and public "common school for all" is basic in the history of modern democracies, where universal education is recognized as essential to universal suffrage; and where, reciprocally, democratic decision-making legitimizes political options, including those having to do with the goals, content, structures, rules and methods of educational institutions.

At the same time however, education and educational systems lie at the heart of crucial tensions between formal civic and legal equality, on the one hand, and the inequality of real social conditions and positions on the other. Inequality is indeed integral to the operation of schools and education systems, because they distribute desirable goods unequally:

- Throughout schooling, students perform unequally in relation to prevailing standards; they receive unequal marks and rewards, obtain access to unequal tracks and curricula, achieve unequal knowledge and competencies, and attain unequal grades.
- After completion of schooling, the returns on investment are unequal, and unequal levels of education typically have major consequences in terms of economic, social and cultural inequality.

Until the 1950s, public education authorities and systems succeeded rather well in appearing predominantly as "neutral arbiters in the competition for educational resources" (Halsey et al., 1997, p. 254). Prevailing principles defined access to schools, achievement and outcome primarily as a function of individual merit, consisting of the addition of intelligence and effort. Under these governing principles, public schools and education systems were more or less generally presumed to allocate resources equally and fairly, and to ensure equal opportunity for all, regardless of birth.

This presumption became contentious during the 1960s and 1970s, as sociological research repeatedly demonstrated that in public education, working-class students, women and cultural, ethnic or racial "minorities" consistently had more limited access to learning and success. Major and systematic educational inequalities appeared not to be exclusively rooted in individual intelligence and effort, but to be related in complex ways to the basic inequality structure of modern societies. A number of prestigious researchers, ranging from Floud and Halsey (1961) to Coleman (1966); from Bourdieu (1966), Bourdieu and Passeron (1964, 1970) to Boudon (1973), Jencks (1972, 1979) and Husén (1975) should be recalled here, with many others, to underline the importance and wide international interest in this research issue. In Chapter 1 of this volume, Luciano Benadusi presents a critical review of the main theoretical approaches in this field. He also underlines the complexity of the question of how and why social cleavages significantly determine the outcome of formal education processes. Research continues, but despite increasing sophistication, as confirmed also by Douglas Cochrane's contribution on the U.S. education scene (Chapter 4), none of these approaches can be considered conclusive.

However, knowledge about the social roots of inequality at school has widened, at least within the circles of social sciences, educational policy and educational institutions, and equity has become a major issue in the educational policy debate. A wide array of policy measures—ranging from delaying the first major options in students' careers to providing increased resources, and from compensating for social and cultural "handicaps" to positive discrimination and affirmative action—aims to prevent, redress or reduce existing inequalities. Prominent examples would include Project Head Start in the United States, Educational Priority Areas in Britain or *'Zones d'éducation prioritaires'* (ZEP) in France.

These reforms have had varied successes in different national contexts, as ongoing observation and research show. But overall, the balance sheet appears ambivalent:

1. In conjunction with favorable economic and demographic conditions, access to post-compulsory levels of formal education and vocational training has increased since the 1970s throughout the industrialized world. The rate at which young men and women attain upper-secondary graduation has risen with each generation. At the end of the 20th century, it exceeds 80 percent in all but eight OECD countries, and in six countries (Austria, Germany, Iceland, Japan, Netherlands and New Zealand), it exceeds 90 percent (OECD 2000a, p. 147). Entry rates into tertiary education have also increased steeply; they reach at least 40 percent in 19 out of 22 OECD countries for which the data are available, and 60 percent or more in 9 of them (ibid, p. 157).
2. Inequality between women and men has diminished rapidly in terms of access, opportunities, achievement and attainment, no doubt under the

influence of rising feminist protest and affirmation. A major part of the above-mentioned increase in post-compulsory enrollments is actually due to women's growing involvement in upper-secondary and tertiary education.

3. Nevertheless, major inequalities of access, opportunities, achievement and attainment remain among students from different socioeconomic, cultural, racial and ethnic backgrounds. Moreover, educational advantages and disadvantages resulting from these factors appear to accumulate within generations and tend to be reproduced over the generation cycles, although to varying degrees from one country to another, as is shown for instance by Noël and de Broucker in Chapter 12.

All groups and classes confounded, the overall level of formal education of the new generations has risen to previously unexpected levels in terms of attainment, and gender inequality has dropped dramatically, indeed, even reverted. Still, considerable disparities remain within all countries, to varying degrees, along the major lines of social cleavage. A comparison of developments in 13 countries by Shavit and Blossfeld (1993) tends to demonstrate that a general rise of attainment levels is by and large compatible with the persistence of major inequalities in opportunities and attainment between social classes and between majority vs. minority groups, whatever their definition[2]. Inequalities also persist between rural and urban areas and among socially differentiated metropolitan areas as demonstrated by Douglas Cochrane in Chapter 15. But with rising numbers reaching higher attainments, the competition for educational goods operates at a higher level, while at the same time the inflation in attainment tends to diminish the differential economic and social value of mid-range diplomas. At the bottom of the scale, attaining what are now minimum qualifications requires higher investments in time and effort on the part of students and families than was required 30 or 40 years ago, but for lower returns than under previous conditions.

2.   Equality vs. equity

Some conceptual clarification is needed here to distinguish between equality and equity. In policy debate as well as in the research literature, the two terms often work as synonyms, particularly in the English-language use. This semantic confusion may signal that all identified inequalities are considered inequitable, but should they be? This critical question can only be addressed if the two concepts are used to define distinct, although interdependent, orders of reality.

2.1. Equality/ inequality

Equality typically designates an equivalence between two or more terms, assessed on a scale of values or preference criteria. Inequality thus characterizes a difference, a disparity or a gap in terms of advantage or disadvantage in material and/or symbolic resources, such as wealth, social recognition, prestige, authority, power and influence. Over the last decade, Bourdieu's (1986) conceptual framework describing and analyzing these resources as a configuration of three major forms of capital (economic, cultural and social) that individuals and groups can mobilize for their strategies, has gained increasing recognition in sociology as well as in educational research:

- Bourdieu refers to *economic capital* as the amount of material resources, mainly income and wealth. These are the most obvious and familiar factors of inequality since they determine access to basic assets such as nutrition, health care, housing comfort and safety, as well as to goods more directly useful at school, such as books, computers or private lessons.

- *Cultural capital* appears in three forms: 1) the *embodied* form consisting of durable competencies and dispositions of mind and body—which Bourdieu calls *habitus*—learned and indeed embodied by individuals, as a kind of "second nature," through lengthy experience and interaction with a given social environment (family, neighborhood, community, school, etc.) and that predispose their future interactions and strategies; 2) the *objectified* form of cultural goods (books, art works, etc.); and 3) the *institutionalized* form, such as academic credits and qualifications. The value of capital will vary with the markets in which it may be more or less advantageously used, and schools and education institutions operate themselves as such "markets." Here the embodied form of students' cultural capital plays a particularly important role, because education systems are culturally not neutral, but privilege the standards of human excellence of dominant social groups and classes. Dispositions and attitudes (language and behavior styles, work ethos, relationship to school, knowledge and learning, etc.), which students have acquired in different family and community environments, are therefore more or less akin to those valued at school, and are more or less rewarded. For school always assesses more than it teaches (Perrenoud, 1984), and the conversion of the embodied form of cultural capital into the institutionalized form depends not only on time and effort, but also on the distance between the culture valued at school and students' *habiti.*

- Finally, *social capital* is embodied in the networks of social relations among individuals and groups. Its volume depends on the size of the networks of inter-connection one can effectively mobilize, and on the volume of economic, cultural and social capital each of these others possesses. Coleman (1987) has added an important dimension to Bourdieu's conception by underlining a more qualitative aspect of such networks, i.e., the role played by variable loyalty, solidarity, trust and faithfulness among and within distinct networks of social relations. In relation to education, school and school work, the amount and quality of social capital in the child's environment (family, community, school) is of primary importance for fostering shared aspirations, mutual aid and support, exchange of information, ability to define and maintain standards and the capacity to mobilize available resources. The professional ethos of teachers as well as the characteristics of peer relationships at school should therefore be considered part of students' social capital. For instance, diversity in the classroom, i.e., the heterogeneity of its composition in terms of social origin and ability, consistently appears to be an important asset for school success of the weakest, without reducing achievements of the strongest (Grisay, 1993, Demeuse et al., in Chapter 2, Vandenberghe, Chapter 11).

Bourdieu would underline that the value of these major forms of capital varies in relation to different markets, including educational institutions, and that they are convertible into each other and can also compensate for each other. It is therefore clearly their combination that counts. This holistic approach opens a full range of new levers and strategies, which schools and education systems can actively develop in order to reduce inequality in access, treatment and results. Last but not least, this approach also allows the definition of a more comprehensive explanatory model susceptible to serve as the basis for relevant statistical measures and indicators, such as the one Luciano Benadusi proposes in Chapter 1.

It should be noted, moreover, that the major relevant preference criteria tend to be widely shared within and across industrialized societies. Thus, most people agree that it is preferable to be wealthy rather than poor, to occupy safe rather than precarious work positions, to be socially prestigious and influential rather than ignored or excluded, to share a wide network of influential social relationships and loyalties rather than to be isolated, etc. This shared nature of the preference criteria gives them a kind of social objectivity since in everyday social, economic or educational interaction they are enacted by most participants as part of the self-evident rules of the game. Individuals can hardly ignore them without cost, nor escape nor change them by their own will. Finally, the fact that they are shared in industrialized societies across national borders—although perhaps with varying emphases—increases the plausibility that a set of internationally comparable indicators can be developed.

2.2   Equity/inequity

In a way, inequality is everyday business in society and economy, and it is a major ingredient in schools' operation and in the experience of students, teachers and parents. However, as modern societies recognize equality as a major value, inequality calls for justification. Every teacher in his or her classroom knows that unequal grades, rewards or degrees require some kind of justification, which in turn presupposes some principles and criteria to judge the fairness, equity or justice of decisions and inequality. Such principles and criteria very often operate in an implicit mode, as part of the shared "tacit knowledge" of scholarly institutions, learned and embodied through the very experience of school rather than through formalized instruction; for instance, according to the meritocratic equation, *success = endowment + effort*. Equity judgments and feelings of being treated fairly or unfairly are therefore persistent components of classroom interaction and school-family relationships, where they are also under ongoing negotiation and debate. They may of course vary across the components of society and change over time.

The concepts of equality and equity thus clearly address distinct issues: the issue of "objective" advantage or disadvantage, in terms of Bourdieu's three forms of capital for instance, on the one hand, and the normative-ethical issue of the fair attribution/acquisition of resources, advantage or disadvantage on the other. Distinct as they are, however, they are intimately associated. The question of equity is pervasive because inequalities persist. But distinguishing between the two concepts is important because it opens up crucial questions: Are all inequalities unfair? And according to which equity criteria or principles are particular inequalities fair or unfair? Or, in less philosophical terms: Are all inequalities considered unfair, throughout social groups and classes and according to the same principles? Two examples may illustrate this point:

- Empirical research consistently shows a positive relationship between educational attainment and income: On average, better-educated individuals earn higher incomes. In other words, cultural capital converts into economic capital. Across OECD (2000a), the earnings premium for persons with a university degree compared to persons with "only" upper-secondary education ranges from about 35 percent (Denmark and the Netherlands) to about 80 percent (Finland, France, Ireland, Portugal, New Zealand, United Kingdom and the United States). Throughout countries, to a varying degree, women earn less than men of the same age and educational attainment. However, the three types of inequalities are not all considered inequitable to the same degree: 1) Income inequality related to educational attainment is hardly contested; education attainment appears to justify higher incomes. 2) Unequal returns across countries also appear socially unproblematic; international equalization of economic returns on education would typically be left to the market. However, 3) women's lower average earnings as compared to men's are strongly suspected to be unjust.
- This latter observation points to another important aspect of the relationship between equality and equity. Within modern societies, educational and other inequalities among individuals are typically considered as basically acceptable, as they are attributed to non-intended

and non-malleable biogenetic factors or idiosyncratic psychological development, and the like. On the other hand, educational inequalities among groups or categories of individuals, such as described by statistics according to gender, or according to socioeconomic, racial, ethnic or cultural backgrounds or geographical areas, are typically perceived as inequitable discriminations. The very existence of educational policies addressed to reduce them signals that they are considered at least partly inequitable and at the same time avoidable or amenable. Conversely, as Denis Meuret argues in Chapter 3, in order to be (considered) inequitable, inequalities must at least be (considered as) avoidable.

Which kinds of equalities are required by educational equity? Which, if any, educational inequalities are tolerable? These are the central questions addressed by Denis Meuret. Equity principles, criteria and beliefs are a matter of normative judgment. They are debatable, but before debate, they ought to be made explicit. Meuret gives an extensive overview of what existing theories of justice have to say about educational inequality, drawing on new developments in political philosophy since John Rawls' *Theory of Justice* (1971).

The by-way through political philosophy may surprise at first glance in the context of an effort on statistics and indicators, but several arguments clearly militate in its favor. Indicators on educational equality and equity must be firmly rooted in the more general, contemporary debate about equity and social justice in modern society. Political philosophy broadens the scope beyond education systems as such, inviting us to deepen and refine our concepts, and it also contributes to a more rational and balanced debate about issues on which polemics fed by interest structure tend to blur the scene. Finally, the philosophical debate on justice theories is one of the best sources for the generation of questions to be highlighted by equity indicators. However, the intention here is not to arbitrate or choose among different justice theories, but to use them for conceptual clarification. This approach permits Meuret to identify the dominant principles of justice that are actually enacted in schools and education systems as they are presently organized, as well as to formulate the kind of quantitative indicators that would suit the measurement of equity from the point of view of differing definitions of social justice. Together with Benadusi (Chapter 1), Meuret also sheds light on the complexity of the prevailing ethical configuration in modern societies, and on the delicate trade-offs between potentially conflicting values, such as liberty, equality, responsibility, effectiveness and efficiency.

3.   Equality and effectiveness

A still not-uncommon representation tends to deem schools and teachers (unfortunately) powerless to counterbalance the effects of pre-existing social and economic inequalities. This rather fatalistic interpretation places the locus of control for socially bound educational inequalities outside the education system; it excludes schools and teachers from responsibility for the problem, but also prevents them from being part of the solution. However, in line with the discussion of the three forms of capital, there is a rising awareness in schools and public opinion that the education system does not play a passive or neutral role in the process by which social, cultural and economic inequalities transpose into scholastic and academic inequalities, which in turn translate into socio-economic inequalities. Increasingly, questions are raised about how education systems deal with the differences between students, on the assumption that, in a diversified, pluralistic and unequal society where life conditions vary considerably, such differences are inevitable. Do education systems ignore, confirm, re-enforce or reduce differences and inequalities? And how do diverse national societies compare in this respect? These are issues on which an improved set of international equality indicators should help to shed light.

As they gradually move from traditional industrial configurations to some new (post-industrial, post-modern, information, consumer, network or knowledge) societal structure, industrialized nations become increasingly aware of the importance of successfully educating subsequent generations. Most at risk are 1) their external economic, scientific, technological and organizational competitiveness in a rapidly changing global marketplace; and 2) their present and future social cohesion against a background of increased segmentation, differentiation, plurality and inequality. For individuals, academic achievement and attainment are necessary—although less and less sufficient—passports to employment in an increasingly knowledge-based economy. The quality of their social and civic life also depends more and more on knowledge and competencies acquired during the early years of schooling, including the capacity for continued learning over the life span.

However, the rising international competition for increasingly mobile capital entails two contradictory constraints on nations and governments: to reduce taxes on the one hand, and to improve the qualifications of the work force on the other. This explains why education remains a top political priority in all countries. But as financial resources, at best, remain the same, new types of political levers and change strategies are being activated. During the 1990s, education policies have become much more output-driven, stressing the issues of quality, effectiveness and efficiency, and accountability, especially in terms of level of students' learning. For the sake of assessment and accountability, many countries have developed national testing of students' knowledge and skills at different stages of their educational careers. At the same time, they engage in international surveys for the sake of international comparison and benchmarking. Three recent examples at the international level underline this trend:
a. The Third International Mathematics and Science Study (TIMSS)

conducted by the non-governmental International Association for the Evaluation of Educational Achievement (IEA), which has measured and compared students' mathematics and scientific competencies at different stages of the education process. A record number of countries (45) participated in this survey, and the results have had strong media and policy impact in all of them.

b. Within its INES program, OECD launched its own Program for International Student Assessment (PISA) in 1997, aiming at the recurrent comparative assessment of knowledge and skills achieved by the end of compulsory schooling within and among participating countries (OECD, 2000b). All 28 member countries of the organization and four others engaged in its first survey cycle focused on literacy skills and self-assessment of self-regulated learning. Within this new framework, the issue of measuring students' outcomes on an internationally comparable and standardized basis gained intergovernmental status.

c. The International Adult Literacy Survey (IALS), initiated by Canada and the U.S., has mobilized some 20 OECD countries (OECD & Statistics Canada, 2000) for the measurement of literacy skills in the adult population since 1994. A new initiative on Adult Literacy and Life Skills (ALLS) is currently under discussion. While, until recently, the stock of "human capital" was measured through the distribution of educational attainment levels in the adult population, this is being completed now by the direct measurement of skills and competencies.

With significant differences across countries, these international studies also consistently highlight unequal achievement levels across social groups and categories. However, several contributions to this volume, drawing on these studies, show that, in reality, there is no necessary trade-off between high average achievements and equality (Demeuse, Crahay & Monseur in Chapter 2; Vandenberghe, Dupriez & Zachary in Chapter 9; Dewitt & Van Petegem in Chapter 14; Wildt-Persson & Rosengren, in Chapter 13). Countries such as Sweden, Belgium and Norway, for instance, show both high effectiveness and low socioeconomic inequality levels.

Despite the increased drive for effectiveness and efficiency, the issues of equality and equity remain among the major education policy priorities. OECD education ministers have emphasized "Quality education for all" (OECD, 1991), signaling clearly that quality cannot be played against equality. There is wide agreement also about the duty of governments to reduce inequality of access to education, learning opportunities and outcomes. Concrete measures are taken throughout the industrialized world, with unequal success under differing conditions. Increased equality remains a goal however and, with improving standards and average achievements, it is likely to be a moving target over the next generations.

Likewise, rather than expressing an egalitarian dream, as in the 1960s and 1970s, education policies on these issues are increasingly rooted in a realistic policy appraisal geared less at complete equality than at "managing the degree of inequality and disparity" in the twin perspectives of social cohesion and international competitiveness. In this sense, for instance, reducing the literacy gap between the most and the least educated, while raising the average literacy level at the same time, is becoming a major goal of realistic and effective education policy for the future, the outcome of which clearly depends on the reduction of educational inequalities across social groups and classes. Put in more statistical terms, and in line with Benjamin Bloom (1979), effective schools and education systems are called on to achieve three major goals:

1. to raise the *mean* achievement level,
2. to reduce achievement *variance* or *disparity*, and
3. to decrease the *correlation* between students' performance and their social background.

In this sense, reducing inequality is integral to fostering the quality of education systems. But as economic and societal conditions change, two additional policy concerns emerge:

First, accelerating trends towards a knowledge economy and society entail a very significant increase in the minimum competence threshold, below which a minimally fair equality of opportunities in the labor market, social life and civil society is simply not warranted. Consequently, whatever disparities remain, nobody should leave school without achieving such minimal standards, which clearly include at least a competent mastery of the basic cultural techniques (the "3 Rs" and computer literacy), as well as a number of social competencies (communicative, cooperative, etc.), and the desire and ability to learn throughout the life span.

Second, in line with the output-driven quest for quality, new policy levers and change strategies tend to modify the governance rules and structures of education systems dramatically under the major key words of "decentralization," "deconcentration," "subsidiarity" or "devolution" of power and decisions from central bureaucracies to local communities and schools. Such changes in governance models for schools and education systems actually represent full-scale experiments in every country, the consequences of which must be carefully and thoroughly analyzed and monitored. They are at risk indeed, not only of increased cultural particularization of individual schools, but also of greater inequality in resources and in the quality of learning conditions between schools. Wildt-Persson et al., make the case for the decentralization under way in Sweden (Chapter 13). Reflecting on New Zealand's recent experience with devolution, Roger Dale (1997, p. 281), raises the question of the *"commitment by the state to ensure the perpetuation of the public-good qualities of education that it alone can guarantee."* He argues for a twofold task confronting Western states if, in the new context, they want to create the basis for shared responsibility for education:

> Firstly, they need to address the question of how equality of resources and outcomes can be achieved under a complex system of governance in which particularism rather than universalism is an important guiding factor in the provision of education. Secondly, they need to address the question of how effective democratic accountability can be introduced into the system (*ibid.*).

4.   Indicators of educational equality and equity

This brings us back to the issue of the knowledge base. Indeed, "effective democratic accountability," in Dale's terms, requires a high-quality public knowledge base to be available for educational policy appraisal, debate and decision. There is an obvious need for more systematic, valid and credible knowledge and information. Reflecting on the history of data gathering and usage on segregation in the United States, Gary Orfield also makes this point in Chapter 6. Democratic governance, he says, accords "a very high value to, and strong protections for, the discussion and debate that help to dismiss error, discover truth, and legitimize the imposition on the minority of majority decisions," and he adds:

> While good information cannot, by itself, produce effective policy, it is very difficult to have a full discussion, to say nothing of good policy, without reasonably reliable information. Often the lack of information on issues of obvious significance is a sign that a society or its government does not want to confront the issue.

Particularly at the macro-level of education systems, the knowledge base on education issues necessarily includes a consistent set—a system—of quantitative statistics and indicators, covering the issues of quality of education as well as of equality and equity.

Until the end of the 1980s, most countries collected educational statistics mainly for the purpose of internal administrative, financial and political accountability, and the types of statistics collected varied according to national priorities and criteria. The development of internationally comparable statistics and indicators on education systems has made considerable progress since 1988, mainly through a shared effort of OECD member countries within the INES program. A whole range of indicators allowing valid comparison between countries has been published annually since 1992 in *Education at a Glance, OECD Indicators*, which has become a top-selling publication of the organization. This remarkable success of an international effort to coordinate conceptual frameworks, categories, criteria and methodological standards as well as resources testifies to a dual shift of education policies from a mainly national to an increasingly international perspective, and from mainly input-driven to increasingly output-driven, governance, stressing accountability with respect to quality.

The success of the INES program is also due to the consistent added value, which derives for every country from international cooperation in the field of education indicators. This added value derives in part from the sharing of the required conceptual groundwork, prior to any data collection—which can moreover mobilize the best internationally available scientific competencies for conception and debate. For the other part, such prior cooperation sets the groundwork for reliable comparison, benchmarking and monitoring of the relative forces and weaknesses of national education systems across diverse historical, cultural, institutional and political national backgrounds.

With respect to educational inequality, in most countries the facts are known through research; such knowledge may, however, be more or less dated and is rarely comparable over time and space. Few countries have developed some systematic and permanent approach for policy and governance-related description and assessment of the current state of inequalities, not to speak of monitoring change in this realm as it occurs over time and across social groups and classes. But, as Gary Orfield (Chapter 6) puts it:

> The more stratified a society is, the less likely there is to be widespread personal contact and understanding of problems, and the more important it is to have reliable data that show relationships and trends. In affluent societies, politics push concerns of the middle class, not of the minority of poor or of different ethnicities. At a time when international markets, growing migrations, and social-policy trends appear to be moving toward increased stratification, and economic opportunity is more directly linked to educational qualifications, such indicators are particularly important.

The goals of a system of equality and equity indicators are therefore, at a national level, to describe, discuss, monitor and inflect the state and change of educational inequalities, paying due account to the state and change of the global inequality structure in society. Such a system must allow for comparison over time as well as space, nationally and internationally. An international indicator system as proposed in this volume will permit comparison, benchmarking and monitoring of the relative educational inequalities across diverse education systems, each with its own historical, cultural, institutional and political background; and taking into account the overall inequality structures of their national contexts.

In a quasi-experimental perspective, the establishment of such a system at the international level can serve as a shared learning tool among countries, helping to answer complex questions such as: How (un)equal are the education systems of countries in comparison with each other, taking into account their diverse existing social, cultural and economic inequalities? How do inequality of access, opportunities and outcomes evolve over time and in relation to changes in other dimensions of social and economic inequality? What is the differential added value of schools and education systems, with respect to reduction of inequality, in different countries? How does inequality evolve in relation to changing structures, institutional arrangements and policy measures? How do recent changes in governance structures and competency devolution in education systems affect equality and equity issues?

Issues of equality and equity have been major concerns of the OECD-led INES program since its beginning, certainly since 1995, when the General Assembly retained them among its five major priorities. In Chapter 7, Tom Healy and David Istance document and review the coverage of relevant existing indicators in this respect. More has been done than might be supposed. In the recurrent editions of *Education at a Glance*, measures of dispersion typically accompany average achievement indicators. Some intergroup differences are also regularly reflected by breaking down indicators by age and gender, and more occasionally by occupation, educational attainment of parents, average income, region or other spatial entities. Moreover, existing data could be more systematically exploited in the perspective of equality, and in the near future, the results from the first PISA survey will be available, which include an internationally comparable measure of students' socioeconomic (SES) family background, and will therefore be of particular interest to those studying equality.

5.   A comprehensive conceptual framework

In the INES program, the guiding conceptual framework is based on a systemic model relating input, process and output of education systems with each other and with the specific economic, social and institutional contexts of respective countries. Building on this systemic approach, a proposal focusing on the issues of equality and equity in education systems is introduced and discussed by Denis Meuret in Chapter 5.[3]

Inequalities in economic, cultural and social capital characterize the context of education systems, and across generations they can be considered inputs to them as well as outputs from them, the question being precisely if and to what extent they succeed in reducing disparities. From this point of view, education systems can be represented roughly by the following figure:

The four categories at the bottom of the figure form the main organizing sections of the proposed framework. As education is not a final good, education systems should be measured not only in terms of what they recognize as their products (internal results), but also with respect to the consequences of these outcomes on individuals' life and on society, economy, democracy, etc. (external results).

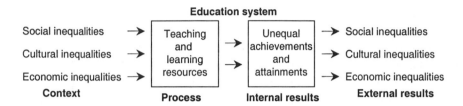

The major inequality structures of society should of course be taken into account by such a framework. Relevant research would identify the following more or less obvious and familiar groups or categories, in particular, as reflecting specific configurations of economic, cultural and social capital: gender, SES, level of education, racial, ethnic, cultural or migrant minorities and majority, sub-national, regional entities or urban-rural zones. Two additional criteria of social differentiation and inequality may be less familiar.

The first relates to the trend of growing metropolization, observed throughout countries, which has been gaining in importance. Metropolitan areas do indeed tend to divide into highly differentiated—often segregated and ghetto-like— environments, in which economic, cultural and social-capital advantages and disadvantages combine and reinforce each other. Douglas Cochrane describes this phenomenon for the United States in Chapter 15. In the development of an indicator framework on educational equality and equity, more attention should be paid to this dimension, as it also points to the close interdependence between urban and education policies.

The second is related to the issue of students with special needs (disabled, handicapped), who should clearly be included among the groups to be considered from the point of view of equality and equity. Peter Evans presents a renewed approach to this issue in Chapter 10, based on a recent review of OECD countries. Special educational needs, he argues, with a focus on the supply side, are

> associated with the need to supply additional educational resources in some form or other (e.g., modified teaching materials, special equipment, extra teachers, etc.). Thus, students with special educational needs are those who are in receipt of additional resources so that they can be helped to access the curriculum and benefit as fully as possible from it.

In this perspective, students with special needs are not only the physically disabled, but all those who may be in need of specialized learning environments of some sort because they are disadvantaged by factors that cannot be manipulated directly by the education system, such as social, ethnic or cultural origin. Evans shows the considerable magnitude of variation among countries in the proportions of students who receive additional resources. He also ascertains consistent differences between male and female students in this respect, throughout the countries that supplied data. But he draws attention to the fact that the attribution of unequal resources must itself be justified, also in the case of positive discrimination. The equitable amount and type of additional resources given to supplement disabled and disadvantaged students' learning needs must be seen in relation to the overall effectiveness and efficiency of education systems. Furthermore, the inequitable situation in which males are provided with more resources than females may be interpreted differently, under different perspectives.

6.   The need for equity indicators

Indeed, in addition to equality, a comprehensive framework must take into account the normative issues of equity, not as abstract philosophical questions but as an empirical issue. Indicators, in other words, should reflect what is considered fair or unfair by different stakeholders, and what are their criteria. To what extent do they agree or disagree among themselves? How do equity judgments, and agreement or disagreement about equity criteria, change over time and space?

This is no doubt the most innovative aspect of the proposed framework. It implies the measurement of the state and change of students', parents', teachers' or citizens' attitudes, expectations and judgments on equity in education, as they can be observed through surveys, for instance. Four main reasons militate in favor of this option:

1. Equity judgments, beliefs, criteria and principles, convergent or conflictive, are part of an education system's context and thereby of its *input*: Parents and students bring them into the school as part of their embodied cultural capital, which also configures their equity expectations. At the same time, they are at least partly learned and/or transformed through the schooling *process*. Feelings of being treated fairly form part of the education experience and they may well influence the students' readiness to comply with the rules of school life and to learn.
2. Differing experiences at school, combined with unequal social backgrounds, will also diversify learning about equity at school and in society. In the long term, this *outcome* dimension is of particular policy relevance for social integration and cohesion in pluralistic and unequal societies. Indeed, there are good reasons to think that the feelings, criteria

and principles experienced at school will have more general consequences on the degree of confidence and trust in economic and social relations and, more specifically, in the public institutions of modern democratic societies.

3. Actually, the policy relevance of equity issues and related indicators is even more immediate, because equity opinions, judgments and feelings— factors in citizens' opinions about policies pursued and in their ideological and partisan involvement—impact directly in the political arena through votes and elections. At the same time, they are malleable through communication and policy debate.

4. Ultimately, numerous observations seem to verify Toqueville's famous paradox: As social conditions improve and people increasingly consider they share the same humanity with equal rights and dignity, inequalities are more deeply experienced as injustices; feelings of injustice and envy occupy a growing place. (Recent developments in the field of gender inequalities may illustrate the case as an example: In many respects, gender inequalities have diminished during the last 50 years, but the closer women's condition comes to men's, the less tolerable residual gender inequalities seem to become—and the more active, imperative and comprehensive is the struggle against them.)

Social cohesion is not related only to "objective" inequalities, but also—and perhaps even more—to people's perceptions and judgments of their fairness. The political consequences of the quest for equity in education may well increase in the near future with the growing significance and impact of individual and collective outcomes and consequences of education systems, and with the growing critical potential resulting from rising levels of education. It seems therefore not only plausible, but crucial that a policy-relevant indicator system on equity issues in education allow for description, analysis and monitoring of the developments on this more symbolic and cultural dimension, within and across national societies.

———————————

There is no generally agreed-upon theory of education systems and educational equality and equity from which a coherent system of indicators could be derived. Any conceptual framework opens a field for the development of relevant indicators and at the same time delimits it. The options presented and discussed in this volume have the advantage of existing, but further clarification, refinement and consolidation will be needed. And this process should involve the scientific community, as well as people and organizations involved in the determination of education policy, because political support will be indispensable to ensure the development of a comprehensive and sustainable system of indicators in this highly sensitive domain.

Geneva, January 2001

Notes

1 Contributors come from Belgium, Canada, France, Italy, Sweden, Switzerland and the United States, as well as from OECD and UNESCO.
2 For a full appraisal of Shavit and Blossfeld's results, see Benadusi in Chapter 1.
3 The development of a comprehensive framework was the main goal set to the group of authors by the INES Steering Group. Meuret's proposal has therefore been intensely discussed within the group and can be considered as fairly consensual among the participants.

References

Berger P.L., Luckmann T.H., *The social construction of reality*, The Penguin Press, 1967.

Bernstein B., *Class, codes and control*, Routledge and Keagan Paul, London, 1971.

Bloom B.S., *Caractéristiques individuelles et apprentissages scolaires*, Labor, Bruxelles, 1979.

Boudon R., *L'inégalité des chances,* Armand Colin, Paris, 1973.

Bourdieu P., Passeron, J-Cl., *Les héritiers. Les étudiants et la culture,* Minuit, Paris, 1964.

Bourdieu P., "L'inégalité sociale devant l'école et devant la culture," in *Revue Française de sociologie, 3*, pp. 325–347, 1966.

Bourdieu P., Passeron J.-Cl., *La Reproduction, Eléments pour une théorie du système d'enseignement*, Minuit, Paris, 1970.

Bourdieu P., "The Forms of Capital," in Richardson J.E. (ed.), *Handbook of Theory of Research for the Sociology of Education*, Greenwood Press, Westport (Conn.) 1986.

Carnoy M., Levin, *Schooling and work in the Democratic State*, Stanford University Press, Stanford (Calif.), 1984.

Coleman J., et al., *Equality of Educational Opportunity*, Government Printing Office, Washington, DC, 1966.

Dale R., "The State and the Governance of Education," in Halsey et al., *Education, Culture, Economy, Society*, Oxford University Press, Oxford, pp. 273–282, 1997.

Floud J., Halsey A.H., "English secondary Schools and the Supply of Labour," in Halsey, A.H., Floud, J., Anderson J., *Education, Economy and Society,* Free Press, New York, 1961.

Grisay A., "Hétérogénéité des classes et Equité Educative," in *Enjeux, 30*, pp. 63–95, 1993.

Halsey A.H., Lauder H., Brown P.H., Stuart Wells A., *Education, Culture, Economy, Society*, Oxford University Press, Oxford, 1997.

Husén T., *Social influences on Educational Attainment*, OECD, Paris, 1975.

Jencks C., et al., *Inequality: A reassessment of the Effects of Family and Schooling in America* Basic Books, New York, 1972.

Jencks C., *Who Gets Ahead? The Determinants of Economic Success in America,* Basic Books, New York, 1979.

OECD, *Education at a Glance, OECD Indicators*, OECD, Paris, 1995.

OECD, *Knowledge Bases for Educational Policies*, OECD, Paris, 1996.

OECD, *Education and Equity in OECD countries*, OECD, Paris, 1997.

OECD, *Education at a Glance, OECD Indicators*, OECD, Paris, 2000.

OECD, *Measuring Student Knowledge and Skills. The PISA Assessment of Reading, Mathematical and Scientific Literacy*, OECD, Paris, 2000.

OECD, *Literacy in the Information Age: Final Report of the International Adult Literacy Survey*, OECD, Paris, 2000.

Perrenoud, P.H., *La fabrication de l'excellence scolaire*, Droz, Genève/Paris, 1984.
Shavit Y., Blossfeld H.P. (eds.), "Changes in Educational Opportunities in Thirteen
    Countries," in Shavit Y., Blossfeld H.P. (eds.), *Persistent Inequality. Changing
    Educational Attainment in Thirteen Countries*, Westview Press, Boulder (Colo.), 1993.

PART I

THEORETICAL APPROACHES AND CONCEPTUAL ISSUES

Chapter 1

Equity and Education
A critical review of sociological research and thought

Luciano Benadusi
Università La Sapienza, Roma, Italia

In this chapter, I will address the question of the relationship between equity and education from the point of view of the sociology of education. My analysis offers a critical review of the different approaches to this question found in the international sociological literature.

Then, in my summary and conclusions, I will draw a general outline of the possible normative conceptions of equity in education and try to show their implications for the choice of indicators. Finally, I will use a descriptive model to identify the most relevant variables in educational opportunity.

I will also try to suggest some indicators that could be constructed to describe and evaluate the functioning of an educational system from an equity standpoint. These indicators vary in a number of ways. Many of them are "objective" but a few are "subjective." Some refer to metric variables (quantitative indicators); others to categorical variables (qualitative indicators). Several focus on variables located outside the school system, while others focus on variables within it. And finally, while most are suitable for international comparison and assessment of entire national systems (that is, at the "macro" level), a few fit only at the "micro" level; that is, for an analysis bearing on single districts, schools or classes. Clearly, the first type of indicator is the most attuned to the general focus of this book, whereas the last could be helpful to local educational authorities and professional staffs evaluating specific equity-oriented micro-policies and instructional strategies.

1.   Different sociological approaches to educational equity

Educational inequality is one of most relevant issues in the history of the sociology of education, even if research has focused on the analytical question regarding the cause of inequalities or their change over time and space, rather than on the normative one (i.e., what people think about the relationship between inequality and equity). Sociologists have almost always assumed—explicitly or implicitly—a single definition of inequality in education and have sought to find empirical evidence of its presence and its dynamics, taking for granted that there is no other valid definition and that inequality is synonymous with inequity. Both beliefs are debatable; nonetheless, sociological research has produced a lot of evidence about how educational inequalities arise and vary (or not) among different countries and over time. We can utilize these findings to elaborate specific policies to reduce inequality and even to debate the legitimacy of inequality from a generally normative point of view. Whether produced by sociologists or by social actors in everyday life, factual (causal) analysis does in fact influence the establishment of value judgments, just as the reverse also occurs. Many conflicting normative views about educational inequalities result from different representations of how and why inequalities arise—not from differences in the principles of equity used. Hence, if as Meuret proposes (Chapter 5 on indicators), we take the traditional set of equality indicators, which tend to be biased by an "objectivist" point of view, and extend them to embrace some indicators about equity beliefs, we need to discover factual representations of relevant social actors, not only normative ones. So, in reviewing the sociological literature on inequality in education, we try to clarify the relationship between equality and equity, and to establish a comprehensive set of possible equity indicators, many of which are also included in the system outlined in this book.

Next we examine four sociological theoretical approaches to educational inequality, characterized by analytical differences and, to some extent, by normative ones (although these last often remain implicit). We are aware that our selection and classification are subject to question, as are all others. The criterion leading to our choice has been the anticipated relevance with respect to equity, the analytical focus of this review. Note also that the lines of research selected are several of the most theoretically characterized approaches and not those more empirically oriented. We could have assembled this second kind of research under the label "methodological empiricism," as others have done, and reviewed the often important results they have reached. We will not do so for two reasons. First, because this would make our work too long and, secondly, because examining the theoretical approaches lets us understand better how differently sociologists deal with the factual and normative aspects of equity and equality in education.[1] We will deal with comparative analysis of inequality of educational opportunity, however, because it is very relevant to the international focus of the book.

The four theoretical approaches reviewed below are:
1. the functionalist approach;
2. the social and cultural reproduction theory;
3. cultural relativism and pluralism; and

4. methodological individualism.

After reviewing these approaches, we will examine one empirical line of research: international comparisons of inequality of educational opportunity.

1.1.   The functionalist approach

This approach emerged within the functionalist theoretical tradition and was pioneered, in the most classic way, by Durkheim and Parsons. Educational inequalities, according to this view, stem from two kinds of factors:

- ascription factors, such as social class or stratum, gender, ethnic group or nationality; and
- achievement factors that are identifiable, on the one hand, with personal natural endowment, and on the other, with the will of the individual to use, cultivate and enrich this endowment (ability plus effort).

Only the second kind of factors were considered functional, and consequently just or equitable, for a modern society, whereas the first were rejected as residual traces of pre-modern society, in which the rules of legitimization were radically different. So, Durkheim (1962, pp. 365–71) contrasted the "constrained social division" dating from ancient society with the "spontaneous social division" that, insofar as it is based on individual merit, is ethically justified and potentially shared by everybody. (Durkheim was speaking about the social division of work, but his theory is equally relevant to the distribution of educational goods.) Within a society said to be characterized by "a growing universalism" (Parsons, 1970), an evolutionist and holistic claim that has often been criticized by the subsequent generation of sociologists, the merit principle is expected to prevail in the end.

In short, we are dealing with a meritocratic interpretation of the principle of equity that seems quite close to the more recent idea of "liberal equality of opportunity," as formulated by Rawls (1982)—who envisions a broader conception of equity relevant for education (see Meuret, 1999)—or to the "just meritocracy" of Bell (1974).

The analytical and normative features of this approach are reflected, in part, in two different lines of empirical research:

- studies aimed at exploring the dynamic of so-called "cultural deprivation," considered to be the main cause of unequal outputs in school and a result of disadvantageous modalities of primary socialization for low-status groups ("deficit theory"); and
- studies aimed at finding out how different variables of ascription or achievement affect attainments—educational, in a first stage, and occupational, in the two subsequent stages (the so-called "social attainment research").

According to the logic behind this and all the sociological studies informed by the structural-functionalist paradigm, equity with respect to output may be taken for granted whenever the dependent variables (with respect to education and occupational status attained) appear to correlate with those independent variables that are linked to achievement (e.g., student's IQ with respect to scholastic attainment and level of education completed with respect to first job obtained). Equity may *not* be assumed when the dependent variables are linked to the ascription pattern (e.g., gender, race, or economic, social and educational status of the student's family). In order to grasp the value of the educational output indicators in terms of equity, the nature of the overall socioeconomic context (level of industrialization, modernization, etc.) should be taken into consideration as well; according to this theoretical approach, this overall context strictly influences the functioning of all social sub-systems, including school.

On the supply side (or, more precisely, looking at the process rather than at the result), one indicator that may be meaningful from this theoretical standpoint is the amount of resources allocated to compensatory education (or, more generally, to policies aimed at increasing equality of opportunity). In such a perspective, we can hold that equity of treatment requires some kind of compensatory policy rather than simply equality of educational provisions. So, another appropriate indicator of equity may be a reverse correlation between public expenditure per student and her/his socioeconomic status.

1.2.   The social or cultural reproduction theory

In spite of Parsons' effort to include a theory of agency[2] within a theory of system, the analytical focus of the structural-functionalist approach remained essentially holistic and, to some extent, deterministic. At the end of the 1960s, as this approach started losing favor, another holistic and (more or less) deterministic approach to the causes of educational inequalities took precedence and prevailed for a long time in the sociology of education (at least in Europe): the social or cultural reproduction theory. The logic underlying such an approach appears similar to functionalism with respect to its methodological aspects, but its propositional and ideological nature is actually the opposite. Here the structural and/or functional constraints determine a strict process of reproduction of social-class hierarchy, instead of responding to the general needs of society. Just as social determinism was evolutionist and consensual from a functionalist point of view, it becomes static and conflictual[3] for the reproduction theorists.

The archetype of equity or justice implicit in these theories is still equality of opportunity among groups (essentially social classes), but with a different and more radical meaning than that espoused in functionalism. Whatever the indicators of educational inequality—unequal access to the school system or to the school's specific levels and tracks, disparity in the final output of schooling (considered in terms of either attainment or achievement[4])—the implicit or explicit theoretical assumption was the same: Inequalities among groups are produced by social constraints and not by genetic endowments and individual choices. No relevance is attributed by this approach to different individual aptitudes. Insofar as they are unevenly distributed among social groups (social classes or fractions of classes), these spring from social privilege and not from natural gifts, as "charismatic ideology" would have us believe (Bourdieu, Passeron, 1971).

Nevertheless, the crucial point is different. Reproduction theorists convert the optimistic attitude of the functionalists into a radical pessimism: All inequalities are inextricably interwoven into the global structure of our society, they say, and no educational reform can break this systemic coercion. Furthermore, it is worth noting that this theory states that educational systems also contribute to the reproduction of unjust inequalities in a "subjectivist" way; that is, by diffusing beliefs that legitimize such inequalities. Functionalist theory, instead, recognized the schools' role in spreading beliefs in tune with achievement values. But, in both cases, the claims were theoretically rather than empirically founded.

We can distinguish two different versions within this approach: one emphasizes the direct effects of structural factors (identified with parent's position in the social division of work), and another underlines the importance of cultural factors that mediate structural effects on individual behavior. Whereas the first direction may be represented by Bowles and Gintis and by Althusser, among others, the second is best represented by Bourdieu, its most influential exponent, and partly by Bernstein who draws a more abstract and complex picture of the cultural reproduction process. I would like to take a closer look at Bourdieu's point of view.

The French sociologist (see Bourdieu, Passeron, 1972; Bourdieu, 1978) is prominently known for the concept of "cultural capital" that has proven to be very useful for understanding the mechanisms determining educational groups' inequalities. It is actually less theoretically loaded with respect to the concept of "habitus" or "class ethos" that is at the heart of his conception of a reproduction process, and implies the individual's total compliance to external forces acting on them without their awareness. Individuals become an instrument of the culture of the group to which they belong and of the structurally based hierarchy between the dominant and dominated cultures. By virtue of its hidden influence, individuals are induced to want what scholastic and occupational status society allows them to attain, as members of particular social classes or sub-classes. A sort of "sour grapes" mechanism (Elster, 1989) operates within every process of social selection inside schools, making the exclusion of dominated groups from the most prestigious educational and occupational positions appear to be self-exclusion.

The concept of cultural reproduction, as formulated by Bourdieu, implies some interesting theoretical and practical consequences:

a) Educational inequalities are claimed to be explained entirely by social inequalities (conceived in such a manner that even disparities in cultural capital are taken into account) and by their effects on youngsters' educationally relevant abilities, behaviors and aspirations.

b) The concept of cultural capital—along with that of social capital that Bourdieu included later in his analytical framework—allows us to explain a broader range of individual variance in academic success than we can accomplish with the conventional demographic indices of socioeconomic status or class and parents' education level (according to Bourdieu, scholastic capital is only a part of cultural capital).

c) Because of the evidence of a moderate relationship between conventional measures of family background and cultural capital indicators, other sociologists (Di Maggio, 1982; Teachman, 1987) have gone beyond Bourdieu's theoretical assumptions, asserting that cultural capital is an element of status culture distinct from class position (Di Maggio, 1982). The relationship is limited because family investments in educational resources for children (or cultural capital) "remain discretionary" (Teachman, 1987, p. 549), as do their investments in social capital.

d) In spite of this widening of the concept of social determinants of unequal attainment in school and relative variables included in the analysis, a not insignificant part of the overall variance remains unexplained, so that we are forced to deduce that inequalities are operating in this domain within groups, not only among groups.

The last two points raise some problems with regard to the coherence of the analytical model adopted by the cultural reproduction theory to its implicit normative model. Point c) weakens the link between social and cultural reproduction built up through the construct of habitus. As to point d), the questions are more relevant and complex. To recognize the existence of important inequalities within a group is to introduce a troubling element for the analytical and normative model we are examining: This model does not enable us to assess these inequalities as unfair in themselves, but, according to the theory of habitus and cultural capital, we are obliged to infer that these inequalities will be unfairly transferred to the subsequent generation. If this is true, we have to conclude that only a society without any kind of social and cultural inequalities—either among or within groups—would be able to eradicate educational inequalities and be called just.

In any case, the concept of cultural capital, as formulated by Bourdieu, stresses the importance of indicators of educational inequalities such as the statistical relationship between parents' level of education and styles of cultural consumption, on the one hand, and children's educational paths, on the other.

This is a relationship that empirical research (using multivaried analysis) has found to be very influential and sometimes growing stronger, in comparison with the net influence of parents' social class or income.

However, it should be kept in mind that, unlike the functionalist tradition, the concept of culture used by Bourdieu is relativistic in essence, as expressions like *"arbitraire culturel"* (arbitrarily selected culture) and *"violence pedagogique"* (pedagogic violence) clearly confirm. Given that, it would be wrong to infer that equalization of school treatment of youths from different social and cultural backgrounds is possible and legitimate, or that it is reachable through a compensatory action that balances the working classes' lesser cultural capital with greater scholastic capital. However, the fact that that the French sociologist has sometimes (see, for instance, Bourdieu, Passeron, 1971) seemed to support a "rational pedagogy" aimed at compensating initial shortages of cultural capital has allowed other less radical (and less deterministic) interpretations to be proposed.

The turn towards agency

Within sociological theory in the last 20 to 30 years, we have observed a turn towards the analytical dimension of agency, which has weakened the influence of the functionalist and structuralist paradigms. Sometimes this tendency has resulted in attempts to combine structure and agency perspectives in a more balanced and comprehensive approach, and at other times, to emphasize the agency dimension in such a way that structural and systemic factors are dropped out or greatly lessened.

To look only at the theoretical versions of this general tendency closest to the focus of our review, we should first of all treat the more open (and less deterministic) models of the reproduction process that have been elaborated by many scholars. Several have stressed the relative autonomy of the democratic state to which school, as an institutional environment, is linked (see, for instance, Bowles, Gintis, 1982; Carnoy, Levin, 1985).

We should also deal with the neo-Weberian theories of credentialism and social closure that drew on a new picture of the relationship between school and the labor market. While functionalists saw the value of educational credentials on the labor market as an indicator of just meritocracy, certain theorists (see Collins, 1979; Parkin, 1985) have seen it as an indicator of ethically and technically unjustified exclusion. On the contrary, from their point of view, a good indicator of equity would be a high rate of intra-generational mobility, independent of the possession of educational credentials. And from the same perspective, we might also consider a high rate of continuing education as a good indicator, independent of the individual's highest education level reached before leaving school (or inversely proportional to it).

Nevertheless, we will now focus our review on the two approaches that seem to be most significant to equity in education (or actually three, because the first may be split into two distinct methods).

1.3.   The cultural relativist and pluralist approaches

Bourdieu's relativist conception of culture leads to, and is sometimes even strengthened by, new approaches to the analysis of educational inequalities. These approaches have emerged within a phenomenological or ethno-methodological or interactionist paradigm, and are generally characterized by a strong emphasis on agency with respect to the construction of the social world, by the use of qualitative methods, such as ethnographic observations, and by a more active perception of the role played by schools in generating unequal educational attainment. Schools do not simply ratify externally generated inequalities, but also produce or actively reproduce inequalities, thereby damaging some groups, especially working class, ethnic minorities and females. In other terms—and here the writer refers to the ethnographically and/or socio-linguistically informed American sociology of education, but this can be applied to the third approach as a whole—"the implication of this line of research for the social production of inequality is clear. It shifts the source of school failure from the characteristics of the failing children, their families, and their cultures toward more general societal processes, including schooling" (Mehan, 1992, p. 7).

This previously mentioned shift leads these approaches away from a functionalist one, while likewise their emphasis on the active role played by social actors in school (teachers and students), making resistance or change possible, distinguishes them from the structural theories of reproduction. In short, we can observe a common tendency in such approaches: a tendency to privilege agency and culture, rather than structure, as sources of inequalities among groups. Insofar as cultural factors are deemed to be autonomous with respect to structural ones, these approaches are defined by a "constructionist" rather than deterministic understanding of social life.

But here we can single out and briefly illustrate two specific traditions of research that appear substantially heterogeneous with regard to other important aspects. These are the "new sociology of education" in the United Kingdom and the "interpretive sociology of education" in the United States.

1.3.1. The English new sociology of education

The exponents of this first line of research (see Young, 1971; Young & Whitty, 1977; and, for a partial revision, Whitty, 1985) share some fundamental assumptions proper to cultural reproduction theory, particularly the more relativist interpretation of Bourdieu's thoughts on education. However, they give them a more politically oriented inflection and reevaluate the role of agency in terms of possible resistance or change.

The most notable contribution offered by these sociologists (calling themselves "new directionalists") is the foundation of a sociology of curriculum. In opposition to a deep-rooted understanding of school curriculum as an objective and neutral instrument of transmission of knowledge, they argue, and sometimes demonstrate in a sophisticated way, that the curricular priorities are biased by conflicting social interests and produce ideological effects.

Because of the present nature of curricula, schools operate as discriminatory institutions exploited by culturally dominant groups (the native white middle-class and *bourgeoisie*), so as to reproduce their dominance over not only the working class but also over ethnic minorities and females, through a process of inculcation and/or selection. As summarized by three English authors (Foster, Gomm, Hammersley, 1996, p. 11) criticizing the cultural over-relativism underlying this sociological tendency and its strong ideological vein: "any attempt to explain differences in educational achievement in terms of students' differential abilities, or the effects of their home background on their motivation or capacity to learn, was ruled out on the grounds that it took for granted the education system's definition of what counted as knowledge, learning, ability, and motivation—definitions which reflected the dominant culture and were discrepant with working-class culture."

In short, authors who adhere to this cultural relativist approach support the claim—more or less explicitly—that fairness in education essentially means differentiated and appropriate curricula for all social groups; that is, equal rights to reproduce their specific cultures and languages through schooling without any dominance or interference on the part of any other groups. Such an idea could be translated into indicators such as the number of students from working-class or minority ethnic groups and the number of females who are enabled to profit by differentiated and appropriate curricula.

In addition to this common normative judgment, several exponents of this tendency—in particular, those trying to combine its phenomenological approach with a neo-Marxist orientation—share the factual judgment that, within our societies, school represents a vehicle suitable only to transmit the dominant culture. It is worth noting that, on the basis of these two judgments, within the present social order, equality of educational outcomes (implying unfair inculcation) means inequity to a no lesser extent than its opposite term, inequality of educational outcomes (implying unfair selection). Typical, by the way, is Willis' well-known analysis of the process of exclusion of working-class boys in one English secondary school (Willis, 1977). His "lads" are positively seen as bearers of an attitude of resistance against school and, at the same time, negatively seen as supporting the process of social and cultural reproduction through their self-exclusion from school. From this point of view, the school's role in our society seems to be radically and unavoidably negative, so that the only valid indicator of equity in education would be the global eradication of social inequalities.

Although this line of research, as a whole, remains firmly anchored to its culturally relativist view of the process of transmission of scholastic knowledge, some ethnographic investigations have begun to draw a more complex and ambivalent picture of the interplay of subcultures within schools. I am referring, for example, to the work by M. Fuller (1980, 1983), which found that girls from one black ethnic group who were successful in school displayed attitudes of commitment to educational achievement and, at the same time, were aware of their place in the social world but not conformist towards it—orientations that led them to a greater commitment to school. Here the "resistance theory" is reshaped in such a way that a potentially positive role of school may be inferred, at least in creating an awareness among disadvantaged students of the damage done to them by unjust inequalities.

In any case, many "new directionalists" argue that an alternative and critical pedagogy carried out by teachers rethinking their curricular choices might stimulate social and educational change, while for others (Whitty, 1985) such a result might be achieved only if a policy aimed at curricular reform takes place also at the "macro" level; that is, within the national political arena.

1.3.2. The American interpretive sociology of education

Research carried out within this second approach—the "ethnographically inspired American interpretive sociology of education" (see, for this definition, Mehan, 1992; see also Cicourel, Mehan, 1985; Cicourel et al., 1974)—wholly considered, is defined by a less rigid and ideologically marked conception of society and culture; thus, its findings are more useful for anyone attempting to build a conceptual and operational framework aimed at supporting a policy of educational innovations or reforms.[5]

Many authors involved in this type of research have shown that the main source of inequalities in achievement at school, damaging minority ethnic groups, is the mismatch between linguistic patterns and socialization practices in the home and the classroom. Here we are dealing with a thesis similar to that advocated by the "cultural deprivation theory," except for the underlying difference in how this phenomenon is judged and the divergent implications of policies designed to eliminate inequalities. For the "cultural deprivation theory," as we have already noted, language use and socialization practices of minority ethnic groups are deficient *in se*, and this deficit has to be overcome through compensatory education policies.[6] On the contrary, "interpretive" sociologists (see, for instance, Heath, 1982a, 1982b; Philips, 1982; Foster, 1989) hold that all kinds of patterns and practices are worth being considered as valid premises for learning, and they propose "a model of mutual accommodation in which both teachers and students modify their behavior in the direction of a common goal" (Mehan, 1992, p. 7).

For example, in his sociolinguistic analysis of the interactions between middle-income white teachers and a community of low-income black children (called "Trackton") in one American elementary school, Heath (1982a) has discovered that students' participation and academic performance in classroom activities improve as soon as questioning styles adopted by teachers become the same as those practiced at home. Thanks to this alignment, these students have been seen to gradually better their ability to answer questions posed in conventional styles. Analogous evidence emerges from other experiments with applying pedagogic strategies to promote a cooperative, rather than competitive, style of learning among minority-group students.

Another important finding stems from MacLeod's ethnographic study of two groups of students from low-status backgrounds who attended the same school (MacLeod, 1987). Notwithstanding their similar experience of poverty, those in the first group (the predominantly black "Brothers") reacted positively to their disadvantageous situation, with high scholastic and occupational aspirations and strong commitment to school learning, whereas the other group (the predominantly white "Hallway Hangers") adopted an anti-school attitude, similar to that of the "lads" studied by Willis. This finding clearly challenges Bourdieu's thesis about the strict dependence of aspirations on an individual's social and cultural class position. Aspirations are not necessarily inherited but can also be constructed, and belief in the principle of equal opportunity has an important influence on structuring or restructuring them.

A third significant contribution of this line of research concerns the organizational and bureaucratic circumstances that generate inequalities within schools, independent of students' individual characteristics and sometimes "beyond the control of the people involved" (Mehan, 1992, p. 13). Therefore, we can state that even unintended effects of the school organizational structure on social inequalities among students must be taken into account.

The crucial point, however, is that the idea of "mutual accommodation" between the school-specific culture and minority groups culture is very different from, and less relativistic than, the idea of an insuperable conflict, as defined by the English "new sociologists of education." As asserted by Spindler, the founder of the anthropology of schooling in the United States, we have to search for a balance between cultural pluralism and educational self-determination, on the one hand, and an open system with some basic competencies that everyone must learn, on the other (Spindler, 1997).

In sum, we can call this point of view pluralistic more than relativistic, as Rawls' latest philosophical stance (see, Rawls, 1994) can likewise be seen.

Actually, we can look at cultural differences within either a multicultural (totally relativistic) normative framework or an intercultural one (that presupposes, to some extent, a persistent universalist outlook). Unlike the first view, the second attempts to encourage dialogue among groups and to respect individual differences and rights, as well as group differences. In so doing, it approaches the respect principle of fairness as (differently) formulated by many authors, be they philosophers or sociologists.[7]

Specific indicators of equity consistent with such a vision should ascertain and measure, as far as possible, how much the pedagogy practiced in school and its organizational mechanisms manages to cope with different styles of learning, to respect cultural pluralism, to promote dialogue and to acknowledge the worth of every individual and group. This implies building new types of qualitative indicators of educational process in tune with a broader and more pluralistic idea of equity of opportunity than that proposed by the "cultural deprivation" approach.

1.4.   The methodological individualism approach

Whereas the previously mentioned line of research that we have called "culturally pluralist" tempers the determinism embedded in reproduction theories by reintroducing the discretionary action of culturally defined groups into its sociological explanations, methodological individualism does so in a different way. Moving from an essentially Weberian matrix, it puts the individual, as an intentional and rational actor whose choices are influenced by social constraints but not completely determined by them, at the center of the analysis. We review this theoretical tendency with reference to two distinguishable versions represented by Boudon and Coleman.

1.4.1. Boudon's stance

The French sociologist conceptualizes students' school careers in terms of a sequence of decision-making processes in which social actors compare benefits, costs and risks connected to each possible choice: to stay in school or to drop out, to enroll in one scholastic channel or track rather than in another, to be more intensely engaged in studying or less so, etc. The choice requires, on the one hand, taking into account objective and subjective resources and, on the other, the goals to be pursued. The amount of available resources, more than the group culture inculcated through primary socialization, is considered crucial to explaining individual choices. But even subjective evaluations about goals have to be taken into account. And the more the social actor is portrayed as *homo sociologicus* rather than simply as *homo economicus,* the more important are these evaluations.

Recent developments with respect to this approach, represented by Boudon's theory of beliefs (1997), actually seem to draw greater attention to the cultural components of the individual's rationality, not only to the economic or strategic ones. In any case, Boudon's analysis of educational inequalities and social mobility precedes his recent speculations about beliefs, and has a more sober and selective shape corresponding to an essentially adaptive conception of how social actors make decisions (Boudon, 1973, 1979). According to this view, inequalities result from the different weights that, through strategic planning, have been variously attributed, within the social stratification, to costs, risks and benefits connected with staying in school instead of going to work. Hence the importance assigned to so-called "branching points"—those times in the school career at which an individual has to decide among alternative courses of action: to stay or to leave, to choose one type of school or curriculum or another, etc. Earlier and later, branching points are characterized by two diverse kinds of mechanisms that engender inequalities. These are linked, respectively, with disparities in abilities to learn and with different perceptions and evaluations of the costs and benefits of continued schooling. What are the consequences of such a theory for the normative approach to inequalities in education and for policy-making aimed at removing or reducing them?

On the basis of Boudon's previous analysis, we might conclude that social stratification, which inevitably affects school careers via abilities and aspirations, can be contained, to some extent, by shifting the first branching point forward; that is to say, lengthening and unifying compulsory school. Another way might be to reduce private school costs for low-income students through a policy of grants and loans, making higher levels of education more accessible.

But two observations should be made. First of all, the methodological individualism approach, particularly in Boudon's view, entails some degree of underevaluation of the institutional dimension and consequently of the role of policy-making in reforming the educational system. Second, Boudon's thinking about equality of opportunity in education and in society appears to become progressively more pessimistic, which brings it closer to Bourdieu's, although it is based on very different factual and normative reasons.

Here we would like to recall what Boudon has recently written about equality of opportunity in education. He has distinguished formal equality of access, which is universally judged as a necessary principle of justice, from substantial or factual equality of access—impossible to reach unless social stratification is ruled out (Boudon, 1997). Even a strict application of the merit principle, in the sense of proportionality between individual performance and rewards, would be an unrealistic solution within a society where the effects of free individual choices, not state arrangements, are the main sources of regulation. This type of regulation also accounts for the apparent paradox described in *L'inégalité des chances* (Boudon, 1979), and represented by the simultaneous significant (albeit limited) reduction of educational inequality and the stability of inter-generational opportunities for social mobility. All these arguments show Boudon's evolving theory of equality and equity approaching the libertarian point of view, as it is theorized, for instance, by the philosopher Nozick (1981). According to this view, full equality of opportunity would imply giving up superior values of liberty on which our society is based—a very different claim from those of other liberal political philosophers like, for example, Rawls (see Meuret, 1999, and in this volume, Chapter 3 on political philosophy).

We point out, however, that despite his different (and disputable) normative orientation,[8] Boudon's theoretical approach has met with growing favor from sociologists involved in empirical research on educational inequalities and social mobility. This has been the case even though his finding that educational inequality of opportunity has been generally reduced over time, and the indicators he used (disparity ratios) have been widely debated. One of the most influential exponents of social-mobility research, Goldthorpe (1996) recently outlined an ambitious theoretical framework (labeled RAT, for "rational action theory") distinguished by its specific application to processes generating educational inequalities. Very significantly, he acknowledged that his framework was broadly inspired by Boudon's methodological individualism.

Another line of research on educational inequalities explicitly modeled on this approach is that represented by a few Italian sociologists, such as Gambetta and Abburrà, among others. However, a distinction has to be made. While, as his assumption concerning the "positional" nature of student aspirations makes clear, Goldthorpe interprets Boudon's rationalism in a context-adaptive and strategic way, the aforementioned Italian sociologists opt for a more inclusive interpretation that manages to encompass both contextual constraints and cultural attitudes. Thus in his work, Gambetta (1990) discovered that something more than merely utilitarian calculations pushes students from superior social classes to pursue high levels of success in school. And in their recent survey on student secondary school choices, Abburrà, Gambetta and Miceli (1996) also included an interesting set of attitude variables.

1.4.2. Coleman's stance

Another influential sociologist of education to whom we can ascribe, in part, the methodological individualism approach is Coleman. However, his analysis of educational inequalities (Coleman, 1990) differs from the preceding one in several important ways. First of all, the American sociologist has paid much more attention to discovering whether supply-side or process variables—be they attributed to inter-school or infra-school differences—matter in generating inequalities in educational outputs. From this point of view, he has more than once demonstrated the crucial roles exerted by the social composition of organizational categories, such as school, class and learning group, though in his later writings, the equalizing effects of heterogeneity are not presumed to work in an unconditional way.

A second, more recent and analytically prominent contribution by Coleman to the understanding of educational inequalities is the concept of social capital (Coleman, 1988). This theoretical construct seeks to complement the individualistic methodological approach, paying greater attention to social and cultural contexts.[9] The concept of social capital is reshaped by Coleman in a broader and more culturally inspired way than in the current "network analysis," insofar as it includes not only interpersonal ties and information but also other dimensions such as values, norms and trust. So it comes to embrace components of student social background not addressed by cultural-capital or human-capital theories. Furthermore, social and human capital are many-sided entities: They operate outside and even inside school. School, indeed, can only confront inequalities in social capital among its students by itself producing more social capital for all.

To demonstrate the validity of the last assumption, we can refer to the findings of some empirical research led by Coleman or others—such as Lee, Bryk, Hoffer and Kilgore—who have shown "that the relationship between social background and academic achievement is weaker in Catholic than in public schools" (Lee & Bryk, 1989); the former are considered to have a more community-like atmosphere and consequently to produce more social capital. However, these findings have provoked a lively discussion among American sociologists.

In addition to its analytical contributions, Coleman's work also contains some important contributions highlighting the normative side of our question. As previously noted, in Boudon's opinion, equality of educational opportunities is simply impossible without dismantling the present stratified social structure and replacing it with an egalitarian and, at the same time, authoritarian one that would be even less acceptable from a social-justice point of view. An analogous belief, if differently motivated, is expressed by Luhmann and Schorr (1988), two sociologists who have worked within a renewed functionalist approach. They assume that in our functional societies where no system is able to dictate its logic to any other, the school is not able to force other systems, like the family, to accept an equal-opportunity principle.

Coleman's (1990) stance appears to be significantly different: Complete equality of educational opportunity is actually considered impossible to reach because it would require a dramatic strengthening of the role of schools to the detriment of family liberty; that is to say, a public policy that is too interventionist and expensive to be accepted by our society. However, a sensible reduction of major existing educational inequalities is possible as well as fair. This presupposes a more active and effective role for schools.

Another relevant indication stemming from Coleman's analysis (1990) concerns the complexity of the idea of equal educational opportunities as well as of the set of indicators needed to ascertain and measure how much they are actually put into practice. On the one hand, following the prevailing direction of sociologists, this is defined as the independence of educational outputs from ascription-patterned inputs, like social class or stratum, ethnic group and gender; in other words, as equal attainment and achievement among groups. On the other hand, this calls for an array of instrumental conditions as well that have to do with school organization: the extension of compulsory education; the heterogeneous composition of school, class and learning groups; equal social-capital production; appropriate pedagogy; and parity or compensatory discrimination in public funding, etc.

A third interesting contribution to the normative conceptualization of equity has a more theoretical scope. Analyzing Rawls' theory of justice, Coleman contended that it should be seen in a particular context, in spite of its claim of universality. Thus, its pivotal traits, among which we can place the equal-opportunity principle, seem to presuppose the existence of such conditions as the provision of some kind of centralized social regulation, and the acknowledgment that, to some extent, human beings are socially interchangeable. We can add that these conditions are both present in a school context, and thereby explain why the ideal of equality of opportunity is so popular in schools.

What ideas can we take from the methodological individualism approach, considered as a whole, to help us choose appropriate equity indicators? I think there is one in particular. If we look at educational inequalities as part of a process determined by an individual's decisions, and subject to influence by external and internal factors, we have to analytically consider the different decision-relevant variables acting on such a process. (These are located on the sides of the resources/attitudes/opportunity triangle, shown on page 58.) We must also control their correlation with collective variables (like social class or stratum, race and gender). To do so means to elaborate a more articulated and contextual frame for equity judgment and equity policy-making.

1.5. International comparisons of equality of educational opportunity

International comparisons of equality of educational opportunity have recently developed within a broader area of sociological research (or two parallel and partly rival areas), aimed at investigating the processes of educational and occupational attainment and social mobility. To mention only a few well-known authors of research relevant for the sociology of education (a mix of first-generation and younger authors), we can cite Blau and Duncan, Featherman and Hauser, Treiman, Jencks and Hout from the U.S.; Glass, Goldthorpe, Halsey, Heath and Ridge from Great Britain; Erikson and Jonsson from Sweden; Ganzeboom from Holland; Muller from Germany; Duru-Bellat and Mingat from France; and Cobalti and Schizzerotto from Italy.

As I have already noted, these kinds of studies were initially stimulated and also influenced by the structural-functionalist approach and its emphasis on the ascription/achievement dilemma, the normative concept of equality of opportunity and the determinant role played by the degree of modernization and industrialization. Later, this original theoretical link was progressively blurred or abandoned, partly because the research findings gave little support to the structural-functionalist hypothesis. On the other hand, though some social-mobility scholars (see Raftery, Hout, 1990) advanced alternative hypotheses close to social-reproduction theory for some aspects, this line of research remained more theoretically open and empirically driven. As specified above, a few scholars currently working in this area are endeavoring to strengthen its theoretical profile and explanatory power, borrowing some constructs from the methodological individualist approach (see Goldthorpe, 1996; Erikson, Jonsson, 1996; Schizzerotto, 1997).

Although these studies have employed different methodologies, they have generally focused, with respect to education, on the relationship between social origins (and other group categories such as gender and place of residence) and educational results, above all represented by attainment—formal levels of education reached by individuals. (Inquiries, including indicators of achievement, related to substantial knowledge and skills acquired in specific scholastic subjects have been rarer.) In doing so, they use increasingly sophisticated statistical techniques designed to weigh the influence of each independent variable on the dependent one, controlling for all the others. The resulting indicators are too refined for a comparison aimed simply at establishing a hierarchy in terms of global levels of inequality, but very pertinent when the aim is an analysis of the more determinant aspects and sources of inequality, which may be significant for elaborating policies.

Within this broad line of sociological research, international comparison has assumed three distinct forms:
- a secondary-level analysis of the findings from different national studies;
- a joint analysis of two or three countries; and
- a joint analysis of a greater number of countries.

In recent years, several important analyses have been carried out. Considered as a whole, they offer the most interesting sociological contribution to the detection of whether and how inequalities in educational success vary over time and across countries.[10] Here we will present the some of the main results and discuss problems of methodology and interpretation.

1.5.1. The trends: A comparison among 13 countries

Above all, we will refer to the comparative study edited by Shavit and Blossfeld (1993a), which is aimed at investigating the long-term trends in the association between social background and educational attainment. Embracing 13 countries,[11] it represents the broadest overview of this field drawn so far.

Results

Only two countries—Sweden and Holland—have shown a general move towards less inequality of educational opportunity among social classes and strata, while the other 11 appear fundamentally stable or changing only in limited and sometimes contradictory ways. Furthermore, the editors note that the timing of the changes found in the two above-mentioned countries suggests that such dynamics were brought about more by the socioeconomic context than by educational reforms. This also tends to disprove the hypothesis of maximally maintained inequality (Raftery, Hout, 1990) because the equalization process occurred before school attendance by privileged groups reached saturation levels. The impact of students' social origin on their chance of passing one scholastic transition point—that is, succeeding to the next academic level (for example, from primary to secondary school)—appears to lessen with the second and subsequent transitions. Finally, the research data reveal a general declining trend in gender inequalities.

A salient conclusion drawn by the editors is that educational expansion does not favor equality of opportunity with respect to social origins, whereas it may do so with respect to gender. This result, however, is challenged by other research, conducted independently from the comparative project that we are examining here. For example, with regard to France, Duru-Bellat and Kieffer (2000) have found a strong diminution of the net effect of social background (father's socioeconomic status (SES) mother's and father's educational levels) on both the highest level of education reached from the oldest to the youngest generation, covered by the applicable database, and on the likelihood of entering secondary school and of completing it. While, over time, inequalities are shifted to upper secondary school, the equalization that has occurred seems to be the direct result of increased school attendance, which generates ceiling or saturation effects. (In other words, since all, or nearly all, of the most privileged pupils reach a particular educational level, only the less privileged pupils may significantly improve their chance of doing so.) A similar result is observable in Italy, where inequalities have diminished in lower secondary school, yet remain constant in upper secondary school (Cobalti, Schizzerotto, 1994; Shavit, Westerbeek, 1997).

Discussion of the definition of equality of opportunity and relative indicators

According to the prevalent current praxis among sociologists, equality of educational opportunity is defined as the lack of any statistical association between indicators of success in students' scholastic careers (such as number of school years completed, highest degree obtained and transition points passed) and indicators of their social origin (such as family income, father's occupational status, and father's or mother's educational level). As to measurement techniques, this research aligns itself with a new practice, largely adopted in the last 20 years by social-mobility scholars, which favors odd ratios or logistical regression models over other, more traditional, methods, such as disparity ratios and linear regression models.[12] But in so doing, it also implicitly narrows the operational definition of inequality of opportunity that had been common within this area of research. This methodological innovation followed the American statistician Mare's proposal (1980) to clearly distinguish between two different processes that remained entrenched and confused in measures previously employed in research on changes in educational inequality of opportunity.

These processes are the expansion of the educational system, on the one hand, and the functioning of selection mechanisms that affect the academic paths of students from different social backgrounds, on the other. Such a distinction, to a certain degree, resembles the distinctions of structural and pure mobility, or absolute and relative mobility rates, previously proposed and discussed within social-mobility research. Odds ratios or logistical regression models, inasmuch as they are insensitive to table marginal values, enable us to put this distinction into practice. Thanks to them, we can understand whether and how much an eventual reduction of educational inequalities, as shown by the trend of disparity ratios, depends on expanded enrollment at higher levels of the school system or on a weaker association between social origin and educational attainment. To make this distinction clearer, we can imagine a case in which the expansion effect has reduced the influence of social origin on the probability of reaching some relatively high scholastic levels (e.g., a complete lower or upper secondary education). However, at the same time, the likelihood of remaining under that level is increasingly affected by social origin because only the children of undereducated people are likely to fall into the shrinking category of undereducated young people. If eventually the two hypothesized effects offset each other, association indices, such as odds ratios or logistical regression parameters, do in fact remain unchanged over time. Something like this actually seems to have occurred in some European countries, while in the United States, the "underclass effect" has been so great as to determine an inter-temporal dynamic of logistical regression estimates involving an increase in the influence of social origin upon an individual's opportunity to complete his or her secondary education (Hout, Raftery, Bell, 1993).

The example we have cited demonstrates that the proposed distinction and the suggested relative indicators represent a significant improvement in techniques designed to measure inequality of educational opportunity. However, it would be wrong to assign them an absolute value and to throw out any other kind of indicators, including disparity ratios or linear regression parameters.

The research led by Shavit and Blossfeld (1993a) actually handled both of these types of indicators: linear-regression effects of social origins on educational attainment (measured as number of school years) and logit-regression effects on school transitions. This choice has been reasonable because, in my opinion, we should avoid placing too much emphasis on the second, more sophisticated, indicators and measurement techniques.

Depending on our different evaluative judgments about what is better from an equity point of view, we can rely on one kind of indicator or another, or adopt a multifaceted perspective using all of them at once. So, let us reconsider the hypothetical case in which, association parameters between social origin and school transitions remaining constant over time, the chances of reaching advanced educational levels become more equal between low- and high-status groups. (But in which, simultaneously, the probability of falling into the small residual minority of under-educated people becomes even greater for the low-status group.)

We contend that this change could be considered positive, negative or neutral from an equity standpoint. On the basis of the definitions adopted by the social-mobility approach, we should really consider it neutral. In fact, the openness of the system—that is, its consistency with the principle of equal opportunities, manifested as the lack of association between social origin and school attainment—would be unchanged over time.

However, the current British social-mobility approach, as represented by Goldthorpe among others, has drawn criticism on this point, particularly with respect to its preference for odds ratios to measure equality of opportunity. Other sociologists (Saunders, 1995)[13] have argued that "there seems no good theoretical reason why improved chances of success for working-class children should be recognized in a measure of fluidity only if there is also a corresponding deterioration in the chances of success of service-class[14] children. Only committed egalitarians would adopt a measure of social 'progress' that demands that those at the top are 'leveled down' at the same time as those at the bottom are 'leveled up'"(p. 26).

There is an important question here regarding the definition of equity or fair equality: May we consider two different methods of equalization—one based on "leveling up" and the other on "leveling down"— as equivalent? Or, to speak in different terms, one associated with an expansion of the educational system and the other with its stability or reduction? If we opt for a strict meritocratic idea of justice, we should think so. But if our conception of justice is different in character—be it, for example, neo-utilitarian or based on Rawls' principle of difference, and we deem education to be also a good in itself (not only a positional one)—the response should certainly be negative.

And again, even though the association parameters between educational results and students' social background are eventually identical, may we view these situations as equivalent, when in one of them some of the people, whatever their social origins, remain below the socially required minimum standard of educational level and basic competence?

As far as we hold basic education to be one of the rights of citizenship, we are obliged to think that to leave people below a reasonably defined social or cultural threshold violates the equity principle, regardless of how many they are and whether they are equally distributed by social origins or not (see also Meuret, Chapter 5 on indicators). In sum, for normative reasons—but also for heuristic ones, a matter into which we cannot enter here—we contend that the different concepts of inequality have to complement each other, and the same is true of indicators and measurement techniques.

From another point of view, De Graaf and Ganzeboom (1993) also argue against a unilateral reliance on logistical regressions applied to single-school transitions, which entail neglecting or abandoning linear regressions for the final output of schooling. These authors hypothesize that the association between students' social origins and their academic success declines across transitions as parental influence on their choices decreases. Thus, the increase in school attendance at intermediate and higher educational levels may contribute to declining trends in OLS regressions of final school output on students' social origin without any change in the transition logit odds. But, they comment, "This explanation of trends over time, in terms of composition effects, is important, but does not mean that trends over time are not important *per se*: Declining parental influence over the total educational outcome is of great social and sociological importance in itself. In events that occur after the completion of the educational career (such as entry into the labor and marriage markets), it is normally the level of completed education, relative to the distribution of the relevant cohort, that counts and nothing else" (p. 98; for a similarly oriented reference, see also Sorensen, 1986).

Discussion of the findings

The research findings show that educational inequalities among social groups are very persistent and cannot be explained by functionalist theories of modernization and industrialization. No general claim about the unchangeable reproductive nature of educational systems seems to be supported by the research data either. Furthermore, insofar as we opt for a multi-criteria approach, we are induced to look at the results of this comparative research on inequality of educational opportunities in a slightly different way, which tempers the idea of an absolute exceptionalism of Sweden and Holland (an idea that other research has called into question, as will be noted later). It is true what Shavit and Blossfeld (1993b) point out: Only these two countries have shown a significant variation of the statistical association between social origin and educational transitions, as is estimated on the basis of logit regression models, over a long span of time (for Sweden, see also Wildt-Persson & Rosengren in this volume). Nevertheless, the evidence resulting from linear regression models, with regard to net effects of social background variables on the number of school years completed, presents, to some extent, a more differentiated picture that should not be overlooked.

Although Sweden and Holland are the only countries where OLS estimates of changing educational stratification document a clear and general trend towards lessening inequality of opportunity, similar (though incomplete or somewhat contradictory) evidence is emerging in other countries. For instance, in the United States, there has been a decreasing influence of the father's occupation, while the father's education influence remains stable.[15] In Japan, the opposite trend has occurred: stability of the influence of the father's occupation, but decrease of the influence of the father's education. This means that status groups' disparities in years of education completed are being diminished in the United States, as are educational groups' disparities in years of completed education in Japan. In these two countries, we discern trends that can be considered intermediate between systematically changing countries, like Sweden and Holland, and countries like Germany, Great Britain,[16] Switzerland, Hungary, Poland and Israel, where there has been no discernable change.

Another observation may be advanced about the way in which the first transition points are treated within our research. As first transition points, we mean, for example, completion of primary school, access to secondary school and completion of low-secondary or compulsory school, which are real points of transition only for the older cohorts; among the younger cohorts, everyone, or almost everyone, passes them. Thus, inter-temporal comparisons covering all these transitions, or some of them, up to the youngest generations are often impossible or statistically insignificant because of the small number of people who fail to accomplish the transit. Often the national case studies included in the cited comparative work (Shavit & Blossfeld, 1993a) have faced this methodological problem, correctly excluding first transition points throughout, or at least relative to last cohorts, because of the doubtful significance of a logit regression analysis applied to so small an amount of young people who have not yet made those transitions. So, it would be inappropriate to expect from this analysis, implicitly centered on higher stages of educational careers, a specific and systematic answer as to whether, across 13 countries and over time, equality of opportunity has increased, decreased or remained unchanged with reference to the first stages of educational careers.

Nevertheless, the general picture of the phenomenon to be described stands to lose some degree of transparency. In particular, it does not adequately highlight scattered trends towards equality in education that occurred over the last decades in many countries: the universalization of mandatory school attendance through the lower or middle-secondary level, a result reached also by virtue of an increase in the minimum age at which one may legally leave school. In addition, in some countries—where comprehensivization of secondary school has taken place— the minimum age at which students and their parents make their first choice about future schooling has risen as well; this is the transition point at which they are allowed to choose among different and stratified school channels or tracks. In these cases, we can hypothesize that educational outcomes, expressed in terms of learned knowledge and abilities, will be more equally distributed than in systems where compulsory secondary education continues to be divided into different channels or tracks, although an empirical test should be made.

In sum, policies directed towards the opening up of educational systems through the prolongation of compulsory education and unification of traditional tracks or channels have played an important role in this process of basic equalization. These seem to have been actually the only egalitarian educational policies to have succeeded almost everywhere they were tried, while the success of policies aimed at equalizing the higher levels of the educational system appears to have been much more problematic and often very disappointing. We can ask whether these policies of basic equalization have been grounded on a previous saturation process of school attendance for higher or middle-class offspring, as has been argued for Italy (Shavit, Westerbeek, 1997), or if such policies have in fact helped to advance this process, as has occurred elsewhere. In the latter case, policies aimed at opening up the educational system may initially increase inequalities.

A third source of problems for this line of research is represented by the presence of unobserved variables that can prejudice the estimates on the effects of background observed variables with respect to school transitions, even when they are not correlated with each other. This contamination occurs because the omitted variables also affect the dependent variables under observation. The same author who first proposed the use of logistical models to study the variation of inequality of opportunity in education across generations, genders, states, ethnic groups and so on, R. Mare, raised this problem and hinted at a broad array of unobserved variables that may be present: "These may be exogenous characteristics of a person's family of orientation, such as wealth or permanent income. They may be endogenous personal characteristics, such as academic ability, motivation, or educational aspirations. Or, they may be aspects of opportunity structures, such as the social and economic opportunities that people expect when they leave school" (Mare, 1993, p. 354).

Unmeasured heterogeneity, in particular, may result in a decline across transitions in the degree of association between social background indicators that are ordinarily used in this research (educational level and occupational status or class of students' fathers) and the likelihood of a successful transit. In this case, such a decline would depend on the impact on the surveyed population of unmeasured variables—for example, measures of cultural capital or social capital not captured by current indicators of social status and educational level of students' parents—which tend to increase across transitions because of cumulative selection. For example, working-class children can be over-selected in the first transition so that they face further transitions with a greater homogeneity of unmeasured characteristics, becoming better equipped to compete with the less selected and more heterogeneous children from privileged backgrounds. In this way, the relationship between social origin and school success may appear to be declining. Whether latent variables are correlated or unrelated with observed ones is irrelevant in order to establish this kind of dynamic.

The hypothesis formulated by Mare may account for a phenomenon—declining inequality of opportunity across transition—which empirical research often displays, even if another plausible and competitive explanation has been advanced: the "life-course hypothesis." This alternative hypothesis figures out that "with increasing age, students will increasingly be able to decide on their own what they want and will rely less on parental resources" (Blossfeld & Shavit, 1993b).

However, it is worth noting that the presence of unmeasured variables affecting transitions can produce distorted effects on comparative analysis concerning the dynamic over time of the relationship between social background and school transitions. For the aforementioned reasons, every other thing being equal, it is important to determine whether when passing from one cohort or country to another a wider part of a social origin-defined student group manages to make a certain transition. If this is the case, we should expect that, relative to other groups, its likelihood of making the subsequent transition deteriorates. To cite as an example something that has actually occurred in many countries: If a first transition, corresponding to the end of compulsory education, has been equalized, we could expect that more inequality occurs over time at the subsequent transition, corresponding to the end of upper secondary school. To the extent that this analytical model holds up, we should reconsider the value of an eventual invariant trend, from an equity point of view.

To avoid the distorting effects of unmeasured variables within studies based on origin-destinations data, as in mobility tables, Mare proposed a model of logistical analysis including an additional variable—school attainment of siblings—under the hypothesis that it can represent unobserved traits that are constant within a family. However, other relevant traits or circumstances varying within families remain unobserved. To capture these variables other less sober models of analysis would be required.

1.5.2. Does Swedish "exceptionalism" exist, and why?

The results of the research outlined above aroused a sharp interest in Sweden,[17] apparently the only country to have displayed a clear past trend towards greater educational equality, as confirmed by other investigations. In subsequent comparative studies centered on Swedish "exceptionalism" (see Erikson, Jonsson, 1996), the dynamics of the relationship between educational careers and students' socioeconomic and cultural backgrounds were tested once more, and new comparisons were made of the trends among some countries and their absolute levels of equality of opportunity.

Searching for changes in the association between social origin and educational destination, and using mainly logistical regression models applied to school transitions, the studies collected in this book confirm that, more than any other country, Sweden passed through a process of progressive equalization, embracing both lower secondary and upper secondary education. This equalization process was particularly pronounced from 1930 to 1970. Moreover, when from an analysis of trends we turn to a static analysis (comparing different countries on the basis of their characteristics in a given time), we discover that Sweden seems to have become one of the most equitable countries, despite its not very brilliant point of departure (Muller, 1996) and thanks to this favorable trend (Jonsson, Mills, Muller, 1996). Some comparisons among countries have found fewer inequalities of educational outcomes in Sweden than in the Federal Republic of Germany, and even slightly less than in Great Britain and in the United States, with respect to the younger cohorts (see Jonsson, Mills, Muller, 1996; Hout, Dohan, 1996). This conclusion, however, awaits corroboration by future research using the same methodology on a larger number of nations, as occurred with the Casmin Project (see Muller, 1996), whose findings need to be updated.

Finally, unlike other countries (notably the United States), Sweden also continues to be one of the best performers in comparisons of equity in educational achievement, as seen in several international surveys of pupils' knowledge and skills (see in this book the contribution of Noël, de Broucker, Chapter 12[18]).

In spite of this significant evidence, the two above-mentioned Swedish editors do not exaggerate in emphasizing "exceptionalism." Actually, other nations, such as Holland, show trends towards more equality of opportunity, although the evidence from different studies or on different aspects of the phenomena is not as convergent as in Sweden. Besides, an analysis included in the same book (Jonsson, Mills, Muller, 1996) demonstrates that there has also been a clear trend towards a lessening of class inequalities in educational attainment in the Federal Republic of Germany, while there is no evidence of this in Great Britain. France and Italy—two countries characterized by greater inequalities of educational opportunity compared to Germany and Great Britain (Duru-Bellat, Kieffer, 2000)—have also experienced significant reductions of such inequalities, although they are limited to lower secondary school, as we have noted above.

Furthermore, the patterns of educational inequality among classes are practically the same in all nations, and the intensity of the association between students' social origin and their success in school is less influential than the global survival rate (connected with school expansion) in determining class-specific probabilities of survival at every transition point. Finally, more recent findings from follow-up and evaluative studies conducted by the National Agency of Education and reported in the Swedish chapter of this book (Wildt-Persson, Rosengren, Chapter 13) indicate that tendencies towards greater inequalities in results and resources among municipalities and schools were surfacing in the 1990s, although, as these authors recognize, in "an international comparison there is yet little evidence to suggest that Sweden should be lagging behind in equity."

What are the factors behind the Swedish long-term trends? Why has Sweden been a pacesetter, in some respects, in educational equality?

The response given by Erikson and Jonsson (1996) is interesting because it is based on an explanatory model that claims a general validity. There are three factors governing educational inequalities among social classes:

- differences among children of different classes in academic ability and performance traceable, above all, to disparity in out-of-school opportunities for learning;
- differences in their propensity to survive in school until they reach the highest levels and to choose the most prestigious tracks; and
- effects of school expansion on the global survival rate.

According to these authors, it is the second factor that counts in explaining the Swedish performance in a comparative perspective (and, in general, international differences in this domain) using Boudon's method of referring to inter-class variations in the costs, risks and benefits of individual choices. The particularity of the Swedish case is deemed to depend on both contextual features and school-specific ones. The relatively substantial equality of socioeconomic conditions and the advanced welfare state existent in Sweden exerted an influence, reducing class disparities in schooling costs. At the same time, the comprehensive educational reform and the lengthening of compulsory education diminished disparities in risks. (The younger the students are when they are called upon to choose whether to stay in school or to leave, and in which track to enroll, the higher the risks of failure if they decide to continue schooling, instead of leaving, and to choose the most challenging tracks.) Both of these long-standing favorable circumstances seem to have weakened since the early 1990s, when the economic crisis narrowed the leeway for income-redistributive social policy, and decentralization in the governance of the educational system made equalization a more difficult goal to pursue, at least in the traditional ways. Thus, Sweden has met the same problems relating to the feasibility of equity policies, albeit later, that other Western nations were forced to face in the 1980s.

2.   Summary and conclusions

2.1.   An overview of some relevant indicators

Table 1 (page 52) summarizes some traits of the theoretical approaches and research lines just reviewed, specifically: a) the normative idea of equity in education, b) the main source of educational inequity in contemporary society, c) the detectable or foreseeable trends and d) the most significant indicators that can be deduced.

2.2.   Attitudes towards equity and fair equality

Sociology of education, like sociology in general, has powerfully contributed to diffusing the idea that inequalities are not (or not only) produced by biological factors, but rather by predominantly social ones that may be removed through social change. In the long-standing dispute between "genetistic" explanations and "environmentalist" ones, sociology of education has made the case for the latter. So, it is striking to observe, in light of the indications stemming from our review, that a quite widespread skepticism towards equity and equality has emerged in the last 30 years.

2.2.1. Equity criticism or skepticism

Various currents, sometimes springing from very distant theoretical and ideological sources, flow into this skepticism (as can be also seen in Table 1).

According to deterministic reproduction theories, an equalization process is impossible in principle without revolutionizing the global order of our society, and education reforms are inevitably ineffective.

The stance of the English sociology of education is similar in some respects, but leaves more space for active resistance from the working class, ethnic minority groups and radical teachers. On the other hand, influential scholars with neo-functionalist orientations, like Luhmann, or methodological individualist ones, such as Boudon, have criticized the very idea of equality of opportunity, respectively claiming that it is in conflict with the systemic requirements of a functionally differentiated society and that it is reachable only at the price of undermining other more important ethical values. Furthermore, the emphasis on the difference among cultures that is so entrenched in the current sociological

Luciano Benadusi

Table 1. Trait of theoretical approaches and research lines

Approach or research line	Concept of equity	Main source of inequity	Trends and leeway for change	Indicators of equity
Functionalism	Rawlsian liberal equality of opportunity	Family cultural deprivation and country level of modernization	Increasing universalism (more equity) Educational reforms may be effective but the evolution of the socioeconomic context is more determinant	Association between student's ability, effort and educational success; no correlation between ascriptive social groups and success
Cultural reproduction theory	No social, cultural and educational inequalities among groups	Cultural capital and habitus	Persistent inequality and inequity Educational reforms are ineffective	No association between educational success and social class or their cultural fractions
Cultural relativism	Equality and reciprocal independence among group cultures	Cultural discrimination through schools	Persistent inequality and inequity Possible resistance on the part of minority groups and teachers	Number of students from working class or minority groups who can profit from the use of differentiated and appropriated curricula
Cultural pluralism	Respect for cultural differences	Cultural and pedagogic distance between home and school	No trends Well-conceived reforms and micro-level policies may be effective	Non-hierarchical differentiation in school
Methodological individualism	Rawlsian liberal equality of opportunity or free choice (formal equality of opportunity)	Different cost, risks and benefits associated with individual decisions about school career Social capital	Different views with respect to: trends: (1) reduction of inequalities; or (2) no trends With respect to policies: (1) well-conceived policies may be effective; or (2) no policy may be effective unless it threatens other more important values	Level of the school's first branching point Social capital produced by family and school
International comparative research on equality of opportunity	No educational inequalities among groups	Students' social origin (class, strata, income and educational level of parents)	Strong persistence of inequality but also some meaningful cases of reduction Effective reforms are possible but they have to be addressed to both socio-economic context and institutional environment of school	Correlation of educational output/ student's social origin measured by odds ratios or logit regressions

debate leads some authors to disdain equality of educational attainment, as simply a "most respectable prejudice" (Murphy, 1990).

Nonetheless, the empirical research, including the most recent international comparisons of trends, proves that equalization in education is a possible, though difficult to achieve, goal. Moreover, equity and fair equality are not necessarily inconsistent with other values such as liberty, social utility, efficacy and respect for cultural difference, but on the contrary, under some conditions, all these values may converge (see Meuret, Chapter 5 on indicators).

2.3. The concepts of equity and equality in education favored by sociologists

Apart from the above-mentioned skepticism or minimalism, we can identify three or four concepts of educational equity/equality within the sociological tradition.

2.3.1. Equal opportunity

The classic and still widespread concept is based on the principle of equal opportunity for students belonging to different types of social groups (class, stratum, race, gender, local community, etc.), meaning that scholastic outcomes must be independent of ascriptive or background variables, which we could call the rule of no social bias.

This conception has appeared, however, in two different versions, as we have seen in our review.

Equal opportunity with merit

The first, which we have seen supported by functionalist sociologists and in some cases by others, falls more clearly within the meritocratic perspective, even if it is adjusted to filter out from the notion of merit the influence of social factors on individual learning ability. Such a concept essentially coincides with the "liberal equality of opportunity" depicted by Rawls, as we have noted above. Fundamental to this conception, therefore, are the distinctions between genetically inherited vs. socially acquired ability, and between freely chosen effort and effort resulting from socially determined aspirations. Bringing together equality and merit, however, makes this conception quite difficult to put into action through appropriate and undisputed indicators.[19]

Simple equality of opportunity

The second version is currently the most widely adopted by sociologists, especially by those involved in quantitative research on educational attainment and social mobility. It distinguishes itself more clearly from the pure meritocratic hypothesis, formulating its own definition of equality of opportunity (synonymous with equity) as total independence of scholastic output from background variables. Conceived in this way, equality of educational opportunity is one important prerequisite of social fluidity; that is, of perfect inter-generational mobility.

Genetic factors and those related to individual discretionary choices are held to exercise an effect only on inequalities within, not among, groups. As only the last ones are considered unfair, a link with the meritocratic idea—albeit subtle—remains in this definition which, having given up the formalization of merit variables, is much easier to put into practice.

2.3.2. Equal rights of citizenship

According to the theory of the rights of citizenship, which has a sociological matrix (Marshall, 1976), the third generation of rights due to the citizen recognized by the contemporary state, following on civil and political rights, are social rights. One of these is education, whose importance varies according to the different national interpretations of the idea of the welfare state, or more precisely, the indispensable instructional foundation required to effectively exercise other rights of citizenship, from political rights to some of the social rights, such as the right to work.

Many sociologists have regarded the equality of opportunity principle more as a citizenship right than as a requisite of just meritocracy. Only a few have also recognized that equality of opportunity is a not sufficient condition from this normative point of view. We have clearly claimed in this book (see Meuret, Chapter 5 on indicators) that inequalities should be considered unjust not only among groups but, to some extent, among individuals as well.

First of all, it is necessary to establish the minimum threshold of instruction and competencies to be guaranteed to all citizens as a basic social right. Any variance from this rule should be considered unfair, according to this conception. The idea of a minimum threshold for all can also be associated with the principle of the generalization of "base capacity" supported by Sen (1994). Along with an increase in the average level of education, the establishment and progressive raising of a minimum standard also allows us to control and possibly reduce inter-individual inequalities without the effects of leveling-down.

2.3.3. Fair respect for differences

This is the most recent concept to have emerged within the sociology of education, and it may be considered somewhat post-modern, whereas the other two are certainly modern. In its strongest version, it holds that all social groups and all individuals—whether expressed mainly in communitarian or individualistic terms—have an equal right to be given instruction (including state-financed instruction) modeled on their own particular ways of perceiving and constructing their educational needs. The relativist nature of such a concept and its potential re-segregationist consequences make it very disputable. However, there is a weaker and more acceptable version of this concept that admits the legitimacy of maintaining a nucleus of universalist values, norms, common goals and common experiences in the school, but postulates a better, more equal relationship of "mutual adjustment" between this nucleus and the various group cultures, individual needs and learning styles. Behind this conception, we can also see the recent contributions from the anthropology of schooling, cultural psychology and theories of multiple intelligence.

Matching the idea of equality with that of difference, this orientation requires the establishment of indicators covering both dimensions. It may be expressed by qualitative indicators, preferably at the micro level. At the macro level, we can utilize quantitative indicators of students' well-being, like those proposed elsewhere in this book (see Meuret, Chapter 5 on indicators), or students' and stakeholders' satisfaction (or perceived quality-of-service) indicators.

The perceived quality may be measured by the degree of satisfaction with respect to educational service, considered on the whole, or specified for single elements. These elements could include: student/teacher relationships and other social climate indicators; curriculum (its cultural, pedagogic and professional value); expectations regarding the future utility of the received education in the labor market; teachers' professionalism; facilities available; and welfare services for students.

2.3.4. An overview of possible indicators

In Table 2, (page 56) we present a synoptic framework of indicators for each concept of educational equity:

2.3.5. The need for a pluralistic approach

The descriptive and analytical work of sociologists should involve all those concepts of equity in education that appear reasonable and significant in our societies, although more or less so, depending on the different contexts. And suitable indicators need to be determined for all these conceptions. An influential, though rare, example of an approach to the analysis and measurement of inequalities, which is pluralistic in its normative assumptions and thus also in the purposes of its data collection, is represented by the major survey that led to the Coleman report (Coleman, 1990).

In particular, equality of opportunity, equal rights of citizenship and fair respect of differences are equity archetypes that may be combined in various ways. In

Table 2. Framework of indicators for each concept of eductional equity

Equal opportunity plus merit	Simple equal opportunity	Fair respect for differences	Right of citizenship
No correlation between students' achievement (educational credentials obtained, years of school completed) and social groups, controlled for aptitude and effort	Independence of outputs (students' achievement and attainment) by social groups	Levels of pedagogical (non-hierarchical) differentiation	Effective minimum threshold for students' attainment
No correlation between students' attainment (competencies acquired) and social groups, controlled for aptitude and effort	Independence of outputs (achievement and attainment) by social groups, controlled for statistical effects of the growth in school attendance	Levels of pedagogical individualization	Effective minimum threshold for students' achievement
Context indicators	Context indicators	Variation in home/school cultural and pedagogic distances by social groups	Statistical dispersion in measures of individual achievement and attainment
Process indicators	Process indicators	Average level of students' well-being or students' and stakeholders' satisfaction with school, and disparities among individuals and social groups	Average level of achievement and attainment

fact, the framework of indicators proposed in this book (see Meuret, Chapter 5 on indicators) brings together concepts from my last three categories.

Finally, I shall move on to consider the question of the determinant variables of inequality of opportunity, which has been the focus in sociology of education. The identification of these variables is crucial for selecting indicators and planning appropriate policies.

2.4.   An explanatory model of inequality of opportunity

2.4.1. The resources-attitudes-opportunity triangle

A good model to describe educational inequalities—or more precisely in this case, inequalities in attainment and achievement among social groups—seems to take the shape of a triangle whose three sides represent personal resources, attitudes and opportunity. Models that are similar in part have been proposed by many sociologists (for example, Sorensen & Hallinan, 1977; Hallinan, 1996; Erikson, Jonsson, 1996). In my opinion, these three variables underlie the decisions or, better yet, the actions that bring about scholastic success or failure. It can be claimed that they mediate contextual variables—like the educational and socioeconomic status of students' families—transforming them into different scholastic outputs. Whereas the last variable, opportunity, is a process variable, the first two—personal resources and attitudes—represent both inputs and outputs of the process because they are transformed through the learning-teaching activity. And in this sense, they may be either equalized or not. It should also be pointed out that in the framework of indicators included in this book, these two variables are treated at the family level and, consequently, labeled as context variables. This is the easiest solution to put into practice, although treating them also at the personal level and longitudinally would enable us to get a proxy measure of the added value produced by school to find whether it is positive or negative, and to what extent, from the equality of opportunity standpoint. In this case, the specific indicator would be the statistical association between the added value and the variables of socioeconomic and educational background (negative association as a standard of equalization).

The construction of this type of indicator would require international longitudinal surveys that are lacking as of now, but it could be more easily implemented at the local level (single school, district and so on) as a complement to current quality evaluation practices.

2.4.2 The sides of the triangle

Our model describing the mechanisms that generate inequalities in scholastic learning, including the three fundamental variables of the triangle, is represented in Figure 1 (page 58).

Competencies and relationships are the two personal resources available to the individual to successfully carry out his or her scholastic career. Both are influenced by the socioeconomic, cultural and educational status of the family and by the school process. The concept of *competence* can simply embrace the abilities and knowledge traditionally included in school curricula or relevant for scholastic evaluation, which in this case is something close to Bourdieu's cultural capital. But this concept evokes a range of new cognitive, meta-cognitive and extra-cognitive (such as social skills) dimensions that often have a cross-curricular character. Interpreted in this way, this concept may differ in certain aspects from the construct of cultural capital and is likely to appear less associated with the level of education, lifestyle and social class of students' parents. Many countries are drafting or implementing reforms in their traditional curricula and quality indicator systems based on this new concept of competencies. The Organisation for Economic Co-operation and Development (OECD) is working on a set of unconventional cross-curricular competencies. However, it may be useful to include this broader and innovative meaning of competence in a

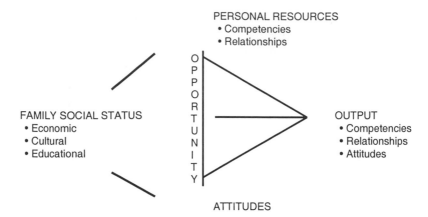

Figure 1. Resources-attitudes-opportunity triangle

descriptive model, provided that it is truly institutionalized and put into practice within the national educational systems.

The concept of *relationships* recalls social capital; that is, the relational network within which each individual is located. Until now, few quantitative studies have been carried out that seek to make the concept of social capital operational as regards education, and the data on which they are based are limited. Now, the PISA project of the OECD is working to incorporate this concept into the construction of a more developed set of SES indicators (see Willms, 1998).

By the term *attitudes* we mean attitudes towards school and commitment to study. This term covers such things as value judgments, aspirations, expectations and motivations that induce individuals to invest their resources and energy into the scholastic learning process (effort) or, alternatively, to do so only a little or not at all. Attitude then is the primary element involved in this decision, understood not only as the deliberation to invest resources and energy or not, but also as the actual act of investing them, and thus "theory in action," rather than just "theory espoused" (Argyris & Schon, 1978).

There is a large body of research showing the critical relationship between social membership factors (especially those related to parental level of instruction, type of occupation, income and ethnic identity) and level of aspiration or expectation, even when ability or scholastic success variables are controlled (for Italy, see, for example, Gambetta, 1987, and Abburrà, 1996; for other countries, see authors cited by Goldthorpe, 1996). But the sociological debate presents two different types of explanations for this relationship: a so-called "culturalist" explanation and a "positional" one, distinguished by different emphases on either intrinsic or extrinsic incentives. The "culturalist" explanation appeals to group norms and identity, whereas the "positional" explanation is based on the relationship between social position (to which ethnic membership

can be added as an autonomous variable) and the determination of the costs
and benefits associated with scholastic decisions. Both of these interpretations
are plausible in principle, but need to be tested by further empirical research.

To avoid overly deterministic interpretations of this concept, we have to
keep in mind that there is a circular relationship between aspirations and the
experience of success in learning, as there is also a circularity between this
experience and the initial level of basic knowledge and skills. From the point of
view of equal opportunity, the school's task should not be restricted to dealing
with competencies, but should also reach out to influence students' and parents'
aspirations and motivations.

The third side of the triangle, *opportunity*, has attracted much attention
from educational scientists. We do not refer here to the learning opportunities
offered by the social environment to which the child belongs, which are included
indirectly in our descriptive model via resources and attitudes. Rather, we mean
the specific opportunities offered by the school system, so that, in this case,
opportunity is synonymous with treatment. By equal treatment, we mean:

- to equalize the quality of the educational service provided by schools and
  districts, or to create a reverse correlation between quality and SES
  indicators in order to compensate for original inequalities;
- to eliminate or weaken the various kinds of hierarchical differentiation in
  secondary schools (for instance, tracking, streaming, traditional European
  channels);
- to establish forms of non-hierarchical differentiation of pedagogical
  practices aiming at a better match with different groups' learning styles
  and motivations;
- to make the SES composition of schools and classes or other educational
  groups more heterogeneous (equi-heterogeneous);
- to extend pre-school education;
- to extend second-chance education (remedial courses and reversed
  curricula; that is, curricula proceeding from vocational towards general
  education); and
- to provide grants and loans to children of low-income parents so that their
  relative costs (costs compared with incomes) of school attendance are not
  greater than those paid by the children of high-income parents.

Many indicators related to opportunities offered by schools are included in
the general framework proposed in this book.

Treatment is the dynamic side of our triangle: The more schools compensate
for society in providing opportunities for students from different backgrounds,
the more equity is guaranteed. This is one of the two strategic paths leading to
a greater equality of opportunity in education; the other is a policy aimed at
modifying the context variables affecting the generation of educational
inequalities, mainly via family social status.

Notes

1 Empirical approaches are examined (with reference to the U.S. literature) in another part of this book (see Cochrane, Chapter 4).

2 In theoretical sociological language, the term "agency" is often contrasted with "system" or "structure" as it means that social actors in principle are able to create the social world, through their intentional actions, and that they are not merely subject to systemic or structural constraints. Here, agency is synonymous with voluntarism, whereas system and (above all) structure is synonymous with social determinism.

3 In the sense that it is viewed as generating conflicts.

4 By achievement, we mean learned knowledge and abilities; and by attainment, educational credentials acquired.

5 A line of research that shares some features of that here examined is the English interactionist sociology of education (see, for instance, Woods, 1983).

6 A partly dissimilar stance has been held by Bernstein who underlined the social advantages of using an "elaborate" socio-linguistic code rather than only a "restricted" one, without sharing all the linguistic assumptions of the deficit theory (Bernstein, 1971).

7 For a more specific reference to education, see Dubet, 1999, and for a somewhat different formulation, see Benadusi, 1990.

8 We can wonder whether methodological individualism and normative individualism are totally independent or not, as I actually tend to think.

9 For Coleman (1988), the construct of social capital "is part of a theoretical strategy that involves use of the paradigm of rational action but without the assumption of atomistic elements stripped of social relationships" (p. 118). It follows that Coleman's stance attempts to conciliate methodological individualism with a sort of methodological collectivism, as his attention to corporate actors, not only to individual ones, confirms.

10 For comparative research on the variation of the degree of association between students' social origin and educational attainment across countries, see Muller, Karle, 1993.

11 The national cases included in this research are: United States, Federal Republic of Germany, Netherlands, Sweden, England and Wales, Italy, Switzerland, Taiwan, Japan, Czechoslovakia, Hungary, Poland and Arab communities in Israel.

12 To make clear this methodological cleavage, we take disparity ratios and odds ratios. To present a very simple example, we imagine that there are two social classes (the upper class, UC, and the lower class, LC) and two educational levels (the upper level, UE, and the lower level, LE). In this case, the disparity ratio between the two classes relative to the best educational result should be formulated so that: (UC:UE):(LC:UE); that is to say, as the ratio between the rate of completion of the upper educational level for the upper class and the rate for the lower class. Whereas, the odds ratio should be formulated so that: (UCUE:UCLE):(LCUE:LCLE); that is to say, the ratio between two distinct ratios. The first is between the number of the upper class members completing the upper educational level and the number of those failing to do so (thus reaching only the lower educational level). The second is the same ratio calculated for the lower class.

13 The debate between Saunders and Goldthorpe focuses on whether the present-day British society is meritocratic or not, as regards social mobility processes, and on the related question of which indicators and techniques of measurement are more adequate in this matter. I think that Goldthorpe's defense of the preference for odds ratios against disparity ratios (Breen, Goldthorpe, 1999) is correct as long as the discussion remains within a strict meritocratic frame.

14 According to the well-known Goldthorpe and Erikson classification, the service class is the

highest and is composed by categories such as entrepreneurs, managers, high public officials, professionals, etc.

15 Other research shows that there has been a great increase in equality of opportunity in the United States, thanks to expanding enrollment in higher education from the early 1960s to the beginning of the 1980s (Hout, 1988; Hout, Dohan, 1996), followed by a period of contraction. An analysis of the 20 years since the Coleman report found a strong weakening of inequalities in achievement for ethnic groups and, to lesser extent, for low-status groups, due however to favorable socioeconomic and educational circumstances that seemed to be likely to disappear (Smith, O'Day, 1991). Subsequent empirical evidence confirms the expected reversal (O'Day, Smith, 1993).

16 But in this country, the data used by the research mentioned are sufficiently up to date to analyze the effects of the establishment and spread of comprehensive schooling.

17 For a specific analysis of the Swedish case, see in this book: Wildt-Persson, Rosengren, Chapter 13.

18 Using data from the Adult Literacy Survey (ALS), these two authors come to discover a lesser influence of parents' educational background on average length of schooling of their children in the U.S. and Great Britain than in Sweden. Such a finding appears to be inconsistent with other research that we have reported here. One of the possible explanations for this discrepancy hypothesizes that the length of schooling is less achievement related in the U.S. and Great Britain than in Sweden and other European countries because of institutional differences inherent to examination mechanisms.

19 The recent English sociological debate about meritocracy has prompted new endeavors to insert merit variables within the statistical analysis of social mobility and equality of opportunity (see Saunders, 1997; Breen, Goldthorpe, 1999).

References

Abburrà L., Gambetta D., Miceli R., *Le scelte scolastiche individuali*, Rosemberg & Sellier, Torino (IRES), 1996.

Argyris C., Schon D.A., *Organization Learning: a Theory of Action Perspective*, Addison-Wesley, Reading (Mass.), 1978.

Bell D., *The Coming of the Post-Industrial Society*, Heinemann, London, 1974.

Benadusi L., "Uguaglianza, giustizia ed equità tra i valori della politica educativa," in *Scuola Democratica, 1*, pp. 4–14, 1990.

Bernstein B., *Theoretical Studies towards a Sociology of Language, in Class, Codes and Control*, Routledge & Kegan Paul, London, 1971.

Boudon R., *Il vero e il giusto* (Paris, 1995), Il Mulino, Bologna, 1997.

Boudon R., *Istruzione e mobilità sociale* (Paris, 1973), Zanichelli, Bologna, 1979.

Boudon R., *La logica del sociale* (Paris, 1979), Mondadori, Milano, 1980.

Boudon R., *L'inegalite des chances; la mobilite sociale dans les societes industrielles*, Colin., Paris, 1973.

Bourdieu P., "La trasmissione dell'eredità culturale" (Paris, 1966), in Barbagli M. (ed.), *Istruzione, legittimazione e conflitto*, Il Mulino, Bologna, 1978.

Bourdieu P., Passeron J.C., *I delfini. Gli studenti e la cultura* (Paris, 1964), Guaraldi, Bologna, 1971.

Bourdieu P., Passeron J.C., *La riproduzione. Sistemi di insegnamento e ordine culturale* (Paris, 1970), Guaraldi, Bologna, 1972.

Bowles S., Gintis H., "La scuola come un luogo di contraddizioni nella riproduzione del rapporto capitale-lavoro: riflessioni sul principio di 'corrispondenza,'" in Cappello R.S., Dei M., Rossi M. (eds.), *L'immobilità sociale*, Il Mulino, Bologna, 1982.

Breen R., Goldthorpe J.H., "Class inequality and meritocracy: a critic of Saunders and an alternative analysis," in *The British Journal of Sociology, 50*, pp. 1–27, 1999.

Carnoy M., Levin H.M., *Schooling and Work in the Democratic State*, Stanford University Press, Stanford, 1985.

Cicourel A.V., et al., *Language Use and School Performance*, Academic Press, New York, 1974.

Cicourel A.V., Mehan H., "Universal Development, Stratifyng Practices, and Status Attainment," in *Research in Social Stratification and Mobility, 4*, pp. 3–27, 1985.

Cobalti A., Schizzerotto A., *La mobilità sociale in Italia*, Il Mulino, Bologna, 1994.

Coleman J.S., "Social Capital in the Creation of Human Capital," in *American Journal of Sociology, 94*, Supplement, pp. 95–120, 1988.

Coleman J.S., *Equality and Achievement in Education*, Westview Press, Boulder (Colo.), 1990.

Collins R., *The Credential Society*, Academic Press, New York, 1979.

De Graaf P. M., Ganzeboom H.B.G., "Family Background and Educational Attainment in the Netherlands for the 1891–1960 Birth Cohorts," in Shavit Y., Blossfeld H.P. (eds.), *Persistent Inequality. Changing Educational Attainment in Thirteen Countries*, Westview Press, Boulder (Colo.), 1993.

Di Maggio P., "Cultural Capital and School Success: the Impact of Status Culture Participation on the Grades of U.S. High-School Students," in *American Journal of Sociology, 47*, pp. 189–201, 1982.

Dubet F., "Sentiments et jugements de justice dans l'expèrience scolaire," in Meuret D. (ed.), *La justice de système éducatif*, DeBoeck Université, Bruxelles, 1999.

Durkheim E., *La divisione del lavoro sociale* (Paris, 1893), Comunità, Milano, 1962.

Duru-Bellat M., Kieffer A., "Inequalities in educational opportunities in France: educational expansion, democratization or shifting barriers?," in *Journal of Education Policy, 15*, pp. 333–352, 2000.

Elster J., *Uva acerba. Versioni non ortodosse della razionalità* (Cambridge, 1983), Il Mulino, Bologna, 1989.

Erikson R., Jonsson J.O., "Explaining Class Inequality in Education: the Swedish Test Case," in Erikson R., Jonsson J.O. (eds.), *Can Education Be Equalized?* Westview Press, Boulder (Colo.), 1996.

Foster M., "It's Cookin' now: a Performance Analysis of the Speech Events in an Urban Community College," *Language in Society, 18*, pp. 1–29, 1989.

Foster P. , Gomm R., Hammersley M., *Constructing Educational Inequality*, Falmer Press, London, 1996.

Fuller M., "Black Girls in a London Comprehensive School," in Deem R. (ed.), *Schooling for Women's Works*, Routledge, London, 1980.

Fuller M., "Qualified Criticism, Critical Qualifications," in Barton L., Walker S. (eds.), *Race, Class and Education,* Croom Helm, London, 1983.

Gambetta D., *Per amore o per forza? Le decisioni scolastiche individuali* (Cambridge, 1987), Il Mulino, Bologna, 1990.

Goldthorpe J.H., "Class Analysis and the Reorientation of Class Theory: the Case of Persisting Differentials in Educational Attainment," in *British Journal of Sociology, 47*, pp. 481–505, 1996.

Hallinan M.T., "Educational Processes and School Reform," in Kerckhoff A.C. (ed.), *Generating Social Stratification*, Westview Press, Boulder (Colo.), 1996.

Heath S., "Questioning at Home and at School: a Comparative Study," in Spindler G.T. (ed.),

Doing the Ethnography of Schooling," Holt, Rinehart and Winston, New York, 1982a.

Heath S., "Ethnography and Education: towards Defining the Essentials," in Gilmore P., Glatthorn A.A. (eds.), *Ethnography and Education: Children in and out of Schools,* Center for Applied Linguistics, Washington, DC, 1982b.

Hout M., "Expanding Universalism, Less Structural Mobility: The American Occupational Structure in the 1980s," in *American Journal of Sociology, 93,* pp. 1358–1400, 1988.

Hout M., Dohan D.P., "Two Paths to Educational Opportunity: Class and Educational Selection in Sweden and the United States," in Erikson R., Jonsson J.O. (eds.), *Can Education Be Equalized?* Westview Press, Boulder (Colo.), 1996.

Hout M., Raftery A.E., Bell E.O., "Making the Grade: Educational Stratification in the United States, 1925–1989," in Shavit Y., Blossfeld H.P. (eds.), *Persistent Inequality. Changing Educational Attainment in Thirteen Countries,* Westview Press, Boulder (Colo.), 1993.

Jonsson J.O., Mills C., Muller W., "A half century of increasing educational openess?" in Erikson R., Jonsson J.O. (eds.), *Can Education Be Equalized?* Westview Press, Boulder (Colo.), 1996.

Lee V.E., Bryk A.S., "A Multilevel Model of the Social Distribution of High School Achievement," in *Sociology of Education, 62,* pp. 172–192, 1989.

Luhmann N., Schorr K.E., *Il sistema educativo. Problemi di riflessività* (Stuttgart, 1979), Armando, Roma, 1988.

MacLeod J., *Ain't no Makin'It,* Westview Press, Boulder (Colo.), 1987.

Mare R.D., "Educational Stratification on Observed and Unobserved Components of Family Background," in Shavit Y., Blossfeld H.P. (eds.), *Persistent Inequality. Changing Educational Attainment in Thirteen Countries,* Westview Press, Boulder (Colo.), 1993.

Mare R.D., "Social Background and School Continuation Decisions," in *Journal of the American Statistical Association, 75,* pp. 295–305, 1980.

Marshall T.H., *Cittadinanza e classe sociale* (New York, 1965), Utet, Torino, 1976.

Mehan H., "Understanding Inequality in Schools: the Contribution of Interpretive Studies," in *Sociology of Education, 65,* pp. 1–20, 1992.

Meuret D. (ed.), *La justice du système éducatif,* DeBoeck Université, Bruxelles, 1999.

Muller W., "Class Inequalities in Educational Outcomes: Sweden in Comparative Perspective," in Erikson R., Jonsson J.O. (eds.), *Can Education Be Equalized?* Westview Press, Boulder (Colo.), 1996.

Muller W., Karle W., "Social Selection in Educational Systems in Europe," in *European Sociological Review, 9,* pp. 1–23, 1993.

Murphy J., "A Most Respectable Prejudice: Inequality in Educational Research and Policy," in *British Journal of Sociology, 41,* pp. 29–54, 1990.

Nozick R., *Anarchia, Stato e utopia* (Oxford, 1974), Le Monnier, Firenze, 1981.

O'Day J., Smith M.S., "Systemic Reform and Educational Opportunity," in Fuhrman S.H. (ed.), *Designing Coherent Educational Policy,* Jossey-Bass Publishers, San Francisco, 1993.

Parkin F., *Classi sociali e Stato* (London, 1979), Zanichelli, Bologna, 1985.

Parsons T., *La struttura dell'azione sociale* (New York, 1937), Il Mulino, Bologna, 1970.

Philips S., *The Invisible Culture: Communication in Classroom and Community on the Warmsprings Indian Reservation,* Longman, New York, 1982.

Raftery A.E., Hout M., *Maximally Maintained Inequality: Expansion, Reform, and Opportunity in Irish Education, 1921–1975,* paper presented to ISA Research Committee on Social Stratification, Madrid, 1990.

Rawls J., *Liberalismo politico* (Cambridge, Mass., 1993), Comunità, Milano, 1994.

Rawls J., *Una teoria della giustizia* (Cambridge, Mass., 1971), Feltrinelli, Milano, 1982.

Saunders P. , "May Britain Be a Meritocracy?" in *Sociology*, *29*, pp. 23–41, 1995.

Schizzerotto A., "Perché in Italia ci sono pochi diplomati e pochi laureati. Vincoli strutturali e decisioni razionali degli attori come cause della contenuta espansione della scolarità superiore," in *Polis*, *3*, pp. 345–365, 1997.

Sen A.K., *La diseguaglianza* (Oxford, 1992), Il Mulino, Bologna, 1994.

Shavit Y., Blossfeld H.P., (eds.), *Persistent Inequality. Changing Educational Attainment in Thirteen Countries*, Westview Press, Boulder (Colo.), 1993a.

Shavit Y., Blossfeld H.P., "Persisting Barriers: Changes in Educational Opportunities in Thirteen Countries," in Shavit Y., Blossfeld H.P. (eds.), *Persistent Inequality. Changing Educational Attainment in Thirteen Countries*, Westview Press, Boulder (Colo.), 1993b.

Shavit Y., Westerbeek K., "Istruzione e stratificazione in Italia: riforme, espansione e uguaglianza delle opportunità," in *Polis*, *1*, pp. 91–109, 1997.

Smith M.S., O'Day J., "Education Equality: 1966 and Now," in Vestergen D., Ward J. (eds.), *Spheres of Justice in Education*, Harper Business, New York, 1991.

Sorensen A.B., "Theory and Methodology in Social Stratification," in Himmelstrand U. (ed.), *The Sociology of Structure and Action*, Sage, New York, 1986.

Sorensen A.B., Hallinan M.T., "A Reconceptualization of School Effects," in *Sociology of Education*, *50*, pp. 273–289, 1977.

Spindler G.T., "Why Have Minority Groups in North America Been Disadvantaged by their Schools?" in Spindler G.T. (ed.), *Education and Cultural Process. Anthropological Approaches*, Waveland Press, Prospect Heights (Ill.), 1997.

Teachman J.D., "Family Background, Educational Resources, and Educational Attainment," in *American Sociological Review*, *52*, pp. 548–557, 1997.

Whitty G., *Sociology and School Knowledge: Curriculum Theory, Research and Politics*, Methuen, London, 1985.

Willis P., *Learning to Labour*, Saxon House, Farnborough, 1977.

Willms J.D., *Proposition pour la composante mesurant le statut economique et social (SES) du questionnaire 'élève'*, paper presented for OECD/PISA, Paris, 1998.

Woods P., *Sociology and the School. An Interactionist Viewpoint*, Routledge and Kegan, London, 1983.

Young M.F.D., (ed.), *Knowledge and Control*, Collier-MacMillan, London, 1971.

Young M.F.D., Whitty G. (eds.), *Society, State and Schooling*, Falmer Press, London, 1977.

Chapter 2

Efficiency and Equity[1]

Marc Demeuse
Université de Liège, Belgium

Marcel Crahay
Université de Liège, Belgium and Université de Genève, Switzerland

Christian Monseur
Université de Liège, Belgium and Australian Council for Educational Research

In democratic countries, instructional systems must be both effective and equitable. These two requirements might be perceived as irreconcilable: Competition within the system and, consequently, its selectivity would be measures of effectiveness. One can, however, ask if it is still valid to pit the effectiveness of a system against its equity. Indeed, in the most developed countries, with the generalization of core curricula, and then of higher education, we find an increasing *de facto* convergence of these two exigencies: In assigning to a system the goal of effectiveness, one obliges it to be fair.

These opposing points of view deserve in-depth consideration. To this end, it is useful to begin with a clarification of concepts: first of effectiveness, then equity. We also examine data from international comparisons in an effort to analyze to what degree instructional systems in industrialized countries have succeeded in marrying these two objectives. Our intention is to put in evidence certain characteristics of systems that are best at articulating the dual requirement of effectiveness and equity, and above all to test some widely accepted ideas, especially with relation to the development of heterogeneity in instructional groups.

1. Effectiveness of educational systems

Interpretations of the term "effectiveness" may vary according to the parameters set up (Scheerens & Bosker, 1997). For our part, we will distinguish four ways of looking at effectiveness: absolute effectiveness, relative effectiveness, subjective effectiveness and efficiency.

1.1.   Absolute effectiveness

Generally speaking, the effectiveness of an educational system is measured in the adequacy of results observed with respect to its assigned objectives. These can bear on the skills to be developed among students, as well as on attitudes. This concept of effectiveness naturally poses a problem of defining the goals that the system assigns to itself and measuring the results actually obtained. After having long-defined curricula in terms of programs that instructors had to apply in terms of pupil attainment goals (de Landsheere & de Landsheere, 1978), current directives tend more and more towards such concepts as basic skills or minimal competencies that all students must master at a given moment in their careers (de Landsheere, 1988; Parlement de la Communauté Flamande de Belgique, 1996, 1997; Ministère de la Communauté Française de Belgique, 1999).

There is no shortage of education research that evaluates the effectiveness of a policy in terms of knowledge growth or performance by students. It is on the basis of such criteria that educational systems are very generally compared in international studies. Then, too, schools have multiple missions: personal growth, citizenship education, development of skills and knowledge, and the training of future workers. For each of these missions assigned to the instruction system, choices must be made. These are highlighted first by political debate and decision. Insofar as defining the end results and objectives of school is concerned, research is not a substitute for moral reflection. Yet the researcher can bring empirical elements that are important to consider into reflection of a philosophical order (OECD, 1995a, 1996). We will show this in illustrations taken principally from two studies of the development of heterogeneity among students in mandatory schooling in Europe[2] (Demeuse & Monseur, 1998; Monseur & Demeuse, 1998) and of preferential treatment systems in French-speaking Belgium (Demeuse & Monseur, 1999), as well as from a composite work edited by one of the authors (Crahay, 2000).

1.2.   Relative effectiveness

1.2.1. The comparative approach and international studies

The comparative approach of the International Association for the Evaluation of Educational Achievement (IEA) and the International Assessment of Educational Progress (IAEP) always comes back to a definition of effectiveness in relative terms even if, instead of just determining the champions among the participating countries, international evaluations try to offer a better understanding of the results and systems that determine them (Bos & Lehmann, 1995; Keeves, 1992). In these types of studies, each education system is situated, not with respect to the goals it pursues, but with respect to an international norm constructed on the basis of a detailed analysis of all national programs of instruction. In this framework, the effectiveness of an education system can be compared with the best in the international ranking system. However, these tests to some extent may obscure the contents and rationale of certain national programs (Beaton et al., 1996; Beaton & Gonzalez, 1997). In this case, a country risks, at the international level, being found relatively ineffective, independent of student results in its own programs (and even less equitable, for, often in this case, students who do better than others on questions outside the national curriculum are those who benefit from a more favorable external environment). It is for this reason that since its first international study of mathematics, the IEA has presented in one form or another results taking into consideration the distance that separates each national curriculum from the international norm. From this point, to correctly appreciate the absolute effectiveness of each system across the results of such studies, one must take this parameter into account, which is not always an easy thing to do.

1.2.2. Added value or the effects of schools and learning themselves

The balance sheet of goals mastered by students in the course of a year or at a particular moment does not constitute an absolute measure of the effects engendered by the educational system, the school or the mechanism evaluated. As concerns educational establishments, we know that they are subject to the effects of aggregation linked to their different forms and recruitment methods. As to the educational systems, they have different cultural and educational histories. Some have had mandatory schooling since the middle of the 19th century; others adopted it at the end of the 20th century. Thus, in the first case, the instructional system is "road-tested" and parents have themselves benefited from a "complete" education; in the second, children from certain groups constitute the first generation to enjoy a formal education and, failing that, to learn to read. To put this another way, instructional systems (or schools or even instructors) do not start from equivalent places. Consequently, a measure of pedagogic effectiveness that does not take into account the starting point of those studied, that is to say their intellectual and cultural baggage and also their conditions of life, is fundamentally biased (Brookover et al., 1979; Webster, Mendro & Almaguer, 1994).

To do this, there are several techniques for calculating gains (such as the gap between the results of a post- and pre-test, residual score, etc.). The difficulty with such efforts rests in the need to use data gathered according to evaluation procedures that are at least comparable, if not identical. The difficulty increases with the size of the application being evaluated. The measure of effects attributable to an instructor in the course of a school year implies subjecting students in their classes to two series of tests a year apart. From the point at which one takes an interest in the school effect or the effects of an educational system, one is immediately confronted with larger samples and, consequently, with procedures that are more costly and require more delicacy to organize.[3]

Rather than look into the change over time in achievements by students who are particularly difficult to measure, other authors are working to relate the achievements of different groups by function of their characteristics of origin. This approach rests on a regression analysis and includes four principal steps, which: 1) measure the level of students at a given moment in their schooling; 2) estimate the average level of achievement by defined and opposing subgroups of students (boys versus girls, natives versus foreigners, students from privileged socioeconomic families versus others, etc.); 3) for each school, calculate what would be the average level of students if, in that school, students performed at the average level of similar students in the larger sample; and 4) finally, calculate the gap between the level observed and the level predicted (for example, Emin, 1995; Thélot, 1996). The nature of the gap (positive or negative) permits identification of schools that produce better or lesser results than those expected for the population being educated.

1.3.   Subjective or perceived effectiveness

The effectiveness of an education system is the goal of societal studies. These can be obtained by submitting questionnaires to people with different roles in education. These are not observed results, but the more or less supported perception that these people have of that which is studied. This perception can prove to be very different from that furnished by objective measures. Thus, an OECD study (Black & Atkin, 1996) revealed that participating countries are all characterized by dissatisfaction with respect to their science and mathematics instruction, independent of results published by the IEA. It is nonetheless interesting to know the effectiveness that actors attribute to the system because this also determines their convictions with respect to the fairness of a particular measure. One illustration can be furnished with respect to grade repetition, which seems poorly founded and unjust to a great number of researchers (Crahay, 1996), but effective and therefore justified to many teachers and parents, at least in the countries where it is authorized. However subjective, these psychological findings have their importance in the development of an education system; their weight is considerable in the success of pedagogic reform. What do you do when the system is ineffective, but teachers and parents are convinced to the contrary?

How do you modernize instruction in reading or mathematics when parents and teachers are persuaded of the effectiveness of methods with which, as students, they were taught? What do you do when parents and teachers worry above all about mathematics, yet objective evaluations indicate that priority ought to be given to overhauling science instruction?

1.4. The efficiency of educational systems

Effectiveness can also be related to the method used by the education system to meet its objectives. The OECD devotes a significant chapter of *Education at a Glance* to the comparison of different costs of education (OECD, 1998, Chapter B: Financial and Human Resources Invested in Education). To the extent that one can relate these two parameters, one obtains a measure of efficiency. It is defined therefore as the relationship between inputs and products of the system, or between agreed-upon methods and results obtained with respect to the desired objectives. Efficiency implies not only the relationship of school results and monetary costs, as Swanson points out (1971, p. 209): "There is, however, a more general definition of efficiency: the ability to produce or achieve a desired effect with a minimum of effort, expenses, or waste. This usage also implies some measurable quantities but quite often involves educational activities in a manner more socially, psychologically, and politically than economically."

Decroly and Buyse, beginning in 1929 and strongly influenced by a period of study in the United States, proposed an analogous definition inspired by physics: "In a machine, the yield is expressed as a relationship between the work expended and the work used; by the same token, in education, the efficiency of a school system is measured by relating the cost, the time and effort spent on school work and the practical results." In physics, it is the term "yield" (*rendement*) that constitutes what French-speaking teachers and economists call "efficiency;" the designated yield, in education, being the total scholastic performance of a given population. An example: the yield of instruction in science at the end of general secondary education, in a country, in a scholastic sub-system (de Landsheere, 1979, p. 235). The term "yield" can be translated in English as school achievement.

2. Equity within education systems

Without any doubt, equity in matters of education has become one of the fundamental requirements of contemporary democracies,[4] leading, as a means of accomplishing it, to a shift in consensus from the right to an education to the duty of education, as indicated by the concept of mandatory schooling. It remains, however, to specify what form of equity is considered when researchers analyze a particular system or when they confront results obtained by several education systems through an international study. The concept of equity is, in effect, subject to several interpretations (Bonami et al., 1997; Meuret, in this work), which correspond to different ethical positions (Crahay, 2000). One can notably distinguish the following interpretations (OECD, 1993):

- **Equity of access or equality of opportunity**: Do all individuals (or groups of individuals) have the same chance of progressing to a particular level in the education system?

- **Equity in terms of learning environment or equality of means**: Do all individuals enjoy equivalent learning conditions? This question is generally taken to mean: Do disadvantaged individuals or groups benefit from a learning environment equivalent to advantaged individuals or groups in terms of the level of training of their instructors and professionals attached to the educational system, rate of enrollment, number and quality of scholastic infrastructures, and quantity and quality of didactic tools?

- **Equity in production or equality of achievement (or results)**: Do pupils or students all master, with the same degree of expertise, skills or knowledge designated as goals of the educational system? Most particularly, are individuals from different social backgrounds given, over the period of instruction of training, equal skills? Or do all individuals have the same chance of earning the same qualifying degrees (for example, a diploma) when they leave and can they do so, independent of their circumstances of origin? This concern about equality in achievement is founded on an ideal of corrective justice (Crahay, 2000) and is inevitably accompanied by a desire to reduce the gap between the strong and the weak in terms of academic performance from the start to the end of a pedagogic action (Bressoux, 1993).

- **Equity of realization or exploitation of results**: Once they have left the system, do individuals or groups of individuals have the same chances of using their acquired skills to realize their individual or group goals in society and validate their skills?

Grisay (1984) has neatly joined the underlying ideas of the four concepts of equity. Her analysis is summarized in Table 1 (page 71).[5]

3.   Effectiveness and equity: Inseparable requirements?

It seems that the dominant social view holds effectiveness and equity in education to be two opposing concepts and, consequently, two irreconcilable

Table 1. Synoptic presentation of pedagogic ideas underlying four different conceptions of equity (adapted from Grisay, 1984, p. 7)

Assumed	Admitted	Admitted	Admitted
Equality of access or opportunity			
The existence of talent, potential or natural aptitude. These define the level or threshold that the individual can hope to attain.	Unequal results, demonstrably proportional to aptitudes at the start. The existence of courses of unequal value. Inequality of treatment.	The fact that merit is not the sole criteria for access to elite courses. Sociocultural biases affecting guidance tests. Imperfections in official evaluations to the point that at the same rank, one student will succeed and another fail.	An objective or scientific search for talents and scientific methods of orientation. Equality in access to extended education, according to aptitude, for children of the most and least advantaged. A balanced system; that is to say, a system with varied options and courses of instruction adapted to the aptitudes of pupils. Assistance for the gifted disadvantaged (scholarships, etc.)
Equality of treatment			
The capacity of all to receive fundamental training and therefore to benefit from basic instruction.	The existence of talent, potential or natural aptitude. Unequal results, demonstrating that students could benefit from learning conditions of equivalent quality.	Unequal quality of instruction, unequal goal management. Ghetto schools, tracking, courses that explicitly and implicitly engender unequal quality of instruction.	One school or comprehensive instruction and, notably, a core syllabus for lower-secondary education.
Equality of achievement and academic success			
Potential for extended learning. Individual characteristics (cognitive and effective) can be modified. Differences in learning styles.	Differences in results beyond essential skills.	The ideology of talent. Negative discrimination (by class level, courses, church and ghetto skills), i.e., all situations where the unequal quality of learning amplifies original inequalities.	Equality of achievement in essential skills. Positive discrimination, teacher training, formative evaluation of all programs that seek to reduce original inequalities.
Equality of social actualization (social output)			
Different individual, motivational and cultural characteristics, none having innate superiority.	Differences in results. The existence of a standard of excellence.	Different types of instruction.	Differences in results. The existence of a standard of excellence. Different types of instruction.

views in practice. To put it another way, effective systems would be by nature not very equitable, and egalitarian systems would inevitably be devoted to ineffectiveness or, more precisely, to poor learners or the lowering of standards (Baudelot & Establet, 1990).

This conception is debatable today and is reconsidered in numerous studies (Crahay, 1996, 2000). As long as school was reserved for the dominant social classes and it seemed acceptable to educate only a limited fringe of the population destined to occupy high positions in the social hierarchy, the problem of equality in education was hardly an issue. Education did not constitute a right for all, but rather a status benefit that the meritocratic and bourgeois state dispensed as a function of birth, so as to maintain the established social order. From the point when mandatory schooling required all individuals to attend school, it became difficult, from an ethical and economic standpoint, to hold that a quality education should be reserved for a small number.

Those who today call for an equitable system do so based on their refusal to attribute to differences in academic results a natural and intangible (or unchangeable) origin, tied to individual aptitudes, and defined once and for all (Fischer et al., 1996; Gould, 1996). Society should be responsible—at least, partially—for inequalities in professional success because school is seen as carrying out a democratic mission: that of diminishing gaps and avoiding the reproduction and increase of differences from one generation to another (Bourdieu & Passeron, 1971). The effects of the academic institution are thus also measured by the extent of its capacity to assure each individual an equitable access to knowledge and, in consequence, to well-being. Seen in this perspective, equity constitutes one of the parameters of effectiveness of the system because it relates to one of its principle objectives, spelled out in legislative texts and political declarations.

Furthermore, the economic arena sustains a similar point of view, essentially by pragmatism. Thus, in a relatively recent declaration, the Ministers of the OECD have proclaimed: "Education 'for all' assumes that one accords higher priority to those who are less well served by the education system: To permit all to benefit from instruction is as important from the economic point of view as under the aegis of social equity and equality of opportunity in education; countries can not be permitted to leave unexploited large reserves of talent" (translated from the French version, 1997, p. 18). From this perspective, the educational system is an integral and necessary producer of knowledge resources and, consequently, of an adequate supply of qualified labor. From this point, equity is not defined as a goal in itself, but constitutes an axiomatic corollary of the profit motive. The student population is a human reservoir of capacities to be developed to the greatest extent possible through initial and/or continued training (Sweetland, 1996). The lack of competence of a more or less sizeable remnant of this population must therefore also be considered as an index of ineffectiveness of the school because it leaves a potential of human resources unexploited or, to put it another way, because it fails to validate the total human capital that is possible (OECD, 1996, 1998b).

One must, at the same time, guard against simplistic approaches. The theory of human capital, which underlies the declaration by the Ministers of the OECD, is easily reconciled with an "exploitation" differentiated by varying individual capacities and, in that way, can be related to pedagogical concepts that adhere to ethics and equality of opportunity. In other words, the return on education can consist of increasing the competence of all, but to different degrees: Some individuals will be led to become specialized technicians; others will be guided to become efficient technocrats, and rational and cold decision-makers. The key question posed here is if one should allocate to all pursuit of the same objectives or if, on the contrary, one should seek to turn out individuals with different types of expertise and earning potentials.

In principal, basic school avoids this difficult line of inquiry: Teachers have a mission of promoting mastery of a range of basic skills, deemed indispensable for any individual to play a role in modern society. Thus, from the point at which one is committed to develop the same skills in all individuals, there is a necessary relationship between efficiency and equity. In effect, if we take as an indicator of efficiency the average results attained by the total number of students and the variation in results as indicators of equity, there comes a point at which an increase in the average implies a reduction in the variation. Let us suppose, for the sake of argument, a skill X, for which the levels of mastery correspond to a scale ranging from 0 to 100 percent; in other words, from total incompetence to perfect mastery. It would be difficult to find that an average of 80 percent mastery of this skill, obtained in a population of 1,000 individuals, is attributable as much to diversity as a finding of 50 percent in an identical population. To the degree that the average of the population rises, progressing for example from 80 to 90 percent, the theoretical margin of variation in this population is reduced.[6]

In the end, the idea of linking efficiency and equity seems consubstantial to the principle of equality of achievement. In this perspective, one will consider as efficient the system of instruction that, while raising the average level of knowledge, reduces the overall variation in results. This is notably the ideal recommended by Bloom (1976) because, according to him, efficient instruction is characterized by three effects related to the completion of each phase of education:

- an elevation in the average result;
- a reduction in the variation of results; and
- a decrease in the correlation between the social origin of students (and, more generally, their initial characteristics) and the result.

Similarly, according to Bonami et al. (1997), "the educational system will be that much more equitable as it reduces, while avoiding the lowering of standards, disparities between the strongest and the weakest, between advantaged and disadvantaged groups."

The will to assure true equality of results implies an admission of the postulate of educability proposed by Bloom (Bloom, 1976; Slavin, Karweit & Madden, 1989) and an acceptance that the school give more to those who have the least. In the plan of action, it is important to assure that the educational system assign such an objective to its end results. Convinced as to which types of student performance are not fixed at a given and permanent level by unchanging aptitudes, those who are committed to these principles try to reduce the size of a series of negative discriminations and seek policies that are shaped by the establishment of positive discrimination (Crahay, 2000; Demeuse & Monseur, 1999; Slavin, Madden, Dolan & Wasik, 1996), whose efficiency is demonstrable (Slavin & Fashola, 1998).

Evidently, it is up to the school to assure a common cultural substratum to all and to guarantee to each the cognitive means to participate actively in democratic life. This fundamental mission implies the development of mastery in reading, but also in arithmetic and many other domains. In this respect, the French community of Belgium, for example, has adopted the concept of core competencies, signifying that there is a range of skills currently judged indispensable for realizing one's potential in modern societies that all must master at a high level of expertise.[7] It is also evident that the school cannot direct all individuals towards the same professional skills. Social progress requires a certain diversification of functions and skills. From the point at which the school assumes its mission of specialized skills, political decisions are imposed, which entail delicate ethical choices. Which individuals should receive specialized training in which professional skills? Once the students are directed towards this or that course, the principle of equality of achievement can be applied within the application of training corresponding to each trajectory of specialization. One cannot see why certain doctors, for example, would *(a priori)* be less competent than others, from the consumers' point of view, while holding the same title and exercising the same functions.

4.   Must schools employ segregation to be effective?

Education research is no substitute for political decision-making, but it can and must inform it. It must especially be invoked against false ideas that could guide this or that social choice—such as the conviction, evoked above, that elitism and selection are the prices to pay for effectiveness. Indeed, there is a great deal of evidence with which to refute this widely held belief.

4.1. Limiting access to training does not improve the results of the "elite," but it does limit the possibility of raising the average level of the population as a whole.

From the first two international studies of mathematics and science by the IEA (1965, 1981, 1971 and 1985), we know that it is useful to interpret in a nuanced way the relation between school retention[8] and average achievement in secondary school. Even if students from countries with strong school retention perform below average, the best students do not suffer from this democratization of higher secondary school (Keeves, 1992; Husen, 1967a and b; Robitaille & Garden, 1989). Thus, the average of the best students in each country (for example, the 5 percent who obtain the highest grades) encompasses fewer differences than the average calculated for the entire population tested. In the second place, the students who attain or surpass a higher threshold of performance represent very similar percentages, not of the school population, but of the school-age population capable of being educated to this level. In other words, the maintenance of a high percentage of young people in higher secondary education does not alter the performance of the best students (Crahay, 1996, pp. 258–263), but raises the level of the population overall.

4.2. With the expansion of mandatory schooling and its extension in some cases to age 18, the mix of students varies greatly among educational systems.

The preceding analysis can be deepened with respect to styles of organized instruction adopted in several member countries of the European Union and data obtained by the IEA from its two last inquiries on reading (1991), science and math (1995). This analysis is all the more necessary now that the expansion of mandatory schooling and its extension—sometimes to age 18, as in Germany, the Netherlands and Belgium—poses the problem in a slightly different way: It now consists of studying in depth the flow within educational systems and not just the access of young people to those systems. This has been undertaken by two of the present authors for European countries (Demeuse & Monseur, 1998).

In the examination of their styles of organized schooling, it appears that these countries are distinguished by their views of heterogeneity of the population as natural endowments unfavorable to the performance of the system or, in contrast, as a source of wealth on which it can draw. This opposition translates into a tendency to reduce heterogeneity within instructional groups, in the first case, and to keep within classes as large a variety as found in the overall population, in the second case.

Following our analysis, Monseur and Demeuse (1998) have used several indicators (Table 2, page 76) to describe national systems as a function of the styles of grouping students within classes, schools and programs, while trying to relate these styles to school achievement.

Table 3 (page 77) summarizes certain practices used by the member states of the European Union to assure greater homogeneity of instructional groups, on the basis of indicators used by the authors and described in the preceding table.

In this table, established with data for the first half of the 1990s, the gray squares indicate a practice more oriented towards the creation of homogeneous instructional groups. The northern countries of Europe (Denmark, Sweden, Norway, Iceland and Finland) have put in place institutional structures that favor organization by heterogeneous groups. In contrast, Germany, the Netherlands and Belgium favor practices that contribute to the formation of more homogenous groups. Between these two groups, some other countries have adopted less segmented approaches: Spain, Ireland and France, on the

Table 2. Variables taken into account in the study by Monseur & Demeuse (1998) with respect to styles of grouping students in mandatory education in Europe

Indicator	Definition and method of calculation	Source
Actual mix of school establishments and classes	Percentage of schools or classes with less than 65 percent of students of the same sex	Upper grades, population 2, IEA-TIMSS, 1995
Automatic promotion or repetition in primary school	Type of promotion of students in primary school from one school year to another	EURYDICE, *Eurybase*,* 1996
Levels of students falling behind at age 14 in 1991 and 1995	Percentage of students who have fallen behind within the sample established for the IEA-Reading Literacy study	Population 2, IEA-Reading Literacy, 1991
	Percentage of students who have fallen behind within the sample established for the IEA-TIMSS study	Upper grade, population 2, IEA-TIMSS, 1995
Distribution at the primary level (school catchment area)	Assignment of students to a public school by function of their residence	EURYDICE, *Eurybase*, 1996
Grouping of students as a function of their age within the school year	Percentage of variance explained by age in the class group within the sample established by the IEA-Reading Literacy study	Population 1, IEA-Reading Literacy, 1991
The importance of specialized schools outside the ordinary instructional track	Percentage of students who, by reason of particular needs or handicaps, attend specialized schools outside of those dispensing an ordinary education	European Commission, *Key data on education in the European Union*, 1997
Level of school retention	Percentage of 17-year-olds still in school	Eurostat, *Education in the European Union—Statistics and Indicators*, 1996

*Eurybase is an online database considered and used by EURYDICE (www.eurydice.org).

Table 3. Indicators of student grouping, in homogeneous instructional groups (Monseur & Demeuse, 1998)

	Real coeducation within schools	Real coeducation within classes	Progression at primary level	Percentage of overaged students (1991)	Percentage of overaged students (1995)	Tracking at 14 years old	School catchment area	Grouping by age	Special education	Percentage of 17-year-olds still in school
Belgium (French-speaking)	73.6%	56.7%	R.	48.9%	35.9%	yes	no	40.1	3.61%	100%
Belgium (Dutch-speaking)	39.2%	30.8%	R.	- - -	23.2%	yes	no	- - -	- - -	- - -
Netherlands	83.1%	67.4%	R.	28.4%	30.7%	yes	no	18.3	4.32%	91%
Germany	77.9%	66.9%	R.	27.2%	22.1%	yes	- - -	17.6	3.29%	93%
Spain	83.3%	71.0%	R.C.	29.1%	28.9%	yes	no	13.2	0.45%	73%
Ireland	55.6%	31.8%	P.	19.1%	16.7%	yes	no	22.1	1.01%	84%
France	92.9%	66.9%	R.C.	47.8%	36.7%	yes	yes	27.2	2.63%	92%
Italy	- - -	- - -	R.	21.6%	- - -	yes	yes	11.6	0.18%	- - -
United Kingdom (England and Wales)	78.9%	59.5%	P.	- - -	1.0%	yes	no	- - -	0.98%	74%
Austria	82.2%	67.7%	R.	- - -	17.8%	yes	yes	- - -	1.58%	86%
Portugal	96.2%	59.2%	R.–	51.7%	39.7%	no	yes	19.4	0.39%	67%
United Kingdom (Scotland)	98.0%	82.7%	P.	- - -	3.0%	yes	no	- - -	0.98%	74%
Greece	96.5%	84.0%	R.–	15.7%	12.6%	yes	yes	13.3	0.91%	57%
Denmark	83.2%	81.9%	P.	6.2%	9.9%	no	no	6.6	0.45%	81%
Sweden	97.8%	72.2%	P.	3.3%	3.2%	no	no	5.0	0.06%	95%
Iceland	75.2%	66.7%	P.	1.1%	0.6%	no	yes	6.0	0.47%	- - -
Finland	- - -	- - -	R.–	5.6%	- - -	no	yes	8.3	1.65%	92%
Norway	92.1%	86.3%	P.	9.2%	1.9%	no	yes	7.7	0.48%	- - -
Luxembourg*	- - -	- - -	R.	- - -	- - -	yes	yes	- - -	0.98%	- - -

*There are too many facts missing to classify this country correctly; R. = it is possible to repeat a grade correctly; R.C. = it is only possible to repeat a grade at the end of each stage or cycle (for example, after completing lower secondary education); R.– = exceptional grade retention; P. = automatic promotion; - - - = no data available.

one hand; and Italy, the United Kingdom, Portugal and Greece, on the other hand, have adopted structures that partially limit the possibility of homogeneous groupings. Certain countries have adopted automatic promotion; others relatively rigid geographic assignments.

The indicators used are relatively stable across the studies considered during the last 10 years, with the exception of Sweden and Portugal which, in the first case, tend to increase disparities, and in the second, to reduce them between 1991 and 1995. These two changes seem associated with reforms in the course of these two systems in the period studied. The PISA[9] study conducted by the OECD will allow, from 2001 on, actualization of the data as well as their extension beyond the limits of the European countries described by the authors.

4.3.   The effectiveness of some styles of student groupings

Scholastic organizations varying on this point, it is interesting to note in what measure these can have repercussions on the degree of effectiveness and equity of the system, notably with the help of the results of international studies such as those conducted by the IEA.[10] In this perspective, Monseur and Demeuse (1998) have also studied, in relation to their effectiveness, some styles of scholastic organization and pedagogic measures such as repetition, free choice of school, and organization of distinct tracks and class levels—measures that can lead to a lessening of heterogeneity of learning groups.

Figure 1 (page 79) describes two systems whose practices, with regard to promotion or repetition, are diametrically opposed. The top chart represents the distribution of ages in a system where promotion is automatic, Iceland, while the lower chart represents a system that practices a significant degree of repetition. This is the French-speaking community of Belgium. The data are from the IEA Reading Literacy study. In the first case, the age of the students, expressed in months, covers a period of a year; in the French community of Belgium, the spread of the ages of students who attend the same school year is much larger. While the Icelandic students of 9.8 years attend grade 3, young Belgians of the same age are enrolled in grade 4 (mandatory schooling begins a year sooner there than in Iceland). In grade 8, Icelandic children are on the average 14.8 years old while the Belgian children are 14.3 years old. If the first group is said to be the expected age, the second is seen to have fallen behind, during the four normal years of schooling, by 6 months, or a half-year of study. The cost of this practice cannot be reconciled with any advantage in the average level of return, nor even in the level of success of the weakest students (Elley, 1994; Lafontaine, 1996).

In systems that practice automatic promotion, one can observe a slight positive correlation between the age expressed in months and school achievement, at least in the early stages of schooling. This signifies that students born first seem to experience a slight advantage in relation to those who, though in the same

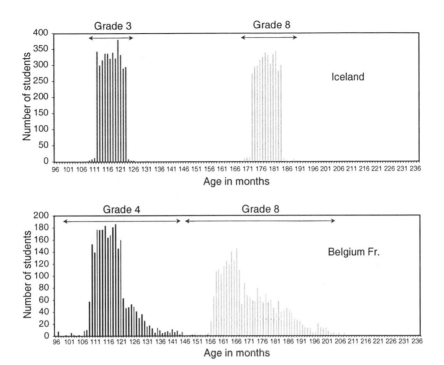

Figure 1. Graphic representation of age differences that can exist between grades tested in each of the countries that participated in the IEA-Reading Literacy study (1991). The age of students is expressed in months (horizontally); the number of students by age group is expressed on the vertical axis. The upper chart shows the distribution by age in Iceland ; the lower, the distribution by age in French-speaking Belgium (Source: IEA-Reading Literacy)

class, were born some months later. In systems where repetition is allowed, and even enforced, this liaison between age and results is inverted—the best results being obtained by the youngest students, those who have not been left back.

There are, within systems that practice repetition, wide differences in school achievement between students who have been held back and students who have not. In contrast, in these systems, the dispersion of student results within a single year of study is slightly less than the dispersion of student results in systems practicing automatic promotion.

Nor do the meta-analyses conducted on these quasi-experimental studies show any gain from the practice of repetition on automatic promotion. In fact, they underline the negative effects of repetition on the emotional and social development of the students who are retained. It is therefore far from such measures that one must seek solutions for the weakest students. One alternative to repetition is to suppress the grouping of students by age, and to organize groups of students from several age categories by function of their academic needs, so as to constitute transitory or permanent groupings (multi-level classes)

(Slavin, 1987, 1990; Slavin, Karweit & Wasik, 1994; Slavin, Karweit & Madden, 1989; Slavin, Madden, Dolan & Wasik, 1996). A review of the scientific literature (Veenman, 1996) worldwide shows no significant differences in favor of classes containing only students of a single year of study. Small-size schools, especially in rural or less accessible areas, may also resort to one class, grouping students of different ages, under the responsibility of a single instructor. However, these do not necessarily bring about the deliberate instructional progress of multi-level classes.

Repetition, conceived as a compensatory teaching method, apart from its notable ineffectiveness (Crahay, 1996), also produces a number of perverse effects. Figure 2 illustrates the relation between "disparity among classes" and "rate of falling behind in different European educational systems." If the rates of students falling behind and the levels of class disparities (percentage of variance explained by the "class level") are rather weak in the different countries of Northern Europe (Finland, Norway, Denmark, Sweden and Iceland), at least one of these indicators is noticeably higher for the other countries. The rate of those falling behind is especially high in Portugal, France and French-speaking Belgium, while the disparity indicator is highest in the Netherlands, Switzerland and Ireland. Some countries, such as Spain or Italy, occupy an intermediate position on the two indicators. In a rather general manner, therefore, in this example, one perceives that when the disparities in results among classes are significant, the tendency to use repetition is also significant. This observation raises a question as to the real nature of repetition: Is it first of all a compensatory

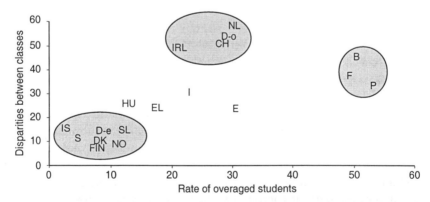

Figure 2. Relationship between the percentage of overage students (at the beginning of secondary education) and levels of disparity among classes for European countries participating in the study* (Source: IEA-Reading Literacy)

* D-o: Germany (old Länder); D-e: Germany (new Länder); IRL: Ireland; NL: the Netherlands; CH: Switzerland; S: Sweden; DK: Denmark; FIN: Finland; NO: Norway; SL: Slovenia; HU: Hungary; EL: Greece; I: Italy; E: Spain; B: Belgium (French-Speaking Community); F: France; P: Portugal; IS: Iceland.

measure for the student who is the "beneficiary" or is it rather to increase the homogeneity of instructional groups in favor of the group itself, even of the instructor who is in charge?

Certain systems link student enrollments in a school to their place of residence; this practice is known, in French, by the term "Carte scolaire" or "sectorisation" (school catchment area). Others, in contrast, authorize free choice among schools, even in public education, sometimes even subsidizing, in whole or in part, private instruction that competes with the public system. The establishment of a system constraining the attachment of students to educational institutions offers some relief, whether to equalize recruitment (the idea of the republican school in France, busing to end racial segregation in the United States; see Orfield in this work) or from a concern about planning for instructional needs. This practice has generally had the effect of rendering schools more similar, while avoiding the creation of ghetto schools. School systems that, in contrast, let the academic marketplace organize itself, sometimes accentuate this approach by publishing school-specific data so that parents can make informed choices. Certain countries take in one or more large networks of private schools, subsidized or not. Sometimes, as in the Flemish community of Belgium, the private subsidized network has a large majority; in this case over 70 percent of all students at the secondary level. There is, however, in countries that practice school mapping, some mobility of students. These students are generally from families that enjoy a socioeconomic level above the average of the school their children would normally attend, who try to enroll them in schools with more privileged students (Castro, 1996; Duru-Bellat & Henriot-Van Zantem, 1992; Lamoure, 1982; Perrot, 1981; Pinçon-Charlot & Rendu, 1988). The geographic assignment of students is less effective as the social division among different residential neighborhoods is itself very pronounced. Countries with very disadvantaged communities, whether or not they use the school mapping system, can establish compensatory mechanisms to assure schools with disadvantaged populations a better environment or greater resources.

If parents take advantage of freedom of school choice, as in the Netherlands, Germany or Belgium, there are strong chances that the schools will appeal to different sectors of the public and have a higher "class effect," as shown in Figure 3 (page 82, from IEA Reading-Literacy, 1991), on secondary education.

The homogeneous grouping of students as a function of their scholastic performance can, according to educational systems, take different forms. The first consists of fixed groups across different courses. One student, as a function of his/her academic results or another measure of his/her competence, is placed in a group and, whatever the subject studied, remains with his/her peers. This category essentially encompasses two large modalities of organization of educational systems, at the school or classroom level. These two modalities are not however mutually exclusive. The second form consists of homogeneous grouping across classes for specific subjects (essentially in reading and mathematics): Students belong to heterogeneous classes, but are grouped for one or more subjects as a function of their results on a test on that subject. The studies examined (Crahay, 2000; Slavin, 1987, 1990) suggest that this type of grouping can be effective provided the duration and pace of learning, as well as the material, are adapted to different groups. This practice, whose positive effects are recognized, is still rarely seen in the educational arena.

The grouping of students in different schools is effected, whether as a function of the reputation of the school or by the choice among options or tracks offered to the student, so that there may or may not be a formal selection for entering. This leads schools to be attended by different segments of the public. The establishment of official projects or organizations on a religious basis in a country where religion and ethnic membership can be confused can also lead to relatively distinct schools, and increase the effect of segregation. Inside the school, the students have many academic similarities, but among establishments there can be great differences.

The division of students can lead to differences in the curriculum and even in the requirements for or value of the diploma. This is notably the case in instructional systems that use one-level classes or tracking. If that is an undesirable effect of one-level classes, then students would in principle have to attain the same level upon leaving school, for the courses are a matter of deliberate policy. One can

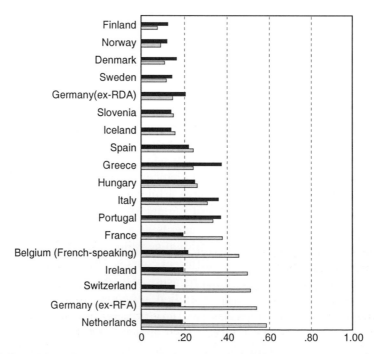

Figure 3. Proportion of variance in results in reading comprehension explained by the "class level" at age 9 (dark bars) and at age 13 (light bars) (Source: IEA-Reading Literacy, 1991)

show other undesirable effects in the system of tracking.

Thus, one can observe an increase in the average age of students in vocational or professional courses determined by negative choices, resulting randomly, after failure in "nobler" courses. Figure 4 illustrates the impact of tracks, in Germany, on the age of students. It is in the professional tracks (Hauptschulen) that one observes the largest proportion of students who have fallen behind, particularly with respect to the academic track (Gymnasium). The less common Gesamtschulen are integrated.

In a domain as important as literacy, notably at the beginning of secondary

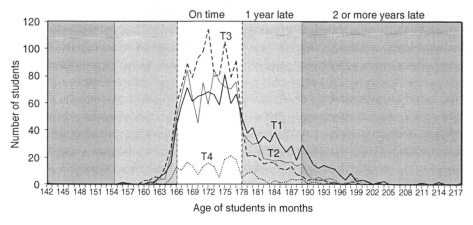

Figure 4. Distribution by age of students (expressed in months, on the horizontal axis) of four types of secondary establishments in Germany (T1=*Hauptschulen*,[a] T2=*Realschulen*,[b] T3= *Gymnasien*[c] and T4=*Gesamtschulen*[d]). The central part of the figure, between the two broken lines, represents the normal age at which students should be at this level (Source: IEA-Reading Literacy, 1991)

a *Hauptschule*: Type of school at lower-secondary level providing a basic general education. Compulsory school, unless pupil is attending a different type of secondary school, usually comprising grades 5-9. (Eurybase, 1998)

b *Realschule*: Type of school at lower-secondary level, usually comprising grades 5–10. Provides pupils with a more extensive general education and the opportunity to go on to courses at upper-secondary level that lead to vocational or higher-education qualifications. (Eurybase, 1998)

c *Gymnasium*: Type of school covering both lower- and upper-secondary level (usually grades 5–13) and providing an in-depth general education aimed at the general higher-education entrance qualification. (Eurybase, 1998)

d *Gesamtschule*: Type of school at lower-secondary level offering several courses of education leading to different qualifications. It either takes the form of a cooperative *Gesamtschule* or an integrated *Gesamtschule*. In the cooperative type, pupils are taught in classes grouped according to the different qualifications available, while in the integrated type, pupils are set in courses grouped according to level of proficiency for a number of core subjects, but taught together as an age group for all other subjects. *Gesamtschulen* can also encompass the upper-secondary level in the form of the Gymnasiale Oberstufe. (Eurybase, 1998)

education (age 14), one can already observe the impact of student groupings on different tracks. Figure 5 also illustrates this phenomenon in the German educational system.

The division of students into tracks can also lead to disparities by sex. Thus,

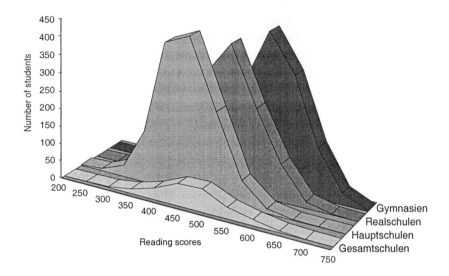

Figure 5. Distribution of scores in reading comprehension as a function of the track (*Hauptschulen, Realschulen, Gymnasien* and *Gesamtschulen*) in the Federal Republic of Germany (Source: IEA-Reading Literacy, 1991)

at the college level in France a unique structure that in principle educates all students between 11 and 13 years of age, 87 percent of the classes are actually coeducational. Beyond this cycle of observation, the use of options and tracks reduces this percentage to 68 percent (TIMSS, 1995).

The tendency of a country to group students according to their cognitive characteristics can be measured by the bias of certain techniques issuing from the analysis of variance. Thus, from the results of students on IEA tests, it is easy to determine the percentage of the total variance explained by membership in a class. Educational systems characterized by large differences among average class levels in the population of 14- to 15-year-old students are also those in which the first academic choice came early, before age 14; the size of the differences among classes corresponds to the differences in level among tracks. Thus, the grouping as a function of future career plans seems associated with the creation of more homogenous groups by performance in reading. This is indeed reflected in a differentiation of results—higher in the general or academic tracks than in the technical or professional tracks.

Observation of the practices of homogeneous grouping of students (instructional tracks, level of classes, repetition, etc.) within a certain number of educational systems, and not in others, leads us to suppose that there is a tendency to seek a certain homogeneous level within the classes of each system. This tendency can also be seen to result from reforms in compensatory programs. Every effort to modify the superficial practices (for example, passage from a system of repetition to a system of automatic promotion) is generally accompanied by a growth in other homogeneous grouping mechanisms that have not been taken into consideration (such as increase in the number of students retained in pre-school, growth of disparities between classes and schools, increase in assignments, special instruction, etc.).

Certain systems organize one-level classes. Schools take in a diverse public, but it is redistributed among different classes as a function of academic performance of the students. This organization can also lead to unwanted results. For example, we have already noted that the organization of such classes can lead to early differences in the official and established curriculum (Burstein, 1993). The two methods of grouping students in schools or in homogeneous classes certainly lead to results that betray this redistribution. When one uses measures effected in several classes within the same schools, it is possible to distinguish the impact of grouping in schools and in classes within them.

By way of illustration, Figure 6 presents these aggregation effects and the levels at which they intervene. Thus, the top part of the figure describes the impact of the "school" and "class" level on the differences observed among students. Of these, 7.8% of the differences alone are attributable directly to attendance at one school rather than another. In other words, the averages of

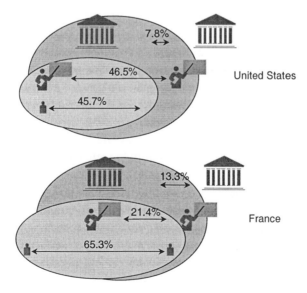

Figure 6. Effects of aggregation at the school and class level in the United States (SIMS), top, and in France, bottom

different schools are relatively similar. By contrast, the averages of different classes within each school vary much more (46.5%). The differences among students within classes reach 45.7%. This figure, drawn from Second International Mathematics Study (SIMS) data for the United States (Burstein, 1993), translates an institutional desire to maintain schools as similar as possible while applying a system of homogeneous ability classes within them.

The lower part of Figure 6 describes, in the same way, the results obtained from a national study in France. If the differences not attributable to school level are similar enough to those in the United States (13.3%), the use of tracking, a practice forbidden by the Ministry of Education, is naturally not as frequent in France. This leads to the observation of a greater heterogeneity within classes in this country (Duru-Bellat & Mingat, 1997).

This model can also be completed in taking into account the organization of tracks.

In a general manner, the practice of homogeneous grouping of students, measured by the intermediary of the aggregation effect between classes, does not seem tied to an improvement in average results in international surveys. In contrast, the secondary analyses conducted with respect to the results of three international studies (SIMS, Second International Science Study (SISS) and Reading Literacy) reveal a slight tendency in favor of countries that do not practice these grouping styles. In comparison, in the Third International Study of Mathematics and Science (TIMSS), an inverse relation, while slight, is noted at this level. The results of quasi-experimental research, synthesized in meta-analyses (Kulik & Kulik, 1984; Slavin, 1987, 1990; Crahay, 2000), confirm the absence of favorable effect linked to homogeneous groupings.

In an experimental situation, where the pedagogic variables are objects of strict control, homogeneous grouping does not produce different effects according to the levels of constituent groups; classes that take in only good students do not progress more than classes composed essentially of weak students (Kulik & Kulik, 1984; Slavin, 1987, 1990; Crahay, 2000). However, in reality, this grouping is accompanied by differentiation of the curriculum, by the fact that the best teachers teach the classes attended by the best students, and by pedagogical practices that favor higher performing students (the Matthew effect). These modifications can then be translated into greater progress among students who benefit from the best learning conditions. These are therefore "parasitic" practices, which lead to a widening of the gap that separates the weakest students from the strongest, and not to an adequate grouping of students.

Conclusion

A conception based more on the selection of students—indeed of schools—by parents than on improvement of the educational system for the benefit of all is hardly compatible with a real democratic ethic. Similarly, the growth in disparities among students and among schools prevents all systems seeking to apply an equitable policy from being fully effective because they neglect at least one of the parameters. This perspective guides research on effectiveness to give a central place to problems of equity, and to not focus exclusively on average levels.

There seems to be a need both to concentrate attention so that desirable change actually takes place with the effective use of additional resources, and to generalize the task of overcoming disadvantage so that it is a national priority, not restricted to isolated "compensatory" measures. Indeed, the more sustained and generalized the priority of addressing educational disadvantage becomes, the less appropriate is the very language of "compensation," with its suggestion of handing over something above and beyond the normal. And the more quality and equity are seen as different aspects of the same educational endeavor, the more mainstream support the pursuit of equity should have as integral to educational improvement, rather than just in the province of "special measures" (OECD, 1993, pp. 83–84). At the same time, a certain number of practices, such as the homogeneous grouping of students, which seem both ineffective and ethically indefensible, must be questioned with regard to the objectives of the system and modified if they are shown to be ineffective or injurious.

In a way, the circle is complete: While we suggested equity in the beginning as a factor of the effectiveness of democratic systems, the OECD and others have shown it to be, "by definition," a necessity. There can be no effectiveness without equity—whether as a matter of deep conviction, founded on democratic values, or because a pragmatic report has tied it to studies conducted since the 1960s throughout the world.

Notes

1   This chapter was originally submitted in French.
2   Europe is understood here to be the European Union, consisting of countries participating in the free trade agreement (i.e., Norway and Iceland).
3   There is also the difficulty involved in measuring the purported lowering of standards, of which most instructional systems are suspected. In this case, the problem is complicated by the degree to which characteristics of the school population are modified. Thus, French high schools (lycées) at the end of the 20th century were subjected to a wave of mandatory schooling, which makes today's cohorts of students difficult to compare with those of 1950 and 1960. Moreover, programs have changed; certain skills or knowledge judged indispensible in the past

are no longer priority goals while others, which were not taught before, have become essential.

4 For example, Article 26 of the Universal Declaration of Human Rights, adopted and proclaimed by the General Assembly of the United Nations in its Resolution 217A (III) on December 10, 1948, states that: "(1) Everyone has the right to education. Education shall be free, at least in the elementary and fundamental stages. Elementary education shall be compulsory. Technical and professional education shall be made generally available and higher education shall be equally accessible to all on the basis of merit. (2) Education shall be directed to the full development of the human personality and to the strengthening of respect for human rights and fundamental freedoms. It shall promote understanding, tolerance and friendship among all nations, racial or religious groups, and shall further the activities of the United Nations for the maintenance of peace. (3) Parents have a prior right to choose the kind of education that shall be given to their children."

5 For an in-depth discussion of this table, refer in particular to the chapter by Meuret in this work or, in the French language, to the book by Crahay (2000).

6 This explanation is valid only with respect to perfectly defined skills in the domains where there is an upper limit that is, at least theoretically, possible to establish (without necessarily implying that it is possible to attain). In practice, goals are supplanted over time: What was supposed to constitute the "summit" in one era can later be judged as just adequate. This does not constitute a decisive element in this demonstration; we have from the start posited the study of efficiency in relation to objectives assigned at a given moment in the education system. To modify goals along the way, even for certain individuals to forego them, poses questions other than the one considered here, linked to education as a status benefit or equality of achievement.

7 The term *"high level of proficiency"* is generally used in English, better expressing the concept than recourse to the French term *"compétences minimales,"* which may be read as pejorative.

8 De Landsheere (1979, p. 237) notes two interpretations of this term: (1) Relationship between the number of students of a given age remaining in school and the total number in the corresponding age group. (2) Relationship between the number of students who finish their studies in an institution and the total number enrolled at the beginning. It is to the first meaning that we refer in the text that follows.

9 PISA: OECD Program for International Student Assessment (www.pisa.oecd.org).

10 A certain number of authors, such as Brown (1998), have vehemently contested the results of IEA-TIMSS type studies and their use at the national level because they compare such different systems of education. Demeuse and Monseur try, in contrast, to use information about the systems and achievement test results so as to better understand the impact of this or that organizational style. This supposes both a good knowledge of the studies themselves (notably their sampling procedures) and the educational systems studied. It is for this second reason that the authors have from the outset limited themselves to the consideration of European educational systems.

References

Baudelot C., Establet R., *Le niveau monte. Réfutation d'une vieille idée concernant la prétendue décadence de nos écoles,* Editions du Seuil, Paris, 1990.

Beaton A.E., Gonzalez E.J., "TIMSS Test-Curriculum Matching Analysis," in Martin M.O., Kelly D.L. (eds.), *Third International Mathematics and Science Study Technical Report, Volume II: Implementation and Analysis—Primary and Middle School Years,* TIMSS International Study Centre, Boston College, Chestnut Hill (Mass.), 1997.

Beaton A.E., Martin M.O., Mullis I.V.S., Gonzalez E.J., Smith T.A., Kelly D.L., "Science Achievement in the Middle School Years: IEA's Third International Mathematics and Science Study (TIMSS)," TIMSS International Study Centre, Boston College, Chestnut Hill (Mass.), 1996.

Black P., Atkin J.M., *Changing the Subject: Innovations in Science, Mathematics, and Technology Education,* Routledge and the OECD, London and Paris, 1996.

Bloom B.S., *Human Characteristics and School Learning*, McGraw-Hill, New York, 1976.

Bonami M., De Ketele J.M., Delvaux B., Deom D., De Ville P., Lietard G., Maroy C., Paquay L., Vandenberghe, *Les modes de régulation du système éducatif: enjeux en terme d'efficacité et d'équité*, Projet interdisciplinaire en sciences de l'éducation soumis au Conseil de la Recherche, Bruxelles, 1997.

Bos W., Lehmann R.H. (eds.), *Reflections on Educational Achievement. Papers in Honour of T. Neville Postlethwaite,* Waxmann, New York, 1995.

Bourdieu P., Passeron J.C., *Les héritiers: les étudiants et la culture*, Editions de Minuit, Collection "Le sens commun" (2ème édition), Paris, 1971.

Bressoux P., "Les performances des écoles et des classes. Le cas des acquisitions en lecture," *Education et formations,* p. 30, 1993.

Brookover W., Beady P., Flood P., Schweitzer J., Wiesenbaker J., *School social systems and student achievement: schools make a difference*, Praeger, New York, 1979.

Brown M., "The Tyranny of the International Horse Race," in Slee R., Weiner G., Tomlinson S. (eds.), *School Effectiveness for Whom? Challenges to School Effectiveness and School Improvement Movements*, Falmer Press, London, 1998.

Burstein L., *The IEA Study of Mathematics III: Student Growth and Classroom Processes*, Pergamon Press, Oxford, 1993.

Castro M., "A Carcassonne: Périmètre scolaire à la carte," *Le Monde de l'Education*, pp. 32–33, October 1996.

Crahay M., *Peut-on lutter contre l'échec scolaire?,* De Boeck, Bruxelles, 1996.

Crahay M., *L'école peut-elle être juste et efficace?,* De Boeck, Bruxelles, 2000.

Decroly O., Buyse R., *Introduction à la pédagogie quantitative. Eléments de statistiques appliqués aux problèmes pédagogiques,* Maurice Lamertin, Bruxelles, 1929.

de Landsheere G., *Dictionnaire de l'évaluation et de la recherche en éducation,* Presses universitaires de France, Paris, 1979.

de Landsheere V., *Faire réussir, faire échoue, La compétence minimale et son évaluation,* Presses universitaires de France, Pédagogie aujourd'hui, Paris, 1988.

de Landsheere V., de Landsheere G., *Definir les objectifs de l'éducation*, Editions Georges Thone, Liege, 1978.

Demeuse M., Monseur C., *Pour accroître l'efficacité des systèmes d'enseignement. recherche des facteurs d'efficacité, Etude comparative des dispositifs de pilotage*, Rapport final, Commission de l'"Union européenne, D.G. XXII, Socrates III.3.1. 96.01-SPE-0406-00, Bruxelles, 1998.

Demeuse M., Monseur C., "Analyse des mécanismes déterminant l'attribution des moyens destinés à la politique de discrimination positive en Communauté française de Belgique," in *Actes du XIIIème colloque de ADMEE-Europe,* Dijon, September 1999.

Duru-Bellat M., Mingat A., *La gestion de l'hétérogénéité des publics d'élèves au collège*, Les cahiers de l'Iredu, Dijon, p. 59, 1993.

Duru-Bellat M., Henriot-Van Zantem A., *Sociologie de l'école*, Armand Colin, Paris, 1992.

Elley W.B. (ed.), *The IEA Study of Reading Literacy: Achievement and Instruction in Thirty-Two School Systems*, Pergamon, Oxford, 1994.

Emin J.C., "La mise en place d'un dispositif d'indicateur pour le pilotage des établissements secondaires français," in OCDE, *Mesurer la qualité des établissements scolaires*, OCDE, CERI, Paris, 1995.

Eurostat, *Education dans l'Union européenne—Statistiques et indicateurs*, Eurostat, Luxembourg, 1996.

Fischer C.S., Hout M., Jankowski M.S., Lucas S.R., Swidler A., Voss K., *Inequality by Design. Cracking the Bell Curve Myth,* Princeton University Press, Princeton, 1996.

Gould S.J., *The Mismeasure of Man*, Penguin Books (2nd edition), Harmondsworth, 1996.

Grisay A., "Quels indicateurs pour quelle réduction des inégalités scolaires," *Revue de la Direction générale des Etudes*, Bruxelles. November 3–14, 1984.

Husen T., *International Studies of Achievement in Mathematics—A Comparison of Twelve Countries,* vol. 1, John Wiley, New York, 1967a.

Husen T., *International Studies of Achievement in Mathematics—A Comparison of Twelve Countries,* vol. 2, John Wiley, New York, 1967b.

Keeves J.P., (ed.), *The IEA Study of Science III: Changes in Science Education and Achievement: 1970 to 1984*, Pergamon Press, Oxford, 1992.

Kulik C.L.C., Kulik J.A., *Effect of ability grouping on elementary school pupils: A meta-analysis*, paper presented at the Annual Convention of the American Psychological Association,Toronto, August 24–28, 1984.

Lafontaine D., *Performances en lecture et contexte éducatif, Enquête internationale menée auprès d'élèves de 9 et 14 ans*, DeBoeck Université, Bruxelles, 1996.

Lamoure J., "La scolarisation en France: de fortes inégalités régionale," *L'Orientation scolaire et professionnelle, 11*(3), pp. 195–213, 1982.

Ministère de la Communautè Française, *Socles de compétences. Enseignement fondamental et premier degré de l'Enseignement secondaire,* Ministère de la Communauté Française de Belgique, Administration générale de l'Enseignement et de la Recherche scientifique, Bruxelles, 1999.

Monseur C., Demeuse M., *The Effectiveness of Educational Systems. Methods of grouping pupils in compulsory education, Thematic report,* European Commission, GD XXII Education, Training, Youth, Bruxelles, 1998 (English translation from: *L'efficacité des systèmes éducatifs. Modalités de groupement des élèves dans l'enseignement obligatoire*; also available in German: *Zur Effizienz der Erziehungssysteme. Methoden der Zusammenfassung von Schülern im Pflichtunterricht*).

OECD, "Access, Participation and Equity," OECD, Education Committee (DEELSA/ED(93)8/REV1), Paris, 1993.

OECD, "Educational Research and Development. Trends, Issues and Challenges," OECD, CERI, Paris, 1995a.

OECD, *Knowledge bases for education policies*, proceedings of a conference held in Maastricht (The Netherlands), September 11–13, 1995b.

OECD, "Measuring What People Know. Human Capital Accounting for the Knowledge Economy," OECD, Paris, 1996.

OECD, *Education and Equity in OECD Countries,* OECD, Paris, 1997.

OECD, *Education at a Glance: OECD Indicators 1998,* OECD, Paris, 1998a.

OECD, "Human Capital Investment. An International Comparison," OECD, CERI, Paris, 1998b.

Parlement de la Communautè Flamande de Belgique, Decret du 24 juillet 1996 sanctionnant les objectifs finaux et les objectifs de developpement du premier degre de l'enseignement secondaire ordinaire, *Moniteur belge,* 14 août 1996.

Parlement de la Communautè Flamande de Belgique, Decret du 15 juillet 1997 sanctionnant les objectifs de developpement et les objectifs finaux de l'enseignement fondamental ordinaire, *Moniteur belge*, 28 août 1997.

Perrot J., "La carte scolaire. Un instrument efficace mais inégalitaire," *L'Orientation scolaire et professionnelle, 10*(1), pp. 83–96, 1981.

Pinçon-Charlot M., Rendu P., "Les hauts fonctionnaires face aux enjeux scolaires de leurs enfants," *Revue française de Pédagogie, 83*, pp. 54–56, 1988.

Robitaille D.F., Garden R.A., *The IEA Study of Mathematics II: Contexts and Outcomes of School Mathematics*, Pergamon, Oxford, 1989.

Scheerens J., Bosker R., *The Foundations of Educational Effectiveness,* Pergamon, Oxford, 1997.

Slavin R.E., "Ability grouping and student achievement in elementary schools: A best-evidence synthesis," *Review of Educational Research, 57*(3), pp. 293–336, 1987.

Slavin R.E., "Achievement effects of ability grouping in secondary schools: A best-evidence synthesis," *Review of Educational Research, 60*(3), pp. 471–499, 1990.

Slavin R.E., Karweit N.L., Madden N.A., *Effective programs for students at risk*, Allyn and Bacon, Boston, 1989.

Slavin R.E., Karweit N.L., Wasik B.A., *Preventing Early School Failure. Research, Policy, and Practice, The first comprehensive, direct comparison of programs designed to prevent failure in early grades*, Allyn and Bacon, Boston, 1994.

Slavin R.E., Madden N.A., Dolan L.J., Wasik B.A., *Every child, every school. Success for All,* Corwin Press, Thousand Oaks (Calif.), 1996.

Slavin R.E., Fashola O.S., *Show me the Evidence! Proven and Promising Programs for America's Schools*, Corwin Press, Thousand Oaks (Calif.), 1998.

Swanson J.C., "Efficiency in Education," in Deighton L.C. (ed.), *The Encyclopedia of Education*. Macmillan Company and Free Press, 1971.

Sweetland S.R., "Human Capital Theory: Foundations of a Field of Inquiry," *Review of Educational Research, 66*(3), pp. 341–359, 1996.

Thélot C. (ed.), *Trois indicateurs de performance des lycées. Baccalauréat général, technologique et professionnel 1996, Résultats lycée par lycée*, Ministère de l'Education, de la Recherche et de la Formation, Direction de l'Evaluation et de la Prospective, Paris, 1996.

Veenman S., "Effect of multigrade and multi-stage classes reconsidered," *Review of Educational Research, 66*(3), pp. 323–340, 1996.

Webster W.J., Mendro R.L., Almaguer T.O, "Effectiveness indice: a "Value added" approach to measuring school effect," *Studies in Educational Evaluation, 20*, pp. 113–145, 1994.

Chapter 3

School Equity as a Matter of Justice[*]

Denis Meuret
Université de Bourgogne, Dijon, France

Educational systems present a considerable number of inequalities. Certain students receive better grades than others, or receive more attention from their teachers, or have more effective teachers, or have shorter school careers, or leave with or without a trade that enables them to find work, etc. Certain categories of students are more successful than others (for example, high-socioeconomic status (SES) children or girls in language tests).

It is evident from this list that certain inequalities may be acceptable, while others are not. Why do unacceptable inequalities exist? Perhaps the causes that produce them are very powerful: Sociologists have put a certain number in evidence (see Benadusi's synthesis, Chapter 1). But if the causes are so powerful that these inequalities must be considered unavoidable, can one still speak of them as unacceptable?

We prefer to believe that, powerful as the forces that cause inequalities may be, they could be changed by collective action. But then a conclusion is imposed: The inequalities that we observe exist because most citizens tolerate them because they find them just, or rather—an important distinction—because they are not so sure that they are unjust enough to refuse to tolerate them.

One can imagine that it is difficult to determine the inequity of this or that educational inequality. If we find it unjust that working-class children are more likely to receive technical than general education, perhaps it is the effect of *petit-bourgeois* ethnocentrism that causes us to look down on the vocational world. If girls surpass boys in schools while teachers give them less attention, which ones are being treated unjustly? The idea that all should receive "equivalent schooling," which was recently introduced in the Swedish education act (see Wildt-Persson and Rosengren, Chapter 13), holds that equality with respect to the learning process does not require that educations be "identical" but of "equal worth," which means something like having "equal effects." But which kind of effects are relevant?

---

[*]This chapter was originally submitted in French.

More systematically, one can justify—or condemn—an inequality between two groups or individuals according to:

- their initial endowments (a sampling of American adults found it fair that disadvantaged children receive more educational resources than others (Hochschild, cited by Kellerhals et al., 1988);
- the fairness of the process that produces the inequality (no one contests that some can pass and others fail a fair exam);
- the effects of the inequality (one accepts that high achievers stay longer in school and therefore receive more public money for their education because of the expected benefit to society; e.g., no one has an interest in producing bad doctors); and
- the side effects of strategies meant to reduce this inequality (they can consume resources that could have been used to address other priorities; they could have negative effects on other things that are valued by society, such as liberty (Gutman, 1999).

The goal of the "theories of justice" is to help us decide which equalities are required by fairness. Indeed, all modern theories of justice rest on the idea that all individuals are equal. But from this assertion of equality, the problem becomes, according to a formula put forward by economist Amartya Sen (1992), "equality of what?" Between libertarians, for whom relevant equality is one of " property rights" and Marx's "each according to his needs," there are degrees of difference.

According to Fleurbaey (1996), a theory of justice is necessarily composed of:

- an ideal; that is to say, the description of a just state, resting on the application of one or several principles of justice;
- a system of arguments explaining why this state is just; and
- a field of application.

These theories evidently do not bear directly on education. They bear on more fundamental goods. Sometimes, the author himself indicates the consequences of his theory for education; sometimes, this must be inferred from what he says about the distribution of the fundamental good that he has chosen as a goal. This inference can take two forms:

On the one hand, the education system is not an end in itself; its function is to introduce young people into the contemporary world. One can thus define educational equity as the quality of an educational system that favors as much as possible what this underlying theory describes as a just society (the "ideal").

But the child or adolescent is not just "a future adult;" he/she is not just a means to an end, which would be his or her state as an adult. The child is also a person, to whom education has to be distributed with equity. Educational equity thus requires also that some rules that hold for adults hold also for young people.

The goal of this paper is to present an overview of what the principal theories of justice have to say with respect to educational inequality, and to see which indicators can be used in each case to determine injustice.

We know that the question of justice has occupied a considerable place at the heart of political philosophy since the publication of the *Theory of Justice* by Rawls in 1971. Moreover, the discussion since then has consisted of a debate around the solution proposed by Rawls. It is therefore convenient to present these theories in relation to him: first, the theories that he critiques; then his own; and then the theories that find fault with or try to go beyond his theories.

1.   Utilitarianism and intuitionism

Rawls dissociates his theory from three principles of justice that are often applied to education: utilitarianism, merit and redress. Utilitarianism—the "principle of natural liberty"—is, in Rawls' view, the principal adversary of his construction.

The latter two are "local" theories, in the sense that they are internal to the educational system. They consider education as a good in itself, without respect to its social effects. For example, the merit approach does not concern itself with the fact that merit can produce considerable inequalities in competence which, in certain circumstances, could threaten the civic equality of individuals. According to Rawls, these two principles grow out of "intuitionist" theory (1971, p. 7). The intuitionist theory holds precisely that it is impossible to construct a universal theory of justice; that we must be content to rely on a series of principles, each valid for a certain type of good.

1.1.   Utilitarianism

It seems at times that the principle of justice that drives education, especially with respect to certain teachers' daily contact with their students, may be a sort of " local Nietzschism," leading them to put the most resources in the service of those with the most aptitude, so as to produce the highest possible appearance of excellence. In France, in particular, one may think of a certain cult of scholarly excellence as the consequence of a desire for a secular/school equivalent of the Catholic notion of holiness (Meuret, 1999). Rawls (1971, p. 67; 1993, p. 5) would probably consider that as an example of the priority of the "Good on the Right" (the rules of equity proceed from the maximization of excellence, here considered as the "Good"), while his "theory of justice" advocates for the reverse priority. Rawls is not opposed to excellence, and not even to giving more attention to the better endowed, but he would certainly not define educational equity as what is necessary to promote their excellence.

At the same time, it seems that the principle of justice most directly responsible for the way the system is currently organized—such as can be deduced from the rules and regulations that organize it—is utilitarianism. This is sometimes rather a "local" sort of utilitarianism, which applies to a particular good (education) the "principle of Pareto optimality," which was originally intended to apply to particular configurations of the economic system.

Pareto's ultimate criterion is the maximization of the sum of utilities of individuals. According to this principle, a situation is optimal if it is impossible to raise the satisfaction of all individuals simultaneously (a strong statement of the principle) or impossible to raise the satisfaction of part of the population without diminishing that of another part of the population (a weak statement of the principle). This condition is often interpreted as meaning that one can only propose changes that improve everyone's circumstances or leave them unchanged; in short, that the only effective improvements in Pareto's mind are those that improve the lot of the unfortunate without destroying that of the fortunate. In fact, Fleurbaey (1996) shows clearly that the logic of the Pareto principle is only "that one can't settle for an inefficient state," and not to forbid any alteration that would reduce one group's happiness for the greater good of another group. The principle does not exclude an economic sacrifice for reasons of justice.

The local version of utilitarianism applied to education points to equalizing the marginal utility of different students—utility being defined as acquired knowledge. In true utilitarianism, however, a student must leave school when the social benefits—private and collective—of a further year of schooling are exceeded by its cost to society. The rule is therefore that one only requires a young person to continue his/her schooling so long as the gain from a supplemental year of schooling will place him/her above a certain threshold, the same for all. If one accepts the lowering of this threshold for certain students, one accepts to lower for their benefit the global amount of transmitted knowledge, and of subsequent social benefits, which is contrary to the principle of effectiveness. It is therefore just to offer less schooling to those who are less capable or less desirous of benefiting from it. Unlike meritocratism (see page 97), utilitarianism would agree that teachers of identical quality are offered to all, but would exclude progressively from the system students who are incapable of deriving more than one (specified) benefit from their teaching. This amounts to a general principle of justice, not to a local one, because the usefulness of a certain sum of knowledge is seen as depending on factors external to the system. It can for example lead to a lowering of the threshold of knowledge that has to be acquired to go on in school, and therefore may keep students in school longer if the evolution of society makes knowledge more necessary for economic or social life.

One indicator inspired by utilitarianism would verify that academic achievement is the only criterion for advanced studies. Another would verify that nobody leaves school before the social cost of a supplemental year of schooling surpasses its social (individual and collective) return. Utilitarianism's strength comes notably from its integration of the idea that resources are limited, and therefore effectiveness matters. One can measure its strength as well in its ability to relate to this principle a large number of arguments that fuel the debates over the democratization of education; for example:

- Is school expansion, egalitarianism or retention detrimental to the effectiveness of the educational system? (See Demeuse, Crahay & Monseur, Chapter 2, and Vandenberghe, Dupriez & Zachary, Chapter 9.)
- Are certain students better "suited" than others for learning that is manual and concrete? If this is the case, one improves their utility by sending them to this type of training. If it is not the case, this is an unacceptable way of justifying an early exclusion from general schooling.
- Is it true that "a year of schooling" has the same quality everywhere? If not, conditions for applying the principle are not fulfilled.
- If, in attending mixed classes, the weak pupils gain more than the strong lose—as has been shown in France for pupils in grades 6 and 7 (Duru-Bellat & Mingat, 1997; see also Vandenberghe, Chapter 11)—an utilitarianist would advocate against tracking and for indicators measuring academic segregation.

1.2. Meritocracy

It is traditional to oppose inequalities linked to circumstances of birth, which would be unjust, to those linked to "merit," which would be just. But one can imagine several forms of justification by merit.

Meritocracy in the strict sense is not a local theory of justice. It affirms the leadership of society by those who are "the most admired" (Bell, cited par Sandel, 1982) and puts the educational system in the service of their discovery and advancement. It would give some external justification to what we have called in relation to education above "local Nietzchism." In this case, one deserves an education all the more if he or she can make good use of it. In this case, the best students—or those with the highest IQs—not only would be authorized to study longer, but would receive from the beginning better school conditions or more attention. One indicator inspired by this approach would verify that it is really superior students and not, for example, the richest who benefit from the best conditions for learning.

One argument against this form of meritocracy is that it presumes to detect "the best" students very early and probably very unjustly. However, as Gutman (1999) says, "in practice, few meritocrats accept the full implication of the standard that they profess" (p. 134). The most commonly understood meaning of "meritocracy" in the current culture of educational systems is simply the "local" (or intuitionist) idea that the possibilities of a school career must be determined solely by the student's past performance. Applied to education, the definition of equity as proportionality between inputs and outputs is inscribed in this framework.

This weak version of "meritocracy" is not very far from utilitarianism, though it is much less complete and more fragile. For one thing, it does not use a single external criterion to determine the level of scholarly competence required to continue one's schooling. For another, it presumes that past school performance is an equitable and reliable indicator of future success: It puts great confidence in the equality of teaching conditions and the fairness of school judgments.

The three criticisms addressed most frequently to the meritocratic principle are:

- Willingness to work itself is determined at least in part by social origin and family circumstances. Therefore, "merit" is socially biased.
- This principle allows considerable gaps in competence between the scholarly elite and others. It can therefore engender a very inegalitarian society, even if all have equal chances of reaching the top whatever their rank at birth. Moreover, it is unstable for it does not create the conditions for its own survival: The more inegalitarian a society, the more those at the bottom will have difficulty rising through education and the more difficult it will be to see this principle applied. It is, in effect, highly disputable to decide that a society can allow uncontrolled growth in inequalities of wealth provided that, through education, all might have equal chances of figuring among the rich.
- It can lead to a "dictatorship of the talented," problematic from a democratic point of view, and as arbitrary from a moral point of view as a dictatorship of the rich. The meritocracy would end in an "unendurable (society), handed over to the tyranny of genes, dominated by an elite of inherited intelligence; it would display before everyone's eyes the value of each one" (Dupuy, 1997, p. 216).

Another problem posed by the meritocracy principle is its rapport with the principle of equal opportunity. One often puts them together, and it is probable that the success of Bourdieu's "reproduction theory" owes much to its proximity with the meritocratic principle—that merit, and not birth, governs scholastic careers.

However, Dupuy (1997) sees—with good reason—a difference between the partisans of meritocracy and the sociologists who criticize unequal opportunity. In effect, meritocrats criticize the fact that external influences (e.g., family, contacts, wealth) blur the effect of the individual's personal worth, but they have no problem with the fact that some inequalities of personal worth originate from financial or cultural inequalities—the latter being the very target of those who favor equal opportunity (see Benadusi in this work). Raymond Aron, for example, who was a meritocrat, held that it is consistent with Bourdieu's criticism of unequal opportunity to want to "suppress the intellectual and moral heritage that only families can transmit;" in short, to preach nothing less than "barbarity" (in *Les désillusions du progrès*, 1969; cited by Dupuy, 1997).

1.3. The principle of redress

In opposition to the meritocracy principle, we find the principle of redress. Rawls (1971, p. 17) presents it this way: "In order to treat all persons equally, to provide genuine equality of opportunity, society must give more attention to those with fewer native assets and to those born into the less favorable social positions. The idea is to redress the bias of contingencies in the direction of equality. In pursuit of this principle, greater resources might be spent on the education of the less rather than the more intelligent, at least over a certain time of life, say the earlier years of school."

This principle is strongly evident for most people. For instance, not even among right-wing parties in France does anyone contest the principle of giving more resources to schools in " priority education zones." In numerous countries, policies of this type have also survived changes in political rule.

Following Rawls' presentation of this principle, one can thus verify that the least gifted, or the poorest, are accorded the largest resources. However, we know that the question of a link between increased resources and the quality of teaching is controversial. So, it is doubtless preferable to measure directly if the quality of teaching is better for the poor or the weak (see Grisay, 1999), thus playing a compensatory role.

Evidently, in the name of meritocracy, one can reproach the principle of depriving the best students for whom justice would suggest equal, indeed better, treatment than others. In the name of utilitarianism, one can reproach the squandering of resources through the lowering of the utility threshold for poor students.

Rawls reproaches the principle of redress for worrying about justice in the educational system without taking into account the social and political effects of the distribution of education. Life in civil society, he says, is not a race with handicaps. It is fundamentally a matter of cooperation, and the question of justice in education is at base whether education contributes to the distribution of primary goods issuing from this cooperation in accordance with the principles of justice.

This is the opposite of meritocracy. For Rawls, it matters little in the end whether the most talented "merit" or "do not merit" becoming richer or more learned. The inegalitarian distribution of talents, being social or natural in origin, has nothing to do with justice. Justice has to do with the allocation of goods that result from the cooperation of these diverse talents. If a longer, more productive and prestigious school career can be the consequence of talent or effort, or if better success in school allows more money to be earned, it is not because it is just or moral to compensate effort or talent, but only because the "distribution of natural talents (is) a common asset" (1971, p. 17).

However, this idea is also contrary to the principle of redress. Not that Rawls rejects this principle: "The need for redress . . . ," he says, "is one of the elements of our conception of justice" (1971, p. 17)—but he refuses to turn it into a fundamental principle.

With a consequence that at first shocks anyone attached to a certain equality of education, **the principle of difference**—which is a fundamental principle—unlike the principle of redress "would allocate resources to education, say, so as to improve the long-term expectations of the least favored. If this end is attained by giving more attention to the better endowed, it is permissible; otherwise, not" (Rawls, 1971, p. 17).

In short, the question is whether we must choose between limited systems of justice in the world of education, which would always be rather easily critiqued for their external consequences, or principles taking into account the external effects of education—at best, inapplicable except to know the most distant social repercussions of educational inequalities; at worst, justifying some truly unjust inequalities for the sake of supposedly positive, unverifiable effects. Does Rawls help us to break through this impasse or is he stuck there?

2.   A theory of justice

Rawl's Theory of Justice strives to consider together the questions of liberty, equality and efficiency. It seeks to create conditions for equitable cooperation that benefit everyone, among individuals who have different conceptions of well-being.

The situation imagined by Rawls is that of deliberation behind a veil of ignorance—by individuals who know neither their own characteristics nor their social position or conception of well-being—on the institutions and rules that form the "basic structure" of society.

According to Rawls, individuals placed in such a situation would only be able to agree on the three following principles, particularly as they would wisely seek to maximize their advantages in case they find themselves among the disadvantaged:

1. Each person is to have an equal right to the most extensive basic liberty compatible with a similar liberty for others ("principle of equal liberty," 1971, p. 11);
2. Social and economic inequalities are to be arranged so that they are both:
   a) to the greatest benefit of the least advantaged ("principle of difference"); and

b) attached to office and positions open to all under conditions of fair equality of opportunity (1971, p. 13).

It is to be noted that the first principle takes priority over the second, and 2b takes priority over 2a.

Rawls' Theory of Justice is distinguished from utilitarianism in three ways (Van Parijs, 1991):

- Utilitarianism takes for its criteria the fate of the average individual, while Rawls' theory concerns the "least advantaged."
- It is not preferences that are used to evaluate the fate of individuals, but the "primary social goods."
- Rawls further submits a just distribution of wealth, riches and self-respect to the observance of principles 1 and 2b, while utilitarianism does not impose any preliminary condition. As a result, not a single argument for efficiency, even in favor of the disadvantaged, can be set in opposition to the equal distribution of liberties, nor to the realization of equal opportunity. One cannot restrain either liberties or opportunities of the least privileged in the name of their well-being. One cannot, for example, diminish the chances of the least privileged of reaching positions of responsibility, even if they:

benefit from the greater efforts of those who were allowed to hold them. They (the least advantaged) would be justified in their complaint, not only because they were excluded from certain external rewards of office such as wealth and privilege, but because they were debarred from experiencing the realization of self which comes from a skillful and devoted exercise of social duties. They would be deprived of one of the main forms of human good (1971, p. 14).

However, this priority of liberty surely means as well that one does not have the right to restrain the exercise of basic liberties of the privileged in the name of a distribution of primary benefits more favorable to the least privileged.

Education occupies an important place in the Theory of Justice, which is not reduced to the question of equal opportunity. For example, it plays a role in the production of reasonable and rational individuals capable of adhering to the principles of justice. We limit ourselves here, however, to attempting to reconstruct the conditions posed by the Theory of Justice to an equitable distribution of education as a private good.

Rawls often evokes education, but its place in his Theory of Justice is not directly defined. Education and knowledge do not figure, as we have seen, in the list of primary social goods, even though there is not one of them to which a successful education does not provide more access. However, Rawls, especially with regard to the second principle, often evokes equity in the distribution of education in order that we may try to construct what could be his theory in that regard. We will do so, evoking successively the two aspects of the second principle, then their elaboration.

Rawls explains his concept of equal opportunity this way "Assuming that there is a distribution of natural assets, those who are at the same level of talent and ability, and have the same willingness to use them, should have the same prospect of success, regardless of their initial place in the social system" (1971, p. 12).

This suggests an indicator to measure the degree of influence of social origin on success or scholastic competence, as is done by Noël and de Broucker, Chapter 12. But the Rawlsian definition of equality of opportunity is perhaps closer still to an indicator used in France by Duru, Jarousse and Mingat (1992): the inequality of opportunity to pass the baccalaureate at the end of high school for children who had the same level of academic skills at the end of grade one. This level of skills would be an approximation of Rawls' "talents, ability and the willingness to use them."

However, as Rawls writes, a perfect application of this principle would lead to the indexing of scholastic and social success only on "the natural distribution of abilities and talents." Thus, "this outcome is arbitrary from a moral perspective. There is no more reason to permit the distribution of income and wealth to be settled by the distribution of natural assets, than by social or historical fortune" (1971, p. 12). "The unequal inheritance of wealth is no more inherently unjust than the unequal inheritance of intelligence" (1971, p. 43).

One thus expects Rawls to propose that the principle of fair equality of opportunity makes up for the "inheritance of intelligence" (extending the application of the principle to inequalities—let us say—in natural aptitude). But he does not; this would be the principle of redress.

From this perspective, one may be tempted to think that the principle of fair equality of opportunity applies to inequalities of social origin, while the principle of difference applies to inequalities of talent. On the one hand, social inequalities would not prevent young people of equal talent and will from succeeding in a similar fashion; on the other hand, unequal talents would be resources that must be turned to the advantage of the "long-term expectations of the least advantaged."

But such is not Rawls' position: The principle of fair equality of opportunity envisions compensating for social inequalities, but the principle of difference envisions natural as well as social inequalities, both being "accidents" that men have decided to use "in view of the common good" (1971, p. 17).

This inelegant position (one can find insufficiently enlightening the idea that a part of inequality in social origin must be compensated by a politics of equal opportunity and another part accepted provided it is to the advantage of the least privileged) is adopted by Rawls for the following reasons:

• It is impossible to effectively root out natural from social inequalities: "The extent to which natural capacities develop and reach fruition is affected by all kinds of social conditions and class attitudes. Even the willingness to make an effort, to try and so to be deserving in the ordinary sense, is itself dependent upon happy family and social circumstances" (1971, p. 12).

• One cannot apply the principle of fair equality of opportunity to compensate for inequalities of talent because it is necessary to consider talents as a common asset.

• One cannot be content with the principle of difference. If the principle of difference is not subject to correction by fair equality of opportunity, this is the system of natural aristocracy, "*noblesse oblige*," in which the most gifted and the best born must put their advantages to the service of the less advantaged (1971, p. 105).

It remains possible only to apply the principle of difference to social inequalities, which thus are guided by two principles. Therefore, it becomes necessary to understand how these two principles combine to address social inequalities.

If equal opportunity takes priority over the principle of difference, it is because it does not envision only to equalize opportunities for access to the material advantages that one derives from elevated social status. Not a single advantage in terms of material well-being can compensate for the denial of access to the realization of self represented by an elevated position in society (1971, p. 14). This self-actualization is indispensable to all having the experience of participating on an equal footing in society, which is a good—indeed a pleasure—in itself (1971, p. 79). It follows moreover from this insistence on cooperation that one can suppose that, for Rawls, the degree of segregation of an education system is one of the measures of equity, and not only because of segregation's effect on equal opportunity or efficiency.

What is required therefore is a politics of equal opportunity to reduce social and educational inequalities—within limits fixed by the first principle—to a certain point until the principle of difference takes over. But where is that point? It seems to me that one can deduce from the economy of the whole Theory of Justice, the following response: One must try to correct social inequality of opportunity in education as long as it compromises application of the principle of difference.

Indeed, if the principle of difference is destined to adjust the limits of the principle of fair equality of opportunity, one cannot condone curtailing the equal opportunity effort before the principle of difference can be applied. Now, if the inequalities of opportunity create two or three quasi-castes that are perpetuated by the school, it is illusory to think that the upper caste will adhere to the principle of difference (i.e., give up its advantages to benefit the lower caste). This is because, in the first place, there is no common humanity between these castes; finally, in more Rawlsian terms, it is because if the members of the higher caste are assured that their children will continue to be a part of it, then the uncertainty about its future social position—necessary to complete Rawls' construction—does not exist.

If this analysis of Rawls' position is correct, one can understand its advantages. One is to give a political justification to the concern about equal opportunity—a justification other than reward for individual merit—that has the advantage of being easily distinguished from meritocracy. Another advantage is to take into account in a realistic way the preexisting social inequalities and to seek in these conditions a solution that also considers the effects of the distribution of education on social cooperation.

We have seen the indicators suggested by the principle of fair equality of opportunity. The principle of difference suggests some others. Rawls writes: "Those who have been favored by nature . . . are not to gain merely because they are more gifted, but only to cover the costs of training and education and for using their endowments in ways that help the less fortunate as well" (1971, p. 17).

This phrase suggests two indicators:

- the degree of utilization for the disadvantaged of the skills of the best-educated professionals, which we will call the "externalities" of the education of the better-schooled (Meuret, Chapter 5); and
- what one calls the "fiscal return" of education, which verifies whether taxes paid by the best educated actually reimburse the expenses that have been authorized by the community for their education.

3.   The debate with Rawls

In a very broad fashion, one can say that the Theory of Justice is open to attack on three fronts: for not sufficiently respecting the rights of a person to self-determination (see, for example, Nozick, 1974), for thinking it is possible to find principles of justice independent of the values of each community (see, for example, Sandel, 1982) and for ignoring that all individuals do not have equal abilities to use primary goods (see, for example, Sen, 1992).

We present here only the libertarian and egalitarian critiques, as the communautarian critique bears on the content of education more than on the equity of its distribution. However, we will also present the position of Walzer, conceived not so much as a direct criticism of Rawls, but which enters into debate with him.

3.1.   Walzer, or the Theory of Independence

The *Spheres of Justice* (Walzer, 1983) opens with a critique of equality: In every equal situation there will arise inequalities that it will be necessary to repress, and that very repression will give birth to another inequality, between those who possess the power of repression and the others. The problem is therefore not inequality, but domination. What justice requires is that no social good be allowed to serve as a means of domination.

The benefits that allow the entrenchment of domination are those with which one can acquire other benefits, such as wealth, power and education. These are the "predominant benefits." "Simple equality," that is to say possession by all of the same quantity of predominant benefits, is impossible. What is required is a "complex equality," in which these predominant benefits are independent of one another; for example, in which money cannot buy education.

Confusion among these spheres is not merely injustice; it is also tyranny. Walzer cites Pascal's *Pensées*: " Thus these discussions are false or tyrannical: 'I am handsome, therefore people trust me; I am strong, therefore they must love me'. . . ."

However, in education, a certain simple equality is required by justice: that which leads to the mastery of a "core curriculum," that "all future citizens need." During this first phase, for Walzer, the goal is equality of results. Not only is it necessary to compensate for social and natural handicaps, but also to strive to compensate for the differences manifested by students in their desire to learn. "Education is distributed equally to each child—or more exactly one helps each child to master the same body of knowledge. This is not to say that all children are treated equally in the same way. . . . Children who lag behind and those who are apathetic probably receive a disproportionate amount of attention from the teacher" (translated from the French version). To the extent that pupils in Sweden "who have difficulties in school" are considered to be pupils "to whom the school has not afforded the opportunity to develop on the basis of their special circumstances" (Wildt-Persson & Rosengren, Chapter 13), Sweden observes Walzer's simple equality.

Beyond this phase, education falls within a more complex equality. It "must adapt to the interests and capacities of students considered individually." During this phase, Walzer distinguishes between general education, conceived more as a pleasure, and professional education, from which the brightest students would logically be drawn to be trained as society's experts.

Independence of the spheres demands that general education be free, but equity requires that it be distributed, not only in scholastic institutions, but also "at the center of ordinary professional life" (Walzer, 1983). For professional education, this presents a problem: The more the first phase succeeds in equalizing knowledge for everyone, the more intense the competition will be for entrance into the professional schools. And the more intense the competition, the more the rich will be inclined to mobilize their resources to gain entrance for their own children.

The way to diminish this competition is, pursuant to the logic of the separation of the spheres, to diminish the consequences of specialized degrees in terms of wealth and power. From success in school, one could draw "praise and pride inside the school, and then in the professions"—and not wealth or power.

This is miles away from the Rawlsian idea of fair equality of opportunity. From Rawls' point of view, one would not wish to see eventual progress in equal educational opportunity "canceled" by a reduction of "credentialism;" that is to say, by a lower social and professional return on the diploma. Walzer, in contrast, would accept lowered credentials as the price of progress towards equal opportunity in education.

It is a little difficult, on first reading, to believe Walzer when he declares he is not " trying to describe schools of saints." At the same time, there are at least two reasons to take his approach seriously. On the one hand, it is correct that the most egalitarian countries are often those where the link between the diploma and the professional situation (credentialism) is weaker. The United Kingdom is an example (Duru-Bellat, 1999). It is effectively possible for the rich to react to a growth in equal educational opportunity with an action aimed at minimizing the role of the school in social reproduction.

On the other hand, it is true that prestige in the professions is generally indexed by the rigor of the studies leading to it, and it has been shown that this relationship is particularly strong in countries where the national educational systems are Malthusian—organized along unequal channels and in which vocational education is strongly developed (Muller & Shavit, 1998). This means that the school systems that are very hierarchical in their own order can effectively build a relatively autonomous extension of the social hierarchy. This is the case in Germany or Switzerland, according to the work of Muller and Shavit. However, in order for this to truly support Walzer's position, it is necessary that the hierarchy of prestige not be correlated with that of power and wealth. But, it is.

It is true that two paths are open to us for actually increasing equal opportunity: that of Walzer, a sort of independence between skill and remuneration, or a solution closer to Rawls. The latter implies a more or less unique social hierarchy in which one aims through equal educational opportunity at access for poor children to "positions of responsibility." But under this concept, children who are bright yet poor have to be equipped with strong professional skills. If they are not, rich people will easily circumvent the schools and hire children from the privileged classes, even those who performed poorly in school. If the poor are well prepared, the social cost of hiring the children of the rich instead of the bright children of the poor for "positions of responsibility" will be higher.

3.2.   Libertarian, or those who criticize Rawls in the name of liberty

With regard to the content of education, Rawls (1993) has developed a position that is very respectful of the values of each community in conformity with the first principle of his theory. However, as we have seen, the distribution of the quantity and quality of education, and the use that the best students can make of acquired skills, are subject to the second principle, not to the first one.

This restriction is founded on the idea that, the distribution of initial gifts being arbitrary, to hold out for a just distribution of primary goods founded on initial gifts is arbitrary as well.

Nozick (1974) disagrees. He does not deny that we do not deserve either our talents or the circumstances of our birth, but he argues that this arbitrariness does not forbid us from being lawful proprietors of these talents. Therefore, to consider individual qualities as a means of serving the collective advantage, or of serving the least privileged, is to treat certain people as a means and not as an end. He considers therefore that the principle of difference violates Rawls' first principle. For him, whatever the size and nature of an inequality, if it has been reached through a process that respected the property rights of each individual, it is just. Some sociologists (Boudon, Luhman) seem to come close to this position (Benadusi, Chapter 1).

According to Nozick, from the moment that "formal" equality of opportunity is created—when no one is deprived of education by characteristics external to education, such as race or religion—justice proclaims that each is free to develop his/her capacities as he/she wishes. Neither the principle of fair equality of opportunity nor the principle of difference is entitled to put limits or conditions on the benefits that each one can derive from his or her education.

For Nozick, "the foundations of merit need not be earned," which Gutman (1999, p. 135) illustrates this way: "Courageous soldiers earn a medal, but they don't earn their courage. In the same way, the most gifted or the most motivated children earn more education, but they don't earn their gifts or motivation."

Rawls responds with two arguments: "On the one hand, it is improper to claim that my goal is a violation or abuse when one of my 'attributes'—my skills, my intelligence—are used for the common advantage. This is to confuse me with the attributes."

On the other hand, "We have the right to our natural abilities and to all that we come to possess while taking part in an equitable social process," and it is precisely on this equitable social process that his Theory of Justice lays down the law. Put another way, property rights are not natural rights; they proceed from a fixed framework of social cooperation.

Nozick would probably measure educational equity in terms of equal freedoms. The availability of "vouchers" in Milwaukee, Wisconsin—even if the results are doubtful from the vantage points of efficiency and equal opportunity (Witte, 1998)—will doubtless improve equity, in his view, because it increases the liberty of the poor to enroll their children in effective private schools. One can suppose that Nozick would reclaim equality for the quality of teaching only for those who have an equal will to invest in learning. The most likely outcome, however, is that it would avoid any intervention of the state in the educational domain, even to render liberties more equal (Kymlicka, 1992).

3.3.   Equalitarian, or those who criticize Rawls in the name of equality

Suppose that the primary goods are delivered according to Rawls' principles. According to those who criticize him in the name of equality, all would not be able to profit equally; thus, justice would not be satisfied. This argument has two versions: a strong version, which raises the fact that Rawls limits the question of justice to the distribution of goods among people capable of cooperating; and a weak version, which invokes the differences in talent among those who are capable of cooperating.

The strong version is represented by the distinction made by Buchanan (1990, cited by Brighouse) between "subject-centered justice" and "justice as reciprocity." As distinct from the second, the first phrase defines the subjects of justice by their needs and interests, not by their ability to cooperate. An argument of Buchanan in favor of the first expression is that the second is arbitrary because the necessary ability to cooperate can vary from one period to another (e.g., dyslexia was not a handicap in preliterate societies). Another argument is that justice as reciprocity is difficult to pronounce on children who are not yet capable of cooperating.

The weak version is represented by authors like Arneson (1989), Cohen (1990), Roemer (1995) and Sen (1992). Like Rawls, these authors distinguish themselves from the classic tradition of the economy of well-being (welfare-ism), which seeks to equalize well-being. Unlike Rawls, they consider that it is necessary to equalize the opportunities for well-being, not to seek equity in the distribution of primary goods. The last three authors lean towards an objective measure of opportunity of well-being while Arneson advocates a subjective approach.

For example, Sen thinks that it is necessary to equalize possibilities of access to "functionings," such as being able to go out in public without shame, being well nourished, etc. "Functionings" relate to the quality of life, not just to the resources that permit it to be lived. Sen reproaches Rawls for penalizing those who derive less than others from the same amount of primary goods.

A pertinent distinction separates that for which individuals are responsible from that which escapes their control. To equalize the chances of access to different pertinent goods, it is necessary that the distribution of "resources" compensates the inequality of talent (social or natural)—in this opinion, the authors are closer than Rawls to the principle of redress—so that only inequalities of will (or of effort) result in inequalities of access.

This position encounters three difficulties: First, if one wants to achieve equality in certain results—that all know how to read, for example—the principle of compensation (for equal effort, equal accomplishments, etc.) does not suffice. It is necessary to accept, like Walzer, that more resources can be offered to those who evidence a weak desire—all the more so, partisans of this principle say—since it has to do with knowledge acquired by the child at an age when it is difficult to hold him or her responsible. This brings us back to the consideration that, as much as the child cannot be considered responsible for his/her effort, the effort must be considered as being a part of his/her talents.

For another thing, it is not simple to distinguish between will and talent; that is to say, to decide exactly where individual responsibility stops and begins (Le Clainche, 1999). This problem is not presented so long as effort and talent are blended, but only when one tries to separate them.

Finally, most authors consider that the obligation to compensate for differences in talent is valid only for the first part of schooling, while a second phase must bow to the " principle of natural compensation,"which holds that "society does not alter the influence of variables of responsibility on individual accomplishments" (Fleurbaey, 1996, p. 140) and which is expressed as "to equal talent, equal resources." It remains to be seen how to determine the moment when it is justifiable to pass from one principle to another, a problem analogous to that which one could encounter in Walzer in passing from simple to complex inequality.

Several criteria have been proposed for determining that moment of passage. Meuret (1997) proposes the moment when the individual has acquired sufficient skill to form a clear judgment about the opportunity to pursue his/her studies or not. Trannoy (1999) proposes, in a fashion very coherent with the nature of the question posed, the moment when skills acquired are sufficiently important to cancel the effects of social origin and natural aptitudes. Gutman (1999) proposes the moment when individuals have enough skill to participate in democratic life. Curren (1995) proposes a "threshold of social inclusion," holding that a state that does not lead young people to a level of education at which they are employable, and can attain a minimal social status, exposes its own citizens to crime and repression, which is unjust.

None of these criteria are, in truth, very easy to put into practice. This is a handicap for theories such as Walzer's, which divide schooling into two phases under two different principles of justice (giving the advantage to theories such as Rawls' or utilitarianism, which refer to the same principle for all schooling), as it is difficult to determine the point at which one ends and the next begins.

But, above all, as Brighouse observes (1999), a complete theory of justice can not content itself with defining a minimum threshold that all must attain. It must address the acceptable level of inequality in the phase that follows. For him, the value of "educational equality" includes the idea that no inequality other than dependence on will is tolerable, but he recognizes that a complete theory of justice must take into account other values besides educational equality (e.g., the family, religious freedom, economic growth).

Sen (1992) also develops a concept of justice that includes a concern for effectiveness as an exterior restraint. For him, effectiveness is not in itself a superior value to equity; the value of equal opportunity may overtake effectiveness. But it cannot totally be ignored either. Sen recognizes that one cannot distribute resources in favor of the handicapped—in our case, those who are less capable of transforming a course of study into a set of skills—without concern for the effectiveness of this expenditure.

It is clear that the very existence of the debate presented—albeit in less than its fullest dimensions and richness—shows that not a single theory has yet proposed a definitive response to the question of equity in education. It is therefore the terms of the debate that must inspire the nature of the variables to measure in order to fuel that very debate. These are the terms that have led to proposals, later in this volume, for a system of indicators that measures not only the independence of scholastic success with respect to social origin, but also the proportion of individuals situated below a minimum threshold of competence, and gaps in knowledge between the least and best educated. These indicators should help us understand the effect of equity in educational systems on the situation of adults, particularly on the least advantaged among them.

References

Arneson R.J., "Equality and equal opportunity for welfare," *Philosophical studies, 56*, pp. 77–93, 1989.

Brighouse H., *School choice and social justice*, Oxford University Press, Oxford, 1999.

Cohen G.A., "Equality of what? On welfare, goods and capabilities," *Recherches économiques de Louvain, 56,* pp. 357–82, 1990.

Curren R., "Justice and the threshold of educational opportunity," *Philosophy of education, 50*, pp. 239–248, 1995.

Daniels N., "Health care needs and distributive justice," *Philosophy and public affairs, 10,* 1981.

Dupuy J.P., *Libéralisme et justice sociale*, Hachette, Pluriel, Paris, 1997.

Duru-Bellat M., Mingat A., "La gestion de l'hétérogénéité des publics d'élèves au collège," *Cahiers de l'IREDU, 59*, Dijon, France, 1997.

Duru-Bellat M., "La sociologie des inégalités sociales à l'école entre engagement et distanciation," in Meuret D. (ed.), *La justice du système éducatif*, de Boeck, Bruxelles, 1999.

Duru-Bellat M., Jarousse J., Mingat A., *De l'orientation en fin de cinquieme au fonctionment du college*, Cahiers du Center de Federal de la FEN, Paris, 1992.

Fleurbaey M., *Théories économiques de la justice*, Economica, Paris, 1996.

Gutman A., *Democratic education*, Princeton University Press, Princeton, 1999 (1st ed., 1987).

Kellerhals J., Coenen-Hutter J., Modak, M., *Figures de l'équité: La construction des normes de justice dans les groupes*, Presses Universitaires de France, Paris, 1988.

Kymlicka W. (ed.), *Justice in Political Philosophy*, 2 volumes, Edward Elgar Publishing, Cheltenham, UK, 1992.

Le Clainche, C., "L'allocation équitable des biens d'éducation et des soins de santé dans une optique post welfariste," in Meuret D. (ed.), *La justice du système éducatif*, de Boeck, Bruxelles, 1999.

Meuret D., "Rawls, l'éducation et l'égalité des chances," in Meuret D. (ed.), *La justice du système éducatif*, de Boeck, Bruxelles, 1999.

Meuret D., "Intérêt, Justice, Laïcité," *Le Télémaque*, Presses universitaires de Caen, Caen, France, 1998.

Meuret D., *Que serait un système éducatif juste, Rapport pour le colloque européen sur l'équité des systèmes éducatifs*, Multigr., 1997.

Nozick R., *Anarchy, state, utopia*, Blackwell, Oxford, 1974.

Rawls J., *A theory of justice*, Oxford University Press, Oxford, 1971.

Rawls J., "La théorie de la justice comme équité, une théorie politique et non métaphysique," *in Individu et Justice sociale*, Seuil, Paris, 1985 (t.f. 1988).

Rawls J., *Political liberalism*, Columbia University Press, New York, 1993.

Roemer J.E., *Theories of distributive justice*, Harvard University Press, Cambridge (Mass.), 1995.

Sandel M., *Liberalism or the limits of justice*, Cambridge University Press, Cambridge, 1982.

Sen A., *Inequality reexamined*, Oxford University Press, Oxford, 1992.

Shavit Y., Müller W., *From school to work*, Clarendon Press, Oxford, 1998.

Thélot C., Peretti C., "L'évolution des compétences des meilleurs élèves depuis quarante ans," MEN, Direction de l'Evaluation et de la Prospective, *Dossiers Education et Formations, 69*, 1996.

Trannoy A., "L'égalisation des savoirs de base: l'éclairage des théories économiques de la responsabilité et des contrats," in Meuret D. (ed.), *La justice du système éducatif*, de Boeck, Bruxelles, 1999.

Van Parijs P., *Qu'est ce qu'une société juste?* Seuil, Paris, 1991.

Whitehead M., *Concepts et principes de l'égalité des chances en matière de santé*, OMS, Copenhague, 1991.

Walzer M., *Spheres of justice, A Defense of Pluralism and Equality*, Basic Books, New York, 1983.

Witte J.F., "The Milwaukee Voucher Experiment," *Educational Evaluation and Policy Analysis, 20*(4), 1998.

Chapter 4

Why Education Matters
Race, ethnicity, poverty and American school-equity research

Douglas Cochrane
American Institutes for Research/Education Statistics Services Institute, Washington, D.C.

More than 30 years of research into specific interventions demonstrate that schools can teach and students learn more than would be predicted by the socioeconomic status (SES) of parents, and that money matters in the delivery of this more effective education. At the same time, the social and cultural context of a student's home and school environment remains an important determinant of educational outcomes. A relevant community-based model that enhances social and human capital, providing economic as well as potential educational benefits, is the metropolitan-wide or regional district. When metropolitan areas practice regional planning, experts find there is increased flexibility to economic downturns and more productivity. Regional planning is considered a necessary condition for cities to acquire "world city" status. The development of such regional districts, when the appropriate educational goals are adopted, would also facilitate the development of desegregated communities and/or schools. The American history of housing segregation based on race/ethnicity and poverty has led to the creation of schools that have been the subject of much debate.

Introduction

Three main research streams developed from the 1966 Coleman report, *Equality of Educational Opportunity (EEO)* and the 1972 reanalysis *Inequality* by Jencks et al.: school-effect studies based on Coleman's EEO report, internal school-process studies and private-versus-public schooling studies. Coleman's surprising finding was that the SES student mix of a school was more important in explaining school outcomes than the schools themselves. School-effect studies and internal school-process studies asked whether schools could teach or students learn beyond expectations set by parental backgrounds—including race, ethnicity and poverty—and if money mattered in the delivery of this education. The private-versus-public school studies attempted to determine if there was social or cultural capital available, particularly in Catholic private schools, which allowed them to be effective where public schools were not. While there is much to be learned and there is less consensus as to what may be the most effective educational intervention(s), the research community now believes that education does make a difference and that money matters.

1.   Background

Following is a brief overview of housing segregation and how it became a catalyst for research on school effects, noting the connection between housing segregation and racial isolation, and the relationship between SES status and race.

The legal structure of the old American South, which enforced separate facilities and services for African Americans and whites in everything from drinking fountains to homes and schools (*de jure* segregation), created very unequal resources and life chances for the descendants of former slaves. It was this lack of access to equal educational resources, which, after decades of effort, prompted the U.S. Supreme Court to apply Southern *de jure* desegregation as a remedy in *Brown v. the Board of Education* (1954).

The South managed its segregated system at the county level (often comprising a combination of urban, suburban and rural jurisdictions). Majority county-based groups collected and distributed education resources to the two race-based systems. A legacy of this Southern county distribution system is that, with very few exceptions, the only county-wide school districts in the country are in the South. There are also many non-countywide districts in the South, but desegregation was not limited to central cities. In fact, county-wide schools were often left intact but integrated as a result of desegregation. Some of these districts were complete metropolitan areas or counties, each containing a central city and surrounding suburban and rural areas, while others consisted entirely of rural counties.

In the rest of the country, residential segregation was maintained by bank and insurance red-lining of certain neighborhoods (that is to say, they were defined as high-risk for purposes of home-purchase or real-estate development loans), and school boundaries were restructured by all-white school boards (*de facto* segregation). Together, these restrictions created similarly inequitable access to education resources. As segregated housing was created and maintained institutionally, rather than by law as in the South, education desegregation court cases outside the South were tried on a district-by-district basis. That is, in each community it had to be proved that residential housing segregation and the corresponding schools were created and/or maintained by institutional barriers in order for legal remedies to be imposed on school systems. Suburban residential barriers for African Americans outside the South were substantial at the time. As a practical matter, this meant that it was almost exclusively central-city districts that were subjected to *de facto* segregation court proceedings.

Residential segregation kept African Americans and the poor disenfranchised from much of the economic development of the country. Good educations and jobs were rarely available in segregated inner-city neighborhoods, and even for those able to acquire an education, pay for the jobs they could find was not commensurate with training. Many metropolitan areas today maintain racial and ethnic residential segregation and schooling. Outside the South, the middle class has continued to desert the central cities, leaving larger proportions of the poor—often African-Americans and Hispanics—to fend as best they could in struggling central-city schools. There was and remains, in spite of a growing African- American and Hispanic middle class, a strong correlation between race/ethnicity and poverty.

The correlation between race/ethnicity and poverty and the associated housing segregation manifest themselves in the schools serving these communities. It is this conjunction of SES, minority status and schools that has been the impetus for research on the effects of schools. The following section will provide some background on these school-effect studies.

There has been much debate over the years on these issues, and, while this debate continues, Grissmer et al. (2000) defines the mid-1900s as a "watershed" for many education researchers. The Tennessee STAR Project class-size experiment provided excellent "proof" of the viability of school-based interventions. Difficulties with quantitative, non-experimental education studies have started to be more clearly defined, and a related frame of reference applying these methods to practical situations has been outlined (Jencks, 2000; Grissmer et al., 2000; Grissmer, 1999). The following is presented not as a debate about whether the equitable goal of reducing the test score gap for poor and minority students can be attained, but as a discussion of the growing consensus within the field with respect to *why* and *how* it can be attained.

2. The studies and the questions they raised

Expecting to find proof of the effects of these poor segregated schools on African-American test scores, Congress commissioned the Coleman (1966) report, which was the largest study of education in the United States at the time. The surprising findings of this study, notably supported in a reanalysis by Jencks et al. (1972) and others, was that variations in test scores were greater within schools than between schools. Differences in test scores appeared to be largely related to the SES mix of students within a school rather than to the resource differences between schools. Coleman (1966) did find evidence that suggested minority students benefited to some extent from schools and their resources.

These findings sparked decades of research and debate on the effects of schools on education outcomes and within school process. Questions about the effectiveness of schools were raised. The suggestion that the SES mix of students, or the family background of students, is the most important indicator of academic success begged the question: Can schools teach? If schools are not able to have an impact on test scores of poor and minority students, is this because these students are not able to learn? Additionally, if it is the SES mix of students rather than the resources available to schools that is responsible for improving test scores, does money matter in the provision of education?

The public school vs. private school debate was initiated by Coleman, Hoffer and Kilgore (1982). Coleman and Hoffer later (1987) concluded that Catholic schools had a differential effect on student achievement compared to public schools, and that this was most pronounced and beneficial for disadvantaged students based on race/ethnicity and poverty. As this difference was associated with Catholic rather than other private schools, Coleman determined that there was social capital available within the internal communities of Catholic schools (Coleman & Hoffer, 1987). The debate then focused on whether this was specific to Catholic schools or whether there might not be public schools with similar characteristics that were effective at teaching, regardless of students' race, ethnicity or gender (Ekstrom, Goertz & Rock, 1988).

3.   Findings

Following is a description of the results, some very recently formulated, of almost 30 years of research, and the value of developing metropolitan or regional school districts.

3.1.   Student learning <u>can</u> exceed predictions.

When questions are raised about the ability of schools to teach or students to learn, or more specifically, about improving test scores, the issue is in part related to how much students' test scores (used as a proxy for IQ) are related to genetics or ability. Recent research on brain development in the early months and years after birth, Bloom's "taxonomy" and Gardner's "multiple intelligence" all have implications for equity goals as they relate to a student's ability to learn. A short background on brain development research is an interesting place to start.

At birth, a baby's brain has almost all its neurons present; however, only the connections related to the functioning of automatic processes, such as the heartbeat and breathing, are operational (Nash, 1997). Particularly during the first two years, and throughout early childhood, the brain experiences remarkable growth and development. At age five or six, a very large number of networks or connections are made in the brain. These are maintained until around the age of puberty, at which point there is another spurt in the growth of connections (D'Arcangelo, 2000).

Contrary to previous research, Wade (1999) reports on Princeton's Gould and Gross and their recent evidence that neurons may also be added later in life to three areas of the brain's cortex. These areas are related to decision-making and visual recognition and are "regions of the brain central to human thought and identity." Not to negate the significance of early childhood, this suggests that learning is also a lifelong experience.

Studies of the value of early childhood enrichment programs, most specifically Head Start, have received a lot of attention for their potential to benefit poor, often minority, urban preschool participants. Entwisle et al. (2000) report that while earlier evaluations suggested that IQ gains amounted to only a couple of points and lasted a fairly short period of time, later evaluations that included all Head Start programs and that concentrated on randomly assigned experimental (preschool) and control (no preschool) groups found the IQ gains to be eight points for those attending Head Start compared with no gain for those who did not. The IQ gains lasted for two to three years, and math scores remained improved through grade five.

The value of Head Start programs follows participants through high school (secondary school) and into the world of work. Of even more importance were gains not identified in early studies. It was found that, compared to the control group, a much smaller percentage of Head Start students were subsequently assigned to special education (specifically designed instruction for students with physical, emotional or psychological handicaps that affect the ability to learn) or held back a grade in school. Thus, Head Start students were not as prone to disabilities that might impede their learning or limit their educational outcomes by failing to prepare them for a decent job. They were less likely to be held back and to drop out of school or experience other educational failures. Many studies have indicated that holding a student back a grade decreases the likelihood that this student will successfully complete his or her education. Additionally, Head Start students were more likely to graduate from high school, and those who were not held back in school were more likely to be employed. They were also able to function better in "mainstream society," and as adults were more likely to be in some type of educational program and to be employed or temporarily laid off.

Burchinel et al. (1997), in a paper based on the combined data of the Abcedarian and CARE Projects at the University of Chapel Hill (UCH), North Carolina (funded in part by the U.S. Department of Education), found that with intensive early educational child care, and responsive and stimulating care at home (including at-home intervention), a child's IQ could be improved—for example, from below average to average. These gains remain through high school. From studies such as these, we now have a better understanding of the potential for specific early childhood interventions in improving test scores.

In these two UCH projects, children and their families were chosen on the basis of the expected low IQ of the child. The mothers came from poor families and many had low IQ's themselves. Children were randomly assigned to one of the interventions or to a control group. There were intensive preschool interventions in a child-care setting; a family-based, school-age intervention; and a family-based intervention from infancy to school age. Three specific educational interventions were used: educational child care from 6 weeks to school entry, home visits from 6 weeks to school entry, and home-school resource services during the first three years of school.

This study and these findings are consistent with the National Research Council (NRC) (1999) and its review of early childhood studies. While there is some debate about the long-term effects of these studies, the debate is related to the fact that studies employing long-term data have dealt with model programs rather than large-scale programs. NRC (1999) states: "A strong consensus has emerged among policy makers, practitioners, and researchers about the importance of increasing investments in the capacity of at-risk students to learn by focusing on the school readiness of very young children, and by linking education to other social services so that the broad range of educational, social and physical needs that affect learning are addressed."

Based on his understanding that all children can learn—provided material was presented in a logical, systematic way—Benjamin Bloom most importantly developed the theory of mastery learning. This theory has been adopted in numerous school districts around the United States and in 12 countries. Bloom was particularly interested in the learning/teaching of poor minority inner-city and rural students. Teachers adopting mastery learning were encouraged to pay more attention to lower-achieving children. Bloom (1956) initially developed, with a variety of researchers, a taxonomy of learning, with three domains: cognitive, affective and psychomotor. These have been broken down within each domain to describe levels of intellectual behavior important to learning. These continue to be used today to develop curricula and train teachers.

Howard Gardner developed a theory of multiple intelligences (MI), which provided frameworks to help understand the variety of intelligences that we possess. Gardner's seven intelligences are linguistic, logical/mathematical, visual/spatial, musical, bodily/kinesthetic, interpersonal and intrapersonal (1983)—an eighth, naturalist, having been added in 1996. Tucker (1999), at Bryn Mawr College's "Serendip" Web site (http://serendip. brynmawr.edu/bb/neuro/neuro99/web3/Tucker.html), describes our current understanding of the complexity of brain development, including a growing understanding of the interaction of both ability and environment as stimulants—rather than determinants—of intelligence and the uniqueness of each child.

In this article, Tucker describes Gardner's MI as a theory of learning that provides an excellent correlation to neurological research. Quoting Armstrong, Tucker finds MI, as a cognitive theory, to be a good representation of how "individuals use their intelligences to solve problems and fashion products. Unlike other models that are primarily process-oriented, Gardner's approach is particularly geared to how the human mind operates on the contents of the world" (Armstrong, 1994).

MI has a number of validated implications for education including the provision of a vocabulary for teachers to use in discussions of children's strengths and weaknesses and in the development of curricula. As both Tucker and Gardner note, there are cautions to be made. Gardner himself perceives MI's variety of intelligences as "categories that help us to discover difference in forms of mental representation; they are not good characterizations of what people are (or are not) like" (Durie, 1997). Irrespective of its limitations, Gardner's theory has provided for the development of rich educational experiences for children from diverse backgrounds.

3.2. Schools <u>can</u> teach more effectively than SES predictions.

The difficulty related to the debate about how effective schools might be in improving a child's test score, beyond a prediction based on the SES of the child's family, becomes clearer with a better understanding of the cognitive development of children. As noted by Tucker (1999), we now believe that the greatest growth in cognitive development takes place by approximately 4 years of age. Schools then have the task of attempting to have a positive impact on an intelligence that, while stimulated by both ability and environment and able to learn throughout life, has already had its greatest growth. To add to the problem, as there are from approximately four to eleven years of age twice the connections between neurons, or twice the networks that will be in place upon further maturity, each child is defined as infinitely variable in how he or she experiences and process information. It is then perhaps little wonder that it has taken some time for a consensus to emerge on this issue, or that in the process the limits of social science and education research have been strained.

To date, the most important school-based intervention with respect to the contribution of schools to the learning of students above and beyond SES expectations is class size (Grismer, 1999). This intervention is most effective for poor children, most specifically African-American and Hispanic children from poor families. Class size as an intervention is a lowering of the number of students in class per teacher. It has been the expectation that in smaller classes, teachers trained to take advantage of this reduced size can provide more time for instruction and devote less to discipline and administrative tasks. Students can also become more involved in class activities and discussions.

Class size was important with respect to the developing consensus on the potential of school-based interventions in the experimental research design used in the Tennessee STAR Project. Numerous smaller random studies had indicated possible improvements in test scores with reduced class size, but the limits of social science and education research made these studies easy to criticize and challenge. The intensity of the debate left policy-makers and some stakeholders unsure as to the interpretation of these studies. The use of easily interpreted experimental design with control groups—the same techniques used in medical research—broke through political dialogue, making it possible for researchers, policy-makers and politicians alike to accept the findings.

The Tennessee STAR Project assigned a complete cohort of kindergarten students to three types of classes: those with 22 to 24 students led by one teacher, those with the same number of students led by a teacher and an aide, and those with 15 to 16 students and one teacher. Students who remained in these schools stayed in these groupings through grade three (i.e., for a total of four years). Students who entered these schools during these years were randomly assigned to one of these groupings. The project covered 12,000 participating students, including late entries and exits. A high percentage of students receiving free lunches as part of a federal program for students from low-income families and a high percentage of minorities were included in the original sample.

Minority students from poor families were found to have had the greatest benefit. Finn and Achilles (1999) found poor minority students had a .40 standard deviation compared with .23–.24 for other students, provided they participated for four years. Kreuger (1999) found the variation to be .30 for minorities vs. .20 for majority white students. While Hanushek (2000) debates how long this intervention is worth the investment, Grissmer (1999) finds, from a review of several studies, that if long-term test score improvements are the primary policy goal, then it is important to maintain this intervention for four years. Grissmer based his conclusion on the finding that those who had four years of this intervention showed the greatest and most enduring benefit. Grissmer noted that this finding was consistent with other early childhood intervention studies that reported that the longer and more intense the intervention, the greater the benefit and the longer the duration of the benefit.

Weckstein (1998) cites Newman and Wehlage (1995) and the Center on Organization and Restructuring of Schools' (CORS) five-year study of 1,500 schools, and Lee, Smith and Croninger's (1995) work on 11,000 students in 280 schools as offering empirical support for such school-process reforms as mixed-ability classes, smaller within-school units (schools within a school), cooperative learning and interdisciplinary teams.

These are all within the framework of providing non-mechanistic, high academic standards based on "authentic student achievement." Authentic student achievement was acquired by "constructing knowledge through disciplined inquiry, to produce discourse and performance that has meaning beyond school."

Weckstein also notes the difficulty failing schools often have in envisioning and therefore successfully implementing restructuring plans. These schools need substantial external support in the process of restructuring. This includes acquiring the expertise of a variety of specialists. Unfortunately, these schools often do not get the appropriate mix of experts. Issues of implementation and integration of effective school reform programs are underrepresented in this chapter. However, they should not be underrated in interpreting the difficulty in providing effective education outcomes for all. Finally, in noting the inability of society to match existing knowledge and desire with successful school outcomes for all, Weckstein outlines the legal federal and state structure available for U.S. children in their efforts to acquire a quality education. This includes the federal Title I of the Elementary and Secondary Education Act; the Individuals with Disabilities Education Act; Title IV of the 1964 Civil Rights Act; Title IV of the Equal Educational Opportunities Act of 1974; the Goals 2000: Educate America Act; the Carl D. Perkins Vocational and Applied Technology Education Act; and the School-to-Work Opportunity Acts.

Many state constitutions provide education clauses that specifically refer to a duty to provide a thorough and efficient education system. Much of the current school-finance litigation in the states has been based on these expectations. Additionally, since the early 1990s, federal law and state education mandates to assure funding have been tailored to standards-based education.

3.3. Per-pupil revenues <u>are</u> important.

The summer 1999 issue of the *Educational Evaluation and Policy Analysis* (by the American Educational Research Association) was dedicated to "Class Size: Issues and New Findings." The Tennessee STAR Project class-size reduction experiment, "the first large-scale experiment done on the major educational policy variables," was the focus. Of some additional interest, the Sage Program—a Wisconsin pilot program in class-size reduction that replicates the Tennessee STAR Project results—was evaluated. Grissmer, guest editor of this issue, noted that this experimental research design had been valuable from a policy perspective, as the "experimental evidence is more understandable, more credible, and more easily explained to policy-makers than is the more complex and often contradictory evidence from non-experimental studies." Hanushek's comments (excepting his own reanalysis of the Tennessee class-size experiment) and Grissmer's conclusion, which responds to Hanushek and summarizes the issue, provide an excellent overview of the difficulty inherent in non-experimental research.

In this most current journal dedicated to the STAR Project, Hanushek's challenge to the project is not based on an analysis of the data, but rather on a listing of all the factors that might lead to a bias in the study and invalidate its results. Grissmer used STAR Project data and information on the study background and implementation to provide an item-by-item response to Hanushek's challenge in this journal, and found that there was no basis for bias and that there were real effects to reduced class size demonstrated by the Tennessee experimental study. He also indicated that a lack of faith in non-experimental design research was setting the stage for more experimental research in education. Jencks (1999) also suggested that descriptive analysis may be some of the most important work we do.

Of relevance is that these results are related most specifically to improving minority and at-risk student test scores. Of additional value over time will be the results of tracking the other educational outcomes from this experiment. Grissmer suggests that the greatest benefit to be derived from smaller classes may be reduced school dropout rates and better labor market outcomes.

In 1998, Jencks, author of the 1972 *Inequality* and perhaps the preeminent sociologist living today. recanted the position he had expressed in that well-known study. In 1972, he had stated that it was not a good investment of public resources to attempt to improve the educational outcomes of African Americans. He came to a different conclusion in *The Black-White Test-Score Gap*, a Fall 1998 publication of the Brookings Institution Press. At a January 1999 conference sponsored by the U.S. Department of Education's Office of Educational Research and Improvement and National Center for Education Statistics on the results of studies on minority education using large NCES education data sets, Jencks, as the invited lead speaker, commented on the state of sociology or education research since Coleman (Jencks, 2000):

> Although educational researchers often felt superior, educators seldom felt inferior. Faced with a study showing, let us say, that children's spelling skills did not improve over the long run if teachers handed out a list of words every Monday and gave a spelling test every Friday, most educators simply dismissed the findings as implausible. Likewise, when studies showed that children learned no more in small classes than in large classes, few educators considered the possibility that the studies might be correct. In most cases, educators did not even bother to dismiss results as implausible. They simply ignored education research entirely. Legislators typically did the same thing.
>
> Educators' indifference to research results convinced many researchers that the people who staffed the schools were unscientific traditionalists, unwilling to consider the possibility that their prejudices were ill-founded. In retrospect, however, the educators' indifference to educational research seems largely justified.

Jencks went on to describe "Type Two" research errors that were consistently made and even today are "disturbingly common." Type Two errors occur when a true hypothesis is rejected as false. Type Two errors occur most often when samples are small and measurements imprecise. He noted a bias among social scientists who have been much concerned about "Type One" errors—accepting a false hypothesis as true. In the policy arena, "if a practitioner were to take such researchers' conclusions seriously, they would often be led badly astray." Additionally, in hindsight, Jencks suggested that if a set of "priors" was developed as suggested by Bayesian theory, it would never have suggested adopting a null hypothesis for policy relevant research. Jencks went on to outline a series of problems with quantitative research, which made it ineffective for policy-makers and allowed it to be marginalized in schools of education for 30 years.

All of this discussion is of some value in understanding the limitations that have affected the use and growth of social science since Coleman. Jencks then noted some of the needs that were being met for better data and practical application of methods, etc., so that there is a better match between social science and practice. He concluded this section with:

> Recent results from analysis of this kind also fit practitioners' expectations better than earlier results did. If this trend continues, researchers may find themselves concluding that conventional wisdom among educators was not as misguided as their predecessors thought. If researchers can then move on to identify the most effective strategies for improving achievement, quantitative research may eventually prove quite useful.

It is interesting to note that this paper was delivered at a conference held to discuss strategies for reducing the minority test-score gap.

Jencks was not alone. Grissmer described the mid-1990s as a watershed for education researchers, many of whom appeared to be no longer asking, "Does money matter?" but rather, "How does money matter?" The National Academy of Sciences (NAS) recently published an influential book by the NRC (*Making Money Matter,* 1999). In this NAS publication, Hanushek (1986, 1996, 1997a) and his summaries on production functions are noted as second only to Coleman (1966) "in persuading people that money (or school) doesn't matter in efforts to improve education." The NRC found it important to note specifically Hanushek's recent statements related to his finding of no "systematic relationships between variations in school resources and student performance." Hanushek (1997b) is quoted: "This finding . . . is, however, very different from finding that schools have no differential impact. A number of subsequent studies (i.e. subsequent to the Coleman report) document rather conclusively that schools have significantly different effects on student achievement, even if the good schools are not necessarily those rich in traditionally measured inputs" (Hanushek, 1997b).

Hanushek, as a result of his own study of Texas teacher preparation, prefers investing in better prepared teachers. The NRC, observing differences in preference for specific education interventions nonetheless reported the consensus of the committee—that money can and should be allocated to make a difference in the education of children, particularly minorities and the poor.

The NRC, among other suggestions, called for urban experiments and quasi-experiments in schools and districts with many low-achieving students. It also recommended that these experiments be funded by the federal government, as the benefit should not be to that location alone but to the country as a whole. The NRC also challenged those who preferred specific interventions to "ensure that specific investments are made," and challenged those who question the implementation of large-scale interventions "to design incentives . . . to encourage each school to make the types of investments that will be best for it given its particular situation."

Grissmer (1999) also outlines additional interventions that are good investments for experimental research. These include increased public pre-kindergarten instruction, higher teacher salaries, better facilities and more resources for teachers, and investment in summer and after-school programs. These are all classroom interventions demanding per-pupil revenue investment, with some substantial demonstrated potential for broad public investment.

3.4.   Catholic/private schools vs. public schools

Coleman has suggested that Catholic schools have been effective in improving minority test scores and suggests that this reflects the existence of cultural capital. However, the culture and processes of Catholic schools have been found to be similar to high-SES public-school processes that have also improved minority test scores This suggests that there is a cultural capital that is not as readily available in the schools many poor and poor minority students attend. This suggests that a case can be made not only for better SES mixes in schools, but also for better information on the communities student live in and their social/cultural capital and human resources.

4.   Regional or metropolitan districts

4.1.   The value of developing metropolitan or regional school districts

Smith and O'Day (1991), Smith (2000), Grissmer et al., (1994), Grissmer et al. (1998) and Hedges et al. (1998) found that the African-American/American-European test-score gap was reduced between 1970 and 1988. Smith found this gap reduction to be much larger for African-Americans in the South and in border states than in the Northeast. Cochrane (1995), using the longitudinal study *High School and Beyond*, found changes in Southern urban African-American test scores to be significantly greater than changes in Northeastern urban African-American test scores during 1980–82. Resegregation started to take place in the South from the mid-to late 1980's through today. Smith (2000), Grissmer et al. (1998), Hedges et al. (1998) and others have noted the negative effect on the test-score gap since that time.

The integration of students in the South during the 1970–88 period was much more thorough than in the rest of the country, and by 1980 the South was the least segregated and the Northeast the most segregated region in the country. As observed by Coleman (1966), and replicated in various experiments involving the transfer of low-income minority students to middle-class suburban districts, the exposure of African-American and Hispanic students to middle-class expectations and resources has a positive effect on education outcomes.

Given the large proportion of poor and minority students in many central-city school districts, the Milliken (1974) ruling that denied the inclusion of suburban school districts in possible metropolitan strategies for desegregating poor central-city school districts was a serious setback. Elsewhere in this publication, Cochrane (Chapter 15) and Orfield (Chapter 6), and Orfield (2000) describe the differences in resources and in human and social capital between poor central-city districts and suburban districts. They also describe the movement of middle-class and majority students to the suburbs, which made the effective integration of schools in many U.S. central cities impossible.

Regional experts, though, are finding that regional or metropolitan areas that have and/or develop collaborative and mutually supporting systems are likely to be more flexible in responding to economic downturns and to provide, in general, healthier economic conditions (Rusk, 1995; Frug, 1999; Orfield, 1998; Pierce, Curtis & Hall, 1994). Internationally, Cochrane (this publication) and Yeung and Lo (1998), describe the region-wide planning focus that is necessary for metropolitan areas to acquire "world city" status.

Numerous large American cities (e.g., Charlotte/Mecklenberg, Minneapolis and Louisville) have been working with their county counterparts in metropolitan efforts to collaborate across regional community boundaries with the goal of improved conditions, including economic development, environmental and growth management, and community services. Improved schools and diversity are often linked with planners' goals as tools for attracting and developing economic partnerships.

Fairfax County in Virginia is a Southern county-wide school system in the Washington, D.C., region that has central-city density and a diversity of race/ethnicity, language, and SES. Because of its proximity to both Washington and the large and growing Reston, Virginia, Internet/technology corridor, a school can have 20-plus languages represented. With a commitment to improving minority test scores in the early 1990s, this county-wide district succeeded in providing the resources and mixture of SES and race/ethnicity within schools to improve test scores for African-American and Hispanic/Latino students. Currently, student participation rates in post-secondary education (93 percent) and Scholastic Aptitude Tests (required for many post-secondary programs (84 percent) are high. Fairfax County's average combined SAT score (1,094) is much higher than that for Virginia overall (1,007) or the nation (1,016). Its dropout rate (2.6 percent) is also lower than the state or national average dropout rate.

Current efforts to mandate metropolitan-wide districts have met with resistance. Frug (1999)—a Harvard law professor and leading expert on metropolitan areas—in his book on the development of cities based on regional integration and cooperation, suggested rebuilding legal and public systems to reward and promote diversity. Organizations and communities that voluntarily adopt integration and multicultural and/or pluralistic missions would be provided with certain legal and economic advantages, perhaps expressed in publicly funded resources or tax incentives. In the process, efforts can be made to voluntarily integrate neighborhoods and their schools. Stone (1998) introduced the concept of civic capacity. Stone described some of the difficulties in developing the necessary civic capacity to adequately integrate schools. In doing so, we start to acquire much-needed information on how to approach this difficult but potentially very valuable process.

There are efforts to develop regional or metropolitan desegregation or integration. McUsic (1999) described a "class integration" model, which was introduced into the *Sheff v. O'Neil* (Conn., 1996) urban Hartford school court case. This model provided for the elimination of high-poverty school districts (in which 50 percent of the students are poor). It was based on the well-documented fact that the "income and education of parents of fellow students is also highly correlated to performance." As most of the "severe poverty is highly concentrated in the major urban areas," this would provide legal grounds for the creation of integrated metropolitan districts. Given the "resonance" of this model with current education finance restructuring litigation, McUsic expected that it would be used with more frequency.

Orfield (2000) reminds us that we have data on Southern county-wide districts, and he encourages further research. Cochrane (1998), using school-district fiscal data, found that metropolitan-wide districts in the South provided greater per student revenue increases during the 1980s than central-city districts around the country, with the exception of the Mid-Atlantic (which includes New York, New Jersey and Pennsylvania).

For the international community, particularly for less developed countries and regions that have fewer resources, the metropolitan integration of ethnic and racial minority students provides an interesting opportunity. While the political effort is demanding and uncertain, the resources needed are those of civic will or capacity rather than financial wealth. These are more attainable resources for many, with a potential for both economic and educational results. Of course, there are areas that need investments, such as teacher training and transportation. However, the solution has economic and educational advantages that would in some cases be prohibitively expensive for many regions, states and nations to achieve through other interventions, or for smaller districts to accomplish by themselves. For evidence of this, we can look to the poor school districts in the American South and at what they were able to accomplish in the 1970s, even with external pressure and internal resistance.

Conclusions

Specific early childhood education or learning-process theories and school-based interventions all have the ability to reduce the test-score gaps of African-American, Hispanic and poor children. These educational outcomes translate into improved life chances and lower state costs related to prisons, health care and social services. There remains much that needs to be learned about each of these types of interventions. Additionally, we do not know what the result would be of using more than one of the types of interventions reviewed here at a time.

There are specific suggestions for investment in further experimental research. Professional development for teachers, curricula, instructional techniques, and summer and after-school programs are included as possibilities. There is also a need for the integration of research from a number of fields into the development of theories to explain why class-size reduction works.

We also know that it will take years and an ongoing commitment to improve educational outcomes for minorities and the poor. In the process, provided educational researchers continue to pay attention to educators in the field and to find out what works—and if policy-makers invest in improving the quality of the data—educational research can be helpful.

It is also the case that schools are assisted in the task of improving test scores when there is a socioeconomic mix in schools. While African-American students in the South experienced improved test scores, relative to majority white and other African-American students around the country—at the height of *de jure* desegregation—the changes in school process and culture have not been well studied. Cochrane (1995) did find that the only region for which increased test scores were not significantly related to SES was in the South. This suggests that somehow, within the South, teachers decided to and figured out how to teach poor minority children.

Given the high concentration of poor, minority students in many central-city school districts, the opportunity to create socioeconomically heterogeneous schools is perhaps best facilitated by voluntary residential and/or school desegregation that is inclusive of a complete region or metropolitan area. The greatest cost for building regional schools is not financial, but entails the development of civic capacity. The motivation is first perhaps the promise of economic success, and secondarily the human development that accompanies regional integration and planning.

References

Armstrong T., *Multiple Intelligences in the Classroom*, Association for Supervision and Curriculum Development, Alexandria (Virg.), 1994.

Bloom B., (ed.), *Taxonomy of Educational Objectives, the classification of educational goals,* McKay, New York, 1956.

Burchinal M., et al., "Early intervention and mediating processes in cognitive performance of children of low-income African American families," *Child Development, 68*, pp. 935–954, 1997.

Cochrane D., *Metropolitan School District Revenues during the 1980s: Did central cities get more?* An unpublished paper presented at the Annual American Education Research Association Conference in San Diego, (Calif.), 1998.

Cochrane D., *American School Desegregation: 1980, A Comparative Regional Investigation of Outcomes,* Dissertation, University of Buffalo, 1995.

Coleman J., et al., *Equality of Educational Opportunity,* U.S. Government Printing Office, 1966.

Coleman J., Hoffer T., Kilgore S., *High school achievement: Public, private, and Catholic schools compared*, Basic Books, New York, 1982.

Coleman J., Hoffer T., *Public and Private High Schools: The Impact of Communities,* Basic Books, New York, 1987.

D'Arcangelo M., "A Wake-Up Call About Brain Research," *Education Update, 42*(4), 2000.

Durie R., "An Interview with Howard Gardner," *Mindshift Connection,* spring 1999.

Durie R., *Mindshift Connection: Multiple Intelligences*, Zephyr Press, Tucson, 1997.

Ekstrom R., Goertz M., Rock D., *Education and American Youth,* The Falmer Press, Philadelphia, 1988.

Entwisle D., et al., "The Nature of Schooling," in Arum R., Beattie I. (eds.), *The Structure of Schooling: Readings in the Sociology of Education*, Mayfield Publishing Company, Mountainview, Calif., London, Toronto, 2000.

Finn J., Achilles M., "Tennessee's Class Size Study: Findings, Implications, Misconceptions," *Educational Evaluation and Policy Analysis, 21*(2), pp. 97–110, 1999.

Frug G., *City Making: Building Communities Without Building Walls,* Princeton University Press, Princeton, 1999.

Gardner H., *Frames of Mind: The theory of multiple intelligences,* Basic Books, New York, 1983.

Grissmer D., "Conclusions—Class Size Effects: Assessing the Evidence, Its Policy Implications, and Future Research Agenda," *Educational Evaluation and Policy Analysis, 21*(2), pp. 231–248, 1999.

Grissmer D., et al., *Student Achievement and the Changing American Family,* Rand Corporation, Santa Monica, 1994.

Grissmer, D., et al., "Why Did the Black-White Score Gap Narrow in the 1970s and 1980s?," in Jencks C, Phillips M. (eds.), *The Black-White Score Gap,* Brookings Institution, Washington, DC, 1998.

Grissmer D., et al., "Improving Research and Data Collection on Student Achievement," in Grissmer D., Ross M. (eds.), *Analytic Issues in the Assessment of Student Achievement,* U.S. Department of Education, Office of Educational Research and Improvement, Washington, DC, 2000.

Hanushek E., "Assessing the effects of school resources on student performance: An update," *Educational Evaluation and Policy Analysis 19*(2), pp. 141–164, 1997a.

Hanushek E., "Outcomes, incentives and beliefs: Reflections on analysis of the economics of schools," *Educational Evaluation and Policy Analysis 19*(4), pp. 301–308, 1997b.

Hanushek E., "Some Findings from an Independent Investigation of the Tennessee STAR Experiment and From Other Investigations of Class Size Effects," *Educational Evaluation and Policy Analysis, 21*(2), pp. 97–110, 1999.

Hanushek E., "The Evidence on Class Size," in Mayer, S., Peterson, P. (eds.), *Earning and Learning: How Schools Matter,* Brookings Institution/Russell Sage Foundation, Washington, DC, 2000.

Hedges L., et al., "Black-White Test Score Convergence Since 1965," in Jencks C., Phillips M. (eds.), *The Black-White Test Score Gap*, The Brookings Institution Press, Washington, DC, 1998.

Jencks C., et al., *Inequality: A Reassessment of the Effect of Family and Schooling in America,* Basic Books, 1972.

Jencks C., Phillips M., "The Black-White Test Score Gap: An Introduction," in Jencks C., Phillips M. (eds.), *The Black-White Test Score Gap*, The Brookings Institution Press, Washington, DC, 1998.

Jencks C., Keynote address at the NCES/OERI conference on issues in the use of large-scale NCES data, 1999.

Jencks C., Phillips M., "Aptitude or Achievement: Why do test scores predict educational attainment and earnings?" in Mayer S., Peterson P. (eds.), *Earning and Learning: How Schools Matter,* Brookings Institution/Russell Sage Foundation, Washington, DC, 1999.

Jencks C., "Educational Research and Educational Policy: An Historical Perspective," in Grissmer D., Ross M. (eds.), *Analytic Issues in the Assessment of Student Achievement,* U.S. Department of Education, Office of Educational Research and Improvement, Washington, DC, 2000.

Kreuger A., "Experimental estimates of education production functions," *Quarterly Journal of Economics*, CXIV, pp. 497–532, 1999.

Lee V., Smith J., Croninger R., "Another Look at High School Restructuring: More Evidence That It Improves Student Achievement, and More Insights into Why," *Issues in Restructuring Schools*, 9, 1995.

McUsic M., "The Law's Role in the Distribution of Education: The Promises and Pitfalls of School Finance Litigation," in J. Huebert (ed.), *Law and School Reform: Six Strategies for Promoting Educational Equity*, Yale University Press, New Haven and London, 1999.

Milliken v. Bradley, No. 73-434, Supreme Court of the United States, 418 U.S. 717, 1974.

Nash J.M., "Fertile Minds," *Time Magazine*, Feb. 3, *149*(5), 1997.

National Research Council, *Making Money Matter: Financing America's Schools,* Committee on Education Finance, Ladd H., Hansen J. (eds.), Commission on Behavioral and Social Sciences and Education, National Academy Press, Washington, DC, 1999.

Orfield G., "The Growth of Segregation: African Americans, Latinos and Unequal Education," in Arum R., Beattie I. (eds.), *The Structure of Schooling: Readings in the*

*Sociology of Educ*ation, Mayfield Publishing Company, Mountainview, Calif., London, Toronto, 2000.

Orfield M., "Metropolitics: A Regional Agenda for Community Stability," Brookings Institution Press, Washington, DC, and The Lincoln Institute of Land Policy, Cambridge, 1997.

Pierce N., Curtis W., Hall J., *Citistates: How Urban America Can Prosper in a Competitive World*, Seven Locks Press, Washington, DC, 1994.

Rusk D., *Cities Without Suburbs*, Woodrow Wilson Center Press, Washington, DC, 1995.

Smith M., "Student Assessment Issues in the Current Policy Environment," in Grissmer D., Ross M. (eds.), *Analytic Issues in the Assessment of Student Achievement*, U.S. Department of Education, Office of Educational Research and Improvement, Washington, DC, 2000.

Smith M., O'Day J., "Educational Equality: 1966 and Now," in Veerstegen D. and Ward J. (eds.), *Spheres of Justice in Education: The 1990 American Education Finance Association Yearbook,* Harper Business, New York, 1991.

Stone C., "Introduction: Urban Education in Political Context," in Stone C. (ed.), *Changing Urban Education,* University Press of Kansas, 1998.

Tucker L., "Connections Between Neuroscience and the Theory of Multiple Intelligences: Implications for education," in *Biology 202, 1999 Third Web Reports* (on-line). Available: *http://serendip.brynmawr.edu/bb/neuro/neuro99/web3/Tucker.html*

Wade N., "Brain May Grow New Cells Daily," *The New York Times*, A.1 (col. 1), October 15, 1999.

Weckstein P., "School Reform and Enforceable Rights to Quality Education," in Huebert J. (ed.), *Law and School Reform: Six Strategies for Promoting Educational Equity,* Yale University Press, New Haven and London, 1999.

Yueng Y., Lo F., "Globalization and world city formation in Pacific Asia" in Lo & Yeung (eds.), *Globalization and the World of Large Cities*, United Nations University Press, New York, 1998.

PART II

EQUITY INDICATORS: A FRAMEWORK, A RATIONALE
AND CURRENT PERSPECTIVES

Chapter 5

A System of Equity Indicators for Educational Systems[1]

Denis Meuret

Université de Bourgogne, Dijon, France

This chapter is founded in a common effort, as evidenced by this volume, to propose a system of indicators capable of permitting comparison of educational systems with respect to their equity. Some international indicators already measure certain inequalities (see, in particular, Organisation for Economic Co-operation and Development Center for Education Research and Innovation (OECD-CERI), *Education at a Glance*). However, these indicators are too few and have too little relationship with each other to lead to a judgment on the equitable character of an educational system. The equity of a school system requires a particular configuration of inequalities and equalities, so that it can be properly evaluated or discussed only according to a system of indicators. For example, a lessening of inequality in access to higher education is without a doubt a characteristic of a more equitable system because education procures intrinsic advantages. However, such a diminution will weigh more heavily in a judgment on the overall equity of an educational system if certain other factors are present (e.g., if the income gap between those who have or have not attended higher education has not declined, or if the children of certain minorities have not been sidelined). The absence of a system of international indicators for equity is not due to the absence of inequitable inequalities in educational systems. The contributions of the second part of this volume bear witness to that, following many other studies. Moreover, the teachers in educational systems are themselves aware of inequities.[2]

Therefore, if the political leaders have not yet decided on a regular course of monitoring, it is that they are not persuaded of the interest in it and of the feasibility of such a system of indicators. We will therefore try:

- to show that there is sufficient (and growing) interest for the governance of modern societies in the use of educational equity indicators.
- to address certain conceptual objections that are raised about such systems (that there is disagreement on the characteristics of an equitable system; that educational inequalities are unavoidable and unchanging; that it is impossible to take account of all the dimensions of equity; and that the

search for equity is detrimental to other, more important goals).

In the course of this discussion, we unveil nine "principles" that seem necessary to guide the construction of a system of indicators, of which a framework will then be proposed.

1.   Equity indicators foster better government

Tocqueville's analysis is well known: When conditions of inequality are lessened, they are always more deeply experienced as injustices; feelings of injustice and envy will occupy a growing place in the hearts of men and render them more and more difficult to govern.

One example of this phenomenon in the educational domain is the following: As long as French schools were content to lead some particularly brilliant children of the lower classes towards secondary education, the essentially elite system appeared to be an instrument of social promotion and equality. Since secondary education was democratized, all children have been enrolled, but the school itself excludes a portion of students from the educational system at the end of compulsory schooling, and thus seems to be an instrument of exclusion and inequality. Having become less inegalitarian, the system nevertheless arouses less recognition and more resentment (Dubet, 1992).

A reduction of inequalities, in effect, can translate into a growth in frustration and not a decline (Kellerhals et al., 1997). The perception of injustice, like envy, can engender violence and destruction of the social bond (Dupuy, 1997). We may recall that, in a story by Friedrich von Kleist, Michael Kohlhaas ends up setting all of Germany afire and leaves it bleeding in his obsession to obtain reparation for an injustice, real but minor, that had been committed against him.[3]

The question of equity therefore has significant consequences for governments and will concern them more and more. Questions of equity in education in particular can be expected to have increased importance, for the following reasons:

- Individuals' stakes in education are growing.[4]
- They see it increasingly as a service that the State owes them.
- The State itself increasingly recognizes this service as one of its major responsibilities. It must therefore expect to be judged, more and more, on the equity with which it renders this service.[5]
- This judgment generates individual and social phenomena in which it is important to contain violence while permitting political expression.

Of course, equity indicators will not be sufficient to guarantee that this expression will take place, nor will they suffice to contain violence or resentment generated by envy, but they can certainly help.

There is more. The common representation of the education equity question is that such an egalitarian system unfortunately finds itself powerless to counterbalance the effect of inequalities that preceded it. But even if social inequalities or aptitudes are partly responsible for educational inequalities, we have some evidence that the educational system has played an active role in their creation. For evidence of this, consider the following:

- The school creates objective inequalities in knowledge far greater than the eventual inequalities in aptitude it inherits. These inequalities are in principle for the common good, but the proof of this claim rests on social institutions (see Meuret, Chapter 3).
- It creates these inequalities not by treating each student independently— as if each were alone in a box and received his/her education with more or less to gain—but by integrating into the educational experience itself comparisons between those who succeed and those who fail, availing itself, with more or less elegance, of comparisons between individuals as an instrument of motivation (Crahay, 2000).[6]
- Finally, it offers to the weakest students, who are often—but not always— the least socially advantaged, a less propitious environment for learning than others. It has been demonstrated that the essential difference in effectiveness among schools has come neither from differences in operation nor from differences in the initial characteristics of students, but in the counter-balancing of these two inequalities, i.e., from the fact that the weakest students attended schools whose operation was less propitious for learning (Grisay, 1999).

It is necessary to add that each educational system creates inequalities through strategies that can often be perceived only in comparison with other systems (Duru-Bellat & Kieffer, 2000). Note that during the period when Bourdieu and Passeron in France came up with their brilliant and soon-to-be globally celebrated Theory of Reproduction[7] (1970), France was said to be one of the most inegalitarian countries in the developed world because it had opened up its secondary education less than others—a highly circumstantial reason, unworthy of attention under this theory.

In sum, scholastic inequalities depend on inequalities of society in general and the educational system in particular, two types of inequalities for which citizens can hold the State accountable. If these inequalities are perceived as unjust, the consequences for social relationships can be considerable, and everything indicates that they increasingly are, to the point that the question of equity in the delivery of educational services could become an increasing focus of the political process.

It is fair to point out that the notion of justice in education has made a re-appearance on the political agenda after a period essentially concerned with efficiency. While opinions diverge on the opportunity for other types of social spending, there is agreement to consider that it is the duty of all governments to give to each person the possibility of remaining employable throughout life, and to have the basic skills for doing so. Governments have recently recognized that they have a duty in this regard towards all citizens. Indeed, it is not unlikely that indicators of educational inequalities will become as important as indicators of economic inequalities are now, with the proportion of the insufficiently educated matching the unemployment rate and the inequalities in acquired skills matching inequalities of resources. Nowadays, educational equity is not merely a concern for intellectuals confronting reality with their principles; it is a concern for the majority of people.

This argues for the existence of a system of indicators with two tracks: one to make education systems accountable to citizens to help them form opinions, as well as to help officials diagnose problems and define their actions (see Orfield, Chapter 6); the other to inform officials about citizens' opinions of what is acceptable and unacceptable—in other words, about citizens' criteria of justice and the judgments they hold about the equity of the system. Of course, if the second group of indicators shows an evolution in the judgment criteria, that can lead to modification of the first.

Hence, our first principle:

(1) The system of indicators must measure inequalities to help citizens and those who govern to judge the equity of the educational system, but it must also identify the opinions of citizens on the equity of the system and the criteria that form the basis for those opinions.

One can object that the measure of opinions may not accurately reflect the real inequity of the system. Indeed, this judgment can be biased by the narrowness of the universe of reference (children or parents in low- to middle-class neighborhoods do not know the conditions of schools attended by students in rich neighborhoods) or by using too short a time frame (underestimating the injustice of inequalities that produce effects over the long term). It is also true that the poor or minorities are likely to underestimate the injustices of which they are victims.

However, we must accept that policy-makers' decisions are shaped not only by reality, but also by citizens' perceptions. The solution for biased perceptions of educational equity is to provide better and more detailed information to the people, not to ignore their judgements.

Paying some attention to the concerns of pupils and parents regarding inequalities, we will have to recognize that they deal very often with criteria that are not frequently measured and not very easy to measure: degree of violence, quality of life, security and conviviality. These are among their declared criteria for choosing a school (Woods, 1993). We therefore have to recognize that inequity in educational systems stems not only from inequalities in attainment or achievement, but also from the inequalities in the life that students experience in school. Individuals nowadays spend a great part of their life in school. Therefore, with respect to equity, the educational experience *matters,* not only the effects or success of the education.

Hence, our second principle:

(2) Indicators must measure not only inequalities in educational results (e.g., knowledge, scholastic careers, social usage of academic titles), but also more immediate inequalities relating to life in school and the way in which students are treated by the institution and its agents.

2. Responses to some conceptual objections

One can conceive of four conceptual objections to the focus on a system of indicators: that there are divergent opinions on the nature of the inequalities that make an educational system unfair; that the educational inequalities are unavoidable and immutable; that they are too diverse to permit measurement of them all; and that the search for equality is detrimental to other more important objectives. These will be examined one by one as we discuss the rest of the principles.

"There are divergent opinions on the characteristics of a fair educational system."

It has been shown that those who argue about equity in education reference not only one but three broad principles: equality of opportunity, equality of treatment and equality of attainment (Grisay, 1984; see Demeuse, Crahay & Monseur, Chapter 2).

However, in this way, the question of equity in education is treated like a local problem of justice; that is to say, by treating education as a good in itself without situating it in relation to more fundamental later gains and to more general principles. To recall the term used by Rawls, equity in education is thus thought to fall in the "intuitionist" category of theories (see Meuret, Chapter 3).

Since the publication of Rawls' *Theory of Justice* in 1971, an ongoing debate in political philosophy has offered several theories, under which it is possible to think of justice in education escaping the limited "intuitionist" approach. There is a general debate on justice in which it is possible to introduce a discussion about education in which "local" concerns are not forgotten but reconsidered. Faced with these theories, those who oppose the establishment of a system for measuring equity argue that it is not worth the trouble because the relevance of any indicator of equality can be challenged by the champions of another principle of justice.

But the argument is flawed. The diversity of the theories does not reflect the incapacity of researchers to provide humanity with a clear and unique conception of equity but, rather, the very existence of a debate on equity among humanity. In other words, the existence of several principles does not lead to some invalidating others, but to the question of justice as it is conceived within this framework. Therefore, it follows from the existence of this debate that an indicator system would enlighten and nurture the debate, not that it would be useless. This reinforces the "political" conception of the indicator system exposed in principle 1, and leads to a third principle:

(3) The indicators must permit debate within the framework of diverse principles of existing justice, and not be inscribed in any one of them.

From this principle, in particular, it follows that the system of indicators cannot limit itself to the measurement of social inequalities in access to the heights of the educational system. These inequalities are certainly important from the standpoint of justice, but they are not the only ones (Meuret, 1999b). Not only can other benefits be pertinent in this respect, categories other than social ones can also be pertinent (e.g., gender, ethnicity, nationality). These inequalities matter according to certain principles of justice—Rawls' principle of fair equal opportunity, Walzer's spheres of justice, meritocracy—but are inadequate or insufficient according to other principles (Sen's "functionings," Walzer's simple equality, Rawls' principle of difference).

These other principles put the emphasis on individual inequalities of two different sorts. The first is that of the deviations among individuals (deviations in competence between the most and least successful, for example). The measure of this type of inequality is justified on several grounds. That is to say:

- If these inequalities are too great, they threaten social cooperation on an equal footing by maintaining a feeling of inferiority among the least educated, which is contrary to an equitable distribution of self-respect (Rawls, 1973).
- They also threaten the feeling of equality that is necessary to the democratic operation of political society (Rawls, 1973).
- Moreover, some policies (called "postmodern" by Stuart Wells et al., 1999) are being put in place, especially in the United Kingdom and the USA, that have the effect of favoring families (poor or rich) prepared to invest in the education of their children. One can expect from these policies a growth of educational inequalities *within* social categories. Such a growth can already be seen in certain countries in other domains; in income, for example.

The second inequality is that of a threshold below which equity requires that nobody fall. One can relate this last type of indicator to Sen's "capabilities" or to the "basic curriculum" that all must master equally according to Walzer. To be below a certain minimum threshold of competence is without doubt the educational situation that can have the gravest social consequences for the individual. In some countries, the law seeks to keep students from dropping out before they reach this threshold. For example, in France it is stipulated by law that the objective of school is to not let a single student leave without minimal qualification. Evidently, the conception of skills that make up this threshold can vary. Several texts of the European Commission relate this threshold to what they call "employability" of individuals by industry. Several authors have proposed other criteria (see Meuret, Chapter 3).

One can therefore propose a fourth principle:

(4) The pertinent educational inequalities for most of the goods distributed by educational systems can be grouped into three large families: inequalities among categories, inequalities among individuals and the proportion of individuals who are below a minimum threshold.

"Educational inequalities are unavoidable and immutable."

The lasting quality of educational inequalities and their resistance to so many policies designed to eradicate them (Meuret, 1994; Vinovskis, 1999) seem to validate the idea that the forces that drive them are too powerful for inequalities to be avoided. But an inequality must be avoidable in order to be unacceptable (Whitehead, 1991) and to be considered as a stake for government action.

Benadusi, Chapter 1, establishes a list of theories on the genesis of educational inequalities, some of which predict a lowering of social inequalities in scholastic careers (let us, for now, limit the question of equity to this dimension); and others, which predict less social inequality in their stability. Among the first is the theory of modernization (Parsons), which claims that the economy cannot long indulge itself with a non-meritocratic scholastic system. Among the second is the theory of reproduction (Bourdieu), which predicts that the upper classes will always be in some way better situated, so that the best places will be reserved for their children.

However, there are some empirical reasons why educational inequalities are not immutable. First, certain inequalities vary, and vary appreciably over moderate periods of time. The positive evolution of success for girls during the last 30 years is well known and spectacular. But other examples are less well known. If one takes for equity criteria the influence of social origin on the highest scholastic level of attainment, France appeared to be one of the most inegalitarian countries in studies ending with the cohort born in 1947 (Müller & Karle, 1993), but this is no longer true when one takes account of the cohort born between 1964 and 1973 (Duru-Bellat & Kieffer, 2000). Another example: In the USA, from the early 1970s to 1996, the deviation in performance at age

13 between white and black students has diminished 20 percent in reading and 37 percent in mathematics (*Condition of Education*, 1998).

Next, certain research on schools or small groups of children suggests that inequalities can vary because they depend on decisions that can be changed by policy modifications. In an already dated study, Bloom showed that all students could acquire similar levels of knowledge provided that they had the time to do so and that adequate schooling was provided (Bloom, 1984). It is also known that certain schools produce fewer inequalities (between weak and strong students) than others (Grisay, 1993; Jesson & Gray, 1991; Thomas, 1997). Numerous actions by schools have been shown capable of compensating, in the time they have been in effect, for the effect of social origin (Fraser, 1989).

Progress has been made in understanding the forces that generate inequalities. It is increasingly understood that these forces are external as well as internal. Sociology has improved our understanding of external factors and today proposes less deterministic theories, which open a greater possibility for corrective action than 30 years ago (see Benadusi, Chapter 1; in particular, what he calls "the American interpretive sociology of education"). Shavit and Blossfeld (1993) conclude that the lowering of academic inequalities observed in a small number of countries (e.g., Sweden, the Netherlands) is better explained by the lowering of social inequalities, or the greater security acquired by the poor in these countries, than by educational reforms themselves.

It is moreover logical to suppose that the greater the inequalities—wealth, social capital, cultural capital—within a country, the greater the inequalities in resources that can be consecrated to education and the greater the mobilization of these resources by those who possess them to assure beyond scholastic success the wealth of their children. The measure of certain contextual dimensions, situated in the source of educational systems, is therefore necessary to understand the educational inequalities and to judge the equity of educational systems: If the educational system of country A presents the same inequalities as that of country B, when country A is much more inegalitarian than B, it will be necessary to conclude that the educational system of A is more equitable than that of B.

Economists have drawn our attention to other types of external factors. If poor people have little financial return for their education (for instance, because of discrimination in the labor market or higher education curricula that do not fit their goals), they will not invest their human capital—even if education is free and its process perfectly equitable (Checchi et al., 1999).

However, we know that internal inequalities matter also. Certain students (the poor, immigrants) receive less attention than others from their instructors (Sirota, 1988). As another example, the later the point in the school career at which students are divided into vocational and academic tracks, the more equitable is the system (see, for example, Boudon, 1973). Further, we know that certain purely internal inequalities have tangible effects: As a result of unequal expectations, students labeled weak and repeaters, regardless of their social origins, receive less attention and a scholarly environment of poorer quality. We know that these differences are translated into differences in achievement (Grisay, 1999, among others).

Educational inequalities are neither unavoidable nor immutable, but they are produced by strong, interwoven external and internal factors. The equity of an educational system depends on its ability to compensate, instead of reinforcing, through internal factors the inequitable action of external factors. So, the evaluation of the equity of an educational system requires the measurement of both internal and external factors.

Hence, a fifth principle:

(5) It is important to measure not only the unequal results of education, but also the inequalities that precede the educational system and those that affect the learning process itself.

"The inequalities are too diverse to permit measurement of them all."

As easy as it is to decide that it would be "interesting" to measure differences among countries with respect to this or that inequality, it is difficult to decide on a reasonably sized list permitting global judgment on the equity of an educational system.

For example, it is rather easy to agree that skills acquired on average towards the end of required schooling are an important indicator of effectiveness of the educational system. To this indicator of effectiveness, it is possible to relate several different indicators of inequality, all having to do with equity of the educational system. One can measure inequalities among individuals or among categories; in the second case, several categories are relevant. Even in the first case, one could use a lot of different measures, each of which may be preferred for non-trivial reasons (Duru-Bellat, 1999).

Evidently there is a great temptation to respond that all these measures are relevant, which happens to be the case. All are pertinent to some degree. But this response only puts off solving the problem because one who confronts a hundred findings must come up with a method of aggregation, which is to say of balancing and combining them, to produce from these findings a judgment about the whole.

To construct a system of indicators, it does not suffice to attack the problems posed by the plurality of principles of justice. It is also necessary to attack those that arise from the plurality of possible benefits and categories. It is doubtless necessary to accept that this choice is imperfect and depends on conceptions of justice only partially determined by reason. For example, the most socially conscious intellectuals would not have seen much inconvenience 35 years ago in not measuring inequalities between boys and girls. In truth, the establishment of pertinent categories in this regard is more the role of political or social movements (see, for example, Orfield, Chapter 6) and public opinion, than of researchers, administrators or philosophers themselves.

What we can hope to shape is a system of indicators that takes stock of what *creates* problems with respect to justice, according to the common conscience of our time. This is challenge enough in the sense that the role of governments is not to treat problems that go unnoticed by the people, but to treat those that people perceive as requiring government action.[8] The role of a system of indicators consists therefore in organizing on rational foundations (those of the principles of justice) comparative measures of goods and categories that matter to citizens (see, for example, Principle 1, above).

However, a specific problem arises when international comparison is at stake: For historical or political reasons, some categories of persons may matter more in some countries than in others. One may think, for instance, that equity towards minorities, which is a fundamental topic in American political consciousness, has its equivalence in Europe and equity towards workers in Europe is important because these were the populations that in their respective region carried out the main struggle for equality and human rights. Another question arises with respect to minorities, which have different status and histories in diverse countries: We would not learn too much from a comparison of the situation of African Americans in the United States with natives of the Maghreb in France, for the history of these two groups of people in their respective countries is not the same. However, what Skrla et al. (2000) write for the United States, based on prior research, is true for most countries: "The inequitable treatment of children of color manifests itself in various ways, including over-assignment to special education, language segregation, low academic tracking, over representation in disciplinary cases, substandard facilities and inadequate resources, disproportionate dropout rates and toxic school climates." Moreover, the relevance of the question of equity towards minorities will very likely grow in all countries. An indicator system that does not deal with this question would be a very poor one.

Other issues to be dealt with are the regrouping of categories (minority girls and boys do not have the same behavior or school careers), and the fact that the benefits that pose problems may not be the same from one category to the other. For example, it is difficult to contend today that girls are disadvantaged from the standpoint of length of studies, though they may be in certain courses or aspects of the process. If girls are often more successful than boys, this may be because they develop particularly strong skills in the "role of student" (Felouzis, 1994), compensating for the reduced attention they receive from teachers. This difference in attention does act negatively however on their self-esteem (Baudoux & Noircent, 1995). One sees therefore that, depending on the benefit under consideration (academic success, attention received, self-esteem), the distribution among girls and boys can appear to be fair or particularly unfair.

There is moreover no guarantee that public opinion in each country will be homogeneous with respect to which benefits matter most. It is likely that men and women, nationals and immigrants, rich and poor will have different views. One can imagine, for example, that an indicator of equality in the distribution of the benefit "to easily find work after school" more nearly addresses the preoccupations of the poor, while equality in the distribution of "finding work corresponding to the qualifications acquired in school" would address the preoccupations of the rich.

How then should one choose among benefits and categories? We will propose here some priorities, but of course only as a contribution to the necessary debate, a debate that should not be confined to academic researchers, but might also be the subject of public opinion polls or local meetings of citizens. The organization of such meetings would be coherent with the political orientation proposed here.

Benefits distributed by the educational system are:
- the immediate results of school (knowledge, attitudes, skills, degrees);
- its mediated results, which include: social position, profession and employability; and
- certain aspects of the educational process (length of school, community expenditures for education), as well as smaller benefits, which through repetition can fashion a powerful experience: punishments, hazing, smiles, friendships with other students, etc.

It would be incoherent with our systemic approach to exclude one of these three categories of goods. So, one has to propose transversal criteria, which could include: those benefits in which inequalities have the heaviest consequences for individuals, those in which inequalities threaten to carry the most damaging political consequences for the democracy, and finally those in which inequalities are found to play a particularly important role in the production of the two first categories of benefits.

For the categories, one can propose giving priority to categories independent of individual will. One supposes, for example, that geographic inequalities are less important than others in the sense that it is possible to leave a poorly equipped region, while it is not possible to change one's social origin, nationality or gender.

Regarding social position, one could also give some priority to income categories, for they are universal criteria—unlike minority status or social class, of which, as researchers well know, the definitions vary from country to country—and because income is also a good index of position on several scales such as prestige or discrimination.

However, income inequalities are not the only social inequalities; others deal with prestige, power, fame, etc. There is agreement that most social hierarchies in which individuals can be trapped are organized around their professional situation (Lévy et al., 1997). Now, an international comparison by social categories is not without problems. On the one hand, some prefer to gather all the social and cultural determinants in the academic success of children into one indicator describing the parents, while we have a preference for separating them (Willms, 1998). However, practically speaking, the nomenclatures are not the same from one country to another. For certain researchers (Erikson et al., 1979) and more recently in the framework of OECD's PISA project, an international nomenclature of social categories has been constructed. With respect to minorities, it would be necessary to establish a category that is valid at an international level, a difficult but highly necessary task.

From this discussion, one might draw two supplementary "principles":

(6) Among the benefits distributed by the educational system, those must be privileged whose equity of distribution matters more for individuals—or for the democratic life of the country.

(7) Among the categories pertaining to the individual, the most important are those from which the individual cannot escape.

"The search for equality is detrimental to other more important objectives."

One frequently reads that the concern for equity in education is in conflict with other objectives or values. Often cited are: educational effectiveness for the average or the best students, the consequences of its decline on economic growth (on the "mind" of the country), freedom and responsibility.

Nobody has an interest in poorly educated teachers, doctors or engineers. Nor would there be much support for a policy that to compensate for inequalities of attention that children receive from their parents would observe, in very minute fashion, life in each home (Kymlicka, 1992). Not even fervent egalitarians could be expected to concur that that those who do poorly should, in every case, be compensated by extra resources (Brighouse, 2000).

All the same, one can respond to these arguments in two ways:
- The first is that they can justify some but not any deviation in knowledge between the elite and the majority; they do not justify that all constraints be rejected in the name of liberty. Modern theories of justice take seriously the challenge to equity posed by the concurrence of other values, but propose some combinations that make it possible to do the right thing with respect to the concern for justice. For example, Rawls accords priority over equality to a certain number of liberties, but not all, and his principle of difference is a way to address the concern for effectiveness

within fair institutions (Meuret, 1999a).

- The second answer is that equity and these other values are not forcibly contradictory. With respect to liberty, it may be argued that a great inequality between the skills of the least and the most educated favors a strong social hierarchy, which in turn is not the best way of enforcing liberty and responsibility. It may also be argued, as Sen (1996, p. 135) does, that the distribution of some basic benefits "tells us something not merely about well-being achieved, but also about freedoms enjoyed," as is shown by the use of expressions like "freedom from hunger."

With respect to effectiveness, there is ample evidence that certain processes favor it as well as equity. Thus, in France, the lengthening of the average duration of schooling and the opening of the educational system permitted growth in the average attainment level of students when they left the educational system, allowed stability or growth of the level of the best students (Thélot et al., 1996), and reduced inequities in access to education among social categories (Duru-Bellat & Kieffer, 2000). Thus also, the average achievement most often grows with the reduction of the gap between the least and most educated (Crahay, 2000; Demeuse, Crahay & Monseur, Chapter 2). The results presented here by Vandenberghe, Dupriez and Zachary show an absence of the relationship between the effectiveness of the education system in mathematics and the influence of social origin on mathematics achievement; in other words, improved social equality for learning in math is not contrary to effective instruction (see also Wong & Lee, 1998).

There is also some evidence that equity in education may foster economic productivity. High-wage firms look for "workers able to work productively with people from different backgrounds" (Lévy & Murnane, 1999), which assumes that their language skills are not too far apart. More generally, there is some empirical evidence that equity in education favors economic growth: One long-term comparison among countries has shown that smaller inequalities in income accompanied stronger economic growth (Persson & Tabellini, 1994, cited by Guellec & Ralle, 1997). The explanation advanced by the authors is that where wage gaps are less pronounced, there is less need for redistribution of revenues, which can be detrimental to growth by withdrawing incentives to invest. In this setting, education is a decisive variable because it is a factor in the wage gap. It can act in two ways: to diminish the ties between social origin and school success, diminishing over time the inequalities inherited from one's parents; and to produce more qualified people by opening the educational system wider, thus diminishing inequalities in salary.

So, the relationship between equity and its so-called opposing values may be more ambivalent or complex than mere rivalry. It is therefore important to be able to see how, in the singular configuration of each country, educational equity and values that can support or thwart it evolve. Hence, the principle:

(8) The indicators must permit discussion about the concern for equality as well as for other values that may seem to oppose it.

This discussion will be possible only if the indicators also explore what happens beyond the educational system. Education, in effect, is not—or not uniquely—a final good. If, for example, one increases equity in education, but through a policy that has negative effects on educational effectiveness and does not produce enough minimally qualified persons, the deviation will grow between the salaries of the most and least qualified. Sure, the knowledge of each group will be more equal, but their salaries will be more unequal (Piketty, 1997).

As Hirschman (1991) has shown, equalizing policies are opposed in the name of effectiveness and their supposedly perverse effects, more than in the name of inegalitarian principles. It is therefore necessary that the system of indicators explores the social effects of educational inequality. With respect to equity, external effects of education include both social mobility and social inequalities.

With regard to education, social mobility may be considered as a contextual element favoring equity (the more mobility between grandparents and parents, the less unequal the educational expectations are likely to be), but also as an effect of the educational system. It depends on the external effectiveness of the educational system (appropriateness of the curricula to the requirements of the labor market and its ability to produce highly qualified job seekers) and on its internal equity (ability to provide high qualifications regardless of social background). The ratio "social position of the child"/"social position of the father" may be seen as the product of two ratios: "social position of the child"/"education of the child" times "education of the child"/"social position of the father."

With regard to education, social inequalities may be considered according to two modalities, individual or collective. The individual modality explores the social consequences for an individual of being at the top or bottom of the school hierarchy. The collective modality explores the effects on social justice of the allocation and utilization of resources—qualified people—that the education system puts at the disposition of society.

Examples of the pertinence of an exploration of individual effects follow: It is observed in comparing certain countries that equality in education is greater where credentialism is weaker; that is to say, where the role of diplomas in access to employment is weaker, as if one could be permitted greater educational equality when it is without consequence on social inequality. Moreover, the relative effects of the diploma on social position matter: If the return for a given diploma is weaker for low-SES (socioeconomic status) people than it is for high-SES ones (Goux & Maurin, 1997), as we have seen, not only will low-SES children not be encouraged to invest in education, but the gaps in educational attainment will be all the more inequitable.

The collective effects of inequalities in education can be illustrated by the following example: Depending on whether the doctors of a country care only for the rich, or for the rich and poor equally, the authorized expenditure for their education may or may not be equitable. The more scientific research allows economic growth that will profit the most disadvantaged, the more equitable the expense of training researchers will be.

Thus, the principle:

(9) Indicators must bear not only on inequalities in education, but also on the effects of these inequalities on social inequalities in general.

From the nine principles that have been presented, one can now propose, not a system of indicators (it is impossible to make such short work of an in-depth discussion on the opportunity and applicability of each potential indicator), but an outline designed to illustrate a certain number of possibilities inscribed in these principles.

This outline, in its simplest form, is presented as follows:

Some observations to facilitate understanding of a presentation based on this outline are that:

An outline of indicators on the equity of educational systems

Context
Social and cultural context
Political context

Process
Quantity of education received
Quality of education received

Internal results
Academic achievement
Personal and social development
School careers

External results
Social mobility
Individual consequences of educational inequalities
Collective conse–quences of educational inequalities

- Its aim is to illustrate the framework, not to propose an account of all existing (see Healy and Istance, Chapter 7, for such an account) or relevant indicators.
- According to the principle of justice that guides the reader, the relation of an indicator to equity can change. For instance, a Rawlsian will be without doubt less inclined than a Walzerian to find that a gap between individuals in mathematics skills at 14 years of age is, in itself, a sign of inequity. At the same time, *grosso modo*, this outline is designed to be read in the following manner: Inequalities affecting internal results and processes will signal an inequity of the educational system all the more when:

—their consequences on the future life of students and on society as a whole are considerable (external results);
—they must be attributed to the operation of the educational system (process) rather than to social inequalities themselves (social and cultural context); and
—they strongly affect the opinion that citizens or users have on the justice of the system (political context).

According to principle 4 (see page 139), we will now present this outline in the form of a table with three columns, each of them corresponding to one of the three types of inequalities: inequalities among individuals, inequalities independent of categories and inequalities experienced by those whose education has left them below a minimum threshold of competence. For each approach, we will present some examples of indicators that could be relevant. Some of these indicators already figure in international systems of indicators. Others have sought international comparisons within the framework of a specific study. Still others have been calculated within the framework of a national study, yet seem relevant in an international perspective. (These are followed by an indication of the country in which they were measured.) Finally, there are others that do not yet exist, at least in the imperfect knowledge of the author.

We must also explore the possibility of calculating, for each part of this outline, a unique index from the available indicators in each country. These indices would evidently be relative. They would permit us to know only if, for this specific section, one country is more equitable than another. This relative approach would permit comparisons among countries even if not all indicators are available for every country.

Below is a more detailed presentation of this outline. Of course, it is imperfect. For instance, it deals mainly with early schooling (see Healy & Istance, for developments on life-cycle patterns of inequality), and the author is not aware of all existing studies on relevant topics. Also, French studies are over-represented. Then, again, some might conclude that from an equity point of view, this last fact may compensate for all papers in which they are ignored. Moreover, many topics are entire research fields in and of themselves (e.g., gender studies, social mobility studies), of which specialists may find the proposed indicators naïve or obsolete. This is only a work in progress and an invitation to specialists to make proposals for their own fields.

3.   Context

Context must be understood to be both social and cultural, on the one hand, and political on the other. The social and cultural context is measured to explain inequalities in internal results, but also to evaluate the system's equity with respect to other countries, according to the perspective defined in the discussion of Principle 5: These indicators would permit us to calculate whether internal inequalities are greater than expected or not, given the social context. The political context is measured for reasons explained in the discussion of Principle 1: to make decision-makers sensitive to the criteria by which the public judges equity in the educational system and also to the opinions that people hold regarding its equity.

3.1. Social and cultural context

We have ample evidence of the relationship of social and cultural inequalities to inequalities in school. Benadusi's synthesis (Chapter 1) of theories on the genesis of social inequalities related to success in school helps to shape the choice of indicators of social inequalities. Among these, expectations (Bourdieu), manner of expression (Bernstein), income (Boudon), cultural capital (Bourdieu) and social capital (Coleman) are designated as benefits that lead to scholastic success. The more unequal the distribution of one or another of these benefits (among social categories or individuals) in a given country, the stronger the influence of these benefits on inequalities in scholarly results.

However, it is not certain that the relationship between social and scholastic inequalities will always be linear; perhaps there are threshold effects—for instance, beyond a certain income and material security, the differences are weak. It is helpful to distinguish here two large categories of resources, social and cultural.

3.1.1. Inequalities in social resources

These resources consist at the same time of revenues, and in the greater or lesser assurance that they will be available for a long time.

3.1.2. Inequalities of cultural resources

These resources are the amount of education of the parents, one of the best predictors of children's careers, but also (to consider culture in the more anthropologic sense) a certain number of values and parental attitudes more or less propitious to children's success in school.

There is an ongoing debate about whether the weakest ambitions or expectations in underprivileged categories are only the effects of alienation or if they are also the effects of indifference (see, for example, Benadusi, Chapter 1); according to the position we adopt in this debate, we will interpret the inequalities in expectation as reinforcing the inequitable outcomes in internal results or, on the contrary, as evidence that they are the result of divergent interests and values. It seems however that the expectations of the different social categories have a tendency to come together, depriving this debate of its pertinence.[9]

3.2. Political context

Unlike the indicators discussed earlier, these serve less to explain the inequalities of results than to interpret them from the political point of view. The *equity criteria* help us to appreciate that inequalities are, according to citizens, school personnel and students, the most important indicators of equity in the educational system. Judgments about the equity of the system help to measure the political effect of actions to improve it. These two dimensions could be captured by an international survey of teachers, students and parents, developed in consultation with educators, philosophers, sociologists and economists specializing in justice.

3.2.1. Equity criteria

One can determine the equity criteria of individuals not only by asking them directly about their principles of justice, but also by asking them about the nature of inequalities that most upset them or by posing moral dilemmas. There is a strong body of research on this topic (Kellerhals, 1997; Hochschild, 1981). It is based mostly on small-scale experiments, but also sometimes on representative samples (see, for example, the International Social Justice Project, reported in Marshall et al., 1999).

3.2.2. Judgments about equity

These judgments would bear principally on the equity of the system, but also on the manner in which the concern for equity enters (or does not enter) into conflict with concerns about other values (see, for example, Principle 9). They would be gathered through surveys of students, parents and teachers.

4.   Process

Measuring equity in the educational process is important in understanding the *origin of* inequalities in internal results. It is important also because numerous inequalities affecting the educational process—inequalities in treatment and well-being, for example—can be inequitable by themselves, independent of their eventual relation with inequalities of results (see, for example, Principles 2, 5). To apprehend inequalities in the scholastic process, it is useful to distinguish their quantity (2.1) and quality (2.2), knowing that it is their combination that explains, all other things being equal, what will have been transmitted to the student by the end of his/her years in school.

4.1. Quantity of education received

For an individual, one can judge the quantity of education by the length of schooling received and by its cost.

4.1.1. Length of schooling

Not one author, to my knowledge, has called for equality among individuals in the length of schooling, but some do propose such an equality in training throughout one's life. They find it inequitable that the less able receive less schooling; that is to say, fewer resources to develop their ability. Most authors measure length of schooling by the "highest level attained" (e.g., Shavit & Blossfeld, 1993). However, the length of schooling is a somewhat different concept, and some studies using it are also illuminating. For instance, Chauvel (1998) found strong and erratic variations of the interdecile intervals of length of schooling in France between 1900 and 1970.

It is often argued that most dropouts *choose* to quit school. However, the International Adult Literacy Study (IALS) collected data on the reasons that people stopped schooling when they did. With the exception of Poland, in the countries that participated, from 53 to 64 percent of respondents declared that they had quit school for reasons beyond their control, such as financial or family problems or illness (Grisay et al., 1995). Another argument for shortening the length of schooling for some students is that "in any case, these students wouldn't learn anything." This is verifiable: The argument supposes that a growth in the length of schooling of the weakest is not accompanied by a diminution of the deviation between the skills of the weak and the strong on their departure from the system, or of the proportion of individuals leaving the system below the minimum threshold of competence. However, such diminutions *were* observed in France, between 1985 and 1993, at the time of the rapid opening up of the educational system (Etat de l'Ecole, 1997), tending to refute that argument.

4.1.2. Spending for education

The amount of spending for education is dependent on the length, but also on the intensity of the instruction (class size, available materials). Inequalities in public spending of that benefit depend therefore on inequalities of access to different "stages" of the educational system, as well as on inequalities in the respective cost of each stage. If a low percentage of young people enroll in higher education, and public spending per student is far higher in higher education than in compulsory education, then the spending for education is likely to be inequitable (Mingat, 1998).

Geographical inequalities matter here. In numerous educational systems, financing is centralized. The geographic and financial inequalities of education are therefore very slight. When financing is decentralized, as in the United States (see Cochrane, Chapter 15), they can be very pronounced. We know that there is a debate on the consequences of these inequalities on unequal results. Several authors concur in their potential importance (for example, Payne et al., 1999; Card & Krueger, 1990).

4.2.   Quality of the education received

With respect to quality, one can distinguish two aspects as well. One—inequalities in conditions of learning—is all that in a given time enables the student to learn or develop, to a greater or lesser degree. The other bears on the scholastic experience, the quality of life in school (see Principle 2).

4.2.1. Inequalities in conditions of learning

Education is considered here as an individual investment. Indicators verify that the institution puts at the disposition of investors—students—resources whose quality corresponds to what is required by fairness.

Numerous studies on schools' and teachers' effectiveness have shown that these have depended not only on the quantity of resources, but also on the quality of schools and teachers. They also have shown that effectiveness tends to be lower in deprived areas, though very effective teachers and schools may be found there. Compensatory policies address this problem, but with less success than expected. Therefore, indicators are required here.

However, we have not tried to measure the extent of these policies with respect to process. Following Grisay (1999), we think that it is better to measure the inegalitarian character (Does it reinforce initial inequalities?) or the compensatory effect (Does it lessen the initial inequalities?) of an educational system than to measure the resources that it devotes to fighting inequalities. Indicators of this sort say nothing about the effectiveness of policies. (Besides, they could designate as very concerned about equity a country that spends a great deal of money for some localized compensatory programs, but whose customary operation is very inegalitarian.)

A debatable question is to what extent "school mix" or "peer effects" are responsible for such inequalities. At the school level, research on this question was often inconclusive (Thrupp, 1995). Recent studies, however, tend to establish a link between scholastic segregation and inequality of achievement. According to these studies, the "peer effect" would have a direct role (influence of students on one another) and an indirect one (through interactions among teachers and students) (see Vandenberghe, Chapter 11). At the classroom level, the evidence is either that weak students do not profit from homogeneous classes (Slavin, 1987, 1990) or are harmed by them (e.g., Duru-Bellat & Mingat, 1997).

The relationship between segregation and inequalities of achievement is not identical in all countries. Sweden and Denmark, for example, present a social segregation among schools equivalent to that in France, New Zealand and the United States. However, the last three countries present much stronger disparities in reading levels among schools than the first two (Raudenbush et al., 1996). In other words, the same degree of segregation will have different consequences according to other aspects of the process in operation in different countries. A consequence of these studies, however, is that the absence of segregation, be it scholastic (Are good students in the same classes and schools?) or social (Are poor students in the same classes and schools?), is likely to have a positive influence on equality of opportunity. Hence, we can distinguish two domains in conditions for learning:[10] inequalities in the school environment and segregation.

4.2.2. Inequalities in quality of life

We recall that Jencks (1972) concluded his great inquiry into inequalities with the idea that to equalize the well-being of children in different schools would do more, considering the time children spend in school, for the equality of conditions in America than any effort to equalize the effectiveness of those schools. Inequalities in well-being cannot all be considered unfair, but it is reasonable to think that the responsibility for proving that they are unavoidable or necessary to learning belongs to the educational system (Meuret & Marivain, 1997). These inequalities can be measured by questionnaires, some of which may have international validity (Williams & Batten, 1988).

One of the principal factors of well-being among students is the quality of the relationships that they have with their teachers,[11] in particular whether they are treated fairly. With respect to our field of indicators, this aspect is especially important. Indeed, apart from the immediate effects of well-being on self-esteem, being treated unfairly in school absolutely affects the confidence that students, soon to be adults, develop in their country's institutions, on the one hand, and in its professionals on the other.

Hence, we will deal with two domains: well-being and the feeling of being treated fairly.

5.   Internal results

Results are defined as the effects of an action by the educational system on the dimensions of its stated goals. We propose to take account of three dimensions: achievement (knowledge and skills acquired); personal and social development (cross-curricular competencies, values and attitudes acquired); and school careers (measured, for instance, by the highest diploma obtained).

With regard to achievement, a good deal of data are available on some subjects through IEA surveys and from the OECD project known as PISA. All these surveys allow for measures of individual inequalities, for the percentage of students under a given threshold (although some further and difficult discussion would be required for countries to agree on a normative threshold) and also for gender inequalities. Some of them permit measurement of the influence of social or educational background on achievement (see Vandenberghe, Dupriez & Zachary, Chapter 9, as well as Noël & de Broucker, Chapter 12, and the PISA project). Regarding cross-curricular competencies, some attempts are made to conceptualize them, but tools capable of measuring them are not yet available.

With regard to attitudes and values, we lack international surveys. However, some national surveys have been conducted on such topics as civic attitudes, sociability, self-esteem and locus of control (e.g., Grisay, 1993, 1997). International surveys could be conducted as well. Social and gender influence on school careers has already been documented by international surveys (Müller & Karle, 1993; Shavit & Blossfeld, 1993) and by a lot of national surveys.

It is when measuring internal results that it is most pertinent to confront equity and effectiveness, as Vandenberghe, Dupriez and Zachary do (Chapter 9).

6.   External results

The greater the negative social consequences of educational inequalities, the more unjust they are. Inversely, if a certain scholarly inequality has no consequence for the rest of life, this inequality is less important with respect to equity. These consequences are of three types, related to: social mobility, and individual and collective consequences of educational inequalities (see, for example, Principle 8).

Social mobility is linked to equity through the principle of equality of opportunity. It does not depend only on educational equity, bur also on educational effectiveness and appropriateness, as stated above. However, this does not mean that it is irrelevant for educational equity, but rather that effectiveness and appropriateness matter to the external equity of the educational system. For example, Checchi et al., 1999, show that in Italy, an education system that is less burdensome for the poor would favor social mobility, but the system does not because, whether due to the nature of Italian society or to skills transmitted by schools, the social milieu and not the school determines professional placement, so that the poor are not encouraged to extend their studies. This is a case in which a policy seeking more equity would have to deal with the contents of learning, which leads to interest in professional placement, more than on the process or resources. Some international surveys on social mobility are available (Erikson et al., 1979).

Individual consequences of inequality bear on the relationship between one's position in the educational hierarchy and one's rank by income or social position. They depend also on knowing if educational position is translated by the possession of goods or non-monetary advantages. Among these benefits are certain skills or knowledge (e.g., literacy) that one is assumed to acquire in school, but whose mastery is in fact not guaranteed even by a lengthy education.

The collective consequences are of two types. The first proceed from educational inequalities that benefit, to a greater or lesser degree, the least privileged or all students. One could call these collective consequences externalities among individuals. The second are those that the community attains as a whole. For example, if confidence in institutions is affected by educational injustice, all can experience the political consequences. One could call these consequences global externalities.

This outline is presented as a basis for further deliberation on an optimal system of indicators, which it is hoped will lead to an optimal program of international studies in this less examined area. It rests on an as yet imprecise knowledge of the factors and consequences of educational inequalities. However, the establishment and regular calculation of pertinent indicators would advance our understanding of the causes and consequences of scholastic inequalities, and lead to a more sophisticated discussion of equity. It would in any case allow us to surpass the actual arena of analysis, in which inequalities among countries are studied in too disparate a fashion for conclusions about equity to be drawn.

More detailed outline of indicators on the equity of educational systems

Inequalities among individuals	Inequalities among categories	Individuals below a threshold
1. Context		
1.1. Social and cultural context		
1.1.1. Inequalities in social resources		
1.1.1.1. Revenues		
Dispersion of revenues among households *(for instance, Gini coefficient; attention should be paid to attempts to measure these inequalities in lifelong earnings).*	Inequalities in revenues among social and ethnic categories Inequalities in wages for the same job, by gender and ethnicity	% of households with children that are below the poverty line Distance between the median income and the 10% poorest *(See discussion on the indicators on poverty; for instance, in Sen, 1996.)*

1.1.1.2. Security

Inequalities with regard to the expectation of "living in good health"	Inequalities between majority and minorities, among social groups with regard to unemployment rate, exposure to illness, etc.	Percentage of adults with accumulated risk factors (e.g., low income, unemployment, weak education)

1.1.2. Cultural resources

1.1.2.1. Education

Inequalities in scholastic careers, among adults Inequalities in reading competence, among adults *(OECD,1998)*	Inequalities between majority and minorities, among social groups and by gender, with regard to scholastic careers of adults	Proportion of adults below the minimum threshold of literacy *(OECD,1998)*

1.1.2.2. Expectations and Norms

Unequal expectations among parents, with respect to children's schooling	Unequal expectations among social categories, minorities and majority	Proportion of parents claiming to distrust schools Gap between the mean expectations of parents and the expectations of those with the lowest expectations

1.2. Political context

1.2.1. Equity criteria

Polls with such questions as:

Should the best students receive better instruction? Should the weakest students receive better instruction? Should all students have the same chance to receive a good education? (Answer for primary, secondary, higher education)	In your opinion, are the reduction of social, gender or ethnic inequalities, or the increase of social mobility important objectives of education?	Which is closest to your opinion: We owe the poorest children a better education. We owe better instruction only to those poor children who try harder. We owe all children the same quality of education.
Among these inequalities, which disturb you the most: Better students *are in school the longest, have better professors, have the richest parents or have the best educated parents?*		

1.2.2. Judgments about the equity of the current educational system

Polls with questions about:

Whether students consider grading, tracking, punishment, rewards, etc., unjust? (For a given country, if such a question is answered on a six-point scale, it is possible to calculate the mean and the dispersion of the answer, but also the gap between the answers of the best and the weakest students.)	In your opinion, does the current educational system: Do what it can reasonably do? Devote (much effort)(little effort) to assure social (gender, ethnicity) equality of opportunity in school? *(Meuret et Alluin, 1998)* Gap between judgments on	Is the current educational system sufficiently (excessively) (minimally) concerned about the weakest pupils? Do students consider grading, tracking, punishment and rewards unjust? (gap between the mean score and the score of the weakest students)

In the present educational system, which of the following statements applies: "Each one succeeds according to merit." "Each one succeeds according to talents." "Each one receives that to which he is entitled." "Each one may acquire the minimum skills he will need."	equity of the system among social, national and gender groups (students as well as parents)	

2. Process

2.1. Quantity of education received

2.1.1. Length of schooling

Inequalities in early schooling Inequalities accumulated in early and continued schooling	Inequalities in length of early schooling according to social origin or to parents' education *(Noël and de Broucker, in this volume; see Duru-Bellat and Mingat, 1993, for a method not requiring the establishment of a common definition of social categories among countries)*	Proportion of students who leave the educational system against their will or for reasons beyond their control *(IALS, see Grisay et al., 1995)*

2.1.2. Spending for education

Spending for higher education as a proportion of total expenditure *(PNUD, 1999)*	By social category and scholastic degree, proportion of a family's income that must be set aside for the education of its children To what extent does public spending for education make the distribution of wealth less unequal? Geographic inequalities in annual public spending for students *(See Cochrane, Chapter 15, USA)*	Proportion of public spending for education devoted to those pupils who have the shortest school careers? to the children of the poorest?

2.2. Quality of the education received

2.2.1. Inequalities in conditions of learning

2.2.1.1. Inequalities in the school environment

Do the best pupils have the best teachers? *(Mendro, 1998, Texas)* Part of the variance in competence among students that can be explained by the initial achievement of the student, by the quality of environment, and by their joint effect *(Grisay, 1997, 1999, France, who takes up the approach of Mayeske, 1972)*	Gap between school quality and teacher quality, according to social background and ethnicity of students Part of the variance in competence that can be explained respectively by social background, by the quality of the learning environment and by their joint effect	Difference between the mean quality of schooling and the quality observed in schools/ classrooms with the weakest pupils

2.2.1.2.Segregation		
Segregation among schools and classrooms, by academic level *(Duru-Bellat & Mingat, 1997, France)* *(See Kalter, 2000, for a discussion on segregation indicators)*	Segregation among schools and classrooms, by social background *(Gorard & Fitz, 2000, Great Britain)* (Same as above, by ethnicity)	Percentage of the weakest and poorest students who are segregated

2.2.2. Inequalities in the quality of life

2.2.2.1. Inequalities in well-being

Inequalities in well-being Are factors of well-being fair? *(Meuret & Marivain, 1997, France; Gil, 1996, Spain)* Proportion of students attending schools where the degree of violence exceeds an established threshold of tolerance	Inequalities in well-being among social, gender and ethnic categories *(Meuret & Marivain, 1997, France)*	Gaps in well-being and violence between the mean situation and those with the poorest and weakest students

2.2.2.2. Feeling of being treated fairly

Poll among students, with such questions as: To what degree do you find your teachers are fair with respect to grading, discipline, distribution of punishments and rewards, decisions requiring students to repeat a grade or to be directed to less prestigious tracks?	Same as the question in the column at left, the answer being aggregated according to social, gender and ethnic categories To what degree do you find that in your class, your teacher favors boys? Girls? Students in the ethnic majority? Minority students? Good students? Poor students? Students from wealthier families? Students from poorer families?	Same as the question in the column at left, the answer being aggregated according to social, gender and ethnic categories

3. Internal results

3.1. Knowledge and skills

Disparities among the weakest and the best students, for different subjects by age group *(IEA studies, Education at a Glance. Taube and Mejding, 1996)* Inequalities in skills tested at the completion of school *(État de l'école, 1997, France, tests taken by those entering military service)* Mean achievement and inequalities considered together *(Demeuse, Crahay & Monseur, Chapter 2)*	Influence of social, gender and ethnic categories on achievement *(Noël & de Broucker, in this volume)* Effectiveness and influence of the social background on achievement *(Vandenberghe, Dupriez & Zachary, Chapter 9)*	Proportion of students whose reading skills are below a standard deviation from the international average *(Education at a Glance, 1993)* Proportion of students leaving school without having mastered basic skills established as necessary to life in society

3.2. Personal and social development

Same as 3.1, for moral or social attitudes, for cross-curricular competencies	Same as 3.1, according to social, gender and ethnic categories	Moral and social attitudes of early dropouts when they leave school

3.3. Scholastic careers		
Inequalities in length of schooling between the longest and shortest school careers Inequalities in school careers among students who were at the same level after one or two years of schooling (a proxy for equality of talent and will) *(Duru-Bellat, Jarousse & Mingat, 1993, France)*	Influence of the parent's education level, income, social or ethnic origin on school career, e.g., on the highest diploma obtained *(Shavit & Blossfeld, 1993; Duru-Bellat & Kieffer, 2000, France; Noël & de Broucker, in this volume)* Ethnic inequalities of school careers, by SES *(Vallet & Caille, 1996, France)*	Proportion of students leaving school without a professional qualification of any kind *(État de l'école, France)*

4. External results

4.1. Social mobility		
	Transitions between income classes, or between occupations ranked according to social prestige, or between social classes *(Atkinson, 1980; Treiman & Ganzebom, 1990; Erikson & Goldthorpe, 1992)*	Social mobility for the poorest individuals *(Checchi et al., 1999, USA and Italy)*

4.2. Individual consequences of educational inequalities

4.2.1. Economic consequences

Unemployment or occupation, according to the highest diploma obtained

Rate of return of a marginal year of education

Inequalities in income among people with the same diploma	Rate of return of education, by social origin, ethnicity and gender *(Goux & Maurin, 1997, France, for social origin; EAG, 1997, for gender)*	Rate of return of education, for early dropouts

4.2.2. Social consequences

Effects of qualifications on position in the hierarchy and prestige of the professions *(Shavit & Müller, 1998)*

Relationship between level of education and risk of imprisonment, outlook on life, situation in the marriage market, reading skills as an adult *(IALS for the latter)*

4.3. Collective consequences

4.3.1. Are educational inequalities to everyone's advantage or to the advantage of the less favored?

Rate of fiscal return of education spending *(OECD-CERI, 1998; Ministère de l'éducation du Québec, 1999)*

Inequalities of income between the most and the less educated, before and after social transfers

Inequalities regarding the use of professional services (e.g., lawyers, doctors, teachers) by income, social classes and ethnicity

4.3.2. Institutional consequences

Confidence in the educational system, institutions, professionals; degree of violence toward institutions and their representatives

Feeling of belonging to society, to the community that delivered the education

To repeat, the nine principles for a system of indicators on educational equity are:

(1) The system of indicators must measure inequalities to help citizens and those who govern to judge the quality of the system, but it must also identify, for the sake of those who govern, the opinions of citizens on the equity of the educational system and the criteria that form the basis of those opinions.

(2) Indicators must measure not only inequalities in educational results (knowledge, school careers, social utility and academic degrees), but also the more immediate inequalities related to life in school and in the way students are treated by the institution and its agents.

(3) Indicators must permit debate within the existing framework of diverse principles of justice, and not inscribe them in only one of them.

(4) The educational inequalities pertinent to most of the benefits distributed within the framework of the educational system can be regrouped into three large families: inequalities among categories, deviations among individuals and the proportion of individuals falling below a minimum threshold.

(5) It is important to measure not only inequalities in educational results, but also inequalities at the source of the educational system that affect the teaching process itself.

(6) Among the benefits distributed by the educational process, priority must be given to those whose distribution is most important to individuals or for the democratic life of the country.

(7) Among those categories pertaining to individuals, the most important are those from which the individual cannot escape.

(8) Indicators must permit discussion between the concern for equality and other values to which it may seem opposed.

(9) Indicators must bear not only on educational inequalities, but also on the effects of those inequalities on social inequalities in general.

Notes

1 This chapter was originally submitted in French.
2 67 percent of French secondary-school teachers believe that "the educational system must do more to assure equal opportunity for students in school," 21 percent believe that the system does in this respect "what it can reasonably do," and only 3 percent think that it devotes "too much effort to it" (Meuret & Alluin, 1998).
3 The newspaper *Le Monde* recounted in this way the evolution of a man tried recently in France for the triple murder of his bosses and a colleague: "Obsessed with injustice, having experienced its effects on public assistance, then in foster homes, and in a multitude of jobs. Obsessed finally with being a just and irreproachable employee . . ." (p. 20, June 21, 1999).
4 For example, it has been established that if the wage gap between whites and blacks in the

United States has increased since 1975, while the gap in their academic competence has not increased, it is because an equivalent gap in academic competence has stronger economic consequences in the 1990s than in the 1970s (Neal & Johnson, 1996, cited by Lévy & Murnane, 1999).

5   Lawsuits have been waged and won in the United States in the name of equity against educational systems in certain states (Kentucky) or school districts (San Francisco), and have led to major transformations of those systems (Khanna et al., 1999; Pedrosko & Lindle, 1999).

6   We know, for example, that teachers have a tendency to grade homogeneous classes in a more dispersed way, simply because they are more sensitive to what distinguishes their students than to the ways in which they are alike (Grisay, 1984). This is not without effect on the progression of students whose differences are thus exaggerated.

7   See Benadusi, in this volume.

8   In that, one could say, paraphrasing Rawls, that the construction of such a system is a political task, neither metaphysical (indicators proceeding from an *a priori* conception of justice) nor technical; the only problem would be to achieve agreement on the most reliable measure and the most valid criteria to be chosen.

9   Evidence of this position, R. Boudon (1984): Egalitarian optimism in matters of education "have led in the end to a politics of education which seems to have neglected the first function of every educational system, its function of training, in favor of a function of . . ."

10 In a very extensive study of the effectiveness of French schools, Grisay, 1997, observes that, among low and middle-class schools, the deviation in quality of learning conditions inside the school is greater than the deviation in parental expectations or ambitions.

11 See, for example, Meuret & Marivain, 1997. One can imagine principles of justice under which certain inequalities among individuals in terms of well-being are equitable; for example, those that are related to academic effort. In this case, the equity of the distribution of well-being depends on the nature of the factors that influence well-being, and not on the inequalities in its distribution.

References

Baudoux C., Noircent A., "Culture mixte des classes et stratégies des filles," *Revue Française de pédagogie*, Paris, 1995.

Bloom B.S., "The two sigmas problem: The search for methods of group instruction as effective as one to one tutoring," *Educational Researcher, 13*, pp. 4–16, 1984.

Boudon R., *L' inégalité des chances*, Pluriel, Livre de Poche, 1984 (première parution, 1973).

Bourdieu P., Passeron J.C., *La reproduction*, Minuit, Paris, 1970.

Brighouse H., "The case for educational equality," in *School choice and social justice*, Oxford University Press, Oxford, 2000.

Card D., Krueger A., "Does school quality matter?," working paper 3358, NBER, Cambridge (Mass.), 1990.

Chauvel P., "La seconde explosion scolaire," *Revue de l' OFCE, 66*, pp. 5–36, 1998.

Checchi D., et al., "More equal but less mobile? Education financing and intergenerational mobility in Italy and in the US," *Journal of Public Economics, 74*, pp. 351–393, 1999.

Condition of Education, 1998, U.S. Government Printing Office, Washington, DC, 1998.

Crahay M., "L'école peut elle être juste et efficace?" de Boeck Université, Louvain, Belgium, 2000.

Dubet F., *Massification et justice scolaires: à propos d'un paradoxe, in Justice sociale et Inégalités*, Esprit-Seuil, Paris, 1992.

Dupuy J.P. , *Libéralisme et justice sociale*, Pluriel, Livre de Poche, Paris, 1997.

Duru-Bellat M., Kieffer A., "Inequalities in educational opportunities in France: educational expansion, democratization or shifting barriers?," *Journal of Education Policy*, *15*(3), pp. 333–352, 2000.

Duru-Bellat M., "La sociologie des inégalités sociales à l'école entre engagement et distanciation," in Meuret D. (ed.), *La justice du système éducatif*, de Boeck, Louvain, Belgium, 1999.

Duru-Bellat M., Mingat A., "La gestion de l'hétérogénéité des publics d'élèves au collège," *Cahiers de l'IREDU*, Dijon, France, p. 228, 1997.

Duru-Bellat M., Mingat A., *Pour une approche analytique du fonctionnement du système éducatif*, PUF, Paris, 1993.

Erikson R., Goldthorpe J.H., Portocarrero L., "Intergenerational class mobility in three western societies," *British Journal of Sociology*, *30*, pp. 412–441, 1979.

Etat de l'Ecole, Direction de l'Evaluation et de la Prospective, Ministère de l'Education Nationale, de la Recherche et de la Technologie, 1997.

Felouzis G., *Le collège au quotidien*, PUF, Paris, 1994.

Fraser B., et al., "Assessing and improving the psychosocial environment of mathematics classrooms," *Journal for Research in Mathematics Education*, *20*, pp. 191–201, 1989.

Gil G., "Analysis of the Williams and Batten questionnaire on the quality of school life in Spain," in *Reading literacy in an international perspective*, U.S. Department of Education, Office of Educational Research and Improvement, Washington, DC, 1996.

Gorard S., Fitz J., "Markets and stratification: a view from England and Wales," *Education Policy*, 2000.

Goux D., Maurin E., "Destinées sociales: le rôle de l'école et du milieu d'origine," *Economie et Statistiques*, *306*, pp. 13–26, 1997.

Grisay A., "Comment mesurer l'effet des systèmes scolaires sur les inégalités entre élèves?" in Meuret D. (ed.), *La justice du système éducatif*, De Boeck, Louvain, Belgium,1999.

Grisay A., "Évolution des acquis cognitifs et socio affectifs des élèves au cours des années de collège," Ministère de l'Education Nationale, *Dossiers Éducation et formations*, *88*, 1997.

Grisay A., Neice D., Jungklaus H., Leuven E., "Que savons nous de l'échec scolaire dans les pays industrialisés?" multigr., 1995.

Grisay A., "Le fonctionnement des collèges et ses effets sur les élèves de sixième et cinquième," Ministère de l'Education Nationale, *Dossiers Éducation et formations*, *32*, 1993.

Grisay A., "Les mirages de l'évaluation scolaire," in *Revue de la direction générale de l'organisation des études*, *XIX*, 8, 1984.

Guellec D., Ralle P., *Les nouvelles théories de la croissance*, La Découverte, Paris, 1997.

Gutman A., *Democratic education*, Princeton University Press, 1999.

Heyneman S.P., Loxley, W.A., "The effect of primary school quality on academic achievement across twenty nine high and low income countries," *American Journal of Sociology*, *88*, 1983.

Hirschman A.O., *The rhetoric of reaction: Perversity, Futility, Jeopardy*, Harvard University Press, 1991.

Hochschild J., *What's fair? American beliefs about distributive justice*, Harvard University Press, 1981.

Jencks C.H., et al., *Inequality*, Basic Books, 1972.

Jesson D., Gray, J., "Slants on slopes: Using multilevel models to investigate differential school effectiveness and its impact on pupil's examination results," in *School Effectiveness and School Improvement*, *2*(3), 1991.

Kalter F., "Measuring segregation and controlling for independent variables," working paper 19, *Arbeitspapiere–Mannheimer Zentrum für Europäisches Sozialforschung*, multigr., available on the Web, 2000.

Kellerhals J., et al., *Le sentiment de justice dans les relations sociales, Que sais je?* PUF, Paris, 1997.

Khanna R., et al., "The history and practice of reconstitution in San Francisco," paper presented at the annual meeting of the AERA, Montréal, 1999.

Kymlicka W., *Contemporary Political Philosophy: an introduction*, Oxford University Press, 1992.

Lévy F., Murnane R.J., "Are the key competencies critical to economic success?" multigr., OECD, Projet DeSeCo, 1999.

Lévy R., Joye D., Guye O., Kaufman V., *Tous égaux? De la stratification aux représentations*, Seismo, Zürich, 1997.

Marshall G., Swift A., Routh D., Burgoyne C., "What is and what ought to be, Popular beliefs about distributive justice in 13 countries," *European Sociological review*, *15*(4), pp. 349–367, 1999.

Mendro R.L., "Longitudinal teacher effects on student achievement," communication to AERA meeting, San Diego, 1998.

Meuret D., "Rawls, l'éducation et l'égalité des chances," in Meuret D. (ed.), *La justice du système éducatif*, de Boeck, Louvain, Belgium, 1999a.

Meuret D., Introduction, in Meuret D. (ed.), *La justice du système éducatif*, de Boeck, Louvain, Belgium, 1999b.

Meuret D., Alluin F., "La perception des inégalités entre élèves par les enseignants du second degré," *Education et Formations*, *53*, 1998.

Meuret D., Marivain T., "Inégalités de bien-être au Collège," MEN-DEP, *Dossiers Education et Formations*, *89*, 1997.

Meuret D., "L'efficacité de la politiques des Zones d'éducation prioritaire dans les collèges," *Revue Française de Pédagogie*, *109*, pp. 41–64, 1994.

Mingat A., Tan J.P., "The mechanics of progress in education, Evidence from Cross-country data," Documents de travail de l'IREDU, 98-01, 1998.

Mingat A., "Mesure et analyse de l'égalité et de l'équité en éducation," *Revue économique*, *1*, 1988.

Ministère français de l'éducation, *L'État de l'école*, 8, 1998.

Ministère de l'éducation du Québec, "La rentabilité du diplôme," in *Bulletin statistique de l'éducation*, février, 1999.

Ministère de l'éducation, USA, *Condition of Education*, 1998.

Müller W., Karle W., "Social selection in educational systems in Europe,"*European sociological review*, *9*, 1993.

OECD-CERI, *L'investissement dans le capital humain*, 1998.

OECD-CERI, *Analyse des politiques éducatives*, 1997.

OECD-CERI, *Regards sur l'Education/ Education at a Glance* (EAG), 1997.

OECD, Statistiques Canada, *Litéracie, économie et société, résultats de la première étude internationale sur l'alphabétisation des adultes*, 1995.

Payne K.J., Biddle B.J., "Poor school funding, child poverty, and mathematic achievement," *Educational researcher*, *28*(6), pp. 4–13, 1999.

Pedrosko J.M., Lindle J.C., "State mandated school reform in Kentucky: Year three of a longitudinal study," paper presented at the annual meeting of the AERA, Montréal, 1999.

Piketty T.H., *L' économie des inégalités*, La Découverte, 1997.

PNUD, *Rapport mondial sur le développement humain*, de Boeck, Brussels, 1999.

Raudenbush S.W., et al., "Social inequality, social segregation and their relationship to reading literacy in 22 countries," in *Reading literacy in an international perspective*, U.S. Department of Education, Office of Educational Research and Improvement, Washington, DC, 1996.

Rawls J., *A theory of justice*, Oxford University Press, paperback edition, 1973.

Scheerens J., *Effective schooling*, Cassell Press, 1992.

Sen A., *Inequality reexamined*, Oxford University Press, paperback edition,1996.

Shavit Y., Blossfeld H.P., *Persistent inequality, changing educational attainment in 13 countries*, Westview Press, Boulder (Colo.), 1993.

Shavit Y., Müller W., *From school to work*, Clarendon Press, Oxford, 1998.

Sirota R., *L' école primaire au quotidien*, PUF, Paris, 1988.

Skrla L., Scheurich J.J., Johnson J., Koschorek, J., "Accountability for equity: Can state policy leverage social justice?" paper presented at the annual meeting of AERA, New Orleans, 2000.

Slavin R.E., "Ability grouping and student achievement in elementary schools: a best evidence synthesis," *Review of educational research*, *57*(3), pp. 293–336, 1987.

Slavin R.E., "Achievement effects of ability grouping and student achievement in secondary schools: a best evidence synthesis," *Review of educational research*, *60*(3), pp. 471–499, 1990.

Taube K., Mejding J., "A nine-country study: What were the differences between the low and high performing students in the IEA RL study?" in *Reading literacy in an international perspective*, U.S. Department of Education, Office of Educational Research and Improvement, Washington, DC, 1996.

Thélot C., et al., "L'évolution des compétences scolaires des meilleurs élèves depuis quarante ans," *Les dossiers Education et formations*, MEN-DEP, *69*, 1996.

Thomas S., et al., "Stability and consistency in secondary schools effects on students' GCSE outcomes over three years," *School effectiveness and school improvement*, *8*(2), 1997.

Thrupp M., "The school mix effect: the history of an enduring problem in educational research policy and practice," *British Journal of Sociology of Education*, *16*(2), pp. 183–203, 1995.

Underwood K., de Broucker P. "An indicator of equity: the probability of attaining a post secondary credential by the level of parents' education," multigr., 1997.

Vallet L.A., Caille J.P. , "Les élèves étrangers dans l'école et le collège français," *Dossiers education et Formations*, *67*, MEN-DEP, Paris, 1996.

Vinovskis M.A., "Do federal compensatory education programs really work? A brief historical analysis of Title1 and Head Start," *American Journal of education*, *107*, May 1999.

Walzer M., *Spheres of Justice, A defense of Pluralism and Equality*, Basic Books, New York, 1983.

Wells A.S., Lopez A., Scott J., Holme J.J., "Charter schools as postmodern paradox: Rethinking social stratification in an age of deregulated school choice," *Harvard Educational Review*, *69*(2), pp. 172–204, 1999.

Whitehead M., *Concepts et principes de l'égalité des chances en matière de santé*, OMS, Copenhagen, 1991.

Williams T., Batten M., "The quality of school life," Australian council for educational research monograph, 12, Hawthorn (Victoria), 1988.

Willms D.J., "Proposition pour la composante mesurant le statut économique et social du questionnaire élève," OECD-PISA, multigr., p. 22, 1998.

Wong K.K., Lee J., "Interstate variation in the achievement gap among racial and social groups: Considering the effects of school resources and classroom practices," paper presented at the AERA meeting, San Diego, 1998.

Woods P. , "Responding to the consumer: parental choice and school effectiveness," *School effectiveness and school improvement*, *4*(3), pp. 205–229, 1993.

Chapter 6

Why Data Collection Matters
The role of race and poverty indicators in American education

Gary Orfield
Harvard University, United States

The United States is a society with vast inequalities of income and wealth[1] (Goldin & Katz, 1999) and a history of deep stratification by race. It is a society with a strong social research capability but deeply rooted ideological views about opportunity and the role that education plays. A central belief in American culture is that everyone has a reasonably fair chance for mobility and that the schools play the central role in assuring that opportunity is actually available. But there has been no significant discussion in American politics since the 1960s about government acting to equalize income or end poverty, and welfare payments for jobless families have been cut and subjected to strict time limits. This highly individualistic perspective and the extraordinary significance of public schools make debates about school policy and how it is linked to opportunity extremely important (Kluegel & Smith, 1986, pp. 1–2).

This paper argues that the addition of data and indicators about poverty and race to education statistics has substantially enriched ongoing debates about educational inequalities and possible solutions. The statistics document dramatic relationships among poverty, race and educational outcomes, forcing attention to issues that would not likely be considered without such information. In a stratified and segregated society with a history of deeply rooted racial stereotypes and recurrent efforts to exploit racial fears in politics, valid data on the complex and changing interplay among race, poverty, isolation, education and equality of opportunity can be very important. In sorting out causes and effects, it is essential to be able to look at the ways in which ethnicity and poverty interact because conditions that relate to class are often treated as impacts of race, and the problems of class differences within races and ethnicities are often ignored. There are very different policy implications if an apparent ethnic difference is actually rooted in social class than if ethnicity is a powerful relationship after controlling for class, and still other issues to consider if class mobility provides an exit from the ethnic stratification that affects poor ethnic minorities.

    The United States did not collect such data through most of its history. Poverty was not defined as a basic category in the U.S. data systems until the mid-1960s; until that time, very limited educational data were collected on blacks and American Indians, and almost no systematic data were collected on the Latino and Asian-American populations. Officials commonly denied that racial and ethnic data were needed, argued that they could be used for discriminatory purposes and claimed that publishing them would further stigmatize the populations because such data would disclose sharply unequal outcomes. The basic idea was that we would be better off not knowing. However, once the civil rights movement stirred the national conscience, and the government enacted and began to seriously enforce anti-discrimination policies, good data were consistently demanded by both governmental authorities and minority rights organizations.

    Other societies coping with signs of stigmatization and unequal treatment of growing ethnic and immigrant minorities may find the U.S. experience instructive, even though the history and scale of their challenges may be quite different. This paper argues that indicators are not merely statistical tools. They also reflect a society's readiness to look seriously at difficult problems, to acknowledge trends, to consider the consequences and, perhaps, to act. Though statistics cannot force policy changes, good data can enable a different level of discussion, permit more effective enforcement of rights, and give awareness and tools to groups whose claims were dismissed before data were available. The absence of, or refusal to collect, data on a basic social cleavage also conveys a very important message: The group that is not counted does not have the power to see to it that its problems are measured. Those in power may fear the consequences of data and probably are not prepared to take action to alleviate group problems because data and tools for the assessment of progress are essential parts of serious reform strategies. Without them, it is difficult to make claims on behalf of the status quo that will be taken seriously.

    In a very large, diverse and fragmented society where the federal government has only a minor administrative role in education, providing only 6 percent of public school funds, national statistics are the only way most Americans can know about educational trends in the country. Education in a society with nearly 47 million public school students, attending 87,000 schools in 14,900 school districts in 50 state education systems (NCES, *Digest 1997*, tables 90 and 91), and another 6 million in private schools, can only be grasped with huge data sets. Indeed, the statistical role of the federal government was its only major role in education in the first century and a half under the Constitution, which contains no mention of education. There were no major federal programs until the mid-1960s and no national ministry or department of education until 1980. Almost all federal resources go out in the form of grants to state and local school authorities, subject to requirements specified by federal laws. The other major responsibilities of the federal government are to enforce federally guaranteed rights that have taken shape in the past half century and address new agendas. Thus, the roles of data and research are important and influential.

1. The role of statistics and indicators

From its origin, the United States has been plagued by issues of race and ethnicity. One of the difficult issues that was compromised in the formation of its Constitution was how slaves and Indians would be counted in the allocation of seats in Congress. The Constitution adopted in 1789 provides for counting a slave as three-fifths of a person and excludes "Indians not counted." These policies were reversed—of course, by Emancipation—by the granting of full voting rights to former slaves in the post-Civil War 15th Amendment, and by the granting of citizenship to all Indians in the 1920s. But the early disputes foretold many disputes to come, up to and including the 2000 Census, both in terms of how the categories are defined and reported, and how the counting should be conducted.

Drawing on the U.S. experience, this paper argues that decisions about data collection, and, more particularly, about creating and reporting new measures of equity are a vital part of both the struggle for rights and recognition of various groups, and of democratic discussion in a complex society. What we know about the situation of various groups has important consequences both for the nature of the policy process and for the ultimate success of the society.

Virtually all theories of democratic governance accord a very high value to, and strong protections for, the discussion and debate that help to dismiss error, discover truth and legitimize the imposition on the minority of majority decisions. In a simple society where citizens have reasonably common experiences and where problems can easily be known and understood, just protecting freedom of press, speech and assembly can do much to reach this goal. In a complex and large society where personal experience and understanding of many problems are necessarily limited, it is very important to have the best possible information collected and made available to inform public discussion.

There is a special responsibility to provide good information about the most disorganized and marginalized sectors of the society because they do not have the tools to bring their perspective effectively into the policy discussion, and are by far the most dependent upon public policy decisions. In the nature of things, much of this information must be statistical, and to be seen and understood it must be accessible. Creation of appropriate new indicators of basic dimensions of the society can be a major contribution to the enrichment of public discussion.

The more stratified a society is, the less likely there is to be widespread personal contact and understanding of problems, and the more important it is to have reliable data that show relationships and trends. In affluent societies, politics pushes concerns of the middle class, not the minority of poor or different ethnicities. At a time when international markets, growing migrations and social policy trends appear to be moving toward increased stratification, and economic opportunity is more directly linked to educational qualifications, such indicators are particularly important in education statistics.

While good information cannot by itself produce effective policy, it is very difficult to have a full discussion, to say nothing of good policy, without reasonably reliable information. Often the lack of information on issues of obvious significance is a sign that a society or its government does not want to confront the issue. In the United States, for example, most of our large cities published virtually no data by race for generations, although anyone who walked through the cities, and saw the stark separation and the striking inequalities, sensed the huge social distance between minority and white communities. Officials could assert that there were no problems of unequal treatment or attainment—and there would be no data to prove them wrong. Critics could be dismissed as self-interested or relying on unrepresentative anecdotes. Denial of problems and refusal to collect or publish data on sensitive issues are typical responses of those wishing to preserve the status quo. Because there are usually many structures and beliefs built around—and tending to perpetuate—patterns of inequality (Tilly, 1998), it is very difficult to change what cannot even be described.

Without systematic data, the failures of particular schools or districts tend to be attributed to individuals and local institutions, not to the social and economic cleavages outside the school. If the diagnosis is wrong, the cure is likely to be misdirected or even perverse, blaming the educators working to serve the most excluded groups, not the external discrimination and inequalities that produce many of the problems within the schools.

Another vitally important reason for objective indicators of serious cleavages in society arises from the increasingly strong relationship between level of education and the competitiveness of a workforce. In an era of global competition, with traditional protections for low-skill, high-wage sectors of the economy being transferred to low-cost economies, advanced societies competing for the most rapidly growing and highly rewarded investment and jobs must be concerned about the skills of the entire workforce.

Without reliable data, many of the key relationships necessary to understand the roots of problems and underlying trends by social sector will not be available. If data are not available, there is likely to be either a costly neglect of the problems affecting disadvantaged sectors, or futile and counterproductive measures, undermining the competitive status of the nation.

The decision to collect statistics reflects a judgment now or in the past that the information collected is important for fostering some goal, mission or responsibility of the agency collecting the data. The United States at the end of the 20th century had a great deal of data on race, ethnicity and poverty—an abundance of information that had not been matched by major policy initiatives for a third of a century, but which had grown out of earlier periods of social and political change whose effects are strong decades later. Although the United States has what is probably the most conservative Western government in many aspects of social policy, such as welfare, incarceration and health care, a great deal of data is continuously collected and reported, sometimes becoming the basis for the creation of major policy initiatives. The data on racial and ethnic stratification and inequalities are particularly extensive, and have turned out to be strongly related to a great many basic educational issues.

2.   U.S. indicators and the politics of equity

This paper analyzes the origin and limits of U.S. data on poverty and race. It discusses some of the social facts and trends that could not have been known without these data. In a comparative context, the racial and ethnic measures may be of most interest because the United States has experienced much more diversity and immigration much longer than the other major industrial nations, and now has more extensive measures built into many of the surveys, studies and reports that the government produces or finances. Many policies, such as school desegregation and affirmative action, have a substantial statistical dimension. They involve plans to change outcomes and produce more interracial schools and workplaces, and their success is evaluated by the actual changes that occur. As other nations become more diverse or old ethnic cleavages become more apparent, they may want to consider similar measures. In the forthcoming Program for International Student Assessment (PISA) survey of the Organisation for Economic Co-operation and Development (OECD), surveying 15-year-olds in many countries, for example, most nations will not collect racial and ethnic data, meaning that they will not be able to look at the possible relationships of many outcomes with social divisions within their country. In the light of recent crises and even armed struggles within Europe over ethnic differences, it would be good to know how these divisions were reflected in the educational system and what could be done to increase equity.

Because of the history of the modern civil rights movement in the United States and the development of legal principles relating to the reporting of data, this may be an area in which the United States is ahead of other nations, in contrast to its very limited policy interventions in the provision of social services and social insurance.

3.   Decisions about data reflect values and goals

The decision to collect and publish data signifies that something is important enough to justify the effort. Often when a group demanding a response to its problem does not have the power to directly win a change in policy, it does have enough influence to initiate the collection of data. If the data justify the group's argument for future policy initiatives, they become part of the process of explaining the situation to the public and policy-makers, and winning assent. Data can also become tools to be used in debates, campaigns, lawsuits and other ways of claiming power, claiming rights and mobilizing movements. If a group seeking equity has neither data nor power, its policy claims can be rejected by opponents as invalid on the grounds that there are no data to prove them, yet this group may continue to refuse to collect data that would illuminate the issues.

Similarly, if a group winning a policy decision believes that there will either be demonstrated benefits or that a situation requires continuous monitoring, a requirement for collecting certain types of data may be written into the policy. In large bureaucratic societies, it is essential to collect at least enough information to show that funds reach their intended targets and to find out how many recipients receive which services. This information is very important for analyzing the equity and efficacy of services needed by various groups. Oftentimes, statistics become basic materials relied on by various parties arguing over the continuation or alteration of a program.

U.S. statistics on poverty and race reflect the social and political movements of the 1960s, and important features of American law, and have become central because of political and constitutional decisions, and the enactment of new laws and regulations that required such data. The data continued to be collected after national politics shifted to the right because the laws and policies were not repealed, in spite of vast ideological shifts, and because opponents never simultaneously controlled the executive, legislative and judicial branches of government. In the absence of a coherent and lasting majority moving in an opposite direction, bureaucratic continuity is the norm, and there is a strong bias to continue to collect and publish tables showing the trends even when poor and minority constituencies have little power.

Another probable reason for the continuity of data is the fact that they have not been used much during periods when opposing political forces were in power—and sometimes have been used to support the very opposite arguments from those they were intended to foster. Also, publication of some kinds of data was stopped, even though the data were still collected. Data collection issues are typically of a lesser order of magnitude than questions about enforcing policies. When controversial policies for alleviating poverty or racism are not being actively implemented and receive little political attention, interest in the data drops rapidly.

Nonetheless, the existence of these data, and a law giving citizens a right to see them—the Freedom of Information Act—have made it possible for the historically disadvantaged to monitor trends. Even in times when neither of the two dominant political parties is interested in an issue, the existence of data may force them to confront it. Data also help maintain the consciousness and motivation of poor and minority advocates.

One of the reasons for the preservation of both the laws and the data systems is that civil rights protections were extended after the civil rights movement to two groups that turned out to have much greater political power than the original beneficiaries—women and the handicapped. These are groups whose needs extend across all social classes. Many women and parents of handicapped children have political and economic resources that poor and minority groups rarely possess, and concerned supporters within all political and economic groupings. With the enactment of prohibition against sex discrimination in employment and all educational programs, and the passage of two sweeping laws protecting the rights of handicapped children, these groups became part of the coalition for protecting those rights and the data needed to enforce them. During the height of the anti-government movement of the 1980s, these groups helped to shield the basic structure of civil rights law and civil rights data collection in battles within Congress and the executive branch. For example, after a more conservative Supreme Court narrowed the law prohibiting discrimination in federally funded programs during the 1980s, Congress responded by enacting a broader law underlining the responsibility of agencies.

4. Poverty data and the war on poverty

Although the most distinctive quality of U.S. data systems is the extensive collection of racial and ethnic information, the idea of defining poverty and using it as a concept in the reporting of many kinds of data is another feature dating from the 1960s. Data on the economic status of families are of course fundamental in almost any data collection system. The United States was very late in collecting any kind of income data, waiting until after the social catastrophe of the Great Depression to include it in the 1940 Census in the administration of President Franklin Roosevelt. The census had long collected data on homeownership, occupation, educational level and other components of social and economic status. What is more unusual is the wide array of information collected about poverty as a category. Income tables and graphs showing all levels of income are full of meaning for social scientists and policy analysts, but convey much less to the public at large, few of whom can understand the meaning of a standard deviation or even decipher a modest chart. The constant change in the cost of living and the value of the currency makes it truly difficult to follow trends over time, and to discern how they are related to education and educational opportunities.

American culture is also extremely individualistic, and suspicious of government intervention, tending to deny class differences. The vast majority of Americans define themselves as middle class, and these include millions who would be considered working class in other societies or who, at the other extreme, rank in the top fraction of wage earners. The modern concept of poverty came from the only other activist administration of the 20th century, which sharply expanded the role of the state in social welfare in the United States, that of President Lyndon Johnson (1963–1968). Johnson decided to launch the "War on Poverty" in 1964, with the goal of abolishing significant poverty in a booming U.S. economy (Johnson, 1971, ch. 4; Levitan & Taggart, 1976; De Plotnick & Skidmore, 1975) on the grounds that the nation was rich enough to wipe out severe economic disadvantage. To do this, the administration needed a definition of poverty and a better understanding of its dynamics.

The politics and policy of this period were based on an understanding that poverty and inequality were linked with many other forces, including discrimination, and that understanding and changing the society required reporting on these variables in many aspects of American life. In 1961, before the "War on Poverty," there were no tables on poverty in the nation's basic compendium of statistics, *The Statistical Abstract of the United States*. By 1973, the book contained 16 tables related directly to issues of poverty and low income (U.S. Bureau of the Census, 1961, 1973). Poverty concepts were also incorporated in many other national data systems.

The American definition of poverty established during the development of Johnson's "War on Poverty" program was designed by an economist in the Department of Agriculture, Mollie Orshansky, who examined the spending patterns of American families and computed the poverty line as three times the cost of food for a typical family, reflecting the ratio of food to other costs in the family budgets of that period (Orshansky, 1965, pp. 3–29).The standard had some real advantages. There had never been a national measure of minimum economic need because each state had set its own standard for public aid to the poor, and most states had substantially lower standards than the new federal one.

The federal poverty level changed with family size and automatically increased as the cost of food rose. There were of course problems with this standard. As American incomes rose, the relative share of family income spent on food declined sharply and the definition of the basic necessities of life expanded, but these changes were not incorporated into the poverty standard. Non-cash services were not counted as income. Poverty is an inherently relative term and this tended to give it a fixed meaning, rooted in a less affluent society.

The advantages, however, were also important ones. The term made sense and the numbers tended to be accepted with relatively little criticism as delineations of who and how many were poor. Because the definition did not count non-cash subsidies for housing, medical care and other programs, it also had aspects that underestimated the well-being of the poor, thus keeping attention on groups that might have been excluded from policy concern if it had been defined more broadly. It kept attention on cash income, which is certainly of central importance in terms of a family having any real choices.

Once the poverty concept was built into federal programs and statistics, it became a very common way of reporting data on many aspects of society and was often used in reporting data on receipt and outcomes of various programs. As the federal system of social provision expanded, concepts of poverty were built into programs ranging from food stamps (coupons that subsidize food costs) to college aid to health care to the largest federal school aid program, which was designed to channel federal dollars into schools with concentrations of low-income students.

One of the most important results of an official definition of poverty was the incorporation of this statistic into standard census reports, drawn from both the national census taken every decade and from many interim (Current Population Survey) reports that released data continuously over the years. These reports provided the country with regular data about the proportion living in poverty, poverty by race, children in poverty, etc., and it is possible to relate poverty to many other forms of inequality. As America becomes increasingly segmented by class and community, these data are among the few regular reminders that the economic boom of the 1980s left poverty almost untouched, particularly for children, as did the most of the expansion of the 1990s. During the 1980s, a period of very active attacks on social programs, such empirical evidence was particularly important. During the 1990s, the data helped focus attention on the need for an increase in the minimum wage and the provision of income subsidies for millions of low-wage workers through the tax system.[2] Had readily understandable data elements of this sort not been built into the statistical system, claims about this issue might well have been dismissed as mere political partisanship.

There were, of course, many attempts to come up with a new definition of poverty, not only by reconsidering the costs of living in the United States, but by adding to cash income some or all of the in-kind services received by households. A number of alternative measures were added to the statistical system, but agencies continued to use the original definition through very sweeping ideological changes in government.

The availability of poverty statistics, together with a sizeable investment in related research in the 1960s and early 1970s, also helped launch many kinds of social policy and social science analysis. In recent years, for example, many social scientists have been exploring the nature and spread of poverty concentrated in the centers of our metropolitan areas and, more recently, in suburban rings that are now also experiencing economic decline and racial transition (Wilson, 1996; Massey & Denton, 1993; Danziger, Sandefur & Weinberg, 1992). Theories about how this spatial pattern may affect socialization, educational and economic opportunity, and the future structure of society are central issues in contemporary social science that are now beginning to be addressed by some policy initiatives.

Schools play an important role in many of those theories of the way in which conditions of poverty shape unequal education, which then become one of the forces that perpetuate inequality between generations. Studies consider, for example, the impacts of peer groups and the loss of jobs in poor neighborhoods on the social supports for academic achievement, and on the economic rewards that may be contingent on location and quality of schooling. Employers seeking well-prepared labor forces often locate jobs in places inaccessible to poor city youth and rarely send recruiters into poor, inner-city schools. (Weis, 1990; MacLeod, 1995; Anyon, 1997; Wilson, 1987). This work is not all statistical in approach and does not derive exclusively from statistical data, but would have been much less likely to have occurred or to have been taken seriously if poverty statistics had not been consistently available.

Poverty statistics are collected primarily by the Census Bureau and its Current Population Survey. These do not provide the information needed to look at issues of school equity for low-income children. Data of this sort have two primary sources, both linked to federal data requirements. One is the system of federal aid to schools that was initially based on the number of children in extreme poverty in a school's enrollment. Data of this sort have been required for the Title I compensatory education program, enacted in 1965, which provides about $8 billion a year for compensatory education. A second national source is the federal program subsidizing school lunches for low-income children. This program sets a standard of need children must meet in order to qualify for subsidized meals. Although this standard is not the same as the national poverty level standard, it does provide a good measure of relative need. School districts must keep track of the number of eligible children and maintain records to receive reimbursement for their meals. Until recently, these data were available only at the school district level in many communities, leaving us uninformed about the relative poverty levels of individual schools and the relationships between concentrations of poor children in a school and academic outcomes. Now, however, the great majority of states submit free-lunch statistics at the school level to the Common Core of Data (CCD) of the National Center for Education Statistics (NCES). The national longitudinal surveys have also created income categories that are very commonly reported with basic data. Many state governments, having attempted to coerce educational improvement by publicizing achievement data at the school level, are now also reporting school poverty data, which are very strongly related to achievement levels. Because achievement tends to be highly related to the percentage of poor children in a school, these data tend to focus attention on the social structural issues affecting schooling. Within such data, schools serving poor children are often simply described as failing schools, shifting the blame to school staffs for inequalities schools rarely overcome.

5.   Poverty and minority status

Statistics on poverty and education in the United States are deeply intertwined with questions of race and ethnicity; the same reform period that gave rise to poverty indicators and research also generated a vast expansion of data on race. If one locates schools of concentrated poverty on a map of a major U.S. city and overlays it with a map showing the racial composition of neighborhoods, there are powerful relationships. Although there are a great many poor whites in the United States, they are much less likely to be persistently poor and very much less likely to live in a community of concentrated poverty. They are less likely than African-Americans to attend schools with very low levels of average achievement, less qualified teachers, more involuntary residential movement, more non-English-speaking children and many other forms of inequality. Scholars have shown that only a small portion of residential separation observed in the United States can be explained in terms of distribution of income; the results cannot be understood without considering the independent impact of racial discrimination and a variety of practices and beliefs that work to perpetuate the impacts of past discrimination (Massey & Denton, 1993; Bullard, Grigsby & Lee, 1994).

A recent analysis of all schools in the United States shows that almost nine-tenths of schools that are 90–100 percent black and/or Latino have concentrated poverty, compared with only one out of 14 schools where less than 10 percent of the students are black and Latino. The strong relationship between these two variables can easily lead to misunderstanding about the causes of poverty and possible remedies.

Because race is an independent factor, yet very substantially related to poverty, both must be measured and great care must be taken not to attribute to race problems that arise out of poverty or to poverty the kinds of limits on educational opportunity that affect much of the minority middle-class. For example, black and Latino middle-class families are now increasing rapidly in suburban rings with large white majorities, yet they are experiencing severe segregation (Orfield & Yun, 1999). Some important, if controversial, research has also suggested that black middle-class students often come under social pressure against academic achievement on the grounds that to be a serious student is to "act white." Because there are still caste-like barriers in social interaction, such students may feel that they are risking exclusion from both the white and minority communities. Studies of minority access to college have shown that poverty works very poorly as a substitute for race if the goal is to achieve a racially diverse class. Poverty statistics can be related in many ways to the rich body of data on race and ethnicity available since the 1960s. Until the 1960s, however, data on race in America were very limited for blacks and American Indians and almost non-existent for other minority groups, including Asians and Latinos. This made it extremely difficult to sort out the forms of unequal resources, discrimination, social pressures and other forms of inequality that were basic substructures of educational inequality (Ogbu, 1988, pp. 163–182).

Before exploring in depth the story of the struggle to obtain data on black-white differences, it may be useful to briefly point out a related story to illustrate the importance of this issue in societies where inequalities are concentrated among ethnic immigrants, not a racial minority. Europeans, for example, often deny the relevance of the U.S.'s racial problems to their societies, though they are being reshaped by immigration. It is important to note that in the very near future the largest minority group in the U.S. population will be Latinos, largely of relatively recent immigrant background. A by-product of the civil rights struggle was the collection of national data on Latinos, beginning in many data systems in the late 1960s and early 1970s. Without these data, the country would have little understanding of a vast social transformation that is projected to lead to a Latino population of almost 100 million by mid-century. The nation had a statistical system in place as a vast migration took shape in the past three decades. The data systems have shown very serious problems of educational and occupational stratification that threaten these communities. Some of these patterns are similar to or even more serious than those affecting blacks.

The fact that some of these problems are as severe as those affecting a caste-like minority should raise very serious warnings for other nations. The data and the many resulting reports, government initiatives, media reports and organizations have also created visibility and a sense of common purpose among populations originally from very diverse nations. They have helped leaders frame issues. This aspect of the U.S. experience deserves close attention in many nations experiencing major immigrations.

6.   How the United States obtained racial data: The impact of a social movement

After the Supreme Court declared racially segregated schools in the South unconstitutional in 1954, attention to data on race increased enormously; however, for more than a decade, all the data on desegregation in the South were collected not by the government, but by a private, foundation-funded association of journalists in the South—the Race Relations Reporting Service. The first major struggle over the issue in Congress after 1954 resulted in the 1957 Civil Rights Act, the first significant legislation on civil rights in 80 years. The law was limited in many ways, but it did set up the U.S. Commission on Civil Rights, which was charged with investigating and producing bipartisan reports on civil rights conditions—reports that would have a major impact on framing many issues in the civil rights struggles of the next decade.

The breakthrough in federal statistics came with the passage of the 1964 Civil Rights Act, which changed the federal government from a passive bystander on racial policy by creating a requirement that no programs or activities receiving money from the national government could discriminate, and prohibiting discrimination in business and employment. There was no way that the administrative agencies could assure nondiscrimination without racial statistics on program recipients. Beginning in the mid-1960s, statistics on blacks and whites were collected systematically across a wide array of federal programs, studies and ongoing data collection systems. By the late 1960s, there was also increased recognition of the need for data on Latinos and other racial groups in a number of federal data systems, beginning with the schools and spreading through many Census Bureau and Bureau of Labor Statistics reports.

The 1964 Civil Rights Act was the most bitterly fought and most consequential legislative victory ever achieved to strengthen civil rights law in the United States. Opponents literally shut down the entire legislative process in Congress for months in an attempt to block the law, but they were defeated by a majority coalition committed to eliminating the laws and practices that had mandated racial segregation (Whalen & Whalen, 1985; Loevy, 1997; Mann, 1996). After it became apparent that the states with such laws would not comply with the Supreme Court's 1954 desegregation decision, civil rights advocates decided that the best way to force change was to cut off federal aid to education for school systems not complying (Watson, 1990, pp. 298–300), and also authorize the Justice Department to sue them.

The sweeping 1964 law, adopted after President Kennedy's assassination, made the federal government an active enforcer of civil rights laws. At the same time, both the courts and administrative agencies were shifting their focus from individual cases of discrimination, which proved to have very little impact, to an insistence on race-conscious policies and plans designed to actually change the status quo and to be measured statistically by results.

Any serious effort to enforce this law required the creation of a data system measuring segregation. There was no other way for a small staff in Washington to know whether school districts were complying. Until this time, most states had no school-by-school racial statistics, so it was impossible to know either the overall patterns and trends or the specific facts of any community or school before the federal government mandated collection of these data from all schools in the country. There was no consistent collection on enrollment of Latino and Asian students. For this law to be administered effectively and applied uniformly and properly in thousands of school districts that had resisted change for a decade after the Supreme Court decision, there had to be statistical definitions and measures.

The law also authorized research and monitoring, including a national study and report to Congress, which became the internationally influential Coleman report, and a broadening of the U.S. Civil Rights Commission's functions. President Johnson then directed the commission to conduct a further big study on urban school segregation issues (U.S. Commission on Civil Rights, 1967). The Coleman report, which included a huge national survey, challenged many basic assumptions about schooling and directed attention away from the traditional issues of equalizing financial resources toward family and peer group influences on achievement. It had very broad impacts on the ways school effects were understood in the United States and elsewhere, and certainly demonstrated the need for data to sort out issues of causation and cure.

The law also provided technical assistance and teacher training to ease the transition to desegregated schools in Title IV of the Civil Rights Act. This was the forerunner of a much bigger desegregation aid program in the 1970s, which included large investments in research and data collection.

Though the desegregation components of the civil rights law were vigorously enforced for only a few years until the conservatives came to power in the White House in 1969, the law led to the establishment of rules and procedures for collection of data on issues of race and national origin that had never been available in much of the United States. During the late 1960s and early 1970s, much of this data was published, empowering minority communities and their representatives to know what was happening and to make demands for change. Many school districts came under civil rights court orders that also directed the collection of additional racial data on key issues. The data collection continued long after the political support for enforcing the law had eroded, contributing good, complete national and local data on some issues.

Many types of data that we now use routinely to measure the racial situation did not even exist before the 1964 Civil Rights Act. There were very little national, state or local data on race and education. Few school districts reported anything, other than total district enrollments by race, to state or federal governments. Southern segregation data were collected in a limited way by the Race Relations Reporting Service, a private association of Southern journalists (Sarratt, Reed, 1966). But by 1967, the government had found it impossible to enforce the nondiscrimination requirements of the 1964 law without such data and imposed requirements on school districts with significant minority enrollments across the country. This was six years before the Supreme Court extended desegregation requirements outside the states where segregation had been mandated by law. Without this information, U.S. policy-makers would not know what has happened in racial terms in our schools and colleges, and civil rights plaintiffs might have faced far greater challenges in court. Though the data were cut back and the whole system severely threatened in the 1980s, and squeezed by budget cuts in the mid-1990s, this framework of racial information has survived and remains critical for policy and analysis.

Data provided under Title VI of the Civil Rights Act, forbidding discrimination in all agencies and institutions receiving federal funds, became important for issues that emerged after the peak civil rights era, such as the vast growth in the nation's Latino enrollment, discriminatory grouping practices (including tracking), bilingual education,[3] unequal provision of courses and qualified teachers and many other questions (Meier, Stewart & England, 1989; Meier & Stewart, 1991). Discriminatory testing has become a subject for enforcement action (Blair, 2000, p. 25). Changes in higher education policies that restrict college access for minority students might be challenged. Other issues surely will come under scrutiny as problems in American society and its schools continue to evolve.

Certainly, enactment of the 1964 law reached very deeply into the operations of many thousands of schools in the United States, created new educational rights and opportunities for millions of students and profoundly changed the nature of American education. The statistical indicators provided under the act were both a reflection of a major change in U.S. society and a very important source for understanding rapidly evolving changes.

7.   School desegregation

A fundamental educational goal of the 1964 Civil Rights Act was the enforcement of constitutional requirements for desegregation. This was debated in Congress and dominated the enforcement process until the Nixon administration. This was also the goal that attracted the most intense attacks. Most of the research on enforcement of the 1964 law deals with this issue.

When the Civil Rights bill went to Congress in 1963, the schools of the South were extremely segregated, very close to what amounted to total racial apartheid, and the issue of school segregation outside the South had barely been explored. The courts were only requiring very small and slow changes in the South and none at all in the North and West. In the 11 states of the Old Confederacy, which had fought the Civil War against the North, less than 1 percent of black students were in desegregated schools. In the heart of the Southern resistance, the three states of Alabama, South Carolina and Mississippi had a total of 30 black students in white schools a decade after the Supreme

Court outlawed Southern segregation (U.S. Commission on Civil Rights, 1964, p. 291). Across the South, no white children were attending traditionally black schools and no black teachers were teaching white children. The concept of desegregation used in the privately collected data of that time relied on very small-scale voluntary transfers of black students between separate black and white systems of schools. Districts with any such transfers were commonly described as "desegregated."

After a year of frustrating efforts to achieve desegregation on a case-by-case basis under the 1964 law, negotiating plans with individual districts, federal officials began to move toward statistical measures of segregation. By 1965, they had defined minimum progress statistically, and by 1966, were requiring substantial annual movement toward interracial schools with integrated faculties. Obviously statistics played a vital role in this process and regular reports from federal officials informed the country about the implementation of these goals (Radin, 1977; Orfield, 1969; Rodgers & Bullock, 1972).

The Supreme Court did not recognize the rights of Latino children to attend desegregated schools until 1973, and little data were collected on that issue. Federal education officials had begun collecting national school data on Latino students six years earlier, and other agencies followed suit in the years that followed. The role of the U.S. Civil Rights Commission in researching and documenting the conditions confronting Latino children would eventually be crucial for the Supreme Court's decision on this issue—the *Keyes* decision—in which the Court would cite the commission's findings (Orfield, 1978, ch. 9).

Whatever the the impact of the enforcement process, the statistics clearly showed large changes during the periods in which the law was seriously enforced either administratively or by the courts. There was also a powerful two-way relationship between administrative agencies and courts, which moved to adopt and reinforce the federal agencies' statistical definitions of desegregation; this greatly accelerated the change in the social composition of schools in the South, which became the nation's most integrated educational institutions by 1970. The transformation of Southern education was clearly a deep and long-lasting impact of the Civil Rights Act. The scale and timing of these impacts would not be known without the data produced under the Civil Rights Act. Without these data, the civil rights enforcement officials could not have implemented and monitored the massive changes. There were also large gains in educational achievement for blacks during this period, particularly in the South, and those were documented because of the Civil Rights Act. In other words, a race-specific history exists that is the raw material for arguments about the efficacy of targeted interventions by government. Without data, this debate would be purely theoretical and ideological.

The impacts of desegregation mandates were very deep and long-lasting. Not only did black desegregation tend to remain at its highest level from the early l970s to 1988, it was not until the judicial appointees of Presidents Ronald Reagan (1981–1989) and George Bush (1989–1993) deeply transformed the Supreme Court that the country began to move back towards greater segregation for black students (Orfield & Eaton, 1996).

Statistics are not a substitute for policy, but they are a powerful tool in battles over the workability of possible policies. Change on a large scale on difficult issues may well require not only clear goals and good measurement of results, but a workable policy, an enforcement process that is serious, political commitment at the top, and both sanctions and rewards for compliance. Publicly available data also permit outside challenges to official claims.

8. Bilingual education

Although school desegregation was the most visible consequence of the Civil Rights Act, it also provided the legal basis for forcing school districts across the country to provide educational services for children who did not speak English. This effort, which became highly important to the nation's very rapidly growing Hispanic and Asian populations, was created by federal civil rights officials and affected the educational policies for millions of students in the largest wave of immigrants ever received in the United States. Statistical measures of ethnicity and language use in various federal data systems were integral to the development and implementation of new policies.

Even as the Nixon administration was shutting down enforcement of school desegregation, it was expanding efforts to deal with the language issue. In 1970, the U.S. Department of Health, Education and Welfare (HEW) announced that it would enforce the little noticed provisions of the l964 Civil Rights Act forbidding discrimination on the grounds of "national origin." The new requirements for special educational programs for non-English-speaking children were directed at school districts with certain percentages of Latino enrollment, which could be identified because of the data requirements (Pottinger, 1970).

The Supreme Court recognized and upheld HEW's authority under the 1964 law to regulate in this area in its 1974 decision, *Lau v. Nichols* (414 U.S. 563, 1974). In 1975, federal officials distributed a document known as the "Lau Remedies," which spelled out the standards school districts were supposed to meet in bilingual programs and would be the dominant enforcement tool for the remainder of the decade. These policies and the related Bilingual Education Act strongly pressed districts to initiate education for children in their native language whenever a certain number of children speaking that language were present in a school. The regulations led to bilingual programs in districts across the country, a large demand for bilingual teachers, state laws and policies supporting the goal and a change in the educational experience of millions of children. They were monitored largely through the statistical reports required under the authority of the 1964 law. It was a very dramatic reflection of the extent of the power granted by the Civil Rights Act and of the ways in which a combination of data, research, politics and policy experimentation could lead to major changes in schools.

9.   Data and research

Race and ethnicity are so much an accepted part of policy discussion, news coverage and research in the early 21st century in the United States that it is hard to realize that it was impossible to make an accurate description of racial conditions and trends within many educational institutions and programs until 1964. That was when the government finally responded to the Civil Rights Act ban on discrimination by requiring the collection of racial data from schools and colleges. Many institutions, including big-city school districts, had not collected or refused to release racial data before these requirements. Few states collected and published such data. That is why it is impossible to say anything about national patterns of school segregation, or unequal provision of resources or curricula, with any precision before the late 1960s; why there was extremely little information available on Hispanic education until the 1970s; and why little could be said about racial conditions at many colleges. In many parts of the United States, there were explicit policies forbidding collection of racial data on the theory that they would be used to discriminate. Once there was a need to actually determine compliance with serious civil rights requirements, however, this policy was rapidly altered.

Data are the most elemental requirements both for understanding racial discrimination and operating a serious civil rights enforcement program. They are also essential for mobilization and policy debate. Their collection and publication made it possible to understand racial trends in U.S. education, describe our successes and failures, target enforcement priorities, and, in many cases, for minority groups and their advocates to create and justify new policy demands. Had the 1964 law not been enacted, the country would now be moving into a period of massive demographic change with much less adequate information.

During the 1960s and 1970s, the Civil Rights Commission produced many extremely important and influential studies documenting the school desegregation process, developing understanding of such neglected issues as the education of Mexican-Americans and strongly influencing the development of the law. Its findings and statistics were frequently relied upon by the courts, as they began to insist on plans that actually worked. During the same period, the federal government seriously supported a number of desegregation studies, under the Emergency School Aid Act[4] and research commissioned by the National Institute of Education. Much of what we know about race relations in American schools and colleges comes out of these efforts which, to a considerable extent, grew out of requirements of the 1964 law and subsequent laws, court decisions and policies.

Perhaps nothing more fundamental could be said about the 1964 law than that it did create, for the only time in U.S. history, a clear public policy against discrimination in all institutions and activities supported by federal funds. The power of the law has been largely preserved and even extended in some respects, though enforcement has been lax and sanctions very rarely used in recent decades. The data and knowledge produced by the law survived long after the will to force further racial change evaporated and may well inform the next large national debates on the subject.

10. School desegregation as an indicator of racial progress or reverse: The battle to provide continuing indicators

Collecting data is necessary but far from sufficient for informing public understanding of changes in conditions, and relationships between those changes and other outcomes. For the data to have impact, they must be made public in a form people can understand. If there are to be discussions about changes and remedies, it is important to have indicators that are intelligible and consistent, and that can be obtained and analyzed. Unfortunately, on controversial issues, the tendency of many agencies is not to publish data on objectives they do not support. However, in this era of cheap computing and transmission of large data sets through Web sites and CDs that cost little or nothing and are readily accessible, it is possible to create indicators outside of government, adding to the information that is available for public debate.

During the early years of enforcement of the desegregation requirements of the 1964 Civil Rights Act, when great progress in desegregation was being made and the national administration supported enforcement of the law, annual reports were issued on the decreases in segregation. Relatively clear information on the scale of desegregation and the trends was available (HEW, 1972). After President Nixon (1969–1973) was elected on an anti-civil rights platform and reversed policy, however, the federal government stopped issuing desegregation statistics; the data collection continued, but no reports were issued after 1972. Nixon fired the officials who had been enforcing the school desegregation guidelines, reversed the government's positions in many court cases (Panetta & Gall, 1971), and took a big step toward reconstructing the federal courts with four appointments to the nine-member Supreme Court, including William Rehnquist, a strong opponent of school desegregation who would later be named Chief Justice by President Reagan (Davis, 1989). Under the American legal system, the Supreme Court has broad authority to determine the meaning of sweeping language in the Constitution, including the key civil rights provision guaranteeing "equal protection of the laws." Between 1950 and the early 1970s, the Court greatly expanded the definition of equal protection rights of minority students, setting off a large political controversy and struggles over appointments to the Court. By 1974, President Nixon's conservative appointments had produced a Supreme Court that was deeply divided; reconfigured, it ruled against the plaintiffs in a key school desegregation case for the first time in two decades, ending significant progress toward desegregated education.

During the next 25 years, statistics on desegregation were issued by a federal agency only during the Carter administration and never by the statistical office of HEW or the Education Department (ED). In Washington and in many states, racial data were collected, but kept isolated from other school data. The results were not reported and not included in the major data sets or tabulations available to the public. The federal data were collected by the civil rights enforcement office, an agency run by lawyers, not researchers; they did not include all school districts, but only those likely to have civil rights problems and a sampling of others. The data were in a very complex and poorly organized format that no one but the federal contractor and a handful of researchers around the country could run. Unpublished data, very difficult to use and with serious flaws in its creation and consistency, posed huge challenges to public awareness of what was happening. But the conservative administrations of the past three decades did not call attention to an issue they did not wish to act on.

The conservatives, however, did not win control of the Supreme Court on this issue until the 1990s, and proved unable to repeal the Civil Rights Act. Though there were no significant expansions of school desegregation requirements by the courts after 1973, neither was there a consolidated majority of Justices supporting civil rights rollbacks until 1991, so the constitutional requirements remained in place. The Democratic Party maintained control of the House of Representatives until 1994 and there was not a time, from 1960 to 2000, when civil rights opponents simultaneously controlled both houses of Congress and the Presidency. Because the Democrats supported the law, this meant that it could not be repealed. The Supreme Court narrowed its interpretation of the 1964 Civil Rights Act's mandate of nondiscrimination in all programs receiving federal aid, but Congress responded by strengthening the law, with the support of a coalition including minority groups, women and handicapped organizations.[5] Although there were serious cutbacks in data collection during the Nixon and Reagan administrations, and no racial data on segregation were published, the government continued to collect them.

One of the problems was that the data on race had not been built into the basic statistical system. They were collected for civil rights purposes by law enforcement staffs, and the research and statistical components of the federal educational establishment, as well as the states who submitted them, did not include them. And no one had the responsibility to report whether the country was realizing or abandoning the goal of desegregated education. The federal government's statistical office relies on voluntary cooperation with state governments and tries to avoid controversial issues. Not until 1987, 23 years after the Civil Rights Act, was race included in the school-level database and, even then, a number of states did not provide this information for the statistical system.

Without planning to do it, I became the source of national indicators on school desegregation for almost a quarter century. During the period from 1976 to 1999, I issued eight major national reports on school desegregation, of which none have been financed or approved by the government, but have provided the only generally available information on these important issues. Each of them has received massive coverage and continuing use in the mass media and many scholarly studies. On many occasions when the government was asked for data on this subject, their experts would refer the inquiries to me. None of these studies required more than a few thousand dollars for computation and my donated time to prepare. The basic reason for this was that the data existed, although usually in a complex and awkward form. I could obtain the computer tapes by making the appropriate legal request, and I was able to find researchers—most of them trained by a desegregation expert, Professor Karl Taeuber, at the University of Wisconsin, a demographer who understood the complexities of the federal data—to work with me on preparing the key tables. A University of Michigan demographer, Reynolds Farley, was another serious user of this data, but for different purposes.

The radically declining cost of computer time, and the increasing ease of analysis after racial data were included in the CCD and made available on CD-ROM, make it increasingly simple for citizens and groups to use data to create their own indicators. This has important democratic implications.

My first experience in this respect came during 1976 when two powerful senators with concerns about the civil rights reversals of the Nixon and Ford administrations[6] asked me to take a temporary leave from my job at the Brookings Institution, a leading Washington think tank, to work with a Senate committee staff to obtain the best available data on civil rights trends in the country. My practice was to canvass the various agencies collecting data, identify possibilities and write letters for signature by these senators, demanding the prompt production of the data. As one of the senators had a powerful voice in controlling education appropriations, these requests produced immediate results. After education officials received the demand for school desegregation data, they asked me to outline which calculations should be done and to define the indicators and regions (Orfield, 1983) in which they would be calculated. The tables were produced by the federal contractor who collected and processed the data for the Office for Civil Rights, and the report was issued in a press release from the senators in 1976 ("Desegregation," 1976). Among the important new social facts presented in the document was evidence of a growing segregation of Latinos.[7] The data were also used for reports produced by a civil rights research organization and a Senate committee report (Orfield, 1977). I did not realize at the time that the statistics I outlined then would become the only continuous indicators available in the United States on this issue for decades.

The next time such data were reported was in 1981, when I was a visiting scholar at the Brookings Institution. I obtained the support of a congressional committee to demand that the data be produced again and scheduled a public hearing on school segregation levels. At that time, the African-American think tank, the Joint Center for Political and Educational Studies, published the results and issued a monograph on the 1968–1980 trends. We were also able for the first time to report data on desegregation trends by metropolitan areas. Most of the remaining segregation in the country was between separate school districts within metropolitan areas, but no data were being systematically collected or reported on this issue because the Supreme Court had blocked orders to consolidate city and suburban school districts.

A series of subsequent reports on these trends grew out of my role in working with the National School Boards Association, a national association of local school authorities. It supplied funds to help with the computation of several subsequent studies, and handled the publication and distribution of those reports through a very strong network. Finally, in the last three reports, my own projects at Harvard have published and distributed the findings, including a report issued in June of 1999 that has received widespread press coverage across the United States (National School Boards Association, 1993; "Deepening," 1997; "Racial Change," 1988; "Status," 1989; "Status," 1992; "Growth," 1993).

The statistics in these reports have been used in hundreds of newspapers and magazine articles, books and journals, congressional hearings, and judicial proceedings in both federal and state courts. The statistics have been used by people and organizations advocating widely varying policies. What policy impact they may have had is unknown, although it is likely that the issue would have largely disappeared, except in isolated local court battles. It is clear, however, that they have added to the discussions important dimensions of information that would not otherwise have been present, and they have been employed by many scholars, journalists and others in assessing the state of race relations. They are frequently used in overview assessments of racial trends.

There are many important facts, trends and relationships that would not be known without this data:

- We would not know that desegregation actually continued to increase for black students almost two decades into the conservative era. Desegregation had been described as a fragile policy that rapidly eroded. It was not.
- We would not know that students in highly segregated black and Latino schools are 11 times more likely than students in highly segregated white schools to be in schools where most of the children are poor.
- We would not know that the segregation of Latino students, soon to be our largest majority group, is more intense than that of blacks and steadily increasing.
- We would not know that the large minority migration to the suburbs is rapidly producing a segregated suburban educational experience.
- In trying to explain the much greater mobility of Asian students, we would not know that they are in schools that are rarely segregated by race or language and where a large majority of their classmates are from educationally advantaged groups (Orfield & Yun 1999) .

These are just a few of the ways in which racial and ethnic indicators, working together with measures of poverty and spatial location, can show relationships and trends that are extremely important in thinking about the causes of educational inequality and possible solutions.

The most recent chapter in this story is the issuance of an official indicator of racial isolation included in NCES' *The Condition of Education 1999*, the first time such an indicator has ever been incorporated into the nation's basic system of education statistics. This seems to close the cycle that has progressed from private data before 1964, to public data publicly reported until 1972, to public data privately reported, to the creation of an official indicator in the public data system in 1999. As one of the authors of this new indicator, I think it is obvious that this is just a beginning and covers only limited issues from a limited perspective, tending in some ways to understate the significance of rising segregation. But it is an important recognition that the issue needs to be seriously considered.

The processing of this indicator produced strong controversy within the statistical agency. When it was released, the document emphasized not the increasing isolation experienced by minority children, but the degree to which the increase could be explained by the rising proportion of minorities in the U.S. population; the continuing high segregation of whites, even in heavily nonwhite areas, was not stressed. Obviously, even when indicators are published officially, there will be choices that will affect the reporting and use of the data in policy debates, and ongoing discussion over which indicators would be the most informative. Thus, the choices and framing of indicators also deserve the closest continuing attention in the scholarly and policy worlds, and there is a continuing need for independent analysis of the data.

11.   Other racial indicators

School desegregation is a special case. Because it has been an intensely controversial policy, with radical changes of stance on the issue among administrations, there were no consistent government statistics. However, it was still possible to provide crucial data on trends and incidence of segregation outside of government using data collected by government. Other measures of racial and ethnic differences have been much less controversial. Many reports and surveys sponsored by the government routinely report racial and ethnic breaks in the data, particularly because Hispanic data were added in the 1970s and the nonwhite category was broken down into component racial groups. Employment, housing, medical and many other statistical systems carry such data. Changes in residential segregation of blacks have been computed by sociologists for decades, and there were many computations of various measures made in the Census Bureau after the last census. The government has commissioned several surveys based on actual tests of discrimination in the housing and employment markets. In education enrollment, graduation, dropouts and data on course taking, resources, etc., are often reported by race, ethnicity and poverty in federal education reports. The United States has much better information in the face of rapid social change than it could have had without the creation of the data elements and their incorporation in a number of continuing reports on trends in various aspects of society and the economy.

12.   Ignorance is not bliss: Problems of policy without appropriate indicators

If there are systemic inequalities relating to social structure and they are neglected in the data systems, policies may well be devised and implemented that will make the situation of the most vulnerable groups even worse, and it may be difficult to know that this is happening until the problems are deeply rooted. If, for example, various forms of prejudice mean that the less qualified teachers are concentrated in schools with disadvantaged, poorly prepared minority students and low levels of peer group competition, but the data do not show that, it might be assumed that the problem is wholly due to a failure of the parents or that the children simply do not want to learn. However, if there are data that show a clear linkage between social status and a set of opportunities that differ in crucial ways across school systems, then the debate is more likely to include more consideration of those issues and ways to overcome them, or broader policies with the potential to actually change them.

The U.S. historic experience shows that covering up problems is the normal response of governments even when the cleavages are very deep and immediately apparent to the outsider, as were our racial divisions in the South and in our great cities. We only have our data on many of these issues because of a vast social movement and a commitment by political leaders to spend heavy resources on social transformation, which led to the collection of data as a necessary precondition for implementing major changes. The fact that we have these data, however, means that we have much greater capacity to understand our problems, and that citizens and groups can follow trends on racial and ethnic issues of educational equity even when the government does not wish to raise such issues. Societies should have variables reflecting their basic social structure in their data sets on opportunity, education and the outcomes of education, employment and housing location. If they do not, there is a high probability that they will neglect dimensions of educational inequality that must be addressed to have beneficial outcomes for the most disadvantaged students.

I believe that the American experience has relevance to a growing number of countries as immigration leads to greater diversity in many nations and to the emergence in many societies of ethnicity as a more basic component of social structure than social class. One need only look at the forces that pulled apart the Soviet Union, destroyed Yugoslavia, create profound difficulties in some nations with two or more major languages, and are becoming apparent in a number of societies where there has been little diversity until recently to know that monitoring of educational opportunities and achievements by groups on all sides of these social cleavages is necessary if educators are to do their work effectively. Those thinking about indicators of equity should start with the basic structure of their society, not as it is reflected in some theory or government document, but with the reality. They should then try to develop and report indicators that are intelligible, as consistent as possible over time, and regularly issued either by government or private institutions to inform debate and policy-making.

13. Impacts and evolution of indicators

Indicators can reveal developing problems, help create consciousness and empower groups that they measure. They also reflect changing consciousness and power and may help shape ways in which issues are joined. Because they play such important roles, there will be continuing controversy over their appropriateness. In many data series in the United States, the historic changes are very apparent. Poverty data collection began in the mid-1960s; black data started in 1966 or 1967; Latino data collection began in the early or mid-1970s; and Asian data, after the huge immigrations from Asia permitted by the 1965 immigration reform, began significantly later. Definitions and data collection procedures become increasingly focused and consistent over time.

The latest change came in the 2000 Census with the creation of data collection rules that permit people to identify themselves as multiracial, reflecting the rapidly increasing numbers of interracial and interethnic marriages in the United States, and the mobilization of interracial families against outdated social assumptions that racial identity is distinct and absolute. The major minority groups—claiming power, representation and influence to a significant degree on the basis of racial statistics—fought these proposals, and many statisticians worried what the changes would do to the analysis of trends (Holmes, 1998; Fiore, 1997). This set of battles clearly demonstrates how important categories are for many objectives. They become reified into what appear to be clearly defined units. They become forces in the distribution of resources and power; vested interests develop around various classifications, and new groups may have to struggle to find a way to produce data about themselves. Statistical agencies have a tendency, once a system is developed, to keep it going because it maintains categories that have been approved and produces comparable trend data.

As societies continue to change, there can be difficulties in deciding how and whether to alter definitions or add new categories to data systems. In the nature of things, there can be no permanent ideal system within communities and societies experiencing major transformations. Everything else being close to equal, there are of course great advantages to maintaining definitions over time to permit measurement of the dimensions of change. The problem comes when the categories begin to obscure important parts of social reality. For example, it was a reasonable approximation of reality to describe race as an absolute and unique category so long as there were extremely few intermarriages and it was understood that anyone with a significant black ancestry would be considered black even if he or she were actually interracial. That kind of rule, however, does not work very well with other racial minority groups that have a much higher rate of intermarriage and in a society without a clear social rule for defining children of such marriages. Eventually, the process of forcing millions of interracial people to define themselves as members of a single race would seriously distort the social reality. In a situation such as this, it is very important to make appropriate changes in the categories to reflect the developing changes in society.

The United States now faces an unusual circumstance. Until national data were collected in the late 1960s and early 1970s, there was very little consciousness of a national Hispanic or Latino community—how to count its members or what the concept meant. As late as the 1970 Census, Latinos were considered a regional group to be identified through "Spanish surnames," and there was no idea that they would take on the characteristic of being identified as a major population to be compared with whites (or "non-Hispanic whites," or "Anglos"). Even today, there is no agreement about whether to call people

"Latinos," "Hispanics," "Hispanos," "Chicanos," "Dominicans," "Puerto Ricans," etc. (Oboler, 1995).

The recognition of this group coincided with a vast immigration and a demographic explosion. About two decades after becoming reasonably identified within federal data systems, Latinos had become 13 percent of U.S. school enrollment and were rapidly overtaking blacks as the nation's largest minority population. In the two largest states, California and Texas, they were moving toward becoming a plurality of the statewide population and a large majority of school-age children. The political and social implications of a group this large and rapidly growing were very significant, though its impact was delayed by the non-voting status of a large proportion of Latinos, due to both their youth and the slow rate of naturalization.

The significance of these statistics is quite different in periods in which the liberals are in power, with minority voters as a central part of their coalitions, than when conservatives are in power, holding it in part on the basis of fear of racial and ethnic change. In the first circumstance, the group itself can use the data to state its claims and needs, and to ask for serious attention. In the conservative eras, discussion of ethnic trends, differences and problems are typically muted, and attention is turned to other issues. In such circumstances, the continuing production of data demonstrating serious problems in access and opportunity is vital to keep attention on the issues, and to make possible the formulation of ideas and proposals for improvement. Without data on Hispanics, for example, we would not know that their high school dropout rate is more than twice as high as that of blacks, they are even more concentrated than blacks in a few of the largest metropolitan areas, and the trends in their family structure or educational and economic circumstances might be responsible for negative and positive changes. We would not know the course-taking patterns and stratifications in educational groupings. Because the Voting Rights Act is race conscious and emphasizes attaining initial representation of identifiable, geographically concentrated minority populations, such data are vital to the political power of Latino politicians and, through them, to the power of the communities. Without college enrollment statistics required by the 1964 Civil Rights Act, it would not be possible to know the consequences of the recent state decisions limiting affirmative action for minority admissions.

Without good data on social cleavages it is not possible to understand and target energy towards some very important educational problems. Data do, however, become a source of claims to power and, as the stakes rise, it is more difficult for those who simply have an interest in clear information on trends and social changes to control the outcomes. Not only is it important for scholars and administrators to fight to get and keep essential indicators of equity, but it is also important that they be prepared for criticism from very different directions, as those who stand to benefit may try to use the data inaccurately to maximize their position or obscure changes. No one should assume that there is any permanent solution in such cases, only that some reasonably thoughtful and consistent measures of change are better and much more informative for public discussion and the making of policy than ignorance. The U.S. experience indicates that it has been possible to develop indicators along some of the most sensitive divisions in American society and to keep them in spite of vast political changes. Moreover, they have been very widely used, sometimes making important differences in public debates, understanding and decisions. These data constitute a most significant legacy of earlier periods of large-scale social reform and one of the most important tools for understanding what is yet to be done in the battles for social justice, and for full and fair development of the talents of various groups in a rapidly changing society.

Notes

1 Income inequality is the highest it has been since income was first measured in the United States in the 1940 Census.
2 This policy is called the Earned Income Tax Credit.
3 The U.S. Supreme Court upheld the authority to require special educational provisions for non-English-speaking students under policies that grew out of analysis of national origin and language data collected under the Civil Rights Act, *Lau v. Nichols*, 414 U.S. 563 (1974).
4 The federal desegregation aid bill was enacted in 1972 and repealed in 1981.
5 The Civil Rights Restoration Act of 1988
6   Edward Brooke (Republican, Massachusetts) and Jacob Javits (Republican, New York)
7 It was possible to compute segregation trends for Latinos because the federal civil rights data, unlike the U.S. census at that time, had already collected consistent data on Latinos since 1968. The census collected such data only in some states, once every 10 years, and changed its definition from one census to the next.

References

Anyon J., *Ghetto Schooling: A Political Economy of Urban Educational Reform*, Teacher's College Press, New York, 1997.

Blair J., "OCR Issues Revised Guidance on High-Stakes Testing," *Education Week*, p. 25, Jan. 12, 2000.

Bullard R.D., Grigsby J. E., Lee C., *Residential Apartheid: The American Legacy*, CASS Publications, Los Angeles, 1994.

Corbett T., "Poverty: Improving the Measure after Thirty Years: A Conference," *Focus, 20* (2), pp. 21–55, Spring 1999.

Danziger S.H., Sandefur G.D., Weinberg D.H., *Confronting Poverty: Prescriptions for Change*, Harvard Univ. Press, Cambridge (Mass.), 1992.

Davis S., *Justice Rehnquist and the Constitution*, Princeton University Press, Princeton, 1989.

"Deepening Segregation in American Public Schools," with Bachmeier M., James D., Eitle T., Harvard Project on School Desegregation, April 1997, in *Equity and Excellence in Education, 30* (2), pp. 5–24, September 1997, reprinted in part in *Southern Changes, 19* (2), pp. 11–18, Summer 1997.

De Plotnick R., Skidmore F., *Progress Against Poverty: A Review of the 1964–1974 Decade*, Academic Press, New York, 1975.

"Desegregation in the Cities—Trends in School Segregation in the 1970's," *Congressional Record, daily ed.,* June 18, 1976.

Fiore F., "Multiple Race Choices to be Allowed on 2000 Census," *Los Angles Times*, October 30, 1997.

Goldin C., Katz L.F., "The Returns to Skills in the United States Across the Twentieth Century," National Bureau of Economic Research, 1999.

The Growth of Segregation in American Schools: Changing Patterns of Separation and Poverty Since 1968, with Schley S., Glass D., Reardon S., National School Boards Association, Alexandria, (Virg.), 1993.

Holmes S.A., "New Census Method Gets Test Run in California," *New York Times,* June 7, 1998.

Johnson L.B., "The War on Poverty," in *The Vantage Point: Perspectives on the Presidency, 1963–1969,* Holt, Rinehardt, and Winston, New York, 1971.

Kluegel J.R., Smith E.R. *Beliefs about Inequality: Americans' Views of What Is and What Ought to Be,* Aldine de Gruyter, New York, 1986.

Levitan S.A., Taggart R., *The Promise of Greatness,* Harvard University Press, Cambridge (Mass.), 1976.

Loevy R.D. (ed.), *The Civil Rights Act of 1964: The Passage of the Law that Ended Racial Segregation*, State Univ. of New York Press, Albany, 1997.

MacLeod J., *Ain't No Making It: Aspirations and Attainment in a Low-Income Neighborhood*, Westview Press, Boulder (Colo.), 1995.

Mann R., *The Walls of Jerico*, Harcourt Brace, New York, 1996.

Massey D.S., Denton N.A., *American Apartheid: Segregation and the Making of the Underclass*, Harvard University Press, Cambridge (Mass.), 1993.

Meier K.J., Stewart J., *The Politics of Hispanic Education,* SUNY Press, Albany, 1991.

Meier K.J., Stewart J., England R. E., *Race, Class, and Education: The Politics of Second Generation Discrimination*, University of Wisconsin Press, Madison, 1989.

National Center for Education Statistics, *Digest of Educational Statistics 1997,* Government Printing Office, Washington, DC, 1998.

Oboler S., *Ethnic Labels, Latino Lives: Identity and the Politics of (Re)Presentation in the United States,* University of Minnesota Press, Minneapolis, 1995.

Ogbu J.U., "Class Stratification, Racial Stratification, and Schooling," in Weis L. (ed.) *Class, Race and Gender in American Education*, State University of New York Press, Albany, pp. 163-182, 1988.

Orfield G., *The Reconstruction of Southern Education: The Schools and the 1964 Civil Rights Act*, John Wiley, New York, 1969.

Orfield G., *Desegregation and the Cities: The Trends and the Policy Choices,* staff report, U.S. Senate Committee on Human Resources, 95th Congress, 1st Session, 1977.

Orfield G., *Must We Bus? Segregated Schools and National Policy*, Chapter 9, Brookings Inst., Washington, DC, 1978.

Orfield G., *Public School Desegregation in the United States, 1968–1980,* Joint Center for Political Studies, Washington, DC, 1983. (Reprinted, in part, in Miller L.P. (ed.), *Brown Plus Thirty*, New York University Metropolitan Center, 1986.)

Orfield G., Eaton S., *Dismantling Desegregation: The Quiet Repeal of Brown v. Board of Education*, New Press, 1996.

Orfield G., Yun J.T., "Resegregation in American Schools," The Civil Rights Project at Harvard, June 1999.

Orshansky M., "Counting the Poor," *Social Security Bulletin*, pp. 3–29, January 1965.

Panetta L.E., Gall P., *Bring Us Together: The Nixon Team and the Civil Rights Retreat*, Lippincott, New York, 1971.

Pottinger J.S., "Memorandum to School Districts with More than Five Percent National Origin Children," Office for Civil Rights, May 25, 1970.

Racial Change and Desegregation in Large School Districts: Trends through the 1986–1987 School Year, with Monfort F., National School Boards Association, Alexandria, 1988.

Radin B.A., *Implementation, Change, and the Federal Bureaucracy: School Desegregation Policy in H.E.W. 1964–1968,* Teachers College Press, New York, 1977.

Rodgers H.R., Bullock C.S., *Law and Social Change: Civil Rights Laws and their Consequences*, McGraw Hill, New York, 1972.

Sarratt R., *The Ordeal of Desegregation*, Harper & Row, New York, 1966.

Status of School Desegregation, 1968–1986. Segregation, Integration, and Public Policy: National, State, and Metropolitan Trends in Public Schools, with Monfort F., Aaron M., National School Boards Association, Alexandria, 1989.

Status of School Desegregation: The Next Generation, with Monfort F., National School Boards Association, Alexandria, 1992.

Supreme Court, 414 U.S. 563, 1974.

Tilly C., *Durable Inequality,* University of California Press, Berkeley, 1998.

U.S. Bureau of the Census, *The Statistical Abstract of the United States,* Government Printing Office, Washington, DC, 1961.

U.S. Bureau of the Census, *The Statistical Abstract of the United States,* Government Printing Office, Washington, DC, 1973.

U.S. Commission on Civil Rights, *Freedom to the Free, A Century of Emancipation*, Government Printing Office, Washington, DC, 1964.

U.S. Commission on Civil Rights, *Public Schools, Southern States, 1963: Staff Reports,* Washington, DC, 1964.

U.S. Commission on Civil Rights, *Racial Isolation in the Public Schools*, Government Printing Office, Washington, DC, 1967.

U.S. Department of Health, Education, and Welfare, *HEW News,* January 16, 1972.

Watson D., *Lion in the Lobby: Clarence Mitchell Jr.'s Struggle for the Passage of Civil Rights Laws,* William Morrow, New York, 1990.

Weis L., *Working Class without Work: High School Students in a De-industrializing Society,* Routledge, New York, 1990.

Whalen C., Whalen B., *The Longest Debate: A Legislative History of the 1964 Civil Rights Act*, Seven Locks Press, Cabin Locks, MD, 1985.

Wilson W.J., *The Truly Disadvantaged: The Inner City, the Underclass, and Public Policy,* University of Chicago Press, Chicago, 1987.

Wilson W.J., *When Work Disappears: The World of the New Urban Poor*, Knopf, New York, 1996.

Chapter 7

International Equity Indicators in Education and Learning in Industrialized Democracies
Some recent results and avenues for the future

Tom Healy
Organisation for Economic Co-operation and Development/
Center for Education Research and Innovation, Paris

David Istance[1]
Organisation for Economic Co-operation and Development/
Center for Education Research and Innovation, Paris

The distribution of education and learning in any country is a matter of profound political, social and economic importance. Yet, measures that demonstrate this distribution in precise terms, and that show whether progress is being made or not, are surprisingly sparse. This is even more remarkable given the prominence that equity now occupies in official statements meant to guide policy in OECD (Organisaiton for Economic Co-operation and Development) countries. In very broad-brush terms, equity policy aims can be characterized as ebbing and flowing in recent decades. An earlier period of prominence in the 1960s and early 1970s, to which the OECD made an important contribution (see OECD 1961, 1971, 1975; Husen, 1975), gave way to a period of disenchantment not only with equity, but with the benefits of educational investment in general. This negativism was fueled by studies purporting to show that "schools make no difference" (most famously, in reactions to the 1972 Jencks et al., study). Since then, the pendulum has swung back somewhat, especially in the recognition of the rights of particular population groups and acknowledgment of the existence of "exclusion." What is less clear is the extent to which actual improvement has occurred in the prospects of the disadvantaged, and indeed whether other guiding policy aims (e.g., improving accountability or the promotion of market mechanisms in education) have supported or counterbalanced the pursuit of equity. A perhaps cynical view is that equity goals, whatever the official statements, are much easier to espouse in the absence of pertinent hard data. Clear comparative indicators can thus make a vital contribution to debate and policy-making on these issues.

Our starting point then is that much greater attention needs to be given, at the national and international levels, to charting the different dimensions of equity in education and learning. In arguing for such a priority, we distinguish among three approaches, each providing its own valuable insights into the understanding of equity: 1) descriptive international measures of different equity dimensions, 2) comparative analyses of the determinants of learning outcomes, and 3) comparisons of national evaluations of the impact of different policy strategies, particularly on the attainment of disadvantaged students (see "Terminology," below). Our focus is squarely on the first of these. This chapter describes the main areas where pertinent data already exist, especially through OECD sources. These could be exploited more thoroughly than they have been to date to enhance our understanding of equity of access, participation and learning outcomes.

There remain major gaps, however. Rather than simply embarking on incremental "gap-filling," it would be preferable for equity indicator development to take place through a coordinated international strategy within an agreed framework. In addressing the glaring lack of comparative descriptive data on educational equity, such a framework should satisfy a further criterion. A great deal of research and analysis relating to educational equity remains firmly focused on young people and on learning opportunities provided them by school systems, colleges and universities. We would maintain that this is insufficient at the outset of the 21st century: Any strategy for international equity indicator development should integrate *lifelong learning* as a core precept. This chapter suggests a framework that, we believe, meets these different criteria. Even within this delimitation of the avenues for further work, there are substantial obstacles, methodological and political, to progress. These obstacles are not insuperable, provided the energy and resources needed to develop indicators in this field can be mobilized.

1.   Terminology: Equity, equality and related concepts

An earlier OECD report, *Education and Equity in OECD Countries*, included a glossary of terms. This set forth some of the distinctions—such as between equality and equity, and disparity and difference—that are relevant to this chapter:

> . . . *Equality/inequality*: At least as commonly employed in its negative form (inequality), this term refers to the condition of being equal, i.e. identical in quantity or quality, of the same value, sameness, evenness . . .

like 'equity' it is open to widely differing interpretations, and it is often an umbrella term rather than anything more precise.

. . . *Equity*: Frequently used as a synonym for 'equality' and, in practical terms, the two raise very similar concerns. . . . Much depends on the interpretation and contents given to the notion of "equity" in practice; frequently it is used as a catchall label rather than in any more precise way. Its political radicalism depends on the substantive interpretation of fairness and justice that lies behind it.

. . . *Inequality/difference*: The distinction can be drawn between a 'difference'—which in educational terms may be a difference of experience, attainment, resources made available or outcome—and an 'inequality.' Some have identified this as residing entirely in the qualification to a given difference that it is unfair.

. . . *Disparity* sits somewhere between the two: neutral enough to be equated with 'difference,' robust enough to be synonymous with 'inequality,' depending on the usage. Such flexibility of interpretation inevitably leaves substantial room for imprecision.

. . . *Diversity*: The moral tone of the concept of inequality is essentially negative; the implication is that when found it should be rectified. In contrast, 'diversity' has essentially positive connotations despite expressing the existence of differences, even unequals (OECD, 1997, pp. 121–127).

Whether or not all would agree with the definitions contained in the earlier OECD glossary, a number of conclusions emerge. First, while some commentators may define terms very precisely, others do not. For many purposes, "equality," "equity," "disparity," etc., provide necessary general labels to identify a broad terrain. Second, and related closely to the first, such terms are often used interchangeably. Whether this is good use of terminology or misuse depends essentially on the context; what can be a critical distinction for philosophical or sociological analysis may be largely irrelevant when the task is to describe families of policy initiatives or statistical measures.

Third, such concepts are essentially value-laden and hence open to differing interpretation within, and especially across, countries. What is unfair for one is acceptable—even desirable—for another. This is especially relevant when defining international indicators. These are fixed measures across time and cultures used to understand a rapidly changing world in which there are no universal values to which all would subscribe. Hence, there are not fixed definitions of equity, but many. For the purposes of this chapter, therefore, the terms "distributional," "equity" and "equality" can be used largely interchangeably to refer to the types of statistical measures we review below.

2.   The policy importance of equity in education and learning

2.1.   Long-standing and new concerns

Education, learning and the acquisition of knowledge and skills have never been more central preoccupations of society than they are today, and will likely be more so in years to come. It is now common to characterize our countries as "knowledge economies" or "knowledge societies" (OECD, 2000). The strong links between learning and "economic health" for individuals through human capital investment are now widely acknowledged in today's highly competitive world (OECD, 1998). Parallel lessons can be drawn for enterprises as "learning organizations," as well as for entire industries, geographical areas and national economies.[2] With rapid change, and hence the continual requirement for new investment in human capital, lifelong learning has come to be recognized as the guiding aim, not only for education but to meet a wide range of economic and social policy objectives.

These developments are frequently characterized as very positive features of post-industrial society. But they have a fundamental reverse side: The consequences for those individuals, organizations or communities who fall behind in learning become the more profound, and can be dire. That the notion of "exclusion" has entered into the mainstream policy vocabulary is testament to how high the barriers to inclusion have become for many. Inequalities have widened in many places since the 1980s (although the nature, timing and direction of change are far from identical across countries), linked *inter alia* to globalization, the freer play of market forces (and hence also of market failure) and the general decline of post-World War II "welfare state" social protection policies (see, for example, Atkinson, 1999).

Of particular relevance for this chapter, education and learning are right at the heart of which individuals become winners and losers. Knowledge, competence and qualifications for work or further study are the predominant currency in the determination of rewards and prospects. The OECD report on human capital investment (1998) indicated just how unevenly qualifications and skills are distributed among the adult population, and the strong tendency for those with high levels of knowledge, skill and competence to acquire more widening existing gaps. Far from diminishing the relevance of distributional issues, the emergence of the so-called "expert," "digital" or "knowledge" society has had the opposite effect.

Changing conditions are thus fundamental to a contemporary understanding of equity. First, there are major social changes—fragmentation, weakening family and community structures—that, we would argue along with others (Carnoy & Castells, 1997), define new roles for educational institutions, especially schools, as generators of social capital. Second, attention is being increasingly focused on the so-called "digital divide"—the gaps between those with technological literacy and those without, and between those with and without the means to build on their formal educational opportunities via access to technology at home.[3] It is still not clear to what extent this divide is simply a reflection of existing inequalities or a major new dimension in its own right. Whichever turns out to be the case, the more fundamental access to and use of communication technology (ICT) become, the more critical will be the barriers experienced by those on the wrong side of the "digital divide."

Third, there is the transformation that has come about through the speed of change itself. What once would have been settled primarily through social origins or educational attainment in each person's early years is now being constantly being revised. Social precariousness is thus more widespread rather than confined to a specific disadvantaged group who are, by the same process, often at acute risk of exclusion. It is natural to see these developments as yet more ammunition to favor more widespread opportunities for lifelong learning. This statement risks being overly simplistic. The growing complexity of learning provision and decision-making—and the wide variety of informal and non-public sources of education for lifelong learning—render the problems confronting those who are not well equipped for the knowledge society still worse. Hence, one of the most intractable aspects of the new situation is that even lifelong learning can be regarded not only as part of the "solution" for socioeconomic inequalities and precariousness, but as an integral part of the "problem" as well.

2.2. The key role of data—national and international

Given the importance of these issues, the dearth of relevant robust evidence of equity or the lack of it represents a glaring weakness, both for public debate and for policy-making. Data are not, of course, entirely absent; international data gathered through the OECD education indicators project, INES, and related activities are reviewed below. However, in view of the considerable challenges involved, we see this area as deserving a much higher priority for indicator development than previously. To realize this priority, the political challenges may be as necessary to address as the methodological ones. To chart accurately the distribution of learning opportunities, participation and outcomes is to compile evidence that reaches into the very heart of equity and cohesion of modern societies. Adherence to laudable policy ambitions, as we noted, is easy in the absence of hard data to substantiate the rhetoric. But issues of equity, inequality and exclusion, as much as any other in education, are the ones in which good, well-organized data can make an immediate and telling impact on policies.

In light of these factors, combined with the absence of extensive existing equity measures, we would argue for a high priority to be given to generating indicators that are primarily *descriptive* of actual patterns and distributions.

This is especially the case with respect to international as opposed to national or sub-national data. Our plea would be that, for the foreseeable future, efforts should concentrate on establishing "international facts." There is a need for authoritative illumination of such questions as: "Who gets excluded from learning opportunities?" "Are disparities widening or narrowing?" "What are the cumulative effects of socio-cultural, economic and educational disadvantage?" "How does our country compare with others in these respects?"

This calls for a distinct, complementary focus from two other common approaches to the analysis of educational equity. First, there is the approach of modeling the relative weight of different "explanatory" variables (e.g., school, home background, location, etc.) on various measures of educational outcome. While appearing to have an advantage over descriptive data, complex analysis and interpretation may well be of less direct policy relevance than sharply focused summaries of educational and social issues. This applies especially to international comparisons. Second, there are evaluations of "families" of policy programs. To know whether a particular category of program initiative (e.g., reading instruction or early childhood intervention) is effective in reaching the disadvantaged, and in which countries, is eminently useful. Even so, this is distinct from the development of international indicators, the focus of this chapter.

3.   Existing international equity data—the OECD contribution

In this section, we review the coverage of existing indicators that shed light on equity in education and learning. More exist than might be apparent at first sight, and could be more effectively exploited. The INES has produced a number of indicators of educational equality and disparity since its inception in the late 1980s. Various editions of *Education at a Glance, OECD Indicators* (*EAG*) since 1992 have shown a range of such indicators. These can be broadly categorized in three ways:
- indicators of dispersion among individuals (intra-group dispersion);
- regular indicators showing differences among various groups—usually by age and gender (inter-group); and
- periodic or occasional indicators showing differences by group—usually by occupation, educational attainment of parents, average income, or region or other spatial unit (occasional inter-group).

Each of these three types of equality measures can be related to the three-way classification of equality perspectives—cross-sectional, trends and lifecycle—that undergird the framework we will put forward in the final section of this paper.

3.1. Intra-group measures of dispersion

The first category typically covers indicators of dispersion or variation for skills of individual students or adults. Examples include measures of disparity among students in achievement in mathematics and science (based on results of the Third International Mathematics and Science Study (TIMSS)).[4] Other examples relate to disparity in adult literacy based on OECD's International Adult Literacy Survey (IALS).[5] Countries vary considerably in degree of dispersion in literacy and student achievement levels. The comparison of results for different age groups (or grade years in the case of the student population) suggests varying patterns of progression (and attrition) in skill acquisition across countries. The following indicators have been included in recent OECD publications:

- measures of dispersion in achievement of mathematics and science (comparing 5th and 95th percentiles) between grades 4 and 8 using TIMSS data;[6]
- distribution of students at age 14 by level of achievement in reading using the IEA[7] Reading Literacy Study of 1990/1991 (*EAG*, 1993);
- proportion of variation in achievement of mathematics of 8th-graders accounted for by school and other factors;[8] and
- distribution of adult literacy for countries participating in IALS in 1994–95.[9]

3.2. Regular inter-group measures of inequality (by age and gender)

3.2.1. Inter-generational

Differences across age groups in levels of educational attainment (as measured by the highest completed level of initial education) have been well documented in *EAG* for the adult population. The rapid evolution in educational attainment in recent decades has initially opened up a sharp divergence in levels of attainment across different age groups. However, as higher levels of graduation from the upper secondary and tertiary levels of education have spread to successive generations, such age gaps have tended to narrow, except for the countries that are "late starters." Published data on attainment are available for the 1990s, but there are few comparable international measures of attainment before this.

However, comparisons have been made of educational attainment by individuals in the adult population with the attainment of their parents to measure mobility of attainment across generations. The IALS provided data making such inter-generational comparisons possible (e.g., the probability of having studies at the tertiary level based on the level of attainment of one's parents). This provides a guide as to whether educational opportunities are becoming more or less equal over time.[10]

3.2.2. Gender

Differences in access, participation, graduation and literacy or student achievement levels between boys and girls, and men and women, have been an important focus of analysis. There has been a recent narrowing of the gender gap in terms of school retention and graduation at the higher levels of education, and indeed a reversal of some earlier patterns. There continue, however, to be significant gaps in rates of labor market participation and in earnings between men and women. Education appears to play an important role in narrowing the gender gap in the labor market. Changing roles, expectations and attitudes accompany a shift in patterns of educational and labor market participation by men and women in industrialized societies. A difference in patterns of graduation by field of study, at the tertiary level, may not necessarily indicate a lack of opportunity or inequity. Many conditioning factors influence individual choices.

The same observation may hold in relation to labor market participation. Hence, value judgments about differences in outcomes or access need to be distinguished from observations of inequality in participation or graduation. A breakdown of many outcome indicators has been shown for men and women in various editions of *EAG* (i.e., student achievement, graduation rates by level and field of study, earnings and labor force participation by gender, and level of educational attainment). Examples include:

*   attitudes of boys and girls about science in the 4th grade (*EAG*, 2000);[11]
*   graduates by level of education and by field of study (various editions of *EAG*), e.g., percentage of university-level degrees in engineering, natural sciences, mathematics and computing that are awarded to women (*EAG*, 1998);[12]
*   levels of attainment in the adult population (a gender index of disparity in *EAG*, 1995, showed the extent to which women were disadvantaged relative to men in the adult population for educational attainment);[13]
*   ratio of average annual earnings by women to those of men, by level of educational attainment (1998);[14] and
*   perceived barriers to participation in job- or career-related continuing education and training, by gender, 1994–95 (IALS).[15]

3.3.   Occasional inter-group measures of inequality (spatial, socio-economic, ethnic or learning needs)

It may be argued that equity requires a removal of differences in outcomes among groups. Once inter-group differences are controlled for, any remaining differences among individuals are a function of innate ability or personal motivation and unrelated to family, social or other group-based factors. Evidence for equality of opportunity, according to this view, would be found when various groups are neither "over-represented" nor "under-represented" relative to their overall position in the population. So, for example, entry to tertiary education by a particular social group (or by men and women) should be in proportion to its size in the overall population.

Equality of opportunity should not be confused, however, with equality of intake or participation in a given level or type of education program. Even when income, prevailing social attitudes and conditioning factors, and other accessibility criteria are taken into account, there will remain important cultural, biological and psychological differences among particular groups—especially with respect to ethnicity and gender—which result in different patterns of participation in learning and the labor market. Even so, measures of participation may provide a clearer picture of the status of access to different levels or types of learning than measures of outcomes, which are confounded by a variety of determining influences.

3.3.1. Regional or spatial equality

Occasionally, indicators have been published on differences among *sub-national* jurisdictions within countries. In many countries, because responsibility for education policy is delegated to sub-national authorities, it is appropriate for some purposes to compare aspects of education for well-defined geographical areas or administrative units (states, lander, provinces, cantons, counties, local school districts, académies, etc.). Differences in funding, school processes and outcomes by geographical unit may well be of interest because national averages can disguise considerable sub-national variation. Characteristics of sub-national units may also be of international comparative interest. Differences between urban and rural areas in actual conditions of teaching, resources, class size, access to adult education, etc., can also vary widely. The main challenge encountered in making such comparisons across spatial units is to define the appropriate sub-national unit. An example of sub-national indicators was contained in *EAG* in 1996: a selection of indicators for spending per student by region[16] and for the ratio of students to teachers[17] (at both primary and secondary levels).

3.3.2. Equality and socioeconomic background

The social status of parents and the quality of the home environment are important factors in influencing students' school and learning outcomes. Education plays an important mediating role in transmitting values, as well as skills and competencies to each generation. To the extent that different social groups have unequal access to learning opportunities or endowments of human, financial and cultural capital, the outcomes for children and students from disadvantaged backgrounds can be significantly influenced. In explaining outcomes related to social background, it is difficult to separate "home" and "school" effects. Coleman (1966 and 1990), and other researchers have found that disadvantage at the beginning of formal education due to social background is exacerbated by the end of formal education.

Differences by socioeconomic group remain a major focus of attention in studies of educational equity. Arriving at a standard for comparing different social classes or socioeconomic groups at the international level is not an easy task. Usually, such comparisons require the specification of an international index of socioeconomic status (SES)[18] based on occupational data. Sometimes, income data are combined with data on occupation to calibrate measures of SES. Frequently, recourse is made to data exclusively on income or on the highest level of educational attainment as proxies for SES.

In the area of adult learning and training, significant inequalities persist related to initial education. The pattern of inequality and skill shortfall is maintained through school and into adult life. The pattern is one of higher rates of participation in continuing education and training for groups with higher levels of initial educational attainment; those with possibly the greatest need for retraining or further education are less likely to participate in such learning. The evidence suggests that work-related training serves to reinforce the inequalities created by initial education. An adult with tertiary education is more than twice as likely on average to participate in training during a 12-month period than one who has not completed secondary school (OECD, 1998). However, while this is true within countries, the least educated adults in some countries train more frequently than the most educated in others. This suggests that there is nothing inevitable about low participation among the least educated.

The effect of these differences in continuing education and training may well be compounded by inequalities in access to informal learning associated, for example, with the growing "digital divide" and the exclusion of a large sector of society from information and learning networks. In IALS, different barriers to learning (e.g., funding, motivation, etc.) have been identified, along with differences in access by group to learning and training with respect to length, content and certification.

Some recent key indicators in this area include:
- student achievement in mathematics in relation to educational resources (whether students had a dictionary, study desk or computer at home) using IEA-TIMSS data;[19]
- student achievement in mathematics at 8th grade in relation to educational attainment of parents using IEA-TIMSS data;[20] and
- participation in job-related continuing education and training in the previous year by employed adults, by highest level of educational attainment and IALS literacy level, 1994–95.[21]

3.3.3. Students with special learning needs

Still further comparisons have been made with respect to groups of students with learning needs. These groups can include not only students with different sorts of physical disabilities, but groups recognized as being in need due to social, linguistic or other "non-biological" factors. Recent work in this area has focused on the allocation of resources to these groups. Further details are provided in the chapter by Evans ("Equity Indicators Based on the Provision of Supplemental Resources for Disabled and Disadvantaged Students"). The relationship between outcomes and funding for specific "at risk" groups is only possible through a more refined breakdown of expenditure data not only by institutional and program categories, but by well-defined "at-risk" groups and targeted resources.

Examples of data used in *EAG* include:

- students at primary and secondary levels with special educational needs (e.g., disabilities, learning difficulties and disadvantages) receiving additional resources distinguished by category of special need);[22]
- ratio of students with special educational needs to teaching staff;
- students with special educational needs receiving additional resources, broken down by location (regular classes, special classes and special schools); and
- students receiving additional resources to access the curriculum as a percentage of all students in primary and lower secondary education, by cross-national categories, based on head counts (1996).[23]

3.3.4. Ethnic or minority-language groups

The growing cultural and ethnic diversity across OECD societies raises important issues for education policy-makers concerned about the integration of different groups, and the provision of opportunities for learning and advancement for those who may be at a disadvantage. It has been difficult to arrive at comparable definitions of ethnic or immigrant groups. Data on adult and student skills can be related to the linguistic family background of respondents. Indicators that have been published in the past include:

- disparities in literacy outcomes between native and non-native language speakers (IALS);[24]
- student achievement in mathematics in relation to the language spoken at home (whether students spoke the language of the test at home) using IEA-TIMSS data;[25]
- disparities in literacy outcomes between persons whose parents were born in the country and whose parents were immigrants (IALS). Similarly, disparities in literacy outcomes between persons born in the country and immigrants (IALS); and
- percentage of tertiary students enrolled who are not citizens of the country of study (*EAG*, 2000).[26]

Table 1, (pages 206–207) summarizes the development of indicators in the various areas mentioned in this section and indicates possible areas for further development (depending on the availability of data and priority to be attached to

206

Thomas Healy & David Istance

Table 1. An overview of equality indicators in Education at a Glance

	Gender	Age	Region/ spatial	Special learning need	SES	Ethnic/ linguistic
Social and economic context in the adult population						
Level of educational attainment in the adult population	R	R				
Labor force participation rate by educational attainment	R	R				
Finance, teaching resources						
Spending on education as proportion of GDP						
Expenditure per student at primary and secondary levels			EAG 1996	EAG 2000	(special)*	(special)
Teaching and other personnel employed in educational institutions	R	R				
Eligibility for public student aid at the tertiary level					EAG 2000	
Ratio of students to teaching staff			EAG 1996	EAG 1998	(special)	(special)
Access to education and training						
Rates of enrollment in various levels of primary and secondary level education	R	R		EAG 1998		
Expected educational attainment (years)	R					
Access to early childhood education and care	R	R				
Access to tertiary education	R	R				
Participation in continuing education and training	R	R				
School and learning environment						
Instruction time at primary and secondary level						
Teacher salaries	R					
Grouping of students by ability at lower secondary level						
Level of differentiation by school and program type						
Grade repetition at primary level						
Participation by parents in school activities by parents' educational attainment level						

See notes at the end of table.

Table 1. An overview of equality indicators in *Education at a Glance (continued)*

	Gender	Age	Region/ spatial	Special learning need	SES	Ethnic/ linguistic
Graduation rates						
Upper-secondary graduation rates	R	R				
Upper-secondary graduation rates—vocational/general	R	R				
Tertiary graduation rates	R	R				
Tertiary graduation rates by field of study/level	R	R				
Student learning outcomes and adult literacy						
Student achievement in mathematics and science	EAG 1998					
Progression in student achievement between 7th and 8th grades	EAG 1998					
Attitudes towards science among 4th-graders	EAG 2000					
Prose, document and quantitative literacy of adults						
Labor market outcomes						
Rate of unemployment by level of initial education (adult population)	R	R				
Earnings by level of initial education	R	R				
Rate of unemployment of recent upper-secondary and tertiary graduates	R	R				

▨ Feasible and desirable new area

☐ Not applicable, not feasible or not necessary in the near future

R (Regular) implies presentation in *EAG* every year, or in most years, since the first edition in 1992.

EAG 2000, *EAG* 1998 or *EAG* 1996 denotes the latest year for which data were supplied with respect to a given category (but the data may not be available for other years).

* *(special)* denotes "under special learning needs."

a given area). The table is not exhaustive and is intended to stimulate reflection on possible areas for priority attention.

4.   Extensions of the data over the short and medium term

The study by Blossfeld and Shavit (1993) of 13 countries linking socioeconomic background to educational attainment and "major transitions" for two cohorts (1910–60) showed:
- persistence of inequality in opportunities in most of the countries studied, as measured by the association between socioeconomic background of parents and length of schooling;
- expansion to the upper-secondary level, with bottlenecks at the tertiary level;
- effects of social origin stronger at lower transition stages, with social selection occurring earlier on; and
- that educational reform appeared to have little or no impact in 11 countries (where "educational reform" related to expansion of education at the upper-secondary level to include all of the main social groups)—the exceptions being Sweden and possibly the Netherlands.

These conclusions reinforce the need for international time-trend data as well as cohort data based on longitudinal sets. These would permit countries to benchmark their own performance and progress towards more equitable outcomes in education against "international best practices" or simply to describe patterns of inequality over time—a useful diagnostic in national policy evaluations. Moreover, marginal or "at-risk" groups—whether ethnic, social or other— tend not to be easily identified in national, let alone international, official statistics (e.g., early school dropouts, under-achieving students, adults with learning and literacy difficulties, etc.). Where a survey is involved, the problem may be related to sample size; in other cases, the data provided by schools or other administrative units may be in a format that does not distinguish among different groups. For analysis of particular cohorts over time, the relative absence of comprehensive or internationally comparable longitudinal studies means that data on lifecycle patterns of learning and equality are limited.

4.1.   Areas for further development

- *Access to pre-school or early childhood education and care.* This remains a difficult area in which to make international comparisons. Data are not readily available on the numbers attending such institutions, let alone by socioeconomic background. This remains an area to be developed.

- *The importance of schools in mediating outcomes for different groups* has been acknowledged, but this information has not been linked to outcomes. The distribution of students among different types of schools (vocational, general, comprehensive, etc.), especially at the secondary level, as well as the streaming of pupils by ability across classes or by group within classes, all have important equality outcomes.

- *The results of the OECD Program for International Student Assessment (PISA)* may throw some light on the relationship of learning environment and school context to learning outcomes. However, caution is needed in drawing conclusions from point-in-time comparisons. Ideally, analysis of progression in achievement in relation to a variety of home, school and classroom conditioning variables would be necessary, using panel data. Differences across school sectors (private, public, comprehensive and specialized vocational) can have profound implications for equality of opportunities and outcomes, as they may interact with other (social, regional, ethnic or religious) factors.

- *The interaction between family and social background and student learning outcomes.* It would be useful to obtain more and better quality information in PISA, IEA or other surveys about the family resources and home environments of students from different social backgrounds, as well as the attitudes and values promoted by home and school in different social contexts. Social capital may play an important role in determining learning outcomes for different social groups.

- *The impact on equality of public subsidies to students at the post-compulsory and especially at the tertiary levels.* It would be valuable to explore the extent to which public subsidies are effective in promoting greater equality of opportunity for students from different social and economic backgrounds. Scholarships and grants in most countries are intended to overcome social disparities and to widen access to tertiary education for students from low-income families. *EAG* 2000 has shown that, in a majority of cases, eligibility for receiving subsidies and the amount awarded are contingent on the student's family or household income (indicator B3.3). The level of subsidy and the overall rate of participation in tertiary education, however, vary considerably across countries.

- *The socioeconomic position of tertiary students* compared with the rest of the population would be useful. Data are available for many countries on the relative intake to tertiary level (especially at the university level) by socioeconomic background. Frequently, this information is provided in the form of "odds ratios" showing the probability of a particular socioeconomic group entering tertiary education, based on its position in the population as a whole.

Constructing a comparable international indicator of entry or participation in tertiary education by socioeconomic background would appear to be a feasible and relevant indicator. Proxy measures for socioeconomic background could be based on occupation, household income or labor force status (employed or unemployed).

• *Adult learning, including informal learning.* Much more extensive use could be made of *existing* IALS data for up to 19 countries (of which 17 are OECD members) to examine the access of individuals from different social, regional and linguistic backgrounds to learning opportunities; the cost and motivational barriers to further learning; and the use made of acquired skills in individuals' everyday lives.

It would be useful to gradually extend the tertiary access analysis to all levels of education (primary through tertiary) showing the probability of entering and graduating from each level in succession for different socioeconomic groups, ethnic groups and regions. Eventually, this analysis could be extended to two points in time to enable trend comparisons.

5.   A framework for comparative equity indicators of education and learning

We have outlined why we believe a high priority should now be given to the development of *descriptive* comparative indicators that can make a clear contribution to the policy process and that shed light on lifelong learning issues. The following three-way framework, we believe, goes a long way towards meeting these criteria. Despite the simplification of focusing primarily on the descriptive, there are, as in all fields of indicator development, substantial hurdles to be crossed. Some of these are also presented.

5.1.   Cross-sectional educational and learning inequalities in access/outcomes in different countries

Indicators in this category address the basic equity questions: "How equal are educational and learning opportunities in different countries?" and "How well do certain groups (e.g., class, gender, minority, age groups) fare in the learning stakes compared with their equivalents in other countries?"

One obvious set of methodological issues that arises with regard to cross-sectional patterns of education and learning relates to the precise dimensions of education/learning most relevant to equity questions as well as to questions about the availability of data on those dimensions. The pragmatic starting point would be to use data on access, participation and outcomes that already exist, at least in some countries, even if they have yet to be fully exploited in an equity perspective.

New measures and data might well be needed, especially if lifelong learning is to be adequately reflected. Expenditure equity considerations—such as the accumulated education/training expenditure *per capita* over the educational careers of different groups of learners—might also suggest a need for new data.

Much more problematic are definitions of population and socioeconomic groupings of students/learners that are both politically meaningful and can command international agreement. While definitions of age and gender are largely unproblematic, internationally agreed-upon SES specifications are far more complex, whether relating to indices of parental SES or to students' own status. Nevertheless, as this volume shows, substantial progress has already been made on these and disability/special needs categorizations. Perhaps the most problematic of all are internationally agreed-upon categories of student/learner by race and ethnicity, one of most critical yet controversial among equity dimensions.

5.2. Trends in cross-sectional inequalities over time in different countries

This category addresses questions such as "Are inequalities getting narrower or wider over time, and in which countries?" and "Are certain groups (class, gender, minority, age groups, etc.) increasingly being left behind or excluded?" These too are fundamental questions.

All the methodological issues arising in relation to the first category, above, necessarily also arise in charting trends over time. To these can be added a host of problems related to definitions and instruments that change over the course of time. There is at least one further set of methodological problems. With the passage of time, the "value" of different educational experiences and qualifications can also change, perhaps markedly. Long-term historical comparisons of the social distribution of university access, for instance, must accommodate the relatively rapid transition from "elite" to "mass" to "universal" higher education. The social meaning of university attendance *per se*, as opposed to type of program or institution, is quite different in the first case compared with the second or third. While complex, this issue too should not be regarded as insuperable.[27]

5.3. Life-cycle patterns of inequality for particular groups or cohorts

This category permits further fundamental questions to be addressed: "How far does the evidence confirm the widespread impression that those with greatest access to continuing education and training are also those who have benefited most from initial education and training?" "Which are the archetypal cases and countries in this respect and which are the exceptional?" "How wide are learning inequalities when this life-cycle perspective is adopted (as opposed to snapshots based on initial education) and what does this tell us about the partiality of measures based exclusively on the initial phase?" Little evidence is yet available on these key issues.

We focus on two thorny problem areas. First, there are the serious difficulties of gathering adequate data on continuing, especially non-formal and informal, learning in ways to permit comparisons across countries. These less tangible, diverse forms of learning are of particular relevance for older age groups, whether as adult education programs, private company or publicly organized training, social and community activities or individualized learning activities. New data collection instruments, including longitudinal sets, will probably be needed.

Second, assuming data are available, the charting of *actual* life-cycle patterns calls for retrospective summaries of learning experiences of those nearing the end of their lives. Such evidence holds relatively marginal policy (if intense scholarly) interest for it provides commentary on educational experiences largely acquired several decades earlier, rendered still more distant in times of rapid social, cultural and economic change. The challenges are indeed imposing but not insuperable. Comparisons of accumulated educational experiences by a certain age (say, 35 or 40 years) is one way forward. Another is the construction of synthetic cohorts based on different age data, parallel to those used for human capital rate-of-return analyses.

Data generated within this framework would supply "core" equity information, whereby countries could be compared on a variety of dimensions, at one point in time and through time. Such a framework does not permit direct analytical comparisons between particular features of each system linked to equity indicators, though the questions so raised attract intense interest. For example, are countries with selective secondary systems more or less egalitarian in outcomes than those with comprehensive schools? What difference does it make to the successful participation of different student groups that there is a highly structured, prescribed curriculum? Does generalized or targeted tertiary student financial aid make a difference to the social profile of the student population? Given the very large number of variables involved in making such comparisons, these can best be made, in our view, as separate *post hoc* exercises once the core descriptive data are in place. That is, it would then be possible to ask if countries that have similar educational features also share patterns of educational equity, and then to contrast the results with those patterns in other countries. These will always be indicative, rather than definitive, comparisons.

We are under few illusions about the scale of the task to be confronted in developing comparative equity indicators. This is a long-term enterprise, requiring patience and new investments of financial and intellectual resources. Yet, the challenges to be faced should not be reason for further delay. With the manifest risks of exclusion from the "knowledge societies" of the 21ˢᵗ century—and as countries return to accord equity such high priority among the different policy aims for education and learning—the need is clear. We hope that this ambitious enterprise will turn out to be one of the major achievements of a new generation of international indicator development in the next decade.

Notes

1   Both authors work in OECD's Centre for Educational Research and Innovation. This chapter expresses their personal views, rather than those of the organization or its member countries.

2   These dimensions are closely analyzed in a Center for Education Research and Innovation (CERI) project on "Learning Cities and Regions."

3   Forthcoming publication from the joint CERI/National Center on Adult Literacy (NCAL) international workshop "Lifelong Learning and New Technologies Gap: Reaching the Disadvantaged," Philadelphia, December 8–10, 1999.

4   TIMSS was conducted in 38 countries in 1995 by the International Association for the Evaluation of Educational Achievement (IEA).

5   The International Adult Literacy Survey (IALS) was carried out in 19 countries over the period 1994–98.

6   "Mathematics achievement of students in 4th and 8th grades, 1995," Indicator F1, p. 315, *EAG,* 1998; and "Change in variation in mathematics achievement as students progress from the 4th to the 8th grade, 1995," Indicator F2, p. 321, *EAG,* 1998.

7   The International Association for the Evaluation of Educational Achievement (IEA).

8   "Decomposition of variance components in mathematics achievement of 8th-graders, 1995," Indicator F3, p. 329, *EAG,* 1998.

9   "Mean scores and scores at the 5th, 25th, 75th and 95th percentiles on a scale with range 0–500 points, prose, document and quantitative literacy scales, 1994–95," Table 1.1, p. 150, OECD, Human Resources Development Canada and Statistics Canada (1997).

10 "Intergenerational change in completion of tertiary education," Indicator A2, p. 46, *EAG,* 1998.

11 "Mean achievement of fourth-grade students, by gender and attitudes toward science (1995)," Indicator F1, *EAG,* 2000.

12 "Percentage of university-level degrees in engineering, natural sciences and mathematics and computing that are awarded to women (1998)," Indicator C4.5, *EAG,* 2000.

13 "Index of gender differences in education," Indicator C02 (B), p. 27, *EAG,* 1995.

14 "Mean annual earnings of women as a percentage of mean annual earnings of men 30 to 44 and 55 to 64 years of age, by level of educational attainment (1998)," Indicator E5.2, *EAG,* 2000.

15 "Perceived barriers to participation in job- or career-related continuing education and training, by gender, 1994–95," Indicator C7.7, *EAG,* 2000.

16 "Inter-regional disparities in expenditure on educational services per student," Indicator F3-R, p. 74, *EAG,* 1996.

17 "Ratio of students to teaching staff" by region, Indicator P32, p. 103, *EAG,* 1996.

18 SES may be defined as the relative position of a family or individual in an hierarchical social structure, based on their access to, or control over, wealth, prestige and power. SES is indexed by occupation. In calculating such a composite index, the results of the International Socio-Economic Index (Ganzeboom, de Graaf & Treiman, 1992) have been used. This study uses

components such as occupational prestige, educational attainment and/or income to assign an SES score to each occupational title. Since these are established, knowing a person's occupation allows the assignment of an SES score to the individual even in the absence of data on income. This is the basic approach adopted in the OECD Program for International Student Assessment (PISA) project. Since the SES of students is the SES of their parents (or guardians or other head-of-household), students are asked to report on the occupation of these members of their family.

19 "Socio-economic background and student achievement in 4th grade," Indicator F4, p. 330, *EAG*, 1998.
20 "The social context and student achievement at the 8th-grade level," Indicator F5, p. 308, *EAG*, 1997.
21 "Participation in job-related continuing education and training in the previous year by employed adults by highest level of educational attainment and IALS literacy level, 1994–95," Indicator C7.4, *EAG*, 2000.
22 "Students with special educational needs (disabilities, learning difficulties and disadvantage)," Indicator C6, p. 221, *EAG*, 1998.
23 "Students receiving additional resources to access the curriculum as a percentage of all students in primary and lower secondary education, by cross-national categories—based on head counts (1996)," Indicator C6.1, *EAG,* 2000.
24 Tables 3.7A through 3.7G (pp. 169–172) in OECD, 1997.
25 "Socio-economic background and student achievement in 4th grade," Indicator F4, p. 333, *EAG,* 1998.
26 "Percentage of tertiary students enrolled who are not citizens of the country of study (1998)," Indicator C5.1, *EAG*, 2000.
27 It represents the parallel methodological difficulty to that confronted by social mobility research with structural changes in occupational "marginals:" the "mobility" generated by growing relative numbers of professionals and white-collar workers in the labor force, and shrinking blue-collar semi- and unskilled positions, which has little to do with society's openness. It should similarly be possible to identify controls for changing educational "marginals."

References

Atkinson A.B., "The Distribution of Income in the UK and OECD Countries in the Twentieth Century," *Oxford Review of Economic Policy, 15*(4) pp. 56–75, 1999.
Blossfeld H.P., Shavit, Y., *Persistent Inequality: Changing Educational Attainment in Thirteen Countries*, Westview Press, Inc., Boulder (Colo.) 1993.
Carnoy M., Castells M., *Sustainable Flexibility: A Prospective Study on Work, Family and Society in the Information Age*, CERI/OECD, Document on General Distribution, OCDE/ GD, p. 48, 1997.
Coleman J.S., *Equality of Educational Opportunity*, U.S. Government Printing Office, Washington, DC, 1966.
Coleman J.S., *Equality and Achievement in Education, Social Inequality Series,* Westview Press, London, 1990.
Ganzeboom H.B.G., De Graaf P., Treiman, D.J. (with De Leeuw J.), "A Standard International Socio-Economic Index of Occupational Status," *Social Science Research, 21*(1), pp. 1–56, 1992.

Husen T., *Social Influences on Educational Attainment: Research Perspectives on Educational Equality*, OECD, Paris, 1975.

Jencks C., et al., *Inequality: A reassessment of the effect of family and schooling in America*, Harper Row, New York, 1972.

OECD, *Education at a Glance (EAG)* and *Education Policy Analysis (EPA)*, Paris, different years.

OECD, *Knowledge Management in the Learning Society*, Paris, 2000.

OECD, *Human Capital Investment: An International Comparison*, Paris, 1998.

OECD, *Education and Equity in OECD Countries*, Paris, 1997.

OECD, *Lifelong Learning for All*, report prepared for the occasional meeting of OECD Ministers of Education, Paris, January 1996.

OECD, *Education, Inequality and Life Chances*, (2 vols.), Paris, 1975.

OECD, Vol. 4, "Group Disparities in Educational Participation and Achievement," and Vol. 7, "Education and Distribution of Income," technical monographs prepared for the June 1970 Conference on Policies for Educational Growth, Paris, 1971.

OECD, *Ability and Educational Opportunity*, Paris, 1961.

OECD/Human Resources Development Canada, *Literacy Skills for the Knowledge Society*, Ottawa/Paris, 1997.

OECD/Human Resources Development Canada, *Literacy, Economy and Society*, Ottawa/Paris, 1995.

Chapter 8

Monitoring Educational Disparities in Less Developed Countries

Vittoria Cavicchioni
UNESCO Institute for Statistics, Paris

Albert Motivans
UNESCO Institute for Statistics, Paris

Concern about educational disparities in less developed countries[1] has emerged as a key issue in development policy debates in the 1990s. A diverse group of voices has called out for greater equality in access to learning opportunities, especially among population groups that are traditionally excluded, such as girls, linguistic and ethnic minorities, rural populations and the disabled. The concern for equity starts with access to primary education (as 99 of every 100 out-of-school children live in less developed countries), but extends to progress in school and to equitable distribution in terms of successful learning outcomes.

At the same time, educational disparity is hardly a new development issue. What accounts for the renewed interest? The increased attention has resulted from the convergence of human rights and poverty reduction strategies that place stress on equitable education systems to maintain individual rights as well as to contribute to broader social goals. In other words, education is more widely recognized as a basic human right and its equitable distribution plays an important role in ensuring economic growth and social cohesion.

The increased attention paid to educational equity comes at a time when global trends threaten to increase inequalities between rich and poor countries. Economic globalization, rapid advances in information and communications technology, and the move towards knowledge-based societies present new opportunities for education systems to address equity issues. However, there is also deep concern that differences in access to information and skills will further polarize rich and poor countries. The gap between countries that are able to convert these developments to their advantage and those that are trapped by lack of opportunity has become increasingly evident in the 1990s.

As well, the contribution of international assistance to development programs has diminished. While the share of international development assistance for primary education has increased, overall levels of aid have declined in the 1990s.

High levels of income inequality across households, although difficult to measure, remain a persistent issue. Cross-national studies show that while rates of income inequality are declining in most countries, the levels are still rather high and reflect sharp differentiation within countries. There is also concern that educational inequalities may arise due to changing public and private roles in the provision of education—especially with regard to decentralization, privatization and other policies that place greater fiscal and governance responsibilities on communities and households.

Assessing equity in education has become a more complex undertaking. The expansion of primary enrollments has continued, although at a slower pace in the 1980s and 1990s. And as a number of less developed countries have made major steps towards universal primary enrollment, this would seem to imply that equity in access to primary education has improved. However, progress in reducing disparities has been uneven, and reflects only part of the picture. Even if enrollment levels are higher, regular attendance and smooth progression may be problematic, and learning outcomes less than satisfactory. Problems also remain with access at pre-primary, secondary and tertiary levels of education. Moreover, it is not only a question of access *per se*, but of equal opportunity to a good quality education. Access, traditionally measured by school enrollment ratios, often fails to reflect these important aspects. And the evidence on equity in process and outcome indicators is scattered and often only from a single point in time.

Thus, the need for more accurate, reliable and policy-relevant equity measures in less developed countries is growing. First, as a result of increased international attention, there is a rising demand for evidence-based policy information on equity issues. The introduction of policies such as privatization, cost-recovery and decentralization in public services has the potential to widen disparities in education. Second, there is the need to monitor equity in light of emerging global trends and the growing "digital divide." Third, with rising enrollments, there is a need to study equity in processes and outputs in order to better guide education policy responses. Further efforts to elaborate group differences and interrelationships are essential to understanding how factors interact to influence participation, completion and learning outcomes. Moreover, assessments of system efficiency and learning are essential to inform policy, particularly where there is a low demand for education.

This chapter is divided into three sections. The first examines the rising prominence of education and equity on the development agenda, and the issues underlying the relationships among educational disparities, rights and public policy. The second section presents evidence of disparities in participation, progression and achievement in less developed countries, focusing on primary education. This focus is taken because many consider the successful completion of primary schooling essential to meeting basic literacy and numeracy needs; moreover, it is a necessary step to continuing to higher levels of education. These examples incorporate a wide range of measurement approaches that include global, regional and country-specific perspectives of educational disparities in developing countries. The final section concludes with a view towards improving the links between indicators and policies, and measuring different aspects of educational equity.

1. Educational disparities, rights and public policy

The emergence of educational disparity as a key development priority has been led by several trends. First, there has been the increasing attention given to the guarantee of education as a basic human right. This has been reflected by a wide range of international conferences and conventions that have created greater awareness of the need to combat educational disparities among girls, the disabled and others facing disadvantage. Second, the 1990s have witnessed the consolidation of more social-centered development approaches and poverty reduction strategies among multi-lateral lending organizations.

From a rights perspective, there has been a long effort to promote social and economic rights alongside the more traditionally conceived civil and political rights, although the effort to implement this vision has faced great challenges. The right to education, broadly defined, was affirmed in the Universal Declaration of Human Rights (UDHR), which was adopted more than 50 years ago. Although not legally binding on states, signatories agree to ensure the provision of education without cost. Article 26 of the Declaration states that "education shall be free, at least in the elementary and fundamental stages . . . education shall be directed to the full development of the human personality. . . "

While the UDHR is not enforceable in the way that, for example, the European Convention on Human Rights is, it does provide internationally accepted minimum standards (Newell, 1991). It can be used together with other relevant international instruments to test and help challenge laws, policies and practices.

The rapid expansion of primary enrollments that began in some parts of the world in the 1950s and 1960s was spurred by pressures from social groups for equity in education, which also resulted in the Convention Against Discrimination in Education (UNESCO, 2000, p. 42). This convention, adopted in 1960, specifically referenced discrimination not only based on race or gender, but also by geographic location, national or social origin, and the household economic situation of children and their families.

The expansion of educational opportunities, while a positive step in terms of greater access, saw the rise of disparities *within* educational systems. Often only a select number of children received education from the most-qualified teachers and had access to learning materials in short supply. For many children, the content of education was below par, and upon completion many were still left without basic skills.

More recently, the Convention on the Rights of the Child (1989) acquired the status of international law in 1990. It is the most widely ratified rights instrument in the world, covering every country except Somalia and the United States. And unlike the UDHR, signatories are legally bound to uphold the articles. In the Convention, the state's responsibilities with regard to education provision are stated:

> State Parties recognize the right of the child to education, and with a view to achieving this right progressively and on the basis of equal opportunity, they shall. . . make primary education compulsory and free to all. . . . (Convention on the Rights of the Child, Article 28)

The impact of rights instruments in developing countries has been difficult to measure. While the obligation to ensure free and equitable education rests with national governments, it is not always clearly implemented. Some argue, as in the case of the Convention on the Rights of the Child, that it allows governments to fulfill rights according to their level of resources; thus, they can postpone, for example, provision of free universal primary education (UNICEF International Child Development Centre (ICDC), 1999, p. 13). Also, rights that have gained the status of international law are not always reflected by national legislation. And even when international rights instruments are reflected by national legal systems, the level of political commitment to implementing legislation has been marginal (Save the Children, 1999, p. 2). Nevertheless, Mehrotra (1998, p. 14) suggests that the level of political will among countries was key to achieving the rapid expansion of primary school enrollments. National and local commitment to improving education and the provision of sufficient levels of resources were seen as more important contributory factors than the presence of compulsory school legislation.

Aside from the issue of compliance of state parties to rights instruments, an important aspect of the Convention and other instruments is that they recognize the multi-faceted nature of the educational process. For example, the Convention notes that the educational system should be concerned with more than simply the individual and social economic returns to be expected from education. The Convention takes a more holistic approach to education and child development:

State Parties agree that the education of the child shall be directed to
. . . the development of the child's personality, talents, and mental and
physical abilities to their fullest potential. . . (Convention on the Rights
of the Child, Article 29)

These goals, in particular with regard to the importance of educational
quality rather than simple access, were emphasized at the World Conference
on Education for All, which took place in Jomtien, Thailand, in 1990. The
right to basic education was at the core of the Declaration on Education for
All. These principles were reiterated at the follow-up meeting in Dakar,
Senegal, in April 2000. Here, special emphasis was placed on ameliorating
inequities in access to education and ensuring that all children have access to
educational opportunities of measurable quality.

The 1990s were marked by a number of international conventions and
conferences that sought to address educational disparities among diverse groups
considered to be at higher risk of exclusion from the benefits of education.
These have included the World Summit for Children (1990), the World
Conference on Special Needs Education in Salamanca (1994), the World
Conference on Women in Beijing (1995) and the International Conference on
Child Labor (1997), among others.

Along with the growth of rights-based approaches, there has also been a
wider recognition of the importance of the social side of the development balance
sheet. The work of Richard Jolly, Amartya Sen and others in the 1980s expanded
the vision of human development and well-being from a narrow focus on macroeconomic trends and income poverty to one more broadly encompassing the
concepts of human "capabilities" and "exclusion." One result has been the
wider recognition of the role of education in enabling people to participate fully
in economic, political and social processes.

Poverty reduction frameworks that build equity in as part of the development
process are recognized as key factors in promoting economic growth and other
positive externalities, such as better social cohesion. Taking account of the
structural, social, and human aspects of development, rather than analytical
frameworks that largely focus on macroeconomic measures, has long been
debated and is increasingly apparent in multi-lateral development strategies.
The World Bank's Comprehensive Development Framework (Wolfensohn, 1999,
p. 13) suggests that the role of education is central to a holistic and strategic
approach to poverty reduction: ". . . all agree that the single most important key
to development and to poverty alleviation is education."

Thus, among multi-lateral agencies, education is recognized as an essential
requirement for a satisfactory level of well-being, although, for practical purposes,
they limit this view to the individual and social returns of education. Minimizing
inequity in education is also important to economic growth and development

because sustained poverty reduction will not be possible without social stability. Poverty reduction strategies target investment or specific actions, particularly in the area of education, as needed to enable the poor to share in the benefits from growth, increase their capabilities and well-being, and reduce their vulnerabilities to risks. How greater efforts to "reach the unreached"—especially those that stress local participation and changing public and private roles—will be reflected in policy formation remains to be seen.

2.   Monitoring equity in the educational process

What needs to be monitored in terms of educational disparities and how best to monitor them? In less developed countries, disparities in access to education have been typically monitored using a traditional set of indicators that are disaggregated by gender, geographic region and so on. However, equity related to differences in environmental factors also influences access to education, school progression and learning outcomes. School-level factors reflect educational quality, i.e., the best-equipped schools, the best-trained teachers, etc. Non-school factors also play an important role. For example, household resources, parental attitudes or their educational attainment can influence access, progression and learning outcomes.

In terms of cross-national comparisons, indicator development has been more or less predicated by the availability of administrative data. Certain population characteristics, such as gender and location, are regularly collected through school surveys. However, the collection of other data, not to mention the conceptual definition of other variables, (e.g., income, poverty) or the identification of special groups (ethnic groups, disabled children), has been more problematic. Although national statistics are often disaggregated by geographical regions or by urban/rural areas—and sometimes by socioeconomic categories, ethnic groups or linguistic and minority groups—international standardization is still elusive. Other types of approaches, typically at the regional or national level, such as household surveys and qualitative research, allow for more in-depth analysis often at the expense of cross-national comparability.

This section focuses on primary education and examines several examples of measures of equity and participation, grade progression, completion and learning outcomes at the global and national levels.

2.1.   Equity and participation in education

The starting point for examining equity issues in less developed countries concerns access to and participation in primary education. Primary education is typically for children 6 to 11 years of age, and in most countries is considered "compulsory and free." However, the idea of "compulsory and free" education appears more often as a declaration of principle than as a reality.

Figure 1 shows the trend in net enrollment ratios in primary education in less developed countries from 1970 to 2000. Impressive progress has been registered in the last several decades, as the proportion of primary-age children enrolled has increased from 63 to 85 percent. However, these figures show that 15 percent of children in less developed regions (12 percent of boys and 19 percent of girls) are still out of school, making universal primary education still a distant goal, particularly for girls. Moreover, as more countries near universal primary enrollment, the pace of improvement has slowed measurably in the last decade.

UNESCO's Institute for Statistics (UIS) estimates for the year 2000 show that 88 million primary school-age children are not enrolled in school.[2] Great inequalities exist between regions and by gender. About half of the total number out of school are from sub-Saharan Africa (43 million) and about 40 percent (34 million) are from Southern Asia. Sixty percent of these children are girls.

Despite impressive global progress, gender inequalities are still significant in certain areas and regions. Figure 2 (page 224) shows net enrollment ratios in primary school by region and gender. The probability of not being enrolled is highest for children in sub-Saharan Africa, followed by those in Southern Asia and the Arab States. In all of these regions, girls are more likely to be out of

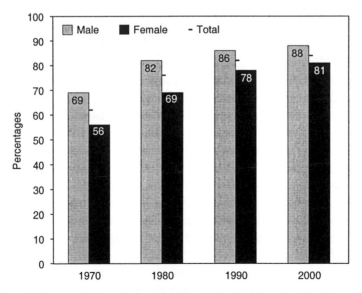

Figure 1. Net enrollment ratios in primary education in less developed regions by gender, 1970–2000 (Source: UIS estimates and projections of net enrollment ratios, April 1999)

Note: These data refer to 97 less developed countries. The list of countries and the composition of regions is cited in UNESCO (2000, p. 112).

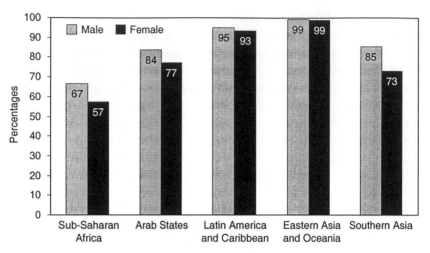

Figure 2. Estimated net enrollment ratios in primary education by gender and region, 2000 (Source: UIS estimates and projections of net enrollment ratios, April 1999)

Note: These data refer to 97 less developed countries. The list of countries and the composition of regions is cited in UNESCO (2000, p. 112).

school than boys. In sub-Saharan Africa, the proportion of girls in the out-of-school population has increased slightly during the last decade, and the trend is projected to continue for the next decade.

However, there are often large disparities among different countries within regions. Thus, in Southern African countries, disparities in education access and participation are often said to be in "favor" of girls. This disparity may in fact be a real discrimination against boys, being more responsive than girls to the demand for child labor. Gender parity and signs of advantage for girls are found in a number of Latin American and Caribbean countries. While net enrollment ratios show that boys are slightly more likely to be enrolled than girls, in most countries of the region, girls drop out less, achieve better learning outcomes and have a higher transition rate to secondary schooling (UNICEF, 1999).

Some consider that socially and culturally, the school effort is seen as something more appropriate for a girl's image than a boy's. The fact that most teachers in basic education are women fails to convey a strong or "male" enough model to the boys (*ibid*). At the secondary level in many deprived areas of developed countries, boys—often bound to some unattractive technical tracks—appear more frequently as "at-risk" students.

Another aspect of global disparity both in terms of regions and gender is illustrated by literacy levels. Sharp disparities are found in literacy levels among less developed regions. According to UNESCO/UIS estimates and projections of literacy, in the year 2000, about three-quarters of the population in less developed regions are literate. However, the proportion of literate adults ranges from almost 90 percent in Latin America, the Caribbean, Eastern Asia and Oceania to 60 percent of the population in sub-Saharan Africa to just over 50 percent in Southern Asia.

The picture is somewhat more optimistic if one considers the younger cohorts. Thus, for the age group 15–24, the overall literacy rate is 85 percent. Significant differences still exist among regions, with literacy rates varying from 70 percent in Southern Asia to 98 percent in developing Eastern Asia and Oceania. In the group of the least developed countries, the rate is close to 64 percent. Gender disparities are reduced, with a female/male literacy ratio of 0.91 compared with 0.81 for the adult age group (men and women 15 years and older.

UNESCO estimates of literacy rates are based on the results of population censuses, which are carried out only every five or ten years, or even less frequently in most developing countries. At the international level, only global comparisons are made. Figure 3 shows literacy rates among urban and rural populations for a selection of less developed countries. The figure shows that for all countries considered, literacy levels are higher in urban than in rural areas. Literacy data also show that gender disparities are higher in countries where the literacy level is low. Rates are generally higher among men, and relative gender disparities are higher in rural than in urban areas.

These generalizations should not hide the fact that persistent pockets of illiteracy are found in urban areas as well. Areas of poverty and exclusion exist

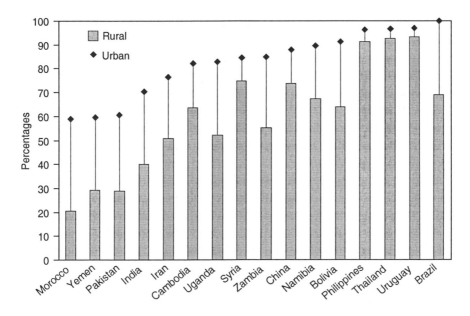

Figure 3. Adult literacy rates by location in selected countries, early 1990s (Source: UIS data base, from national censuses)

in large urban areas in developed countries; for instance, in North America, as noted by Douglas Cochrane in Chapter 15. In less developed countries, Denzil Saldanha (1999) has described the difficulties that literacy programs face in urban areas of relatively high literacy (70 percent and over) and rural areas within underdeveloped regions in India. In high-literacy urban areas, there seems to be a "saturation effect," with low growth in literacy rates and residual illiteracy difficult to eradicate. On the other hand, the rural areas (with literacy rates below 45 percent) are regions of mass illiteracy with particularly low levels of female literacy.

In high-literacy urban areas, non-literates are typically older women, the homeless and recent migrants who are difficult to reach. The situation is comparably more favorable to literacy campaigns in the regions of medium-literacy and in rural areas, where illiterates constitute a majority; this mass base helps to facilitate mobilization of the population. The need to modify the campaign approach was noted in regions where gender, community/caste and class relations reinforce each other (*ibid*).

In India, as in other developing countries, addressing disparities between urban and rural zones is recognized as a challenge. Programs are more readily targeted regionally/geographically, as in the case of literacy campaigns, but the more individualized (and thus, cost-intensive) approach is needed to address disadvantages that are more difficult to identify or in areas with higher living standards. Moreover, sustainable change often requires intervention that goes beyond the narrow scope of the educational system to a more macro-level approach. It is not possible to confront mass illiteracy in low-literacy areas without major socioeconomic interventions, such as land reform, access to income-generation schemes and addressing issues of the status of women.

Sufficient levels of public and private resources, of course, are vital to the effectiveness of an educational system. As shown in Figure 4 (page 227), in the sub-Saharan African countries with the lowest GNP per capita, most pupils are unlikely to complete primary education. At the same time, these figures show that resources are a necessary but not sufficient condition for achievement in the educational system. For example, despite the high GNP per capita in Brazil relative to other less developed countries, the average pupil has a probability of staying in school for about 11 years.[3] This is also true in the Philippines, Swaziland and Iran, where the GNP per capita is markedly less.

2.2   Equity and school progression

Universal primary education is not the only challenge for many countries. Late entry into school, repetition and dropping out—events that influence successful learning outcomes—are prevalent in certain less developed countries. School-based administrative data that record these flows are

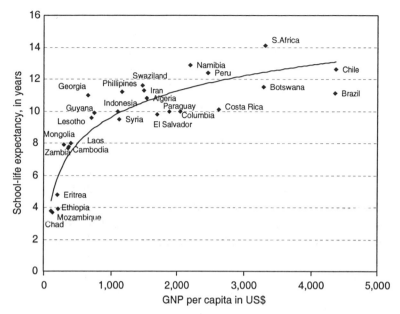

Figure 4. GNP per capita and school-life expectancy, in selected developing countries, mid-1990s (Source: UIS database)

collected as part of annual surveys and can often be disaggregated by gender or location.

As highlighted by UNESCO statistics based on these administrative data, a high proportion of pupils who enter primary schooling do not complete it or even reach grade 5.[4] In regions like Southern Asia, sub-Saharan Africa and Latin America and the Caribbean, one-third of the cohort of children who entered grade 1 in 1994 did not reach grade 5 (Education for All Forum [EFA], 1998). The low overall survival rate to grade 5 in the Latin America/Caribbean region is unusual in a region that, with respect to economic development and access to school, is more advanced than the other two regions. The pupils who drop out of school are likely not to have mastered basic literacy skills and thus face higher risks of marginalization.

Gender differences in survival rates are slight. For the less developed regions as a whole, the survival rate is 76 percent for boys and 74 percent for girls (*ibid*). These differences are most pronounced in Southern Asia (67 and 62 percent, respectively), are practically nil in sub-Saharan Africa and are in favor of girls in the Latin America/Caribbean region.

Educational attainment ratios, calculated on the total school-age population instead of only on the cohort who actually entered primary education, as in the survival rate, show lower levels of gender disparity. This illustrates that in many countries the central problem for girls is access to school rather than progression or performance. This conclusion can also be reached by comparing two measures:

the school-life expectancy as defined earlier and the school-survival expectancy (UNESCO, 1995; UNESCO, 1997). To simplify the relationship between these two measures, it can be said that the school-survival expectancy is basically a school-life expectancy for children who have actually gotten into school.[5] In countries where all children get into school, as in more developed countries, the two measures are equal. Available data show that for countries characterized by low levels of access to school, the disparities in favor of boys are more pronounced when measured with school-life expectancy than with school-survival expectancy. In other words, once girls get into school, their "survival" in the system may be expected to be as good or better than that of boys.

Although data collected by international organizations like UNESCO have the advantage of covering a large number of countries, they present two major limitations. First, they are generally collected at the macro level, i.e., consisting of national mean averages; second, as they are based on administrative data, it is not possible to directly analyze the relationships between education and other variables, such as income, socioeconomic categories, etc. For this type of analysis—which is more relevant to the study of disparities and equity—household or individual data collected by sample surveys are necessary. Several examples of possible analyses using household survey data are presented below.

Socioeconomic disparities are among the most important factors underlying access to and smooth progression in education. However, as noted earlier, there are significant obstacles to the measurement of income and expenditure, particularly when attempting cross-national comparisons. Analyses of enrollment and graduation in secondary and tertiary education by "social origin" are regularly carried out in some developed countries, and the results published as part of annual school survey results. As for developing countries, information on the socioeconomic status (SES), educational attainment or occupation of parents is rarely collected in the annual school surveys.

One approach to overcoming these difficulties is through the use of more readily available indicators to serve as a proxy for the SES of the household. One example of this is the "asset index,"[6] which was first used as a proxy for household wealth as part of a study of educational attainment in Southern Asia (Filmer & Pritchett, 1998). Further elaboration of this approach was applied to the analysis of a series of cross-national Demographic and Health Surveys (DHS), allowing for the analysis of overall patterns in enrollment and attainment of children by different characteristics. This study compiled household-level data on educational attainment from the DHS conducted in 41 countries (Filmer, 1999).

The results echoed those of the national aggregates in that, generally, gender disparity in educational attainment is mostly in favor of boys. Such disparities are higher in poorer countries and, within these countries, are higher among the poorest parts of the population. At the same time, school attainment is higher for girls than for boys in some Latin American and Caribbean countries (e.g.,

Brazil, Colombia, Nicaragua and the Dominican Republic). Girls attained higher levels of education than boys in certain Southern African countries (e.g., Namibia, Kenya, Rwanda and Tanzania), and are practically at the same level as boys in Asian countries, such as the Philippines and Indonesia.

The study showed that low primary school-level attainment among the poor is driven by two distinct patterns of enrollment and dropout. In the case of Southern Asian and Western and Central African countries, many of the poor never enroll in school, and those who do very rapidly drop out. About 40 percent of those who enroll do not complete grade 1 and only 25 percent complete grade 5. In Latin America, primary enrollment is almost universal, but dropouts are so high that the median attainment by the poor is lower in Latin America than in certain Western African countries.

On average, figures show that in countries where there is a significant gender gap, it is wider in terms of enrollment than in terms of attainment of a given grade, suggesting that once girls are given access to school they generally progress at the same rate as boys. Another important finding is that the "wealth gaps" in attainment vary enormously across countries.[7] The gaps are very high in Southern Asia (e.g., Bangladesh and Nepal), high in Latin America and Western/Central Africa (e.g., Benin, Burkina Faso, Chad, Central African Republic, Niger, Senegal, Togo, etc.) and low in Eastern/Southern Africa (e.g., Kenya, Tanzania and Zimbabwe).

Niger is a country with high levels of disparities between rich and poor, and between girls and boys. As shown in Figure 5, gender and household wealth can have a compound effect on the levels of disparity in enrollments and progression through primary education. Data from a DHS survey in 1997 show

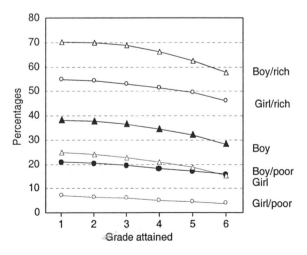

Figure 5. Educational attainment by grade, by gender and wealth, Niger, 1997 (percentage of 15- to 19-year-olds) (Source: Derived from Filmer [1999])

that boys were more than two times as likely (among low- and middle-SES households) to attain five grades than girls. Children from "rich" households were almost three times as likely to attain five grades compared to children from the "poor" and "middle" households.

Comparing these results with those from an earlier DHS study conducted in 1992 shows that the situation has worsened. Disparities based on household wealth as well as gender tended to increase. A greater proportion of both girls and boys from high-SES households reached grade 5, while among those in low-SES households, only the proportion of boys increased slightly.

A report on the education situation in Niger, prepared for the EFA 2000 Assessment, acknowledges that the goal of universal primary education is still elusive, despite slight progress in the 1990s (République du Niger, 1999). Globally, the gross enrollment ratio has increased less than one point per year since 1990, to reach just 32 percent in 1998–99. The gender parity index of this ratio has improved, from 0.57 to 0.65. This progress is appreciable considering that during the same period the share of public primary education expenditure on GNP has decreased (from 2.0 to 1.7 percent); this suggests an increase in efficiency of the system, but also a greater inequity if private efforts have to compensate for decreasing public resources. Disparities are considerable among geographical/administrative regions and between urban and rural areas. For example, the gross enrollment ratio is 52 percent in urban areas compared to 25 percent in rural areas. The gender parity indices are 0.87 and 0.52, respectively.

A certain improvement is also registered in indicators of female participation and achievement in literacy programs. This improvement has been attributed to the introduction of literacy centers solely for women. Improvements have also been noted in the internal efficiency of the education system. School wastage, defined as the pupil years spent on repetition and drop-out, seems to have been reduced from 1989–90 to 1997–98. The repetition rate decreased slightly during the 1990s, from 15.2 to 13.4 percent, with reductions greater for girls (-2.1 points) than for boys (-1.1).

Other studies on the relationship of school access and progression with household income have been conducted in Latin America and the Caribbean. The UN Economic Commission for Latin America and the Caribbean (ECLAC) has elaborated some analyses of educational attainment by SES based on the results of national household surveys. These analyses suggest that despite high levels of enrollment and graduation, there will be major shortfalls in rural areas. In urban areas, by contrast, the goal of achieving a fourth-grade completion rate of more than 80 percent for all children, and a primary education completion rate of more than 70 percent, will have been met overall, and in certain cases exceeded (ECLAC, 1998).

With regard to socioeconomic stratification, by the end of the 1990s, there will have been a slight narrowing of the gaps across different groups.

Nonetheless, children from the poorest 25 percent of all households will still be at a considerable disadvantage in relation to the average and higher income households. The countries with the highest levels of inequality in income distribution face difficulties in providing all children with minimum educational requirements (*ibid*).

In the ECLAC studies, income groups derived from household surveys are used as a measure of SES categories. Incidence analysis is used to assess equity in the completion of four years of primary school across quartiles of household income. A summary measure—"index of inequality"—is then constructed based on the cross-classification by educational attainment and income quartile of the households.[8] As shown in Table 1, the index provides a useful comparison of trends in inequality over time and across countries.

Brazil presents an important case study from the South American region— first, because the size of its population and primary enrollments represent half

Table 1. Percentage of children aged 12–13 years who have completed at least four years of schooling, whether or not they are currently attending school, by household income quartile

| Country | Year | Total | Income quartiles | | | | Index of inequality |
			Q1	Q2	Q3	Q4	
Brazil	1990	63.8	42.3	65.3	82.3	90.9	34
	1996	71.5	52.4	76.2	86.8	95.0	29
Costa Rica	1990	85.5	79.3	86.9	90.6	93.0	9
	1997	86.0	83.4	84.1	85.3	97.1	13
Honduras	1990	78.4	75.1	72.2	81.3	91.0	16
	1997	85.8	82.3	83.3	91.6	90.0	6
Paraguay	1990	91.8	87.3	91.1	95.3	94.3	4
	1995	89.4	81.4	88.1	96.6	95.9	10

Source: ECLAC (1998), Table V.6, On the basis of special tabulations of household survey data collected in urban areas

of the total in South America; second, because the extent of disparities varies widely by region. According to the EFA report, the median number of years of attainment has increased from 3.3 nationally in 1990 to 4.4 in 1996 (INEP, 1999). In the same period, the median number of years changed in favor of women, from 5.1 to 5.7 for men and from 4.9 to 6.0 for women.

Obviously it is not possible to intervene with policy measures on the basis of average values that conceal enormous geographic and socioeconomic disparities. The median number of years of educational attainment varies from 6.6 in the Southeast region to 4.4 in the Northeast, which is the most disadvantaged region of the country. The net enrollment ratio in basic education (grades 1–8) varies from 96 percent in the South to 89 percent in the Northeast. The repetition rates in the first grade are 7 percent in the Southeast compared to 24 percent in the Northeast. Data on teachers' wages show similar variation: A primary

school teacher in the Southeast region earns almost three times the salary of a
teacher in the Northeast region.

Within the Northeast region itself, large disparities exist among different
economic categories. Filmer and Pritchett's analyses of results from the DHS
conducted in 1991 and 1996 illustrate certain aspects of these disparities. In
both years and in all categories, grade 5 attainment is higher for women than
for men. As in many Latin American countries, the disparities are at the
disadvantage of boys who tend to drop out of school too early, often to enter the
labor market or to join the ranks of street children. Even in a poor region like
the Northeast, large gaps can be observed between the poor and the middle
and rich categories.

There has been a considerable improvement for children across household
wealth categories between the two periods, despite the persistent gap between
the poorest and better-off households. The share of each category in this progress
is confirmed by data referring more precisely to the shortfall for completion of
grade 5, as illustrated in Figure 6. The overall shortfall, or difference between
an optimum situation where all enrolled children complete five grades and the
number actually completing five grades, was reduced from 65 to 52 percent
during this period. In other words, the share of children completing five grades
increased from 35 to 48 percent. However, this progress did not benefit children
from different backgrounds equally.

Figure 6 shows the proportion of non-completers by wealth category. It
indicates that those who benefited most were children from the richest category
(their share of total non-completers dropping from 17 to 3 percent) and the
middle segments (their share falling from 34 to 16 percent) of the population.
While the number of children from poor households reaching grade 5 increased

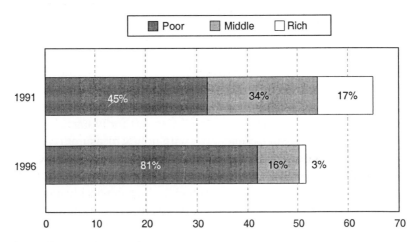

Figure 6. Proportion of the shortfall in grade 5 completion, by income category in Northeast
Brazil, 1991 and 1996 (Source: Derived from Filmer [1999])

during the study period, it was at a much slower rate than children from other groups. The share of total non-completers from poor households grew sharply, from 45 to 81 percent. This is evidence of the "queuing effect," which suggests that the poor are the last to benefit from the expansion of public services, such as primary education (Vandemoortele, 2000, p. 12).

This overall improvement can be seen as a result of the different measures that Brazil has taken to increase school attendance in difficult areas, either in cooperation with international organizations (the World Bank in the case of the *Projecto Nordeste)* or with state and municipal governments (INEP, 1999). The Northeast project was launched to correct the extremely disadvantaged situation of the Northeast region. The project consisted of the application of substantial resources to municipal and State programs of reforms, school construction, teacher training and school equipment.

The Brazilian government actually pursues several such strategies:

- To reduce the phenomenon of exclusion due to economic reasons, a system of scholarships (*Bolsa Escola*), linked to school attendance, has been established by several city governments to supplement the revenues of the families of poor children (*ibid*).
- The *Fundo Nacional de Manutenção e Desenvolvimiento de Ensino Fundamental e Valorização do Magisterio* (FUNDEF) aims for a more equitable distribution of federal resources.

The latest school survey seems to show that this second strategy is effective, as the growth of primary enrollments in the poorest regions is higher than in the rest of the country. However, these results should be interpreted cautiously. The EFA report also indicates that because the incentives are allocated proportionally to the number of primary pupils in states and municipalities, the significant increase in the number of pupils in primary education may be due to the tendency to report pre-primary pupils as primary enrollments. In fact, statistics on pre-school enrollments show a corresponding decline.

2.3. Equity and learning achievement

Finally, we turn to monitoring equity in learning outcomes. While measures of school attendance and completion are important, the outcomes of the educational process represent the real goal of the educational system. However, the measurement process is a complex and often difficult task; therefore, deriving conclusions about the equitable distribution of learning outcomes is also difficult.

The growing importance of assessment of learning achievement in more developed countries has been reflected by the large number of national assessments carried out in the 1990s. International initiatives include the Third International Mathematics and Sciences Studies (TIMSS) in 1995 and 1999, the latter of which included 41 countries (although none from the less developed countries). The nature of assessments has also become more comprehensive, often going beyond measures of traditional academic subjects (e.g., literacy and numeracy) to encompass "functional literacy" and "life skills," as in the International Adult Literacy Survey (IALS), Program of International Skills Assessment (PISA) and the International Life Skills Survey (ILSS) developed by the Organisation for Economic Co-operation and Development (OECD) and Statistics Canada.

In recent years, however, a number of international assessments have been undertaken to involve less developed countries in cross-national measurements. These include the Monitoring Learning Achievement project and several regional studies in sub-Saharan Africa and Latin America.

- Monitoring Learning Achievement (MLA), a joint UNESCO-UNICEF project, is a large-scale study of learning achievement being carried out in 40 less developed countries that tests literacy and numeracy goals specific to each country' s national curriculum, as well as knowledge of health, hygiene and nutrition.
- The Southern Africa Consortium for Monitoring Educational Quality (SACMEQ), founded by national education ministries and the International Institute for Educational Planning, conducted an assessment that analyzed the reading levels of pupils in grade 6 in Southern Africa. Mauritius, Namibia, Tanzania (Zanzibar),[9] Zambia and Zimbabwe took part in 1998; and Kenya and Malawi participated in 1999. A follow-up study among 15 countries is scheduled for the year 2000.
- Under the Program of Analysis of Educational Systems (PASEC), established in 1991, studies of achievement in math and French in grades 2 and 5 have been carried out in nine francophone African countries.
- Finally, the Latin American Laboratory for Assessment of Educational Quality (*Laboratorio*), also sponsored by UNESCO, is a network of assessment systems in 18 Latin American countries; it carried out a first study of students in grades 3 and 4 in 1997 in 13 countries.

While there have been an impressive number of new initiatives in less developed countries, the extent to which results have been disseminated and, more importantly, had an impact on education policy has varied widely.

How can the monitoring of learning achievement impact policies related to educational equity? In both more and less developed countries, steps have been taken to improve educational quality and efficiency through assessments of learning outcomes. Large variations in learning outcomes are commonly found across regions, types of schools and groups of students within a specific country. Understanding the factors underlying these variations is crucial to policy-making that aims to improve the performance of schools and minimize disparities in outcomes.

Among less developed countries, the SACMEQ study of literacy at grade 6 in five Southern African countries—Mauritius, Namibia, Zambia, Zimbabwe and Zanzibar (Tanzania)—shows differences in learning outcomes among countries that have achieved or are nearing universal primary enrollment. All countries recorded primary enrollment rates of 90 percent or higher in the 1990s. Moreover, participation in primary school is equitably distributed by gender. In 1995, the number of girls enrolled in primary school ranged from 92 per 100 boys in Zambia to an equal number of boys and girls in Namibia (UNESCO, 1999).

The results revealed both startlingly low levels of overall learning achievement and significant disparities across the group of countries. The share of students tested who met *minimum* literacy standards ranged from 56 percent in Zimbabwe and 54 percent in Mauritius to only 26 percent in both Namibia and Zambia. Moreover, the share of students reaching *desired* literacy standards ranged from 37 percent in Zimbabwe to only 3 percent in Zambia.

As shown in Table 2, disparities within individual countries showed a mixed picture relative to gender. In countries with the highest shares of students meeting minimum/desired literacy levels, namely Zimbabwe and Mauritius, girls showed better results than boys relative to the national mean. Among the remaining countries, outcomes among girls were poorest relative to boys in Zambia—the country posting the lowest literacy scores.

Literacy scores among pupils grouped according to an index of household assets show a much stronger relationship than by gender. This index is based on the ownership of specific consumer goods and serves as a proxy measure of household SES. In all countries, test results were markedly low among children in households with low SES. Differences were also large between socioeconomic categories, and were most pronounced in Namibia, where children from high-SES households were five times more likely than those from low-SES households to meet minimum literacy standards (see Table 2).

Table 2. Literacy achievement by gender and SES[a] relative to national mean scores (among 6th-graders meeting minimum mastery standards)

	Gender		SES		
	Boys	**Girls**	**Low**	**Middle**	**High**
Mauritius	94	107	73	101	123
Namibia	107	93	43	64	202
Zambia	109	90	82	105	114
Zanzibar, Tanzania[b]	102	98	84	106	111
Zimbabwe	98	102	83	98	123

Source: Derived from SACMEQ reports (1998)
[a]SES is based on an unweighted index of household assets.
[b]For Tanzania, the SACMEQ report relates to Zanzibar only.

3.   Monitoring educational disparities in a changing world

As shown in this chapter, in the 1990s educational equity has become a more prominent issue in less developed countries. This has been driven by growing international support for more equitable education systems, the apparent willingness of governments to respond (as signatories to standards-setting instruments), and concern about the rapid change in global demographic and economic contexts and their impact on equity. This renewed interest and the implied data requirements provide the motivation for better and more extensive monitoring of equity issues.

However, there are many challenges. For example, moving towards more equitable educational systems demands both political commitment and the resources commensurate to needs. Although there are a number of positive examples of the progress that countries have made in terms of educational equity, for many other countries, efforts have been largely the result of external pressure. Thus, one important part of the monitoring process is to help build demand for such indicators among potential users within countries. This can be achieved by creating greater awareness among policy-makers about the impact of inequity on development and the uses of equity indicators to inform political debate, policy design, scientific research and analysis. At the same time, there is a need to be selective in the choice of indicators, so as not to overburden national statistical services and spend great amounts of resources in collecting overly detailed data, which are then costly to process and analyze.

One way to achieve this would be to use an approach that incorporates some measure of equity in the calculation of existing indicators. For example, the United Nations Development Programme's (UNDP's) *gender-equity-sensitive indicator (GESI)* utilizes the harmonic mean between the male and female indicators, which is equivalent to using equity-sensitive weights on the achievements of males and females.[10] The harmonic mean has the property of taking into account both the overall level of the indicator and, to a certain extent, the disparity between males and females. It is possible to modify the calculation of the indicator to make it more sensitive to gender disparities and to apply it to other types of disparities.

Keeping in mind that there can be significant difficulties associated with the measurement of equity, and great diversity in conditions across less developed regions, four general areas of agreement have emerged as a result of ongoing attempts to measure equity in less developed countries:

First, it is important that indicators of equity are relevant to changing contexts and new policy approaches.

Approaches to measuring equity should be pragmatic, as the types of disparities found in developing countries vary widely. And often they confound stereotypes about educational equity in less developed countries. For example, while girls' education is a striking disparity in one region, in another region, girls outperform boys in terms of participation and achievement. However, the issue is not just about access to schools, but access to learning opportunities, especially those that enable advantage in changing labor markets, and promote healthy behaviors and participation among young people. For example, who gains access to training for skills that are particularly relevant to labor market success? Who has access to formal or non-formal efforts that disseminate information about health behaviors and risk, such as nutrition or HIV?

Changing public and private roles in education have become more evident across developing regions; these changes can influence levels of equity. Reallocating responsibilities for the finance and governance of education from the central government to local authorities may put poorer regions at greater risk; likewise, efforts to expand instruction will have to rely on greater private financial contributions by communities and households. What are the impacts of such policy shifts on equity between regions, districts, towns, schools and households?

Second, while there should be efforts to improve measures at the level of primary education, in countries nearing universal primary education, there should be more concentrated efforts to examine equity at other levels of education and the equity dynamic relative to processes within schools.

While enrollments in pre-primary, secondary and tertiary educational levels in most developing countries are often quite small, the disparities in access may be large. As the situation becomes more equitable in terms of access to primary education, inequality may persist in other ways. In almost every country, inequality in educational systems is progressive; the further one advances, the more selective access to certain learning opportunities becomes. This is particularly relevant with regard to early childhood development programs, which are considered by many as a positive intervention for children, particularly those from disadvantaged backgrounds. Disparities are especially evident in higher levels of education, which are often key to successful outcomes in later adulthood. Do children from disadvantaged backgrounds have access to early childhood development programs? Would they be more likely to enter and complete primary education after attending such programs? Does gender parity in secondary school or the labor market necessarily follow from gender parity in primary school?

Third, it is important to maintain and improve existing measures of access to educational opportunities, but to also focus on process and outcome indicators.

In less developed countries, the focus on disparities in access to primary education should not overshadow issues related to progression/efficiency or outcomes/quality that may influence demand for education. While the set of international indicators compiled by UNESCO provides some direction in this area, data collected at the individual and household level (as shown by the examples of Niger and Brazil) help to assess interaction and possible interventions at the national level.

Finally, it is important to examine how conditions outside of the school affect equity.

Clearly, the emergence of rights-based approaches has made the quantification and identification of out-of-school populations increasingly important. As these groups are not covered by school-based surveys, it is important that other approaches, such as household surveys or qualitative research, are used to help define the characteristics of this population. The economic welfare of the household (which is central to targeting policy interventions in poverty reduction frameworks) is an important place to start. It is also important to consider parental and community attitudes and perceptions of education quality, the benefits of education, and the direct and indirect costs of education.

The larger task is first to improve the quality of administrative data, such as school surveys. These data enable analyses of basic components of education through the study of access, internal efficiency and outcomes. However, available data provided by school registers and records do not always allow the analyses of internal disparities. Nor do they address many of the internal processes or outcomes at the individual level. Thus, research based on surveys or qualitative approaches gives a vital perspective to the study of equity and is an essential complement to administrative data.

In order to incorporate measures that seek to be policy relevant, cover different levels of the educational process and examine school and out-of-school factors more closely, it is necessary to develop complementary data sources and improve data relevance. However, the demand for more accurate, reliable and policy-relevant equity measures must be balanced with needs and feasibility.

Notes

1   For the purposes of this chapter, the terms "less developed regions/countries" or "developing countries" refer to the classification system used by the UN and UNESCO. These terms may include countries that reflect, in terms of development or educational attainment, levels similar to those in "more developed regions." The list of countries and the composition of regional groupings are cited in UNESCO (2000).

2　The estimated number of children out of school based on data from the Education for All 2000 Assessment was 110 million in less developed countries in 1998. This estimate was based on a similar methodology, but took into account the latest enrollment figures and used different sources of population data.

3　The school-life expectancy, or expected number of years of formal education, is the number of years a child is expected to remain at school or university, including years spent on repetition. It is the sum of the age-specific enrollment ratios for primary, secondary and tertiary education.

4　See EFA Forum (1998) for regional estimates. See UNESCO (1999) and UNESCO (2000) for individual country data.

5　See the two UNESCO documents for more detailed definitions of the school-life expectancy and the school-survival expectancy.

6　The weight of the different assets is determined using the statistical techniques of principal components. The "asset index" derived first from the Indian National Family Health Survey has been validated using data from Indonesia, Pakistan and Nepal, which include statistics on both consumption expenditures and asset ownership. Results seem to prove that the asset index is more stable and less affected by measurement errors as a measure of long-run wealth than, and performs as well as, traditional measures of consumption expenditures.

7　Individuals were sorted by the asset index into three groups: the top 20 percent (rich), the middle 40 percent (middle) and the bottom 40 percent (poor).

8　For the calculation of the index of inequality, see ECLAC (1998), Box V.11, p. 172.

9　For Tanzania, the SACMEQ study is limited to Zanzibar.

10　The formula of the harmonic mean H is: $H = n/S(1/xi)$. For more information on the calculation of gender-equity-sensitive indicators, see UNDP (1995), *Human Development Report*, Technical Notes.

References

Chu S.K., "Education data in demographic surveys," mimeo, UNESCO, Paris, 1999.

EFA Forum Secretariat (EFA Forum), *Education For All Assessment,* statistical document, UNESCO Institute for Statistics (UIS), Paris, 2000.

EFA Forum Secretariat (EFA Forum), *Education for all:status and trends. Assessing learning achievement*, EFA Forum, Paris, 2000.

EFA Forum Secretariat (EFA Forum), *Education for all: status and trends. Wasted opportunities: when schools fail*, EFA Forum, Paris, 1998.

Filmer D., Lant P., "Estimating wealth effects without income or expenditure data—or tears: educational enrollment in India," *World Bank Policy Research Working Paper No. 1994*, DECRG, The World Bank, Washington, DC, 1998.

Filmer D., Pritchett L., *The Effect of Household Wealth on Educational Attainment. Demographic and Health Survey Evidence,* The World Bank, Washington, DC, 1998.

Filmer D., "The structure of social disparities in education: gender and wealth," *Gender and Development Working Paper No. 5,* The World Bank, Washington, DC, 1999.

Hammarberg T., "A school for children with rights," *Innocenti Lectures*, International Child Development Centre, Florence, 1998.

Instituto Nacional de Estudos e Pesquisas Educacionais (INEP), *EFA 2000: Educaçao para todos: Avaliaçao do Ano 2000*, INEP, Brazil, 1999.

Mehrotra S., "Education for all: policy lessons from high-achieving countries," *UNICEF Staff Working Papers*, Evaluation, Policy and Planning Series, No. EPP-EVL-98-005, mimeo, 1998.

Micklewright J., "Education, inequality and transition," *Economics of Transition*, 7(2), pp. 343–376, 1999.

OECD, *Education and equity in OECD countries*, Paris, 1997.

OECD, *Investing in education: analysis of the 1999 world education indicators*, Paris, 2000.

République du Niger, *Education pour tous: bilan à l' an 2000*, Ministère de l'éducation nationale, Niamey, 1999.

Ross K. (ed.), "The quality of education: some policy suggestions based on a survey of schools," *SACMEQ Policy Research Reports Nos. 1–5 (for Mauritius, Namibia, Zambia, Zanzibar and Zimbabwe)*, International Institute for Educational Planning, Paris, 1998.

Saito M., "Gender vs. socio-economic status and school location differences in Grade 6 reading literacy in five African countries," *Studies in Educational Evaluation*, 24, p. 3, 1998.

Saldanha D., "Residual illiteracy and uneven development," *Economic and Political Weekly*, pp. 27–29, Delhi, 1999.

Save the Children, *Children's rights: reality or rhetoric?*, International Save the Children Alliance, London, 1999.

UNESCO, *World education report*, Paris, 2000.

UNESCO, *Statistical yearbook*, Paris, 1999.

UNESCO, *Gender-sensitive education statistics and indicators: a practical guide*, Paris, 1997.

UNESCO, *World education report*, Paris, 1995.

UNICEF, *State of the world's children*, New York, 1998.

UNICEF ICDC, "Basic education: a vision of the 21st century," Innocenti Global Seminar: summary report, UNICEF International Child Development Centre, Florence, 1999.

United Nations Development Programme (UNDP), *Human Development Report*, New York, 1995.

United Nations Economic Commission for Latin America and the Caribbean (ECLAC), *Social panorama of Latin America*, Santiago, Chile, 1998.

Vandemoortele J., "Absorbing social shocks, protecting children and reducing poverty: the role of basic social services," *UNICEF Staff Working Papers*. Evaluation, Policy and Planning Series, No. EPP-00-001, UNICEF, New York, 2000.

Wolfensohn J.D., "A proposal for a comprehensive development framework," a discussion draft, The World Bank, Washington, DC, 1999 (accessed at: http: //www.worldbank.org/html/extdr/cdf/cdf-text.htm)

World Bank, *Education Sector Strategy*, Washington, DC, 1999.

PART III

INTERNATIONAL COMPARISONS ON EQUITY ISSUES

Chapter 9

Is There an Effectiveness-Equity Trade-off?
A cross-country comparison using TIMSS test scores

Vincent Vandenberghe
Université Catholique de Louvain, Belgium

Vincent Dupriez
Université Catholique de Louvain, Belgium

Marie-Denise Zachary[1]
Université Catholique de Louvain , Belgium

Equity and effectiveness are priorities commonly assigned to educational systems across most Western countries. The aim of this paper is to present the results of a simple empirical analysis that measures simultaneously the levels of effectiveness and equity (both socioeconomic status (SES) and gender equity) prevailing at the beginning of secondary education (seventh and eighth grades) across a sample of OECD (Organisation for Economic Co-operation and Development) countries. The results shown and discussed here all come from the Third International Mathematics and Science Study (TIMSS) 1995 database and suggest that there might be no effectiveness-equity trade-off as some countries or regions manage to be highly effective and simultaneously limit the level of SES or gender inequity.

1.   Measuring effectiveness and SES equity simultaneously

Let us consider the relationship between the predictor variable of achievement (typically a student's SES) and his or her actual score (in mathematics or science achievement). Suppose we have "centered" SES by subtracting the international mean for each student. Referring to Figure 1 (page 244), we can represent achievement as a function of the "centered" SES index. This function shows two parameters that are particularly interesting: its intercept (a) and its slope (b).

We see that the intercept (a) of the line is indeed the mean (mathematics or science) achievement the country would get if its average SES were equal to the international mean, while the slope (b) captures the sensitivity of achievement to changes in terms of SES.

Let us now consider separate lines for two hypothetical countries ($j=1,2$). Country 1 and Country 2 differ in two ways. First, when controlling for SES, Country 1 has a higher (expected) mean than Country 2. This difference is reflected in the two intercepts in which clearly $a_1>a_2$. If in Country 1, SES is less predictive of (expected) achievement than in Country 2, then this difference should be captured by the two slopes with $b_1<b_2$. Confronted with these (hypothetical) results, we could say that Country 1 is both more "effective" and more "equitable" than Country 2. The higher (expected) mean level of achievement in Country 1 indicates the greater effectiveness ($a_1>a_2$). The weaker slope indicates the greater equity ($b_1<b_2$).

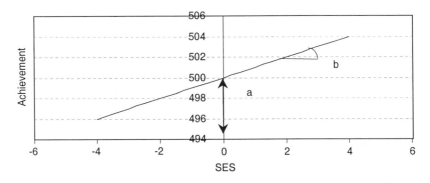

Figure 1. Effectiveness and SES inequity

2.   How to measure effectiveness and both SES and gender equity

This simple model can be modified slightly in order to improve the assessment of equity. Equity is indeed a multidimensional concept. Independence of achievement from SES background is one dimension of equity—typically the one captured by the slope of the achievement/SES regression line. But there are many other dimensions. Independence of achievement from gender, for example, is often presented as a crucial condition for equity. This additional dimension of equity can be very easily introduced into the analysis (Fox, 1997). For instance, consider Figure 2 (page 245) with two separate lines: one for boys and another for girls. The distance (*c*) between the two lines (be it negative or positive) actually captures the difference between the average achievement of boys and girls. If girls were disadvantaged relative to men in country *j*, then c_j would be negative. The reverse would occur if girls were achieving better than boys.

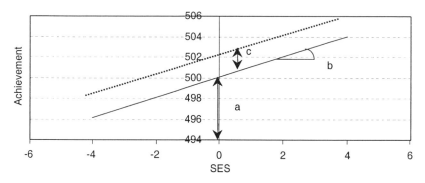

Figure 2. Effectiveness and SES and gender inequity

3. The TIMSS database and the SES index

All the scores used come from TIMSS.[2] This study, carried out in 1994–95, is one of the largest and most ambitious international studies of student achievement ever conducted. Students were tested in mathematics and science, and extensive information about the teaching and learning of mathematics and science was collected from students, schools and principals. TIMSS also gathered contextual and socioeconomic data that we used to create an SES index. We also know the gender of the students.

To build the SES index, we followed a fairly typical procedure. Background characteristics that generally influence education are [1] parents' education, [2] parents' income and occupational status, [3] family structure (whether the child lives with both parents) and [4] immigration/language use. Looking at the items in TIMSS, it seems that all of these can be constructed, more or less, with the exception of [2]. But there is evidence that possession of material objects is fairly strongly correlated with income and occupation. So it makes sense to use items available in TIMSS on calculators, computers, study desks, dictionaries and books. The latter will deliver a good proxy for earnings and occupation.

We took all these items available in TIMSS, standardized them (i.e., applied a technique for removing location and scale attributes for the set of data) and created the composite SES as the mean of the separate items. By standardizing, we imposed the values to be centered to a mean of 0 and a standard deviation of 1. Note also that centering is done on the international mean of the SES components, meaning that we refer to an absolute SES scale and not to a country-specific one. Consequently, the method used here to evaluate effectiveness *a priori* controls for inter-country SES differences: The (expected) mean scores displayed in section 4 reflect each country's performance assuming its average SES equals the international average SES.

4.   Results

The results shown here describe the situation at the beginning of secondary education[3] (seventh and eighth grades[4]). Countries/regions for which we have been able to carry out the analysis are Australia, Belgium (Fl), Belgium (Fr), Canada, France, Germany, New Zealand, Norway, Sweden, Switzerland, England, Scotland and the United States.

4.1.   Science

Figure 3 displays simultaneously the results in terms of effectiveness—expected mean score in science for boys—and SES inequity for pupils attending grade 7. The comparison of Belgium (Fr) and Switzerland seems to support the idea that there is a trade-off between effectiveness and equity: The higher the effectiveness, the more sensitive achievement is to SES differentials. Yet, the situations in Norway, Sweden and Belgium (Fl) go against this assertion. Those countries are characterized by high effectiveness (high expected mean scores) and low SES inequity levels. The same results are visible in columns 2 and 3 of Table 1 (page 247).

It is worth looking at column 4 as it also contains information about gender inequity. It turns out that in most countries, girls perform poorly compared to boys in science. Controlling for their SES, we see that their (expected) mean score is 8 to 20 points lower than that of boys. Australia, and to a lesser extent Germany, are the only countries where girls do as well as boys in science. Similar results are visible in Table 2 (page 247) for grade 8 pupils.

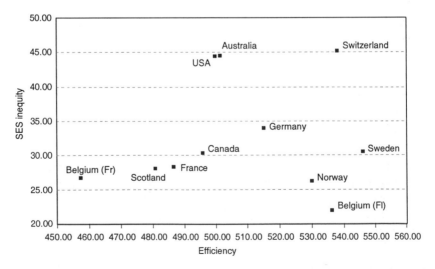

Figure 3. Level of effectiveness (expected mean score for boys) vs. SES inequity, grade 7, science (Source: TIMSS 95)

Table 1. International science scores (grade 7), expected mean achievement for boys plus sensitivity to SES and gender differences

Grade	Country j	Intercept (mean score for boys) a_j	SES inequity b_j	Gender inequity (mean score differential for girls) c_j
7	Sweden	546.08**	30.51**	-14.48**
7	Switzerland	538.10**	45.22**	-14.03**
7	Belgium (Fl)	536.32**	21.98**	-13.09**
7	Norway	530.05**	26.24**	-11.02**
7	Germany	515.13**	33.98**	-8.18*
7	Australia	501.51**	44.55**	-2.51
7	USA	499.89**	44.41**	-11.41**
7	Canada	495.85**	30.39**	-10.27**
7	France	486.61**	28.27**	-18.53**
1§	Scotland	480.76**	28.08**	-19.94**
7	Belgium (Fr)	457.39**	26.72**	-20.69**

§Presumably equivalent to grade 7 in other countries
*Statistically significant at 5%
**Statistically significant at 1%
Source: TIMSS 95

Table 2. International science scores (grade 8), expected mean achievement for boys and sensitivity to SES and gender differences

Grade	Country j	Intercept (mean score for boys) a_j	SES inequity b_j	Gender inequity (mean score differential for girls) c_j
8	Switzerland	578.25**	50.46**	-20.34**
8	Sweden	576.75**	35.18**	-4.30
8	Belgium (Fl)	571.46**	24.11**	-17.57**
8	Germany	556.30**	49.65**	-14.98**
8	Australia	542.83**	38.78**	-11.69**
2§	Scotland	530.12**	37.53**	-21.72**
8	France	527.89**	23.66**	-16.86**
8	Canada	526.55**	30.90**	-14.19**
8	USA	525.05**	47.83**	-10.20**
8	England	512.98**	31.04**	-22.12**
8	New Zealand	494.63**	38.89**	-13.66**
8	Belgium (Fr)	487.84**	34.72**	-13.54**

§Presumably equivalent to grade 8 in other countries
*Statistically significant at 5%
** Statistically significant at 1%
Source: TIMSS 95

4.2. Mathematics

The results in mathematics displayed in Figure 4 definitely confirm the absence of an automatic and systematic relationship between effectiveness and equity. As with science scores, Sweden, Belgium (Fl) and France get relatively high mean scores, but display a limited sensitivity of score to SES gradients. By contrast, Switzerland still combines high effectiveness and low SES equity.

Tables 3 and 4 (page 249) tend to confirm the results of Figure 4. But the information these tables contain about gender inequity is also very interesting. Contrary to what we find with respect to science, mathematics is not synonymous with a large (and statistically significant) gender gap. Girls have similar results as boys, except in Switzerland, Scotland and England where they still perform poorly relative to boys.

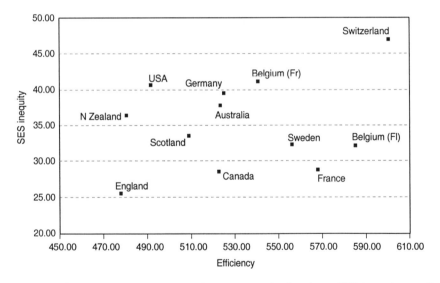

Figure 4. Level of effectiveness (expected mean score for boys) vs. SES inequity, grade 8, mathematics (Source: TIMSS 95)

Table 3. International mathematics scores (grade 7), expected mean achievement for boys and sensitivity to SES and gender differences

Grade	Country j	Intercept (mean score for boys) a_j	SES inequity b_j	Gender inequity (mean score differential for girls) c_j
7	Belgium (Fl)	558.23**	25.56**	2.60
7	Switzerland	555.58**	41.38**	-5.07**
7	France	526.47**	32.67**	-7.63**
7	Sweden	521.99**	28.69**	-0.81
7	Belgium (Fr)	519.76**	30.43**	-12.25**
7	Norway	503.03**	24.42**	-3.77**
7	Germany	496.06**	32.75**	-0.98
7	Australia	491.91**	38.36**	6.58**
7	Canada	489.34**	27.34**	-2.74**
7	USA	467.85**	39.58**	-5.05
1§	Scotland	466.78**	29.48**	-4.11**

§Presumably equivalent to grade 7 in other countries
*Statistically significant at 5%
** Statistically significant at 1%
Source: TIMSS 95

Table 4. International mathematics scores (grade 8), expected mean achievement for boys and sensitivity to SES and gender differences

Grade	Country j	Intercept (mean score for boys) a_j	SES inequity b_j	Gender inequity (mean score differential for girls) c_j
8	Switzerland	600.05**	47.08**	-9.84**
8	Belgium (Fl)	584.75**	32.15**	-1.21
8	France	567.43**	28.84**	-6.20*
8	Sweden	555.53**	32.36**	4.42
8	Belgium (Fr)	539.99**	41.15**	-3.93
8	Germany	524.12**	39.50**	-0.65
8	Australia	522.42**	37.84**	2.49*
8	Canada	521.84**	28.57**	-1.69**
2§	Scotland	507.80**	33.56**	-15.11**
8	USA	490.56**	40.71**	-3.45
8	New Zealand	479.54**	36.41**	0.09
8	England	476.70**	25.58**	-15.33**

§Presumably equivalent to grade 8 in other countries
*Statistically significant at 5%
** Statistically significant at 1%
Source: TIMSS 95

Conclusion

Equity and effectiveness are at the forefront of the political debate in many OECD countries and elsewhere in the world. By analysing TIMSS 95 results in math and science, we have been able to measure simultaneously the level of effectiveness and equity prevailing at the beginning of secondary education (seventh and eighth grades) across a sample of OECD countries. The results suggest that there might not be any effectiveness-equity trade-off. Indeed, some countries or regions succeed in ensuring a relatively high achievement level on average without showing a high sensitivity of achievement relative to SES. By contrast, other countries display poor results with respect to both criteria. The other striking result is that there continues to be a gender gap, especially in science. On average, girls still perform less well than boys. But again, there are exceptions to this tendency suggesting that there is no strict determinism.

Notes

1 This research was financially supported by the convention ARC N° 97-02/209 and the Collinet Foundation. The usual disclaimer applies.
2 We indeed used variables BIMATSCR and BISCISCR. These are the international mathematics and science achievement scores that should be used to report achievement at the international level. Not only do they allow for comparisons across countries, but they also take into account the specific difficulty of items attempted by each student ant their relative difficulty internationally. For further details, the reader should refer to TIMSS (1997).
3 All results shown here come from the so-called population 2 sample.
4 The results based on grade 7 are likely to be less reliable than those based on grade 8 given the sampling technique and the way the TIMSS study was implemented. The reader should bear this in mind hereafter.

References

TIMSS, *User Guide for the TIMSS International Database, Primary and Middle School Years, Population 1 and Population 2, Data collected in 1995*, TIMSS International Study Center, Boston College, Chestnut Hill (Mass.), 1997.
Fox J., *Applied Regression Analysis, Linear Models, and Related Methods*, Sage Publications, London, 1997.

Appendix

Analytical Presentation of the Effectiveness-Equity Measurement

Let us consider the relationship between the predictor variable of achievement (typically a student's socioeconomic status (SES) (X_{ij})) and his or her actual score (mathematics or science achievement (Y_i)). Suppose we have "centered" SES by subtracting the international mean $X_{..}$ for each student $(\tilde{X}_{ij} = X_{ij} - X_{..})$. We can specify Y_i as a function of $\tilde{X}_{ij}$ (Equation 1) with intercept α_j and slope β_j (term ε_{ij} represents the random component or the measurement error of the score).

$$Y_{ij} = a_j + b_j \tilde{X}_{ij} + e_{ij} \tag{1}$$

We see that the intercept α_j of Equation 1 is indeed the mean (mathematics or science) achievement the country would get if its average SES were equal to the international mean, while the slope β_j captures the sensitivity of achievement to changes in terms of SES.

Let us now consider separate regressions for two hypothetical countries $(j=1,2)$. Country 1 and Country 2 differ in two ways. First, when controlling for SES, Country 1 has a higher (expected) mean than Country 2. The difference is reflected in the two intercepts, i.e., $\alpha_1 > \alpha_2$. Second, SES is less predictive of (expected) achievement in Country 1 than in Country 2 as suggested by the comparison of the two slopes, i.e., $\beta_1 < \beta_2$. Confronted with these (hypothetical) results, we could say that Country 1 is both more "effective" and more "equitable" than Country 2. The higher (expected) mean level of achievement in Country 1 indicates the greater effectiveness $(\alpha_1 > \alpha_2)$. The weaker slope indicates the greater equity $(\beta_1 < \beta_2)$.

This simple model can be modified slightly in order to improve the assessment of equity. Equity is indeed a multidimensional concept. Independence between achievement and SES background is one dimension of equity—typically the one captured by the slope of the achievement/SES regression line. But there are many other dimensions. Independence between achievement and gender, for example, is often presented as a crucial condition to get equity. This additional dimension of equity can be very easily introduced in the analysis (Fox, 1997). For instance, consider a simple binary variable (generally referred to as a "dummy variable") D_{ij} coded 1 for girls and 0 for boys. Equation 1 becomes:

$$Y_{ij} = \alpha_j + \beta_j \tilde{X}_{ij} + \gamma_j D_{ij} + \varepsilon_{ij} \tag{2}$$

Thus for boys, the model becomes:

$$Y_{ij} = \alpha_j + \beta_j \tilde{X}_{ij} + \gamma_j(0) + \varepsilon_{ij} = \alpha_j + \beta_j \tilde{X}_{ij} + \varepsilon_{ij} \tag{3}$$

and for girls:

$$Y_{ij} = \alpha_j + \beta_j \tilde{X}_{ij} + \gamma_j(1) + \varepsilon_{ij} = (\alpha_j + \gamma_j) + \beta_j \tilde{X}_{ij} + \varepsilon_{ij} \tag{4}$$

In Equation 2, the coefficient γ_i for the dummy variable (gender) gives the difference in intercepts for the two regression lines. Because these regression lines are parallel, γ_j also represents the constant separation between line, and it may, therefore, be interpreted as the (expected) mean achievement differential accruing to girls when SES is held constant. If girls were disadvantaged relative to men in country j, then γ_j would be negative. The coefficient α_j gives the intercept (i.e., expected mean achievement) for men for whom D_{ij} is nil.

Chapter 10

Equity Indicators Based on the Provision of Supplemental Resources for Disabled and Disadvantaged Students

Peter Evans
Organisation for Economic Co-operation and Development/
Center for Education Research and Innovation, Paris

Following the "difference principle" outlined by John Rawls in his *Theory of Justice* (Rawls, 1971), which argues that institutions should be structured with a built-in bias in favor of the disadvantaged, there seems to be little doubt that equity in education should not be based on an equal distribution of resources to all students. Disabled students, for example, need additional resources if they are to access the curriculum on anything like an equal basis with non-disabled students and thus be able to profit, as other students, from "the benefits that education provides opportunities for" (Brighouse, 2000). For instance, deaf students frequently need signing interpretation, which requires an additional assistant in the classroom.

On the other hand, students with severe learning difficulties are unlikely to attain the same outcome levels as non-disabled students no matter how many additional resources are supplied. For this reason, Harry Brighouse (2000) goes on to argue that equity, conceived of as the attainment of equal outcomes for all students, is also undermined by considering the inevitably low educational achievements of severely mentally disabled students. Thus, a simple reduction in inequality in performance cannot be considered an adequate indicator of equity. The focus should more properly be on the degree of inequality that is acceptable.

Such considerations have led to the possibility of considering minimum thresholds of achievement (e.g., Benadusi, Chapter 1) for employability and inclusion into the normal elements of democratic life (Guttman, 1987; Curren, 1995; Demeuse & De Zanet, 1999). Although these threshold conceptions are less demanding than the equality of outcome approach, they still present substantial challenges to most educational systems. Relevant also are Bloom's contentions that an efficient education system should raise mean achievement levels, reduce achievement variance, and decrease the correlation between the student's performance and social background (Bloom, 1976). A full discussion of these issues is beyond the scope of this chapter, but the implications are important for the interpretation of quantitative indicators.

Providing additional resources for disabled students also raises the question of "bottomless pit" funding. It would not be equitable to supply endless resources to students who are most unlikely to ever attain even average levels of achievement at the expense of most other students in the system. Again, this proposition follows Rawls "difference principle:" If the distribution of goods were to be so extreme that this would lead to a general disadvantage, it would be neither fair nor just.

It should be clear that there is philosophical disagreement about how much extra to provide to disabled and disadvantaged students. But there is agreement, among advocates of the two kinds of theory (threshold theory and equality theory), that considerably more resources should be provided to disabled and disadvantaged students than to other students, and for the present this must suffice to inform existing policy. This may be seen at a pragmatic level, where for instance providing additional resources is a central focus of policy-making, in formula funding approaches (Hill & Ross, 1999). Clarity in the philosophical debate would help further to inform decision-making on the resources distribution front, and this would clearly be a goal for the future, but it is a problem that will not be resolved in this chapter, which approaches the issue from a quantitative perspective.

The value of appropriate resourcing levels for improving educational outcomes is also becoming better appreciated. For instance, research in Sweden (Borhagen, 1999) shows that 40 percent of the variance between mean grades can be explained by a resources variable. Cochrane (Chapter 4) also argues that a decrease in class size associated with improved outcomes for students in minority groups is correlated with increased resources. In addition, in the Francophone community of Belgium, government policy has been working towards developing models of resource distribution that will positively discriminate in favor of disadvantaged groups (Demeuse, Crahay & Monseur, Chapter 2). Thus, what is at stake is not the principle but, as suggested above, the extent of the additional resources to be supplied and their distribution among the groups concerned.

As Brighouse (2000) argues:

> A full and principled account of educational equality would say something about how much more must be devoted to children with disabilities than to ordinarily-abled children. Even among students without disabilities there is a range of ability levels, such that, assuming that the same level of resources is devoted to each, those in the top ability levels simply have more prospects for the rewards of the labor market than those in the

bottom ability levels. So the account must also be able to guide the distribution of resources among more and less able children within the ordinarily-abled group. If the same resources should be devoted, the account needs to explain why, and why such differences do not merit the same response as the differences between the ordinarily-abled and disabled. If on the other hand, differential resources should be devoted, this needs to be explained.

Two additional points are worth raising. First, the inclusion of disabled students in mainstream schools identifies a further facet of equity. If equity policies should promote educational opportunity for all, and this is seen in terms of access to employment and to involvement in life in general, then education in segregated provision could be inequitable if it prejudiced access to these opportunities. And this is almost certainly the case because of different curricula covered by students in segregated settings, different networks developed, employer prejudice towards the disabled, different experiences of the human condition had by disabled and non-disabled students, etc. Thus, in some countries, such as the United States, the aspiration of full inclusion is driven by a human-rights agenda.

Second, Orfield (Chapter 6) has pointed to the importance of gathering statistical data for informed policy-making. Given the additional costs of educating disabled and disadvantaged students, it is important to ensure that funds are efficiently and effectively spent. Informed policy development is greatly strengthened if appropriate data are readily available. For many countries, in the field discussed in this chapter, this is simply not the case, as OECD (2000) reveals.

In this chapter, data will be presented in a number of key areas relating to the education of these students, in terms of overall resources provided, place of education—i.e., special schools, special classes in regular schools, or regular classes in regular schools—and gender. In the conclusion, some key issues will be identified for further discussion. International comparisons of this type should serve to inform the debate on the balance that should be struck in the appropriate allocation of resources.

A resource-based approach to international comparisons for identifying disabled and disadvantaged students

Earlier work (OECD, 1995) brought together data on students with special educational needs from 21 OECD member countries. It showed clearly that international comparability based on national descriptions of those with special educational needs was severely hampered by different definitions in use among countries of the concept "special education," and in the varying categories through which students with special needs were described and data gathered.

For instance, the term "special education" is used in some countries to refer only to those students with disabilities, while in others it covers a much broader range of students including the disadvantaged, ethnic minorities and even gifted students (OECD, 2000). The number of categories used to describe special-needs students also show no pattern. At one extreme, some countries have a non-categorical approach with only one category (e.g., the United Kingdom), while other countries have several categories, such as Switzerland with 19. Furthermore, definitions of categories vary substantially from one country to the next. A summary table is provided in OECD (2000) that reveals clearly the range of definitions and terminology in use. Given the complexity of the picture, a means was needed to provide a coordinating framework, which is described in the next section.

1.   Disability, disadvantage and special educational needs

Before introducing the approach taken in this chapter, it is necessary to be absolutely clear about how the issue relating to disabled and disadvantaged students is being approached. Descriptions of *disability* are frequently if not invariably made in terms of factors relating to individuals' impairment; for instance, in terms of sensory, physical or cognitive dysfunction, or all three. These impairments normally imply that a specialized learning environment must be supplied. But whether or not a student has *special educational needs* depends on the extent to which the current educational arrangements can meet those needs as part of the normal provision made for non-disabled students. It follows from this that a student may have a *disability* but not a *special educational need.*

A similar argument can be advanced with regard to the disadvantaged. Definitions of disadvantage are usually couched in terms of essentially non-educational variables such as ethnic status or poverty—factors that cannot be manipulated directly by the education system. Such experiences may indeed lead to students with these backgrounds being in need of a specialized learning environment of some sort, or they may not. Thus, as with disabled students, students from disadvantaged backgrounds may or may not have special educational needs.

What both of these groups have in common is that a special educational need is associated with the requirement to supply additional educational resources in some form or other. They would be intended to help these students access the curriculum; for example, through modifications to teaching materials, extra teachers or different forms of computer hardware and software. In this chapter, the issue is approached in exactly this way. The assay is made on the basis of the additional resources supplied by countries. Thus, students with special educational needs are those who are in receipt of additional resources so that they can be helped to access the curriculum and benefit as fully as possible from it.

Additional resources are defined as follows:

"Additional resources are those made available over and above the resources generally available for students who have no difficulties in accessing the regular curriculum" (OECD, 1998). Resources may be of many different kinds. They may be *personnel* (e.g., extra teachers), *material* (e.g., specialized teaching materials), or *financial* (e.g., funding formulae that are more favorable to those with disabilities or disadvantages). Financial resources will, of course, include the costs of personnel and materials (OECD, 2000).

Such a definition provides a supply-side approach based on countries' own identification of those perceived to need additional provision to offset or compensate for disadvantage of one sort or another. It allows for the broadest possible numbers of students to be included and is not dependent on idiosyncratic categorical descriptions. Furthermore, such an approach is commensurate with the revised International Standard Certificaiton of Education (ISCED) 97 classification definition of special education (UNESCO, 1997).

2. Cross-national categories A, B and C

While the additional resources supplied provide a practical means of identifying the wider envelope of special-needs students who are receiving additional support, it is at the same time clear that students are included in this definition for different reasons. Students with disabilities and those with disadvantages can have very different types of problems in terms of accessing the curriculum, and the causes of these problems have different roots. Different policies may determine the resources provided for the different groups.

In order not to lose sight of these differences, and their significant policy implications, it then becomes necessary to subdivide those covered under the additional resources definition in a relevant way. It was agreed by member countries of OECD that this could be done in terms of three cross-national categories, named A, B and C.

Category A: Refers to educational needs of students where there is substantial normative agreement—such as in the case of the blind and partially sighted, deaf and partially hearing, severely and profoundly mentally handicapped, and those with multiple handicaps. These are conditions that affect students from all social classes and occupations. Typically, adequate measuring instruments and agreed criteria are available. These are considered in medical terms to be organic disorders attributable to organic pathologies (e.g., related to sensory, motor or neurological defects).

Category B: Refers to educational needs of students who have difficulties in learning that do not appear to be directly or primarily attributable to factors that would lead to categorization as "A" or "C" For instance, students with learning disabilities, as defined in the United States, are classified here.

Category C: Refers to educational needs of students that are considered to arise primarily from socioeconomic, cultural and/or linguistic factors. There is some background factor, generally considered to be a disadvantage, for which education seeks to compensate.

3.   Some comparative data

During the work conducted at OECD/CERI, a great deal of data has been gathered in different areas. In consideration of a discussion on equity as described at the outset of this chapter, comparative data will be presented that inform this debate. Thus, information is supplied on the numbers of students identified as receiving additional resources, on gender and on inclusion as indicated by the place in which they are educated, i.e., special schools, special classes in regular schools or regular classes in regular schools.

3.1.   Additional resources made available

Countries were asked to provide data in terms of the resources definition of special-education needs as described above. The numbers of students they reported as falling within this definition expressed as a percentage of the overall school population in each country are presented in Figure 1 (page 259).

As may be seen from the table, countries vary substantially in the extent to which additional resources are made available. In the United States, 35.5 percent of students receive additional resources in contrast to 0.41 percent in Turkey. The table also shows these data broken down by cross-national categories A, B and C. It reveals substantial differences among countries in the numbers of students in these categories who are receiving additional resources.

It is important to note that these data *per se* do not allow us to conclude that one country's provision is more or less equitable than another's. A great deal more information would be needed to determine this. However, the data do provide a comparative basis for further inquiry.

3.2.   The location of education

Countries were also asked to report on where special-needs students were educated, whether in special schools, special classes or regular classes. Figures 2, 3, 4 and 5 (pages 260–261) show the data for each of the three cross-

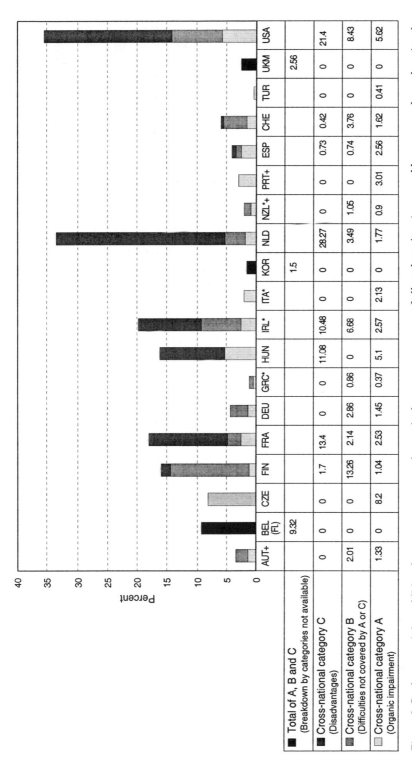

Figure 1. Students receiving additional resources to access the curriculum as a percentage of all students in primary and lower secondary education, by cross-national categories (based on head counts, 1996) (Source: Education at a Glance, OECD, 2000)

+Cross-national category C not available. Cross category B not available for Portugal.

*Public Institutions only.

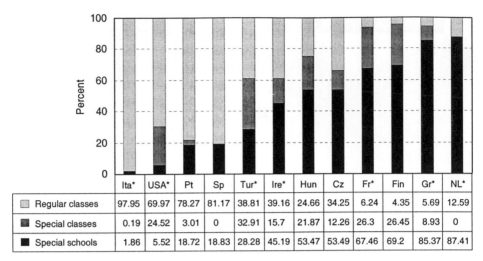

	Ita*	USA*	Pt	Sp	Tur*	Ire*	Hun	Cz	Fr*	Fin	Gr*	NL*
Regular classes	97.95	69.97	78.27	81.17	38.81	39.16	24.66	34.25	6.24	4.35	5.69	12.59
Special classes	0.19	24.52	3.01	0	32.91	15.7	21.87	12.26	26.3	26.45	8.93	0
Special schools	1.86	5.52	18.72	18.83	28.28	45.19	53.47	53.49	67.46	69.2	85.37	87.41

Figure 2. Proportions of students in cross-national category A by location (Source: Education at a Glance, OECD, 2000)

*Greece, Ireland: Public institutions only; Italy: Special classes and regular classes are public institutions only; France, USA: Estimated figures; Turkey: Turkish data refer only to compulsory school period (ISCED1); Netherlands: The data for regular classes are estimated

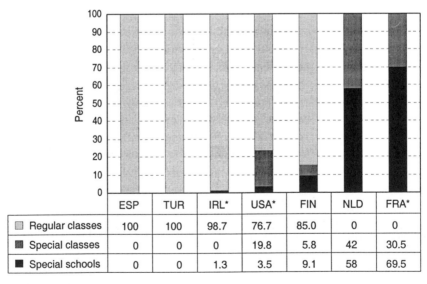

	ESP	TUR	IRL*	USA*	FIN	NLD	FRA*
Regular classes	100	100	98.7	76.7	85.0	0	0
Special classes	0	0	0	19.8	5.8	42	30.5
Special schools	0	0	1.3	3.5	9.1	58	69.5

Figure 3. Proportion of students in cross-national category B by location (Source: Education at a Glance, OECD, 2000)

*Ireland: Schools only; France, USA: Estimated figures

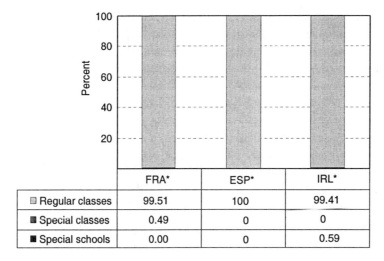

	FRA*	ESP*	IRL*
☐ Regular classes	99.51	100	99.41
▨ Special classes	0.49	0	0
■ Special schools	0.00	0	0.59

Figure 4. Proportion of students in cross-national category C by location (Source: Education at a Glance, OECD, 2000)

*Ireland: Public institutions only and data on children of refugees in regular classes are missing; France, Ireland, Spain: Data are estimated

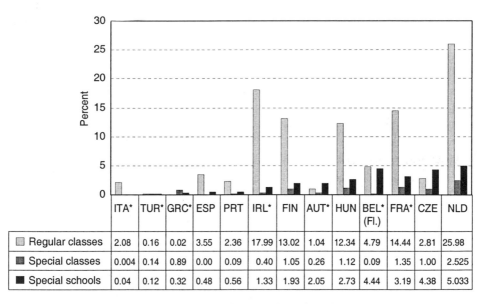

	ITA*	TUR*	GRC*	ESP	PRT	IRL*	FIN	AUT*	HUN	BEL* (Fl.)	FRA*	CZE	NLD
☐ Regular classes	2.08	0.16	0.02	3.55	2.36	17.99	13.02	1.04	12.34	4.79	14.44	2.81	25.98
▨ Special classes	0.004	0.14	0.89	0.00	0.09	0.40	1.05	0.26	1.12	0.09	1.35	1.00	2.525
■ Special schools	0.04	0.12	0.32	0.48	0.56	1.33	1.93	2.05	2.73	4.44	3.19	4.38	5.033

Figure 5. Number of students with special educational needs within resources definition as a percentage of all students in primary and lower secondary education, by location and by country (Source: Education at a Glance, OECD, 2000)

*Austria: The data in regular classes are estimates; Belgium (Flemish Community): Includes upper secondary students (ISCED3); France: Estimated figures; Greece, Ireland: Public institutions only; Italy: Special classes and regular classes are public institutions only; Turkey: Turkish data refers only to compulsory school period (ISCED1)

national categories separately and for all students added together.

The figures clearly reveal major differences among countries in the place of education for students with special educational needs. It is clear that in cross-national categories A and B, students perceived to need additional resources to access the curriculum might be in special schools in some countries but in regular schools in others. The limited data available for category C students show that the majority of these students are in regular schools.

Again, on their own, these data do not allow the conclusion that segregated education is more or less equitable than inclusive approaches. Further data, for instance on differential availability of opportunities for students in the different settings, would be needed.

3.3. Gender

Countries were also asked to provide breakdowns of data by gender. Figures 6, 7, and 8 (below and page 263) show how gender is distributed in special schools, special classes and regular classes for countries that were able to supply data.

The figures show clearly that in all countries providing data, boys are in the clear majority by a ratio of around 3:2, and by implication as a group are receiving more resources than girls to help them gain access to the curriculum. Such large differences seem unlikely to be wholly due to "natural," randomly distributed biological factors.

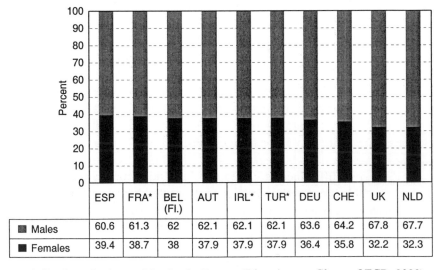

	ESP	FRA*	BEL (Fl.)	AUT	IRL*	TUR*	DEU	CHE	UK	NLD
■ Males	60.6	61.3	62	62.1	62.1	62.1	63.6	64.2	67.8	67.7
■ Females	39.4	38.7	38	37.9	37.9	37.9	36.4	35.8	32.2	32.3

Figure 6. Gender ratios in special schools (Source: Education at a Glance, OECD, 2000)

*Ireland: Public institutions only; France: Estimated figures; Turkey: Turkish data refers only to compulsory school period (ISCED1).

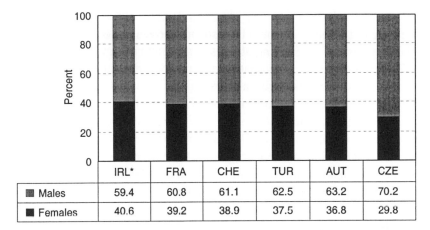

Figure 7. Gender ratios in special classes (Source: Education at a Glance, OECD, 2000)
*Ireland: Public schools only.

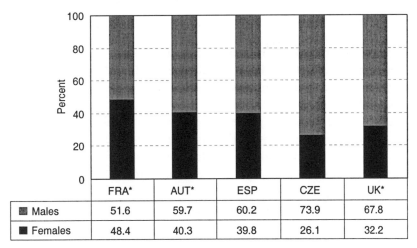

Figure 8. Gender ratios of students with special educational needs in regular classes (Source: Education at a Glance, OECD, 2000)

*Austria, France, UK: Estimated figures.

Whether these differences are inequitable or not depends on knowledge of other factors. This issue is discussed and interpreted further in the next section.

4. Discussion

What do these data tell us about issues of equity for disabled and disadvantaged students and provision for their special educational needs? The three indicators will be commented on individually followed by a brief general discussion.

Resources supplied—First, it is clear that in all the countries that provided data, the idea that resources should be distributed equally does not hold. Thus, in general terms, a positive discrimination is practiced in recognition of educational needs. However, there is wide variation among countries (and although the data do not show this, there is regional variation as well) in the extent to which students are given this additional support. This variation raises the question of the adequacy of this additional support. This point touches on the issue of the bottomless-pit question raised by Brighouse (2000) and others on the degree to which substantial additional resources should be given to supplement disabled and disadvantaged students' learning needs. It emphasizes also the importance of quantifying the extent of additional resources being supplied—and ultimately their link with outcomes. The empirical approach adopted in this chapter offers a start in providing such a quantification from which more effective policies, for instance pertaining to the most cost-effective use of resources, could be developed.

Location of education—The location of a student's education raises rather different issues. Here, the provision of additional resources is a given. Thus, the equity argument rests more on whether such provision provides equitable access to the opportunities provided by education. These might be, for instance, to the world of work; to the ability to participate in a democracy; to the possibility of developing friendships; or, more generally, to the avoidance of social exclusion (e.g., Sen, 1999).

As noted above, the data gathered so far cannot address this issue in any direct way, but they do point to the significantly different experiences that students with the same disabilities would receive in different countries. These are quite substantial and likely to lead to different post-school outcomes. Comparative data, collected within the present framework, have not been gathered, so little more may be said conclusively. However, data from individual countries (OECD, 1999) would suggest that segregated settings provide few advantages in many areas of normal life. For instance, students are often educated outside their own communities, thus inhibiting the development of friendship opportunities. Segregation separates the general public from disability; this alone does nothing to reduce prejudice and improve employment opportunities or other social involvement. Access to post-compulsory education may also be hindered, partly because of frequent differences in curricula in special schools. Certainly from this perspective of equity, segregated provision would be viewed as inequitable, additional resources notwithstanding.

Gender—Educational equity for males and females has been a central policy issue in many countries for many years and, at least in terms of access, has been achieved in OECD countries. However, the finding here of a ratio of around 3:2 males to females, for both disabled and disadvantaged groups of students, raises questions of interpretation because it appears that an inequitable situation has arisen where males are provided with more resources than females. Such a situation may arise because of different social and educational expectations of males in contrast to females, or because males or their parents express their dissatisfaction with education in a different and more aggressive way than females.

Following other arguments for positive discrimination for disabled and disadvantaged groups, this unequal distribution would not be inequitable if males were genuinely more in need than females of additional support to access the curriculum and benefit equally from education. There is a hint from Swedish data to support this view (Hard, 1999). This study showed that schools were better at preparing females than males for life in a democracy, covering areas such as willingness to take responsibility, tolerance of minority groups, solidarity with those outside the group and attitude to immigration policy. Thus, if curriculum goals are becoming more accessible to females (at least in part due to changes in content driven by globalization, societal changes and current labor market demands), then additional resources to help males would not be inequitable.

Conclusion

Equity in education can be usefully seen in terms of the way resources are distributed to disadvantaged groups, an approach firmly situated within the theory of justice outlined by Rawls (1971). This supply-side model of equitable provision has the major advantage of being quantifiable, and for this reason can provide a data-based approach to policy development in this field (the significance of which has been discussed by Orfield (Chapter 6), for issues on race and poverty). For instance, it should help to determine whether additional resources are being used efficiently or effectively in segregated school settings in achieving equality of opportunity in access to the labor market. Or, as has been shown, it can provide an additional perspective on the differential resources supplied for males and females. These examples point to the multi-dimensional nature of equity issues and the need for data in making rational decisions for resource distribution that will lead to an equitable education for all.

Comparative approaches have much to offer in this regard. The large range of differences that exist among countries in the way resources are allocated to different disability and disadvantaged groups should help to identify key aspects for policy development for improving equity. However, the paucity of good data in this area is also a considerable barrier, and a major effort to improve data quality is required.

References

Benadusi L.B., "Equity and Education," Chapter 1, this volume, 2000.

Bloom B.S., *Human Characteristics and School Learning*, McGraw-Hill, New York, 1976.

Borhagen K., "Overview of studies from the equity perspective in Swedish child-care, pre-school and school," presentation to the OECD/INES ad hoc project on equity, Geneva, 1999.

Brighouse M.H., *School choice and social justice*, Oxford University Press, Oxford, 2000.

Cochrane D.R., "Why Education Matters," Chapter 4, this volume, 2000.

Curren R.R., "Justice and the threshold of educational equality," *Philosophy of education, 50*, pp. 239–248, 1995.

Demeuse M., "La politique de discrimination positive de Commaunauté française de Belgique: une méthode dáttribution des moyens supplémentaires basée sur des indicateurs objectifs," presentation to the OECD/INES ad hoc group on equity in education, Geneva, 1999.

Demeuse M., Crahay M., Monseur C., "Efficiency and Equity," Chapter 2, this volume, 2000.

Demeuse, M., De Zanet, F., *Equity and Efficiency,* Unpublished paper presented at the OECD Ad Hoc Group on Education Equity Indicators, Geneva, 1999.

Guttman A., *Democratic education,* Princeton University Press, Princeton, 1987.

Hard S., *Equity and democracy*, presentation to the OECD/INES ad hoc group on equity in education, Geneva, 1999.

Hill P.W., Ross K.N., "Component 3: Student supplementary educational needs," in Ross K.N., Levacic R. (eds.), *Needs-based resource allocation in education—via formula funding of schools,* IIEP, UNESCO, Paris, 1999.

OECD, *Integrating students with special needs into mainstream schools*, OECD, Paris, 1995.

OECD, *Education at a glance*, OECD, Paris, 2000.

OECD, *Education at a glance*, OECD, Paris, 1998.

OECD, *Inclusive education at work—students with disabilities in mainstream schools,* OECD, Paris, 1999.

OECD, *Special needs education: statistics and indicators,"* OECD, Paris, 2000.

Orfield G.,"Why Data Collection Matters: The role of race and poverty indicators in American education," Chapter 6, this volume, 2000.

Rawls J., *A Theory of Justice,* Harvard University Press, Cambridge, 1971.

Sen A., *Development as freedom*, Knopf, New York, 1999.

UNESCO, *International standard classification of education*, UNESCO, Paris, 1997.

Chapter 11

Educational Equity
Social interactions might matter

Vincent Vandenberghe
Université Catholique de Louvain, Belgium

This paper discusses the importance of social interactions at the school and classroom level (the so-called peer effects) as determinants of achievement. It comments on the results of a statistical analysis aimed at estimating the impact of peer effects on science and math test scores. The study is based on the Third International Mathematics and Science Study (TIMSS) created in 1995 by the International Education Agency (IEA) for grade 7 and 8 students across OECD (Organisation for Economic Co-operation and Development) countries. This study confirms the importance of peer effects, but also suggests that their intensity may be subject dependent. This paper also explores the nature of peer effects as it reviews different theories about their *modus operandi*.

Introduction

It is clear that education requires a certain number of monetary resources (Nye, Hodges & Konstantopoulos, 1999). Yet, people like Hanushek (1986, 1992, 1994) have highlighted the fact that some incentive and organizational problems also need to be solved to maximize achievement. Another promising idea, when it comes to education policy design, is to consider that a child's ability to learn is also influenced by the characteristics of his or her peers. Education inevitably takes place in classrooms where pupils are together and interact. In turn, these classrooms are part of a school where pupils tend also to interact, generating what pedagogues call "peer effects;" sociologists call "contextual effects;" and economists call "social externalities." This idea was initially put forth by Coleman et al. (1966) in the educational context, but this phenomenon has been extensively documented in several areas including urban security and crime, drug addiction and teenage pregnancy (Jencks & Meyer, 1987; Corcoran, Gordon, Laren & Solon, 1990).

1.   Peer effects' measurement and stakes

1.1.   Existence of peer effects

Several empirical studies have attempted to measure the peer effect phenomenon. The issue has been addressed by sociologists (Coleman, 1966, 1988; Jencks & Meyer, 1987; Willms & Raudenbush, 1989), pedagogues (Slavin, 1987; Grisay, 1993; Gamoran & Nystrand, 1994) and also some economists (Henderson, Mieszkowski & Sauvageau, 1978; Hanushek, 1986; Brueckner & Lee, 1989; Bénabou, 1993, 1996).

Most researchers have concluded that peer effects exist in primary and early secondary education: The higher the proportion of high-achieving pupils in the classroom, the higher everybody's achievement. In other words, the higher the average ability of classmates, the higher the local social spillover to a pupil's benefit. Willms and Echols (1992), using Scottish data, estimate that peer effects (also called contextual effects) range from 0.15 to 0.35 of a standard deviation. A child whose ability is at the national average (NA) has an expected attainment about one-quarter of a standard deviation higher when moved from a school where the mean ability is one-half of a standard deviation below the NA to a school where it is one-half of a standard deviation above the NA. This is a substantial effect. This result was already present in previous studies: first in Coleman (1966), then in Henderson, Mieszkowski and Sauvageau (1978). It is also to be found in more recent studies in the United States (Duncan, 1994; Link & Mulligan, 1991; Dynarski, Schwab & Zampelli, 1989; Willms & Echols, 1992) and in France (Leroy-Audouin, 1995; Duru Bellat & Mingat, 1997).

1.2.   Peer effects and ability-grouping policy

Our own research confirms the existence of peer effects, but also highlights the political stakes they carry. Indeed, if peer effects matter, distribution of heterogeneous individuals between strictly delimited entities (such as schools and classrooms) becomes a critical issue regarding not only equity but also effectiveness. Average education outcomes might be directly affected by the way heterogeneous individuals are distributed. And the cost of an egalitarian objective aimed at equalizing educational achievement can be influenced by the way peer effects are distributed among schools.

The first question worth assessing relates to the marginal contribution of peer effects on achievement. Knowing that peer effects matter, we might want to know whether redistribution of this particular "input" among schools and classrooms amounts to a zero, negative, or positive sum game. In other words, does the presence of an additional high-achieving pupil in School 1 generate peer-effect (teaching climate) improvement that is equal, inferior or superior to the negative consequences of the presence of an additional low-achieving pupil in School 2?

The second question has to do with the interaction between the level of peer effects prevailing in a classroom or school and the socioeconomic profile of a pupil. Are low-socioeconomic-status (SES) pupils equally, less, or more sensitive to peer effects than their more privileged comrades?

It is rather intuitive—but can also be shown analytically (Vandenberghe, 1996)—that desegregation (i.e., mixing of abilities; also called whole-class instruction) will be socially preferable to segregation when, simultaneously, the marginal contribution of peer effects is decreasing and low-achieving pupils are more sensitive to peer effects (teaching climate) than their comrades.

1.3. Peer effects and TIMSS data

The data we used to answer these two questions come from the 1995 TIMSS project. This database contains the test scores of pupils attending grade 7 or 8 across OECD countries. These pupils are ensconced in classrooms within schools (two classrooms were sampled in each school). In addition, the database contains information about the pupils and their classrooms. To carry out our analysis, we pooled information from 19 countries and regions—Australia, Austria, the Flemish-speaking Community of Belgium, the French-speaking Community of Belgium, Canada, France, Germany, Greece, Japan, South Korea, the Netherlands, New Zealand, Norway, Singapore, Spain, Switzerland, England, Scotland and the United States. This gave us a total of 124,125 pupils ensconced in 2,849 classrooms. We also standardized the scores so that, for both math and science, we have a cross-country mean of 500 and a standard deviation of 100.

Preliminary work involves the creation of a SES variable. It was done here by aggregation of information from TIMSS regarding education of the parents, immigration status, correspondence between the test language and the language used at home, family structure and a series of material possessions acting as proxies for disposable income: calculator, computer, study desk, dictionary and a number of books. The aggregation procedure is fairly typical (Gamoran, 1996). It consists of building dummies or categorical variables (e.g., possession of a computer means the computer dummy = 1, and 0 otherwise) and then taking the mean of the existing components. The resulting aggregate is then standardized (mean = 100, standard deviation = 10).

Estimation[1] results are displayed in Tables 1, 2 and 3 (see appendix). Focusing on Table 1, we observe that the peer effect term has a positive but decreasing marginal contribution to both math and science achievement. Yet, only the coefficients of the science regression are statistically significant. Thus, in the case of sciences, our results suggest that the presence of an additional high-achieving pupil in School 1 generates peer-effect (teaching climate) improvement that is inferior to the negative consequences of the presence of an additional low-achieving pupil in School 2. This is in line with some of the observations made in the U.S. context and surveyed by Mosteller, Light and Sachs (1996).

Note also that the impact of the peer-effect proxy (average SES of the classmates) does not seem to vary with a pupil's own SES level. In other words, peer effects affect low-, middle- and high-skilled pupils equally.

The other results worth mentioning are that attending the upper grade (grade 8) logically means a higher achievement as suggested by the coefficient of the UPGRADE dummy. Gender also seems to matter, particularly in science as the GIRL dummy is synonymous with a significant drop in score (-17.726). There is a gender gap in math also, but of lower magnitude (-8.719). Finally, it is no surprise to see that pupils who are older (possibly because of grade repetition) achieve less well (see negative coefficient of the AGEY variable).

This analysis confirms the importance of non-monetary inputs like peer effects and the need for an efficient allocation of those resources. If peer effects really influence achievement, as most empirical work seems to confirm, they must be properly used. As their (direct or indirect) productive contribution is local by nature, they must also be properly allocated among schools and classrooms. Using 1995 math and science scores across OECD secondary education systems, we observe that optimal skill-grouping practices are subject dependent. Skill-mixing (whole-class) instruction seems to be the best option to maximize average outcome in science. When it comes to math, however, average achievement does not seem to be affected by skill-grouping practices.

2.   How do peer effects work?

Most researchers have thus come to the conclusion that peer effects exist. This being said, the question of the *modus operandi* of peer effects is still largely debated.

Some works known as "microeconomics of the classroom" help us understand the potential link between skill-grouping practices and educational output. Mulligan (1984) develops a queuing model to explain how in desegregated classrooms[2] low-skill pupils force their more able classmates to wait longer before moving towards the next topic. This might be beneficial to the former, but could also come at a cost for the latter, as the curriculum they eventually cover is less complete than in the segregation case.[3] But there are other explanations of peer-effect phenomena. Some sociologists and pedagogues (Hallinan, 1990; Hallinan & Williams, 1990) talk about "behavioural contagion" in which high-skilled pupils act as "models" for their classmates. Their willingness to learn helps the teacher establish a "learning" climate favorable to the knowledge-transmission process.

In his survey of experimental studies testing the impact of various schemes of skill grouping, Slavin (1987) concludes that the latter have *per se* very limited effects on educational achievement. Yet, Oakes, Gamoran and Page (1962) argue very judiciously that the real issue at stake is the "curriculum differentiation" process, a direct corollary of "real" skill grouping practices. In other words, Slavin neglects some part of the reality because the experimental studies—typically what he looks at—neutralize the curriculum variable. Quite invariably, Hallinan (1990) observes in her work that non-supervised skill-grouping practices lead to a dramatic differentiation of curricula.

According to this line of reasoning, peer effects would simply correspond to the implementation of programs and teaching content structured by skill-grouping practices. If the classroom is entirely composed of low-skilled pupils, the teacher tends to significantly lessen the complexity of his/her teaching content and his/her demands and expectations. On the contrary, if the classroom is composed of "gifted" pupils, the teacher seems invariably inclined to become more demanding and to revise his/her expectations upwards. This very troublesome empirical observation has led several "liberal" pedagogues to question the opportunity presented by greatly personalized curricula. Uniform programs and content wrongly assume that all pupils are identical. But personalized curricula often lead to excessive differentiation, practically synonymous with unrestrained classification and implicit ranking (Grisay, 1993).

To mix "bright" and "dumb" pupils consequently generates curricular adjustments. Dahllöf (1971) describes this process as follows:

> In the comprehensive classes the bright pupils reach the same level of objectives in the same effective time as their counterparts in the positively selected classes. Having done this, they must wait in some way or other for their slower peers in the steering criterion group. This waiting time may be filled by other types of work...so-called enrichment exercises...more difficult from a formal point of view...but of the same general type as in the common core. With regard to fundamental learning, enrichments of this type very soon become overlearning with no further gain. The pupils in this area of the skill distribution may be busy, and certainly do not cause any disciplinary problems, but they are not learning anything more of substantial value in the curriculum unit under treatment. Otherwise bright pupils in comprehensive classes would excel pupils in positively selected classes in elementary curriculum units.

Dahllöf's description seems to confirm the idea that skill mixing entails curricular adjustments that are favorable to low-skilled pupils and unfavorable to high-skilled pupils. Successive interruptions caused by less able pupils tend to add up and eventually come at a cost for their more able peers. A teacher's allocated time is indeed limited.

Conclusion and educational policy implications

The capacity to mobilize non-monetary (social) input is probably important when it comes to educational achievement. In the school context, these social inputs amount to social interactions called peer effects—some people also use the term "contextual effects." In other words, education is one of those numerous human activities characterized by social spillovers. This means the implementation of socially optimal education policy is conditional on the identification of the optimal allocation of individuals (by type or skill level) across schools. Empirical evidence from TIMSS 95 suggests that mixing might be socially superior to tracking for topics like science, while skill-grouping practices seem to matter less for math.

Note finally that educational policy also depends heavily on the skill of decision-makers to get individuals (the pupils and their parents) to accept a certain kind of allocation. As suggested by Mosteller, Light and Sachs (1996), if results on the importance of peers hold up under further investigation, decision-makers may face a dilemma. Parents of highly skilled children may advocate for schools to group their children according to skill, while parents of less skilled children may prefer the opposite

To persuade families with high-achieving pupils to voluntarily attend desegregated schools and classrooms might be difficult, but not impossible. A first decisive step might simply consist of reassuring the public about teachers' capabilities to cope with a diversity of skill levels. It is indeed important for teachers to be trained to teach heterogeneous classrooms and cope with diversity. Imposing skill mixing on ill-prepared teachers might create undesirable curricular adjustments and increase discipline problems. Both phenomena are likely to reinforce the belief, widely present among some families, that mixing inevitably comes at a certain cost for their children. Second, international comparisons might significantly help to identify policies and practices that successfully combine whole-class instruction and high achievement, even for high-skilled pupils. Japan, for example, provides a very interesting case (National Institute of Student Achievement and Assessment, 1998). The Japanese insist on mixed groups and skill-mixing arrangements through primary and secondary education. And in spite of these mixed classes, Japan consistently has scored in the top group of OECD countries.

Notes

1   Obtained with HLM 4.0 software
2   Some people use the word "mixing."
3   Often referred to as "tracking" (in the U.S.) or "streaming" (in UK).

References

Bénabou R., "Workings of a City: Location, Education and Production," *The Quarterly Journal of Economics*, pp. 619–652, August 1993.

Bénabou R., "Equity and Efficiency in Human Capital Investment: The Local Connection," *Review of Economic Studies, 63*(2), pp. 237–264, 1996.

Brueckner J.K., Lee K., "Club Theory with Peer-Group Effect," *Regional Science and Urban Economics, 19*, pp. 399–420, 1989.

Bryk A.S., Raudenbush S.W., *Hierarchical Linear Models*, Sage Publications, London, 1992.

Coleman J.S., "Social Capital in the Creation of Human Capital," *American Journal of Sociology, 94*, Supplement, pp. 95–120, 1988.

Coleman J.S., Campbell E.Q., Hobson C.F., McPartland L., Mood A.M., Weifeld F.D., York R.L., *Equality of Educational Opportunity* (OE-38001), U.S. Office of Education, U.S. Department of Health, Education and Welfare, Washington, DC, 1966.

Corcoran M., Gordon R., Laren D., Solon D., "Effects of Family Community Background on Economic Status," *American Economic Review, 80*(2), pp. 362–366, 1990.

Dahllöf U.S., *Ability Grouping, Content Validity, and Curriculum Process Analysis*, Teachers College Press, New York, 1971.

Duncan G.J., "Families and Neighbors as Sources of Disadvantage in the Schooling Decisions of White and Black Adolescents," *American Journal of Education, 103*, pp. 20–53, 1994.

Duru Bellat M., Mingat A., "La gestion de l'hétérogénéité des publics d'élèves au collège," *Cahier de l'Iredu, 59*, IREDU, Université de Bourgogne, Dijon, France, 1997.

Dynarski M., Schwab R., Zampelli E., "Local Characteristics and Public Production: The Case of Education," *Journal of Urban Economics, 26*, pp. 250–263, 1989.

Gamoran, A., "Student achievement in public magnet, public comprehensive, and private city high schools," *Educational Evaluation and Policy Analysis, 18*(1), pp. 1–18, 1996.

Gamoran A., Nystrand M., "Tracking, Instruction and Achievement," *International Journal of Educational Research, 21*(5), pp. 217–231, 1994.

Grisay A., "Hétérogénéité des classes et Equité Educative," *Enjeux, 30*, pp. 63–95, 1993.

Hallinan M., "The Effects of Ability Grouping in Secondary Schools: A Response to Slavin's Best-Evidence Synthesis," *Review of Educational Research, 60*(3), pp. 501–504, 1990.

Hallinan M., Williams, R., "Student's Characteristics and the Peer-Influence Process," *Sociology of Education, 63*, pp. 122–132, 1990.

Hanushek E., "The Economics of Schooling: Production and Efficiency in Public Schools," *Journal of Economic Literature, 24*, pp. 1141–1177, 1986.

Hanushek E., "Improving Educational Outcomes While Controlling Costs," *Carnegie-Rochester Conference Series on Public Policy, 37*, pp. 205–238, December 1992.

Hanushek E., "Money Might Matter Somewhere: A Response to Hedges, Laine, and Greenwald," *Educational Researcher, 23*(4), pp. 5–8, 1994.

Henderson V., Mieszkowski P., Sauvageau, Y., "Peer Group Effects and Educational Production Functions," *Journal of Public Economics, 10*(1), pp. 97–106, 1978.

Jencks C., Meyer S.E., "The Social Consequences of Growing Up in a Poor Neighborhood," in Lynn L.E., MacGeary M.G.H. (eds.), *Inner-City Poverty in the United States*, National Academy Press, Washington, DC, 1987.

Leroy-Audouin C., "Les modes de groupement des élèves à l'école primaire, catalyseurs des performances," *Cahier de l'Iredu , 95009*, IREDU, Dijon, France, 1995.

Link C.R., Mulligan J.D., "Classmate Effects on Black Student Achievement in Public School Classrooms," *Economics of Education Review, 10*(4), pp. 297–310, 1991.

Mosteller F., Light R.J., Sachs, J.A., "Sustained Inquiry in Education: Lessons from Skill Grouping and Class Size," *Harvard Educational Review, 66*(4), pp. 797–843, 1996.

Mulligan J.G., "A Classroom Production Function," *Economic Inquiry, 22*, pp. 218–226, August 1984.

National Institute of Student Achievement and Assessment, *The Educational System in Japan: Case Study Findings*, U.S. Department of Education, Office of Educational Research and Improvement, Washington, DC, 1998.

Nye B., Hodges L.V., Konstantopoulos S., "The Long-Term Effects of Small Classes: A Five-Year Follow-Up of the Tennessee Class Size Experiment," *Educational Evaluation and Policy Analysis, 21*(2), pp. 127–142, 1999.

Oakes J., Gamoran A., Page R.N., "Curriculum Differentiation: Opportunities, Outcomes, and Meanings," in Jackson P. W. (ed.), *Handbook of Research on Curriculum*, American Research Association, Washington DC, 1962.

Slavin R.E., "Ability Grouping and Student Achievement in Elementary Schools: A Best-Evidence Synthesis," *Educational Policy, 57*(3), pp. 293–336, 1987.

Vandenberghe V., "Functioning and Regulation of Educational Quasi-Markets," thèse de doctorat, nouvelle série N° 283, CIACO, Louvain-la-Neuve, Belgium, 1996.

Willms D.J., Raudenbush S.W., "A Longitudinal Hierarchical Linear Model for Estimating School Effects and Their Stability," *Journal of Educational Measurement, 26*(3), pp. 109–132, 1989.

Willms D.J., Echols F., "Alert and Inert Clients: The Scottish Experience of Parental Choice of Schools," *Economics of Education Review, 11*(4), pp. 339–350, 1992

Appendix

Table 1. Estimation of fixed effects, OECD countries, TIMSS 1995 test scores

Variable	Math achievement Mean=500, Std=100		Science achievement Mean=500, Std=100	
	Coefficient	*P-value*	Coefficient	*P-value*
For INTRCPT1				
BASELINE	476.293	*0.000*	480.351	*0.000*
PUPSTAFF	23.806	*0.000*	30.193	*0.000*
MEANSES	14.207	*0.119*	46.220	*0.000*
MEANSES²	-0.050	*0.262*	-0.202	*0.000*
PUPSTAFF*MEANSES²	-0.236	*0.000*	0.305	*0.000*
For SES slope				
BASELINE	0.943	*0.000*	1.089	*0.000*
PUPSTAFF	0.054	*0.000*	0.029	*0.000*
MEANSES	0.260	*0.311*	0.183	*0.476*
MEANSES²	-0.001	*0.277*	-0.001	*0.376*
UPGRADE	51.763	*0.000*	50.191	*0.000*
GIRL	-8.719	*0.000*	-17.726	*0.000*
AGEY	-15.932	*0.000*	-10.548	*0.000*
# level 1 observations (pupils)	*124,125*			
# level 2 observations (classrooms)	*2,849*			

Table 2. Estimation of variance components (math achievement), OECD countries, TIMSS 1995 test scores

Random effect	Std dev.	Var. component	df	χ^2	P-value
INTRCPT1	61.722	3809.68229	2716	67801.476	0.000
SES slope	1.000	1.00177	2717	4331.797	0.000
level-1 random term	76.129	5795.70596			

Table 3. Estimation of variance components (science achievement), OECD countries, TIMSS 1995 test scores

Random effect	Std dev.	Var. component	df	χ^2	P-value
INTRCPT1	49.001	2401.128	2716	37323.978	0.000
SES slope	0.872	0.761	2717	797.023	0.000
level-1 random term	82.945	6879.924			

Chapter 12

Intergenerational Inequities[1]
A comparative analysis of the influence of parents' educational background on length of schooling and literacy skills

Sylvain Noël
Centre for Education Statistics, Canada

Patrice de Broucker
Centre for Education Statistics, Canada

In societies demanding high levels of competence, educational pathways and certain intellectual capacities are important factors in professional and social fulfillment. The number of years of schooling is a measure of the human capital of individuals, on which access to the most specialized and best-paid jobs very often depends. As to literacy skills, retained here as a measure of intellectual capacity, they are also an important determinant in professional success for they offer an appreciation of the ease with which individuals can analyze information pertinent to their jobs, learn, improve and become multi-skilled in their workplaces. Recent studies suggest that the economic return on basic skills would be even higher now than in the past.[2]

Length of schooling and literacy skills are influenced by a complex group of factors. Among them, we find inherited and familial factors. The parents' education is a good example. In fact, the probability of a young person attaining a high level of education and developing strong literacy skills varies significantly according to whether the parents attained a high level of education or not.

To observe that national systems of education do not permit equalization of chances for success through active participation in economic and social life is a troublesome finding. This raises an important question for public policy since, in several countries, a number of social and economic policy measures seek directly or indirectly to reduce inequalities among individuals.

Inequality is, however, a question of degree. It is therefore useful, before putting policies into operation and then trying to assess their effectiveness, to be able to measure the extent of the phenomenon for an overall perspective, using time and space comparisons. It is because of the absence of such indicators elsewhere that the present research becomes particularly pertinent.

By referring implicitly to theoretical and sociological analyses of equity in education, we postulate, in this study, that the parents' education is one of the important hereditary and familial factors that impact on the level of schooling and literacy skills that a person attains and develops by adulthood. Our objective is to develop indicators to measure its influence, then to use them in a comparison across countries.

1.   Analytical framework

As expressed in Chapter 5, by Meuret, and Chapter 1, by Benadusi, in this volume, family background—whether measured by the parents' level of education or by their profession—has been a key element in recent attempts to explain inequalities in education. Without claiming to be exhaustive, let us recall some points of established theory to fashion a backdrop for our essentially empirical work:

- The functionalist approach postulates that educational inequalities come essentially from two types of factors: fixed demographic and social factors, such as socioeconomic status, sex, ethnic group or nationality; and factors of individual ability, such as aptitude and the will to succeed. By focusing our analysis on the influence of two factors important to this theoretical approach (sex and the level of schooling completed by the parents), we find a point of reference.
- According to the theory of social and cultural reproduction, of which P. Bourdieu is one of the most eminent proponents, the educational system functions as if to reproduce inequalities of birth linked to characteristics of family, cultural and social environment. In two complementary approaches, this theory puts the emphasis either on the direct effects of structural factors (e.g., socioeconomic status of the family, education level of the parents) or on the importance of cultural factors that intervene to influence the effects of these structural factors. Our empirical study takes up the important notion of cultural capital, while reducing it by constraint of the data on parents' education.
- The modeling presented here is also allied with traditional studies of academic attainment level and abilities, which relate social origin to academic performance.

These theoretical references and our empirical approach link the indicators developed to several elements of the system of indicators on the equity of educational systems proposed in this volume by Meuret:

- contextual indicators bearing on cultural inequalities and social mobility;
- process indicators designed to provide information about inequalities in

length of schooling and on the quality of the education received; and

- outcome indicators of external and internal results, to the extent that one of the essential goals of this analysis is to quantify the influence of social origin on the results of the educational process (total years of schooling and literacy skills).

In this text, we will be led to explore several dimensions of intergenerational inequality that we make explicit at the outset:

- *Inter-familial inequality*: This inequality reflects differences in the number of years of schooling and individual reading abilities, according to the intellectual capital residing in the family milieu (represented here as the level of education attained by the parents).
- *Inequality between the sexes*: This measure represents the inequality that one would find, with regard to duration of schooling and literacy skills, between individuals of different gender whose parents had attained the same educational level.
- *Inter-cohort inequalities:* This measure represents the evolution of inter-family inequalities between two different age groups.

A survey such as the International Adult Literacy Survey (IALS), conducted in a generally similar manner in numerous countries, provides an invaluable source of data for international comparisons.[3]

In a perfectly egalitarian social and academic context—that is to say in which the system would provide the same opportunities for academic success to all individuals whatever their family characteristics—one would not expect differences in the intellectual capital of families to contribute to differences in the number of years of schooling or in literacy skills. Consequently, the more our model can explain differences in length of schooling and literacy skills, the better will be our understanding of the factors that influenced them. The development of our indicators of inequality is based on a model formalized statistically and described succinctly in Appendix A.

2. Analysis of results[4]

The models that we have used permit measurement of the influence of the education of parents on both the length of schooling of respondents and on their literacy skills, while controlling for the influence of other factors. Indeed, we measure, on the one hand, the average number of years of schooling; on the other, we measure the average literacy skills of persons having similar characteristics with respect to four factors contained in this model: sex, age, level of schooling of the parents and immigration status/language. We deliberately decided to include in this model only descriptive variables totally external to the individual to better understand their direct effect, clear of influence by other more endogenous personal characteristics. The central element of this analysis is the relationship that the model exposes between the parents' level of education and the number of years of schooling and literacy skills of their children. We are also interested in the differences that this relationship can show us between the sexes and on the evolution of this relationship over time.

Because we face a high number of combinations of variables in this model, we will not comment on all the elements that can be drawn from it. We are most particularly interested in the relationship for one age group (36- to 45-year-olds) and in the analysis of the change over time for two age groups (26- to 35-year-olds and 46- to 55-year-olds), which reflects a change between two generations. Apart from this, the model takes into consideration the mother tongue and immigration status. In the present document, we will discuss inequalities only within the framework of a population that is homogeneous in this respect; that is, the population of respondents whose mother tongue is the official language of the country and who were born in the country. In all countries, this constitutes the largest proportion of the population, ranging from 71 percent of the population in Australia to 97 percent in Poland.

2.1.   Inequalities in length of schooling are reproduced within families, though to different degrees from one country to another.

In every country studied, we note a tangible influence of the parents' level of schooling on the average length of schooling of the children. The average number of years of schooling of a New Zealander (male) from 36 to 45 years of age whose parents have obtained a post-secondary diploma is 13.2 years (Figure 1, page 281). It is only, in this instance, about a year and a half more than for a New Zealander of the same age whose parents have not obtained a secondary diploma. One can therefore consider this inequality in the duration of formal schooling low in comparison to what is observed in other countries. In contrast, Swedes from the same age group who while presenting a similar situation to that prevailing in New Zealand for those whose parents do not have a secondary diploma (11.6 years of schooling), have a substantial advantage if their parents reach the post-secondary level. The Swedes in this group accumulated on average 15.8 years of schooling, amounting to more than four extra years in school.

All other countries fell between these two extremes of inequality. We find relatively lower levels of inequality among 36- to 45-year-old men in New Zealand, Australia, the United States and the United Kingdom; in all these countries, the gaps in duration of schooling between those whose parents have a post-secondary diploma and those whose parents do not have the secondary diploma is less than three years. In contrast, the same gaps are relatively more significant in Sweden, Ireland, the Netherlands, Belgium,

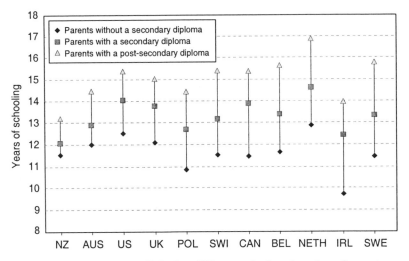

Figure 1. Inequalities in education linked to differences in the education of parents, men, age 36–45

Canada and Switzerland; in these countries, the gaps are greater than three and a half years.

One cannot, however, totally judge the weight of these inequalities without making reference, on the one hand, to characteristics of the educational systems and, on the other hand, to the relative proportions of parents at each of the levels of schooling by country. It is also useful to weigh the importance of the role of the parents' education level (and of other factors taken into account in this model) in relation to the whole group of factors that can influence the time their children will spend in school.

An interesting point of reference with respect to the characteristics of educational systems is the average number of years of education pursued from primary school to the end of secondary school (Table 1, page 282). The duration varies from one country to another, from 14.1 years in Australia to 12 years in Sweden. One can thus measure the gap between the average number of years of schooling attained according to the level of education of the parents and this average duration, which reflects a characteristic of the national education systems. In the Netherlands, the United Kingdom and the United States, the average length of schooling for men 36 to 45 years of age whose parents do not have secondary diplomas is nearly equal to the number of years needed to complete secondary school. This leads us to suppose that a good many of these persons have themselves completed their secondary education. In the other countries, except for New Zealand and Australia, the majority of men whose parents have a secondary diploma exceed the number of years of school required to complete secondary school.

Another contextual factor to consider: When the parents of the respondents who were 36 to 45 years of age at the time of the study were in school, the

Table 1. Average length of schooling to the end of secondary school

Country	Number of years
Australia	14.1
New Zealand	13.6
Belgium	12.9
Netherlands	12.9
United States	12.7
Ireland	12.5
Canada	12.2
United Kingdom	12.1
Switzerland	12.1
Sweden	12.0
Poland	n.d.

Source: OECD, *Education at a Glance*, 1998.

academic "norm" was not yet attainment of a secondary school diploma. The IALS easily demonstrates this state of affairs: In most of the countries studied, a great majority of the respondents' parents had not completed secondary school.

But it is also useful to note that if the level of education of the parents appears to be a significant factor in the determination of the length of their children's education, it cannot be seen as the only intervening factor. The statistics accompanying the results of the modeling exercise give us some interesting information in this respect. The model used to produce the indicators presented in this document "explains" a different proportion of the variations in number of years of schooling by country. This model explains about 37 percent of the variation in duration of schooling of the respondents in Canada, but only 14 percent of the variation in New Zealand. This indicates that—in the case of Canada, for example—63 percent of the variations must be sought in other factors.[5] (This is natural in this type of analysis, but it is counterbalanced by the statistically very significant character of the contribution of the parents' education.)

2.2. These inequalities are of a fairly similar magnitude among men and women.

Figure 2 (page 283) shows the inequality in the educational attainments of women 36 to 45 years of age. As a comparison with Figure 1 will show, the inequalities are in most countries of a similar magnitude. The statistical model indicated to us that this was the prevailing situation in almost all countries. From this fact, the ranking of countries in increasing order of inequality remains largely unchanged for women. Four countries have differences between the sexes that merit our interest. In Sweden, the inequality seen in the situation of women whose parents have not finished secondary school in relation to those who parents have obtained a post-secondary diploma is less than that found among men—essentially because women from 36 to 45 years of age whose parents have obtained a post-secondary diploma have had, on the average, more than a year less education than men in the same age group. One can advance the hypothesis that women would have entered shorter post-secondary career tracks. In Flemish Belgium, the inequality is visibly greater among women, principally because women whose parents had little schooling have themselves had, on average, shorter educations than men (more than a year of difference). In Switzerland and the Netherlands, it is not so much a matter of greater inequalities among women, but rather a shift downward of the overall distribution of school years at each level of education attained by the parents, to the disadvantage of women—in these two cases, resulting in differences of a year to a year and a half.

2.3. Inequalities are somewhat reduced among younger cohorts who were educated more recently, but marked differences remain among countries in this regard.

These inequalities evolve over time, under pressure from numerous social and economic factors. The demand for education, which generally can be seen in longer attendance among the youngest age groups, is stretched by economic needs for greater productivity and the value added by gray matter. It is also pushed by individual desires for the greater personal—as well as intellectual or economic—satisfactions made possible by higher incomes generally associated

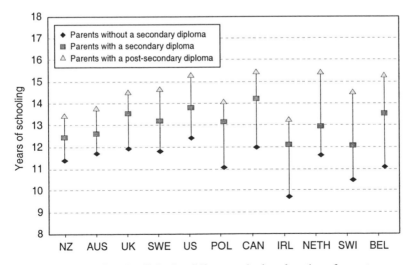

Figure 2. Inequalities in education linked to differences in the education of parents, women, age 36–45

with higher levels of education. Indicators reported in Figures 3 and 4 (below and page 285) broadly convey this phenomenon for men and women separately. These two figures were established from comparisons of the data for two age groups framing that which served as the basis for the preceding analysis, those from 26 to 35 years of age and from 46 to 55 years of age. These permit measurement of the change in inequality over time: the *inter-cohort inequalities*. For each of the figures and each country, the column on the left indicates the change in the degree of inequality in 20 years, which separates the two age groups for persons whose parents did not possess secondary diplomas. The central column measures the same change in degree of inequality for those whose parents did have secondary diplomas, while the column on the right measures the change for those whose parents had post-secondary degrees. Each column pointing towards the bottom (towards the top) indicates an increase (a reduction) of inequalities for the group concerned in comparing the situation of the youngest to the oldest.

These two figures indicate that the patterns of change in inequalities over time are visibly different from one country to another, but in practically no countries were different trends detected between genders—even though men and women may have been affected to different degrees. In all countries, except the United States, the handicap that most particularly affected individuals whose parents had not finished secondary school has been reduced. This reduction has been most evident in Belgium (Flanders) (nearly two years), Canada and Ireland (nearly one and a half years), Sweden (more than a year, but only for men), Poland (more than a year and a half for women, a little less than a year for men), and in the Netherlands (two and a half years for women and more

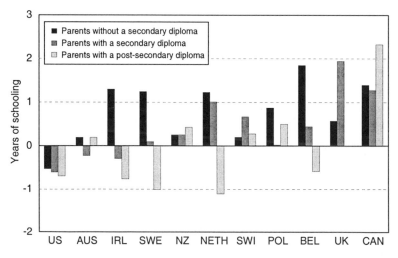

Figure 3. Inter-cohort gaps in education by parents' level of education, men, age 26–35 and 46–55

than a year for men). The situation of persons in the 46–55 age group was the least favorable in these six countries, compared with other countries; obviously, countries in which this older cohort had achieved higher levels of education have made less tangible progress in this regard. One can certainly relate this phenomenon of convergence to the force of compulsory education policies, now present in all of the countries, to at least 15 years of age, often more. The impact of these policies is also felt in the increase—though generally not as strong—in length of schooling among persons whose parents had indeed obtained a secondary diploma.

The situation appears more disparate among countries when we consider the contribution of positions most favorable to inter-cohort inequality. In several countries, there are only minor changes (less than a year) of comparative advantage for persons whose parents held a post-secondary diploma. This is the case in the United States, Ireland, New Zealand, Australia, Switzerland, Belgium (Flanders) and the United Kingdom. In Sweden, we pick up a relatively pronounced decrease in length of schooling (a year for men, more than two years for women), which could be explained by a significant development of shorter post-secondary courses. In Poland, most particularly among women, the average number of years of schooling has increased more than a year. In the Netherlands, while there has not been any tangible change for women, the average length of schooling for men has fallen about a year, albeit from a very high level. There, as in Sweden, it is possible that the development of post-secondary education was effected principally to the benefit of shorter programs. In Canada, a strong expansion of participation in post-secondary education caused the average number of

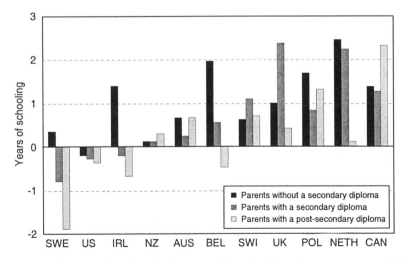

Figure 4. Inter-cohort gaps in education by parents' level of education, women, age 26–35 and 46–55

years of schooling to climb by more than two years for men, as well as for women whose parents had earned post-secondary diplomas. Canada is one of the only countries where—the number of years of school having risen more visibly among persons in this category than among those whose parents had not completed secondary school—the inequalities between the two groups have increased somewhat.

2.4. An education level at least equal to secondary school appears decisive in the development of literacy skills.

The analysis of inequalities in literacy skills gives us a more qualitative perspective on the transmission of intellectual capital between generations, complementing the more quantitative expression of number of years in school. In international comparisons, a number of years of school is not necessarily proof of a similar experience. The density of the experience (number of days per year, number of hours per day) varies from one country to another, as can curriculum coverage. In contrast, one of the major contributions of the IALS is the comparison of skills measured directly by tests administered identically in several countries. It is certain that the skill—here the capacity to understand schematic texts—develops from multiple sources and is maintained over time within the context of personal and professional life. As for years of schooling, the model used here is far from being able to furnish an exhaustive explanation of the variations found in literacy skills (ranging from 10 percent in Ireland to 34 percent in the United States). But it does indicate a significant relationship between reading capacity and the level of education of the parents. Figures 5 and 6 (page 287) present a measure of the inter-familial inequalities for men and women, 36 to 45 years of age.

This method of charting the inequalities permits a concrete interpretation of the reading levels recorded. In fact, the scale adopted on the vertical axis is a direct representation of the levels, which permits easy interpretation of the data: Level 3 reading abilities (there are five levels in all) are considered as being at the threshold beyond which one is considered to be reading at a reasonable and satisfactory level. Following this line of interpretation, one may be somewhat surprised by the limited nature of inter-familial inequalities in several countries: In four countries—the Netherlands, Australia, New Zealand and Sweden—whatever the parents' level of education, the descendants all achieve on average a level of competence of at least level 3. We also notice that in all countries except Poland, persons whose parents have at least a secondary diploma have on average literacy skills of level 3. One cannot say as much for those whose parents did not successfully complete secondary school: In six of the 11 countries examined, the literacy skills of these persons do not exceed level 2, and indeed are only at level 1 in Poland. We note also that these

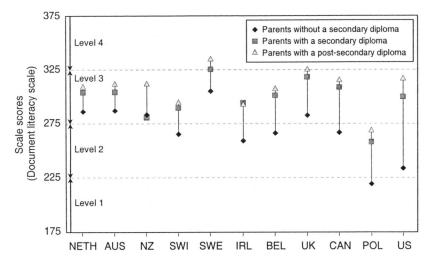

Figure 5. Inequalities in average literacy skills by parents' level of education, men, age 36–45

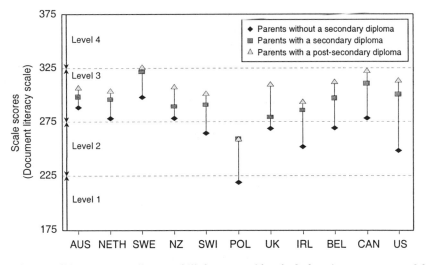

Figure 6. Inequalities in average literacy skills by parents' level of education, women, age 36–45

countries are in general those in which inter-familial inequalities are relatively more pronounced.

If we now consider the situation of persons whose parents have obtained post-secondary diplomas, we are struck by the low "value added" contribution in this situation compared with persons whose parents hold secondary degrees. This relationship seems remarkably stable among countries, among women as much as men. It is confirmed when we measure the inequalities among the youngest group, 26 to 35 years of age. This analysis tends to indicate clearly the positive effect of policies promoting the completion of secondary school among young people. This seems to be the crucial turning point for equipping young people with fundamental literacy skills at an acceptable level. Satisfaction in personal as well as professional life is largely dependent on these skills.

It can therefore be seen that if inter-familial inequalities are often less pronounced than those encountered for length of schooling, the intrinsic influence of the parents' education level is less accentuated. Comparing Figures 5 and 6 shows us also that there are no significant differences between men and women in this regard.

2.5. Over time, the parents' level of education plays a less and less important role in attaining a decent level in literacy skills.

If inter-familial inequalities are only moderately severe, one can add that they have the tendency to be reduced in most countries, when one compares the situation of the parent-child relationship for persons 46 to 55 years of age with those of young people 26 to 35 years of age (Figures 7 and 8, below and page 289).[7] As we have previously seen, this type of graph is read first—each column individually—as the difference in literacy skills between two age groups for a type of family in which the parents have similar education levels. Then, for a given country, we measure the change in inequality from one age group to the other by comparing the relative heights of the three columns.

Only in the United States do inequalities seem to have increased, principally among men and essentially because of the degradation of the situation of persons whose parents did not finish secondary school. In all other countries, one finds

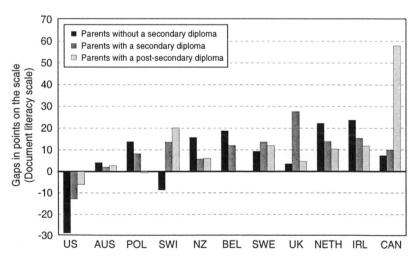

Figure 7. Gaps in inter-cohort literacy skills by parents' level of education, men, age 26–35 and 46–55

gains in literacy skills—even if often modest—for all education levels of the parents. But it is only in six countries—Ireland, the Netherlands, Belgium, New Zealand, Poland and Australia—that these gains are expressed by a reduction of the inequalities between those whose parents did not finish secondary school and those whose parents have post-secondary diplomas.[7] It is interesting to note that, in these six countries, the gains in literacy skills among persons relatively disadvantaged by their family environments have accompanied more pronounced gains in number of years of schooling for this same group (see also Figures 3 and 4). One can only suspect that this is more than coincidence.

2.6. More schooling is not always synonymous with greater competence—or of quantitative and qualitative aspects of education.

It would be tempting to establish a direct relationship between the number of years of schooling and literacy skills, which would permit us to state that more time in school would contribute to better literacy skills. If such an assertion is probably justified on the national level, where the skill level generally progresses with the number of years in school, one is however wise to question the relative effectiveness of national education systems in inculcating skills when we find significant disparities in competence level for a similar number of years of schooling among countries. Certainly, margins of error in the data can be a disturbing factor of these comparisons, which would lessen their worth. But this can not be a sufficient argument when we are in the presence of recurrent results. Following are two examples from the youngest cohort, the latest to have left the school system, permitting the best appreciation possible of the

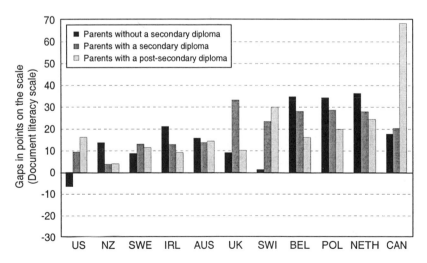

Figure 8. Gaps in inter-cohort literacy skills by parents' level of education, women, age 26–35 and 46–55

systems in a recent period:

- In Sweden, men 26–35 years of age from families where the parents have not finished secondary school have on the average 11 and a half years of schooling and an average literacy skill score of 316 points. This score is superior to that obtained, on average, by persons from families in which parents have obtained post-secondary diplomas in seven of the 10 other countries. In these seven countries, the average number of years of schooling of young adults from relatively privileged families varies from 12.7 years to 15.4 years; in other words, always tangibly more than the 11.5 years of schooling of the young people from the least privileged families in Sweden.

- In five of the 11 countries, women 26–35 years of age coming from families in which their parents have not finished secondary school do not attain, on the average, level 3 in literacy skills. These include Poland, the United States, Ireland, Switzerland and the United Kingdom. In these five countries, the average number of years of schooling for these same women varies from 10.6 years to 12.3 years.

In two countries, Belgium and the Netherlands, the age of compulsory schooling has been raised to 18 years. One cannot help relating the observed changes in inequality to this fact: The strongest increases in number of years of schooling as well as in literacy skills are produced among persons coming from the least privileged families, permitting a tangible reduction of inter-cohort inequalities. We see here the tangible effect of one measure of education policy.

Certainly the school year cannot be considered as a reliable measure from one country to the other of the "quantity" of education received within the formal framework of the education system. In fact, from one country to another, the number of days in a school year as well as the density of experience in the school day vary. Nevertheless, the "qualitative" gaps put in evidence lead to some questions. To make them better understood, we have constructed a "learning effectiveness index" (LEI) (Figure 9, page 291). This index is the average measure of progress in literacy skills for each year of school. It is calculated in the following manner:

$$LEI = \frac{\text{Average score in literacy skills (Men + Women) / 2}}{\text{Average number of years in school (Men + Women) / 2}}$$

Calculated for the 26- to 35-year-old age group, this index permits reflection on the learning gains that would be rather strongly linked to the experience within the formal system of education, as well as to the contribution of intellectual capital in the family milieu.

This index is presented for each of three situations relative to the parents' level of education. But we put the emphasis here on the value of the index in the case where respondents came from a relatively underprivileged family milieu.

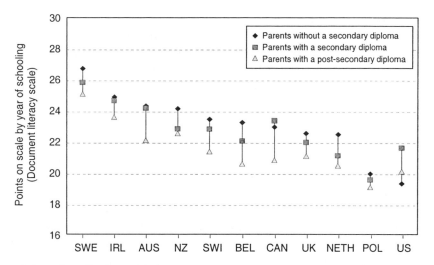

Figure 9. Learning effectiveness index

Note: Countries are classified in descending order on the index of effectiveness of time in school for persons whose parents do not have secondary diplomas.

It is this situation that would best take stock of the real effect of the school system, to the degree that, according to the theoretic tradition in which we join our empirical research, there would be less support that is culturally exterior to and independent of the school. The diminution in the value of the index when the family's cultural capital is higher—a situation found in all countries except the United States—means that supplemental years of schooling, at least beyond a certain threshold, have a marginal negative return in terms of the acquisition of literacy skills, which can only be partially compensated by the greatest cultural richness of the family environment. The size of the diminution of the marginal return (measured in Figure 9 by the distance from the black diamond to the triangle) is moreover practically identical from one country to another.

Thus, one notes a tangible difference in the effectiveness of the time in school between two extremes, Sweden and the United States; the index for Sweden would be nearly 40 percent higher than that of the United States. That means that a year of attendance during initial schooling procures average gains in literacy that are about 40 percent higher in Sweden than in the United States (gains of 27 points in Sweden vs. gains of 19 points in the United States). The classification of countries between these two poles depends, understandably, on two factors: the recorded level in literacy skills and the average number of years of school of a given group. So, for example, the position of Ireland (second place) is explained by the weaker relative position of the country with respect to the average number of years in school, rather than for literacy skills.

Conclusion

In this document, we have sought to quantify inequalities in the duration of schooling and in literacy skills, which would be associated with the education level of the parents. In all the countries examined, tangible inequalities appear according to the intellectual capital of the family environment. Although literacy skills and level of schooling are correlated, the influence of the parents' education on these two characteristics is not exactly the same: It is relatively stronger on length of schooling.

By observing these intergenerational relationships for two distinct cohorts spanning some 20 years, we can effect a reading of the evolution of inequalities over time. While these changes vary from one country to another, we note nevertheless a tendency towards global convergence: The countries where the inequalities were largest tend to see them diminish, while inequalities tend to rise, albeit moderately, in countries where they were lowest.

The length of schooling plays a fundamental role in the distribution of values and knowledge within the society. Do schools everywhere play the role of equalizer of opportunity, opening up opportunities regardless of family environment? In a world that is more educated and more dependent on the written word, the marginalization of those who attain low levels of education and literacy skills is a disquieting phenomenon, for their chances of professional, economic and social success grow constantly smaller.

We have seen that certain policies in matters of education could achieve qualitative objectives and objectives of equity at the same time. In the two countries, Belgium and the Netherlands, which have extended mandatory schooling to age 18, it is the least privileged who benefit most; moreover, their most tangible progress is in literacy skills. Another important element put in evidence: Attainment of the secondary school diploma seems crucial in the transmission of good literacy skills. Policies seeking to reduce dropouts would therefore have one of the most significant effects, not only for the well-being and the personal and professional prospects of the young, but also to assure better prospects for their descendants.

Notes

1   This chapter was originally submitted in French.
2   See, for example, Murnane et al. (1995).
3   All the same, it is regrettable that the inclusion of a large number of questions is left to the discretion of national authorities. The analysis presented here would have been richer if we had been able to use a larger number of variables common to all countries.
4   Detailed results are available from the authors. Any request should be addressed to Patrice de Broucker (*debrpat@statcan.ca*).

5 Here it would have been interesting to be able to use a larger number of variables common to all participating countries. Past studies of Canada have shown an added explanatory capacity associated with the parents' occupation.

6 One element to keep in mind in this analysis, and that has been found by analyses using the same IALS data, is that literacy skills are not necessarily acquired once and for all, but rather that, for an individual, they can vary over the course of a lifetime, largely by the extent of their use. Skills deteriorate if they are not used, but they can also be improved through the regular practice of activities requiring those skills.

7 The vertical column for Canada reflecting the situation of people whose parents had a post-secondary diploma seems to result from an aberrant value in the score obtained by the parameters of the model for men and women, ages 46 to 55. Because of this, the result with regard to inter-cohort inequalities for this country is difficult to interpret. All the same, the values obtained in the two other situations suggest that the rise in scores from one age group to the other presents a similar size; therefore, a certain stability in inequalities over time.

References

Bourdieu P., Passeron J.-C., *La reproduction. Éléments pour une théorie du système d'enseignement,* Minuit, Paris, 1970.

de Broucker P., Lavallée L., "Intergenerational Aspects of Education and Literacy Skills Acquisition," in Corak M. (ed.), *Labour Markets, Social Institutions, and the Future of Canadian Children*, Statistics Canada and Human Resources Development Canada, Ottawa, 1998.

de Broucker P., Underwood K., "Intergenerational Education Mobility: An international comparison with a focus on postsecondary education," *Education Quarterly Review 5*(2), Statistics Canada (No. 81-003), 1998.

Human Resources Development Canada, Organisation for Economic Co-operation and Development, *Literacy Skills for the Knowledge Society: Further Results from the International Literacy Survey,* OECD, Paris, 1997.

Murnane R.J., Willett J.B., Levy F., "The Growing Importance of Cognitive Skills in Wage Determination," *Review of Economics and Statistics,* 77(2), pp. 251–266, May 1995.

OECD, *Education at a Glance: OECD Indicators,* OECD, Paris, 1998.

OECD, *Human Capital Investment,* OECD, Paris, 1998.

OECD, *Literacy, Economy and Society: Results of the First International Adult Literacy Survey,* Statistics Canada, Ottawa, 1995.

U.S. Department of Education, National Center for Education Statistics, Murray T.S., Kirsch I. S., Jenkins L.B. (eds.), *Adult Literacy in OECD Countries: Technical Report on the First International Adult Literacy Survey,* U.S. Department of Education, Washington, DC, 1998.

Appendix A: Source of data and analytical method

Source of data

Our analysis is based on microdata from the International Adult Literacy Survey (IALS).[a] The IALS was conducted between 1994 and 1996 in 12 countries. The participating countries are Germany, Australia, Belgium (Flanders), Canada, Ireland, New Zealand, the Netherlands, Poland, the United Kingdom, Sweden, Switzerland and the United States.

In the present article, the data for the United Kingdom are based on combined estimates for Great Britain and Northern Ireland, where two distinct studies were conducted. Similarly, the data for Switzerland are based on combined estimates for the French- and German-speaking cantons of Switzerland (the Italian- and Romansche-speaking cantons not having been part of the survey). Finally, the data for Belgium (Flanders) relate to the Flemish community, with the exclusion of the city of Brussels.

Germany was not included in this analysis because of problems in the collection of data on some levels of education important to the present study.

Analytical method

The objective of the indicators developed here is to measure the influence of the education level of the parents on the education level attained by their children and on the literacy skills that they will have developed by adulthood. Recourse to the regression method permits us to take into account other variables in the socio-demographic context that may also contribute to length of education and literacy skills.

To measure the length of schooling, we use the number of years of formal education that the person has completed, without counting repeated years. Although educational systems vary from one country to another and, in each country, from one period to another, the number of years of attendance represents a realistic approximation—and one that is often employed by analysts—of the intellectual capital of individuals.

The IALS defines literacy skills as "the ability to understand and employ printed information in daily activities at home, at work and in the community to achieve one's goals, and to develop one's knowledge and potential." According to this definition, literacy skills present more than one dimension. The dimension we have used here as a complementary indicator of intellectual capital is document literacy.[b] This skill is measured on a scale ranging from 0 to 500 points, which permits the classification of individuals in five levels of competence.

The main explanatory variable with which we seek to explain education and literacy skills is the level of education of the parents. In order to have a sufficient sample size by level of education achieved, we aggregated the data bearing on the education of parents on three levels: schooling below the second cycle in secondary education, completion of the second cycle and post-secondary diploma. When both parents do not have the same level of education, we codify the variable on the education of the parents, so that it corresponds to the education of the parent who has attained the highest level. In two-thirds of these cases, this is the level of education of the father.[c]

To take account of the effect of other factors, measured in the survey employed, on the length of schooling and literacy skills, we introduce other variables in the regressions. Considering the optional nature of several questions in the survey, we find only a very limited number of pertinent explicative variables common to the 11 countries considered. We must therefore limit ourselves to the following control variables: sex, age and situation of mother tongue with respect to test language and immigrant status (determined by place of birth).[d]

For different reasons, we have been led to exclude certain observations from the available sample at the start. In each country, we retained the optimal samples relevant to the analysis.[e]

All the results presented in this document come from the following models:

$$YSCHL = a + b\,SEX + c\,AGE + d\,PAREDU + e\,IMMILANG + f\,SEX*AGE + g\,SEX*PAREDU + h\,AGE*PAREDU + i\,SEX*IMMILANG + j\,AGE*IMMILANG + k\,PAREDU*IMMILANG$$

$$DOC = a + b\,SEX + c\,AGE + d\,PAREDU + e\,IMMILANG + f\,SEX*AGE + g\,SEX*PAREDU + h\,AGE*PAREDU + i\,SEX*IMMILANG + j\,AGE*IMMILANG + k\,PAREDU*IMMILANG$$

where:
YSCHL = number of years of education claimed by the respondent;
DOC = score obtained in tests of comprehension of schematic texts;
SEX = sex of the respondent;
AGE = age of the respondent (respondents are divided into five age groups);
PAREDU = level of education completed with success by the parents (this variable takes three possible values, plus one which regroups the respondents who do not know the level of schooling attained by at least one of their parents); and
IMMILANG = composite variable created by joining the linguistic status of the respondent and his or her immigration status.
SEX*AGE, SEX*PAREDU, AGE*PAREDU,
SEX*IMMILANG, AGE*IMMILANG, PAREDU*IMMILANG are variables of interaction among primary variables permitting one to take account of possible effects of interactions on the dependent variable.

For four countries (Belgium/Flanders, Ireland, Poland and Sweden), we have retained the two models above without the variable of interaction involving IMMILANG inasmuch as situations represented by these interactions did not exist in the collected data.

Appendix notes

a To obtain information on the objectives, methodology and general results of the study, the reader is invited to consult the three following publications: OECD & Statistics Canada (1995), HRDC & OECD (1997), U.S. Department of Educaton, National Center for Education Statistics (1998).

b This is defined as the "knowledge and skills required to locate and use information contained in various formats, including job applications, payroll forms, transportation schedules, maps, tables and graphics."

c For fuller details on the choice, see de Broucker & Underwood (1998).

d A similar study conducted with the same source of data to analyze the Canadian situation was able to use other variables, not being constrained by the requirements for international comparisons [de Broucker & Lavallée (1998)].

e Details of the technical considerations leading to the definition of the sample employed are available from the authors.

PART IV

NATIONAL POLICIES AND THE USE OF INDICATORS

Chapter 13

Equity and Equivalence in the Swedish School System

Anna Wildt-Persson
Skolverket/Swedish National Agency for Education, Stockholm

Per Gunnar Rosengren
Skolverket/Swedish National Agency for Education, Stockholm

The formation of a country's education system takes place in a historical context and comes to reflect some national characteristics. Equity is a main concern in Swedish policy-making and has been so since the end of the 19th century when Fridtjuv Berg formulated his idea of elementary school as a basic school for all. The Swedish Education Act[1] provides a basis for equity in the school: "All children and young people shall, regardless of gender, geographical residence, and social or economical situation, have equal access to education in the public school system for children and young people." The education provided within each type of school should be of equivalent value, irrespective of where in the country it is provided. National goals specify the norms for equivalence. However, equivalent education does not mean that education should be the same everywhere or that the resources of a school should be allocated equally.[2] The act stipulates that consideration must also be afforded to pupils with special needs. The school has a special responsibility for those pupils who, for different reasons, experience difficulties in attaining the established educational goals.

The links between education and the rest of society are widely recognized, and one task of the school system is to foster in children a spirit of equality and democratic values. The Education Act specifies that education should "provide pupils with knowledge and skills, and, working together with their families, promote their harmonious development towards becoming responsible human beings and members of society."[3]

Sweden has tried to promote equity through a variety of educational policies. Studies have also shown that inequalities in Swedish society have diminished over the last century in the sense that the influence of a number of background factors important for educational attainment—parents' class or social position, cultural capital, type of community and gender—have been reduced.[4] But is this the result of educational policies, welfare policies or a combination of both?

Concerns have been raised about a trade-off between equity, in terms of socioeconomic status, and effectiveness, in terms of achievement. Studies in many countries seem to suggest that such concerns are valid. However, according to an analysis of the Third International Mathematics and Science Study (TIMSS) results presented in this anthology, some countries, among them Sweden, are characterized by both high efficiency and low levels of socioeconomic inequity.[5]

In a decentralized educational system, such as Sweden's, follow-up and evaluation are of central importance in monitoring equity. This paper shows some attempts to establish a conceptual framework and to find tools to accomplish this. To give the reader an understanding of the Swedish notion of equity, with respect to the administration and organization of the Swedish education system, a brief description of the system is provided in section 2. The section includes discussions of equity and socioeconomic status, the roles of evaluation and follow-up, and some international comparative studies. In section 3, the term equivalence is introduced, together with some examples of how equivalence can be translated into a set of areas of reference for evaluating equity. The first example, presented in section 3.2, is a conceptual model, identifying critical areas for the measurement of equity. Another example, given in section 3.3, is the development of indicators referring to equity in preconditions, process and results. The establishment of such educational indicators is also an attempt to achieve a balance between monitoring and promoting school development. The system of indicators, now being developed in Sweden, is one tool to promote school development and represents a shift in focus from the central to the local level. Finally, the paper summarizes the situation today in the Swedish school system and in society as a whole, pointing to some areas of concern for the future.

The paper does not claim to provide a complete description of policy and research in this area, nor does it include any new research. It does, however, describe and provide examples of how Sweden is working with particular methods to measure and monitor equity in its education system.[6]

1.   Objectives and organization of Swedish educational policy and programs

1.1.   Organization of the Swedish education system

The Education Act regulates early childhood education and schooling up to the university level. Preschools to upper-secondary and adult education have national curricula, and different types of schools have national syllabi. The goals in the curricula are derived from principles laid down in the Swedish constitution. The constitution speaks of "respect for the equal value of every individual and for the freedom and dignity of the individual."[7] This sentence maintains that all people are of equal worth, but also that the state should remain neutral in questions of values, i.e., with respect to the fact that different citizens hold different values and have their own individual goals in life. An important principle in achieving equity has been and still is the compensatory principle, i.e., that the state should *not* remain neutral in issues relating to equal opportunity. Differences among geographical regions, social or economic groups must not be attributable to any form of discrimination that would indicate that the principle of equality has been neglected.

Early childhood education is regarded as the first step in the Swedish educational system. Its guidelines were drawn up at the beginning of the 1970s and have since then developed with the aim of providing universal child care of good quality, organized mainly by municipalities and financed by public funds. Legislation assures equal access to child care as municipalities are required to provide it without unreasonable delay.[8] As a result, 75 percent of all children between the ages of 1 and 5, and 66 percent of school children in the 6- to 9-year-old age group are enrolled in early childhood education and supervised after-school programs.[9]

To assure good quality, child-care activities follow guidelines laid down in national curricula for preschool and other child-care programs, including after-school activities for children up to 12 years of age. These national guidelines contain objectives, which are linked to those of the curriculum for compulsory school. The Organisation for Economic Co-operation and Development (OECD) has recently published a review of early child-care policies and programs in Sweden, in which it concluded that these services reflect societal values like democracy, solidarity and equality, with theoretical and pedagogical understandings of childhood permeating practice and policy.[10] Early childhood education and care programs form the first part of a lifelong learning process. In the present text, the focus will be on the Swedish school system and reforms undertaken during the last decade.

Since the appointment in 1946 of a commission of Parliament members on a comprehensive school system, the Swedish education system has moved towards a comprehensive public school. In 1962, a nine-year unified compulsory school program for all children ages 7 to 16 was introduced. A few years later, a new upper-secondary school and technical-vocational school were established. The 1970 reform brought the technical-vocational schools and vocational education together into a single administrative unit, integrating all forms of academic and vocational education in what was designated as the upper-secondary school, for pupils between the ages of 16 and 19. In the curriculum of 1994, the government introduced core subjects with more theoretical content into the curriculum of the upper-secondary school, giving students in vocational training basic eligibility for higher education.

Adult education is another important aspect of equity, as it allows for retraining and further study later in life. One example is a special, large-scale government initiative, parallel to the regular adult education system, to provide adults who are under-educated, or have educational deficiencies, with remedial instruction and an education corresponding to the upper-secondary level.

Equity carries a particular significance for children with special educational needs. The majority of these children are integrated into regular child-care activities, compulsory schools and upper-secondary schools. There are, however, eight special schools for pupils with hearing/vision and physical disabilities, as well as some schools for the mentally handicapped. A total of 1 percent of all pupils in the compulsory and upper-secondary school levels are in such segregated settings. This is a small share in an international comparison, but a tendency towards a growing number of pupils in segregated settings have been observed during the last decade.

At the end of the 1980s and the beginning of the 1990s, the education system went through great changes. The school system was decentralized, with the idea that, the school system would become more receptive to change and more sensitive to its interest groups. A new financial system was introduced, which essentially moved resource allocation from the national to the local level, combined with a new type of steering and control mechanism. Since 1991, the school system has been under municipal management. Overall responsibility for the implementation, development and financing of school activities now devolves on the municipalities (there are 289), which are governed by political representatives, elected every fourth year. The former system of state control of schools through the medium of regulations and resources has been replaced by goal- and achievement-referenced guidance, based on objectives of the National Education Act and other statutory instruments dealing with education and curricula. The purpose of this decentralization has been to achieve a school system that is governed by national objectives, but rooted at the local level. The ultimate responsibility for schools still lies, however, with the State, which is responsible for guaranteeing equity of education, a goal laid down in the Education Act.

The reform also brought changed financial conditions for private schools. Private schools, which were approved as meeting compulsory schooling standards, are now entitled to public grants. The aim was to revitalize the school system through diversification and increased freedom for children and parents to choose their schools. As a result, the share of pupils in private schools in the compulsory level has increased from 1.9 percent in 1991 to 3 percent in 1999. The number of private schools has also increased accordingly, from 94 in 1991 to 331 in 1998, but private schools are still, as in the past, most common in the metropolitan areas.

In 1994, a new grading system was also introduced in Sweden. According to the new system, grades are to be given according to nationally formulated criteria denoting certain qualities of knowledge and skills corresponding to the syllabus for a given subject. The possible grades are: "pass," "pass with distinction" and "pass with special distinction." When a student in compulsory school fails to meet the criteria of the syllabus, no grade is given; in upper-secondary school, the grade "fail" is given. The criteria, however, are to be based on curricula and syllabi, without reference to the accomplishments of a pupil's peers. This system of grading is referred to as absolute in comparison with its predecessor, a relative system, in which grades were awarded on a Gauss curve denoting the normal performance for a given age group of pupils. The possible grades had been 1, 2, 3, 4 and 5, with 5 denoting the best performance. The new grading system has influenced the debate about equity in Sweden. The new system, with only three possible grades in the compulsory school level and four in the upper-secondary level, distinctly shows failure or inadequate work on the part of the school or its students, as the grade "pass" is determined by the fulfillment of basic requirements for a school's work.

Because education is based on a system of objectives and results, it is of the utmost importance that follow-up and evaluation are carried out on the national as well as the local level. The school system's current official guidelines assume that differences exist between the municipalities and schools as a consequence of local political and professional decisions. The decentralization, together with an introduction of more actors, (i.e., the increasing number of private schools), has led to greater variance, and the issue of whether there is a conflict between decentralization and equity. In other words, has decentralization led to variation between schools and student achievement (which could violate the equity objectives)?

The National Agency for Education is the central administrative authority for the locally administered school system and child-care activities in Sweden. Its principal task is to actively encourage the realization of the goals and guidelines laid down by the government and Parliament. The national agency has performed this task by compiling empirically based material on the national level through evaluation, case studies and supervision. The national agency also maintains a national follow-up system containing information about individual students' performance, socioeconomic background, ethnicity and parents' education, as well as the resources, location and average student performance of schools. Follow-up studies show a large variance in results and resources among and within municipalities. Evaluations also demonstrate that the increased choices among compulsory schools, and the establishment of more private schools, have introduced tendencies towards segregation in areas of different socioeconomic status. Parents with a higher average educational level are more likely to choose a private school, than are parents with a lower average educational level. The possibility to choose another school also indicates the persistence of socioeconomic differences among school populations.[11]

1.2. Performance of the Swedish education system in an international comparison

The level of educational attainment is relatively high in Sweden compared with that of many other countries. On average among OECD countries, the proportion of people, ages 25 to 64, who had attained at least an upper-secondary education in 1998 was 61 percent; 21 percent had attained at least a tertiary education. The corresponding values for Sweden were 76 and 28 percent, respectively, in 1998.[12]

Sweden has participated in several international surveys of pupils' knowledge and skills. TIMSS is one example. This study of student achievement in mathematics and science was carried out in 1994–95 covering more than 40 countries. The survey showed 13-year-olds in Swedish compulsory schools to be above the international average for science, and in line with the international average for mathematics. In mathematics, there was little or no difference in results between boys and girls in Sweden. However, in several other countries, boys performed better. In science, the average result for boys was better than for girls in Sweden, as well as in a majority of the participating countries.[13] Results from the TIMSS study for students completing upper-secondary education showed that Sweden was one of the top countries among the 21 participating countries.[14] Swedish students scored well in mathematics and science, and Sweden has improved its position from previous years.

The International Association for the Evaluation of Educational Achievement (IEA) Study of Reading Literacy, carried out in 1990–91, with 31 participating countries, showed favorable results in literacy for Swedish 9-year-olds.[15] Results from another comparative study of France, Spain and Sweden, carried out in 1996–97 and measuring pupils' knowledge of English, showed that the Swedish pupils possessed better knowledge of English than their French and Spanish peers.[16]

The International Adult Literacy Survey (IALS), carried out in 12 of OECD's member countries in 1995, measured adult literacy, or basic proficiency and competence in three areas. Among these were the ability to understand and interpret printed and written information, and to use information from different sources to carry out basic calculations. Among the participating countries, Sweden exhibited the best performance, but also the lowest variance in results, in all three tests. Even adults with a low level of formal education were found to have good results in basic literacy.[17]

As this volume went to press, Sweden was also preparing to participate in PISA (Program for International Student Assessment), together with over 30 countries. Students born in 1984 are assessed in reading literacy, mathematics literacy and science literacy. PISA surveys are planned for 2000, 2003 and 2006, and in each of these surveys, one area will be studied in depth. Data from this large international survey, containing indicators of students' knowledge and skills, as well as context and trend indicators, will form a basis for further comparative studies.

1.3.   Sweden, socioeconomic status and equity

A student's education can be helped or hindered by his or her societal circumstances. Evaluation shows that background factors such as the educational level of the parents, a student's ethnicity, and other socioeconomic variables correlate strongly with student achievement. According to a study of the relationship between resources and performance results (in terms of students' average grades) of schools, 42 percent of the variation in average grades among all Swedish schools in the 1994–95 school year was explained by five background variables.[18] These five factors reflected different resource-related preconditions for school activity. The strongest explanatory variable was the average educational level of the parents of those attending the school.

Other explanatory variables at the school level were gender (the higher the percentage of boys, the lower the achievement at the school level); the percentage of pupils with foreign backgrounds (the higher the percentage, the lower the achievement of the school); school size (the larger the school, the lower the achievement of the school); and the number of teachers per pupil. The first four variables have a relatively simple relationship to grading. The fifth, teacher resources per pupil, presents a more complicated connection. Because the Swedish school system follows a policy of compensatory resource allocation, less favorable preconditions often lead to more teacher resources per pupil. At the same time, more teacher resources have a specific positive effect on average grades for individual schools; the net effect, after allowance has been made for the negative compensatory connection, is estimated to be positive.

Our extensive system of redistribution of income aims to equalize or at least moderate the differences in background factors that give rise to differences in achievements. As mentioned above, additional resources are allocated for the support of students with more difficult preconditions, and for schools with below-average grades, and redistribution takes place within the education system, as well as in the society as a whole. Have the policies encouraging equalization produced any effects over time? Jonsson's findings[19] suggest that the influence of a number of background factors significant to educational attainment, such as the social position of parents, cultural capital, type of community and gender, has diminished over the last century.

According to Jonsson, the class equalization with regard to educational attainment in Sweden must be characterized as pervasive. The most disadvantaged classes have improved their situation the most, and equalization is not restricted to certain classes. There are several reasons why equalization has taken place. Reforms in the education system—for example, study allowances, non-selective admissions and the possibility to continue one's education later in life (reducing the risk over time for pupils from low-educated homes)—are contributing factors. Expansion of the education-equalized standards of living and changes in the labor market also play a role. How much significance each variable plays is yet to be determined.

A finding underlining the importance of socioeconomic equity in relation to educational achievement is shown by Vandenberghe et al. (Chapter 9). The authors demonstrate a low correlation between socioeconomic status and educational achievements, using results from TIMSS, in Sweden. These results may well be unusual in an international context. For instance, the United States and Switzerland were found to have high degrees of correlation between results and socioeconomic status (SES). The compensatory principle as it is implemented in the educational system, and other aspects of Swedish society, may well account for Sweden's low correlation between SES and educational results.

Variance in achievement among groups of students is observed though the national follow-up system. Students with foreign backgrounds receive lower average grades than do their peers, fewer qualify for higher education and they have a higher dropout rate from upper-secondary education. There are also differences in achievement between girls and boys. Girls receive higher average grades in the majority of all subjects in compulsory and upper-secondary school.[20] Results from national examinations in compulsory and upper-secondary school support this difference in the subjects Swedish and, to some extent, English, but show no difference in results in mathematics. Variance in achievement among schools is relatively low in an international comparison.[21] There is, however, from a national perspective and with respect to the goals in the national guidelines, evidence of differences among schools and tendencies towards segregation in Sweden. In the study "Stimulating Competition,"[22] the National Agency for Education followed 4,000 pupils in compulsory education in 1974–75, and found segregation between schools. The study showed that the residential areas in which students and their parents lived were highly linked to SES. Because schools recruit pupils locally, the student body also tends to reflect the social status of the neighborhood. The study divided students into two groups, one encompassing students from a high-status area and one containing students from a low-status area: 80 percent of the children of parents with academic education went to schools where 80 percent of the children of working-class parents did not go.

The socioeconomic composition of residential areas thus becomes visible in the student body and is also reinforced by the students' own choice of courses and teachers' organization of instruction. Studies have indicated that residential areas around larger cities are rather segregated. Areas with major differences in level of household income tend to have a higher proportion of pupils attending private schools. The same conditions apply to areas where a number of different ethnic groups or religious beliefs are represented.

In the society at large, there are also indicators suggesting a move towards greater socioeconomic inequalities. Since Sweden is characterized by relatively even distribution of income and wealth, compared with those of other countries, a sizeable proportion of government expenditures consist of transfer payments to households, and social expenditures constitute about a third of the gross domestic product. In the early 1990s, Sweden experienced a deep recession. Employment rates fell, leading to an increase in demands on cash support, for example, in the form of unemployment compensation, in turn leading to a rapid weakening of public-sector finances. Decreased income transfers were followed by heightened demands for social spending, and for several years in the beginning of the decade, average household incomes fell. Demographic changes have also increased the pressure on the welfare system, increasing segregation (in terms of ethnic division among residential areas) during the 1990s. The economic crisis thus meant a sharp deterioration in public finances at the beginning of the 1990s. Towards the middle of the decade, the situation stabilized, bringing about a moderate increase in public financing and household incomes, however, not to pre-crisis standards. The decade has been characterized by large-scale changes in the organization and delivery of public services, in which the key words have been decentralization and privatization.[23]

2. Evaluating equivalence

2.1. The concept of equivalence

This paper uses three terms central to the concept of fair chances in education: equity, equality and equivalence. The terms are related, but do not carry the same meaning and need to be more closely defined.

Equity is a general term indicating "fairness;" for example, that principles of justice have been used in the assessment of a phenomenon. The term says nothing, however, of the principle used to make that assessment. Different principles of justice can be applied to evaluate a situation and still be viewed as "fair" depending on the principle. However, the principles of justice vary. For example, the principles of giving to each person according to his or her ability, or purchasing power, can be viewed as compatible with equity, but they may still not correspond to the expectations a group of people or a society may have of equity. That education should be accessible according to purchasing power is not generally regarded as fair in Sweden.

Equality is another term describing fairness, but carries a slightly different meaning. Equality indicates fairness by application of a comparison. If the relationship between the sexes, for example, is equal, it means that men and women must have the same rights. The term therefore assumes a certain degree of conformity as it implies that a certain standard must be achieved before a situation can be regarded as equal.

Equivalence is used to mean "of equal worth," and does not imply a strict criterion for comparing two objects, but does assume comparability. Educational paths, for example, can be equivalent, but do not necessarily have to contain identical courses and subjects to have the same worth.

An article by Lindensjö[24] questions the notion of one school with a common curriculum for all. Lindensjö argues that education is not of equal worth for all. Interest in education, and perceptions of the benefits of education, do vary among people. But he also notes that the reforms in Sweden have led to the insight that it is difficult to attain true equity without promoting uniformity, which in turn is seen as negative. Therefore, the term equivalence has become central in the Swedish Education Act and has thus come to replace equality as the adjective describing the principles of equity.

Meuret discusses principles of equity (Chapter 5). He states that the goal of the theories of justice is to help us decide which inequalities are acceptable and which are not. Benadusi (Chapter 1) argues that the origins of these inequalities stem from powerful forces in society. Meuret suggests that educational equity can be defined as the method of operating an educational system that favors students as much as possible.

As stated in the Introduction of this chapter, the Swedish principle of fair education is equivalence, and it is operationalized in the school act, which states that all children between the ages of 6 and 16 should, regardless of sex, economic means and location of residence, have equal access to education. The school act also holds that the education process should be equivalent and the outcomes of equal worth. The national curriculum (LPO 94) states that: "education shall be adapted to each pupil's circumstances and needs. However, equivalent education does not mean that the education provided within each type of school shall be the same everywhere or that the resources of the school shall be allocated equally. Furthermore the school has a special responsibility for those pupils who for different reasons experience difficulties attaining these goals."

The school act does not hold, however, that results should be equal. Results may vary within the system, and education may still be regarded as equivalent, but if the system systematically discriminates against certain groups such as women or immigrants, then it fails to be equivalent.

The term *quality* is also a central term in this paper, and it will be used in conjunction with the other three. Quality is often used in a descriptive sense, stating for example that an object possesses a certain quality. However, in this paper quality will be used in the normative sense as in "all good qualities." The term requires a more precise definition to be usable in this context. The definition given to quality by the National Agency for Education is goal attainment or high attainment of the goals for education established by Parliament and the government. The government stated in its last development plan[25] for the education system that the goal of equivalence must be founded on quality awareness at all levels of the school system. More measures must be taken to assure quality in all parts of the system. If schools do not perform at a certain standard, then the system fails to promote equivalence and individual students will receive an education that does not meet the national standard.

In curricula and syllabi, the *goals lay* the foundation for[26] the desired development of quality in the school and thus support the fundamental guidelines for school performance. Quality in relationship to these goals is, then, determined by the extent to which a school works to attain them, measured both in terms of results and the steps it takes to keep working in the right direction. Quality in relation to *goals to be attained* should be assessed in accordance with the extent to which pupils attain or surpass them. That assessment should be made based both on the average results and the variation of results. It should also be assessed according to which steps are taken to achieve the results.

This last aspect is related to the concept of equivalence, the National Agency for Education states that the school must operate in such a way as to allow each student to develop optimally according to his or her ability. At the core of the national guidelines lies the requirement that schools will always strive for development and innovation, important dynamic elements.

However, it is also relevant to discuss quality and equivalence in relation to nationally established prerequisites for school work, such as teacher competence and the guidelines for the work of the school, i.e., the pedagogical process. Such demands are set forth in the school act and other national documents.

Quality cannot always be assessed in relation to national goals, though of course this may make assessment more difficult. In such cases, quality must be assessed in relation to research or evaluations, where an analysis of the causes for different degrees of goal attainment makes it possible to find connections between the school organization and the results (quality).

Finally, there may be an inherent contradiction between national goals and guidelines, stemming from political decisions on the one hand, and the results of research and evaluations on the other. If the latter are used as criteria for assessments, they cannot, in the short term, contradict that which is nationally decided. Such a situation may of course lead to changes in national goals and guidelines. It is an important task of the National Agency for Education to inform Parliament and the government of research and evaluations that indicate that national goals and guidelines must be altered so that such contradictions may be removed.

A decentralized system with several actors, in which all have the capacity and the right to act independently of each other, requires monitoring of the quality of the instruction offered. The Swedish government stated in its last development plan—describing the general direction of government policy for a period of three years—that the goal of equivalence is hollow if it is not combined with quality,[27] and that more measures must be taken in order to assure quality in all parts of the educational system.

The following sections provide some examples of how the national agency works to monitor and evaluate equivalence.

2.2.   Equivalence—a conceptual mode

In order to monitor equivalence, the National Agency for Education has tried to make the term equivalence operational by dividing it into three aspects (see Figure 1). Instead of formulating a precise definition, the national agency identified critical areas relating to it: equal access, equivalent education and the equal value of education. The first column addresses prerequisites for equal access to education (i.e., it must be accessible regardless of gender, geographic location, social and economic circumstances). The second column implies that the education process should give students an environment for learning in accordance with their needs, and that schools should be sensitive to students with special needs. It also relates to adults entering the educational system. Finally, in the third column, "the equal value of an education" relates to the possibility of leaving school qualified for further work or studies, i.e., the results of education must be comparable for all.

Columns one and two are thus associated with what is commonly referred to as equal opportunity or the right to have access to education and the possibility to choose. Equal opportunity is also related to equal treatment in the school according to the criteria of the curriculum, which really states that the school should be compensatory. The third column is related to equality of outcomes. The national agency has chosen to work with all three aspects of equivalence, although one could argue that the school acts holds that equal opportunity should be the main concern of the agency, not so much equality of outcomes.

Figure 1. Equivalence in schools

Prerequisites	Process	Results
Equal access to education	Equivalent education	The equal value of an education
Regardless of:		With respect to:
Gender	Within every type of school	Further study
Geographical location	Wherever in the country a	Society
Social circumstances	school is run	Working life
Economic circumstances		

Some of the factors that can be considered as central to the matter of equal access to education are:

Equal access

- *Educational options:* What do the actual educational options look like in different parts of the country? How well do pedagogical leaders cooperate in order to increase the number of options for pupils?
- *Information regarding current options:* How do educators and guidance counselors inform pupils and parents about educational options, and can that information change traditional patterns of choice?
- *Admissions and the selection process:* Are schools really open to all? What kinds of admissions regulations and selection criteria are in place? Do schools have fees?
- *Gender:* Does everyone have equal access to education, regardless of gender? How can schools work to change traditional gender patterns with respect to the choice of educational fields and careers?
- *Social circumstances:* Does everyone have access to educational options, regardless of individual social circumstances? How does residential segregation influence actual opportunities to gain access to education? Why do pupils and their parents make the choices they do?

Equivalent education

Other central statutory conditions for ensuring equivalence in education include:
- *Education offered:* Is a broad range of subjects and courses offered with respect to, for instance, language choice and the students' interests? Is instruction in Swedish offered to immigrants, as well as instruction in the immigrants' own language and Swedish as a second language?
- *Teaching carried out in accordance with the relevant curriculum, program targets and syllabi:* Is instruction planned accordingly?
- *Sufficient time for learning:* Are students offered the amount of time in class that is guaranteed in the school act? This is considered to be a minimum requirement for students to be able to meet the goals of the curriculum.
- *Trained staff:* Does the municipality use teachers who are trained in the subjects they teach and who have pedagogical know-how?
- *An effective school principal:* Does this person effectively monitor, evaluate and supervise operations? Research shows the importance of effective school management.
- *Support for students:* Does the school provide students with the support they need to meet the goals of the curriculum? Are action plans developed

for those who require special support? This is a key point in a school without tracking or selection.

- *Pupils evaluated on an equal basis:* Are pupils evaluated in accordance with the relevant grading criteria?

Equal value

Below are some of the areas that can be considered central to the equal value of educational programs.

- *Further study:* Do the upper-secondary schools provide pupils with the knowledge they need in order to go on to higher studies? Is the education provided in upper-secondary schools equally valuable with respect to both university and college admissions? How are admission regulations and selection criteria determined? To what extent do pupils go on to higher education from the different educational programs?

- *Society:* Do schools manage to live up to their goal of communicating and instilling in pupils the values upon which life as a member of society rests: the inviolability of human life, the freedom and integrity of the individual, the equal worth of all human beings, equality between men and women, and solidarity with the weak and vulnerable? Do schools communicate the more durable knowledge that constitutes the common frame of reference that all members of society need? Are pupils provided with the basis for lifelong learning?

- *Working life:* Do the upper-secondary schools manage to deepen and develop students' knowledge in preparation for future participation in the workforce?

The first two perspectives were developed into a model for the inspection of schools and municipalities. Because the National Agency for Education opposed using an exact definition of equivalence, the model for inspection had to be focused on assessing whether a municipality had the prerequisites for equivalence rather than assessing whether the said municipality really offered equivalent education. The municipalities inspected were assessed in reference to a number of criteria, corresponding to those cited above. Depending on these findings, some municipalities were criticized if they failed to meet the requirements of any of these criteria.

Inspecting municipalities in reference to these criteria became unwieldy; it was difficult for the inspectors to achieve a balance between the depth needed to assess the complexity of equivalence and the perspective needed to reach a conclusion based on all criteria. The agency therefore adopted another method of inspection in which follow-up and evaluation (equivalent education) constituted a criterion, always linked to two or more from the first group (equal access). That criterion—monitoring—has become one of the most important.

However, inspection is not the only way for the national agency to monitor equivalence. Studies using a different approach have been used to measure such issues as, the differences between small and large schools, ways to organize classes and choices of study in upper-secondary school.

2.3. Equivalence and quality

A decentralized system with several actors, in which all have the capacity and the right to act independently of each other, requires monitoring of the quality of the instruction offered. If parts of the educational system do not adhere to a certain standard, the education system itself will fail to promote equivalence. One of the tasks of the National Agency for Education has so far been to show variance with respect to preconditions and results, thus providing policy-makers with a basis for decision-making. The national follow-up system provides this information. Its purpose is to supply objective, empirically founded input data for the assessment of goal achievement in Swedish schools, for State control of the sector, and for local development work by the educational providers (i.e., municipalities and private schools), as well as for public debate generally. The system contains information about the organization, resources and results within the school system, which is published on a yearly basis. The data provide opportunities for comprehensive analyses at both the national and municipal levels. Many variables are also available at the level of schools and individuals. Those available at the school level include particulars about the extent of school management resources, teaching resources and grading. Grading data are also available at the level of the individual, as are data concerning, for example, teachers, students' SES and students' ethnicity. The follow-up system provides a basis for description and comparison, as well as opportunities for quantitative and qualitative analyses.

As previously stated, follow-up and evaluation in Sweden show growing inequalities and variance of results among schools and pupils. These results, together with a decentralized education system, offering significant freedom of action, have shown a need for a new type of information to supplement the information on preconditions, resources and results.

A system of quality indicators would illuminate qualitative aspects of the preschool and school sectors, for the ultimate purpose of contributing towards development of quality in the core activity. To establish a link between equivalence and equity, and provide policy-makers, parents and students with the information they need to make appropriate choices, more qualitative information must be gathered. Such information would make the education system more transparent. The National Agency for Education already collects much data from the municipalities and therefore sees a need to limit the collection of quantitative information in favor of qualitative information.

This being so, a national quality indicator system should be viewed as a national development instrument, aimed at influencing local educational development. This means that the indicator system must be serviceable at all levels of the education system, i.e., at the operative level in preschools and schools, at the district or municipal level and at the national level. The requirement is for the system to supply relevant information at all levels, but above all to those directly responsible for activities. This in turn means that information obtained at the operative level must be capable of aggregation into a municipal picture, which in turn can be aggregated with national data.

A good deal of the data concerning preconditions, and operational goals, are already available within national follow-up systems. Much of these data are more in the nature of analytical variables than concrete indicators of quality. Nonetheless, a reason for choosing to include them in the system of indicators is that, on their own or together with other information, they can help to explain outcomes in other parts of the indicator system.

2.4.   Structure of the indicator system

The intention in creating a system of quality indicators has been to develop the follow-up needed for quality development in the school system. As work on the system has progressed, the emphasis has changed from simply supplying information about quality development at regular intervals to developing indicators that can also supply information about how a school might work towards a specific national goal. The indicator system must be able not only to supply relevant information at the local and national levels, but also to supply information about quality development.

Pursuant to this discussion of quality and equivalence, quality has been defined as goal fulfillment. The goals are provided in the curricula and they are numerous. The indicators must therefore be relatively comprehensive in relation to the national goal documents. The indicator areas are governed by those goals that are specially highlighted in curricula, syllabi and general recommendations, and that the agency, on the strength of supervisory activities, has reason to believe are central to equivalence; for example, local evaluation. Factors such as evaluations and research—which we know from experience have an important bearing on the qualitative development of preschool education and school activities, and also on potential achievement by individual students—should determine indicators, as should knowledge and experience concerning the qualitative development of activities. The indicator system has a basic structure of three general areas: prerequisites, process and results. Those related to prerequisites are not really indicators, but rather more variables for analysis. They are included because these, together with other relevant information, can help to explain results in other parts of the indicator system. Indicators with respect to the *preconditions* consist mainly of quantitative data obtained through the regular collections of national follow-up data.

Examples of indicators of preconditions include the number of preschool children eligible for childcare because their parents work or study full- or part-time. The supply of education (elementary school and upper-secondary school) is related to the possibility to choose a school and to proximity of education (i.e., distance to school and availability of busing). There are also a number of indicators related to staffing. For elementary school, these are density (teacher/ pupil and staff/pupil ratios), continuity (turnover of employees, sick leaves, etc.) and training (training in subjects, pedagogical training and development of competence). Another set of indicators reflects pupils' prior knowledge as measured by parents' formal education and pupils' special needs when starting school. There are also indicators for expenditures, specific allocations and the physical resources, such as teaching aids, available to a school. Indicators of process consist of assessments of quality, on a scale from 1 to 6, to show how schools are working to realize their national goals. Assessments can be made by national inspectors or through self-assessment by the staff.

The indicators relating to the education process are formulated as goal areas in which each indicator is based on one particular goal of the curriculum. Each goal is followed by a set of reference points indicating a work or education process of high quality in a school. The reference points draw on the results of evaluation, research and verifiable experience. The goal areas are in most cases identical, regardless of school, but the reference points are according to the age of the children/pupils and type of school. The agency has decided that it is necessary to use national inspectors for the collection of such data to assure objectivity.

An example of a process indicator related to preschool children in need of special support would, for example, show the extent to which the pedagogical environment is adapted to those children with special needs. Two points of reference among several areas follows:

• The administrator of the preschool uses special pedagogic competence when planning the environment of the preschool; the goal is that each child should be able to play and learn in his or her normal environment.

• The greater part of the professional support for the child is carried out within the scope of regular activities. Children with special needs and handicapped children are integrated into the group and participate in most activities. Those persons who are responsible for support have the competence and the time needed.

There are several indicators related to the educational process, which are divided into three general areas, the first of which deals with working procedures and working environment. This area contains the following indicators: children's/ pupils' participation and influence; children's/pupils' personal and social development; pedagogical work; support for children/pupils with special needs;

pedagogical uses of the physical environment; school-family interaction; staff-pupil interaction; staff cooperation; interaction among different types of schools/activities; interaction between working life and the community; the pupils' working environment (including, for example, established safety routines or procedures); the staff's working environment; and legal safeguards. The second general area is management and leadership, which includes goal documents, responsibilities and duties of the pedagogical leader, responsibilities mandated by the curriculum and decision-making. The third area is quality control/development, in which control of activities and quality development are the two indicators.

Indicators relating to goal achievement are of two kinds. Indicators for the goals to be pursued (according to the curricula) are obtained in the following assessments on a four-point scale, while indicators for goals to be achieved (according to the curricula) are obtained through quantitative data collected through the national follow-up system.

Here are examples of indicators relating to goal achievement in basic democratic values:

• The curriculum constitutes a "living" document, which is the starting point of all activities.

• The staff and children show that they have the ability to discover and reflect upon ethical dilemmas in everyday situations.

The following are examples of indicators related to students' results or outcomes that are common to both preschool and compulsory schools. The first three goal areas are assessed by using points of reference (as in the example of process indicators above). The first of these three indicators consists of operative goals, which relate to the overarching goals of education, i.e., the norms and values of democracy and solidarity. The second of the three includes basic value goals related to social and personal development; the third, encompasses such overarching fields of knowledge as environment, internationalization, and awareness of the hazards of drugs and alcohol. The following outcome indicators are measured through grades in individual subjects: such as Swedish, English and mathematics, and through educational goals. Also relevant is the ratio of the percentage of pupils who advance to upper-secondary education, out of all pupils enrolled in compulsory education.

This indicator system is currently being tested in a number of schools and municipalities. It has not yet been fully developed, but preliminary results indicate that it is having a salutary effect on pedagogical discussion and goal achievement. The schools involved in testing the system found that the strong link between the curricula and quality is very important, and makes the national task of the schools clearer. This tool has a natural place in the continuing work at the local level. The system can be used in all parts of local work, namely goal formulation, development, evaluation and assessment of goal attainment, and formulation of new goals.

The system contains a great number of indicators and, if all are used, they will require access to resources beyond what schools usually have at their disposition. The agency has therefore decided that schools may select indicators according to local priorities or to suit the particular requirements of municipal monitoring. The schools should, however, choose indicators from all three areas: preconditions, process and results. The National Agency for Education believes that indicators from all three areas render the assessments fair and multidimensional, but of course they will also make benchmarking more complex. As this book went to press it had not been finally decided when the system would be implemented.

Conclusions and discussion

The aim of this chapter has been to describe the status of equity in Swedish education politics, discuss the importance of education system reform in this matter, and explain how Swedish follow-up and indicator systems are structured in order to monitor equity and variations within the system.

Equity and equivalence have been the main policy concerns in Sweden during the last decades. Policies of redistribution in society at large and in education have been used to achieve them. Studies have confirmed a decreasing influence of background factors, such as parent's position in society, gender and type of community, in educational attainment as a result both of educational and other welfare policies. The relative effects of the different factors are, however, difficult to estimate. Research seems to indicate that the education system cannot on its own increase equity in educational attainment and the educational level of a population.[28] It is, consequently, not enough to provide the opportunity for an individual; social patterns must also be influenced.

The 1990s have seen increasing inequalities in socioeconomic standards and segregation by place of residence. Families with children have been particularly affected as reductions in spending have occurred in those public services provided for children. The Swedish education system has gone through great changes. The shift from decentralization to municipal administration, the establishment of more private schools, and a new goal- and achievement-referenced operating system have led to greater variance in results and resources among schools and municipalities, as well as to a tendency towards segregation or at least to the persistence of socioeconomic differences among school districts.[29] As the new education system allows a greater degree of variance, the importance of monitoring and follow-up increases. This paper reflects the importance that the government has attached to national and local follow-up and evaluation.

The principal questions are: Is equity possible in a decentralized system? How large can these variations inherent in a given school system be without threatening the concept of equity? This is, above all, a political concern and a matter to be taken up in public debate. But it is also a question for Sweden's National Agency for Education, as it relates to the task of providing, by means of evaluations and other knowledge, a basis for evaluating equity. As we pointed out earlier, the school system's official guidelines currently assume that differences exist between municipalities and schools as a consequence of local political and professional decisions. Thus, any evaluation of equivalence will, to a considerable degree, need to consider whether the actual variation that is found should be deemed permissible within the framework of an interpretation of equivalence. Such an evaluation must also provide a basis for taking or promoting action with political implications. In this respect, the question of equity is linked to the way in which schools are managed at every level of the school system.

One way of answering the question is to compare Sweden with other countries. In an international comparison, there is yet little evidence that Sweden is lagging behind in terms of students' results or knowledge equity. The variation in educational attainment between students is still relatively low.[30] Results from international studies also demonstrate that Swedish students compare favorably to international students. In the UK and the United States, it seems that the gap between goals and results is larger than in Sweden.[31] However, if we study development of results over time, we cannot disregard the fact that the variation between schools and student achievements, and resources seems to increase.

A second point in this discussion is that society itself has changed rather dramatically during the last 10 years. Sweden is no longer a homogenate society with small differences between various groups and classes. Sweden is now a multicultural society, and class differences are increasing. These differences tend to effect variations within the education system. Variations or inequalities—the distinctions between these concepts are vague—in the education system are not necessarily effects of education reform; they could be the result of societal change. However, the challenge for the future in Sweden is to meet these changes in preconditions and still guarantee equivalence in the education system. Sweden has developed a broad follow-up system and quality indicators in order to monitor changes within the system. These systems could describe differences and variations within the system, but the crucial question, not yet answered, is when variations turn into inequalities.

A third reflection concerns the conceptual framework. Equality, equity, equivalence and quality are overlapping concepts. They are also empty if they are not related to resources, needs, results, etc. In the Swedish debate, and in the discussion in this paper, slightly varied interpretations are applied. On top of this, the different equity concepts are also connected to concepts of justice, fairness and liberty. The aim of this article is not to explore and analyze concepts and ideas. But it should be kept in mind that there is no political or official unanimity around central concepts, and that this confusion to some extent explains the lack of focus and the broad approach in the quality indicator system.

One distinction could be made between equity with regard to preconditions (chances) and equity with regard to results (outcomes). This distinction reflects two different concepts of fairness and, in a way, two quite different political ideologies. The quality indicator system, based on preconditions, process, and outcome, tries to include both aspects of equity. One advantage of this strategy seems to be that all necessary information is included in the quality indicator system, which builds a good foundation for debate about equity issues. Since there are various interpretations of the equity concept and no interpretation seems to be superior, the best strategy may be to provide extensive information and knowledge about the system. Unfortunately, we cannot really determine when the system provides equal value to all and when it does not. This depends on whether you stress equity with regard to preconditions or equity with regard to outcomes.

Notes

1 The Education Act, Chapter 1, § 2.
2 The curriculum for the compulsory school, the preschool class and the after-school center, Lpo 94.
3 The Education Act, Chapter 1, § 2.
4 See Eriksson R., Jonsson, J., *Ursprung och utbildning 85*, SOU, 1993; see also, for example, Jonsson J., in Shavit, Blossfeld (eds.), *Persistent Inequality*, 1989.
5 See, for example, the TIMSS report or the article of Vandenberghe et al., Chapter 9, in this volume.
6 The paper is partly based on report no. 110, *Likvärighet–ett delat ansvar, kap. 1 och 4* (*Equivalence–a shared responsibility*), Chapters 1 and 4, National Agency for Education, 1996.
7 Swedish constitution (Regeringsformen), Chapter 1, § 2.
8 The Education Act, Chapter 2 a, § 7.
9 *Barnomsorg och skola i siffror 2000: 2 (Child care and school statistics 2000: 2 Children, Staff, Pupils and Teachers)*, National Agency for Education, report no. 185, 2000.
10 OECD Country Note, *Early Childhood Education and Care Policy in Sweden*, revised December 1999.
11 National Agency for Education, report no. 109, 1996.
12 *Education at a Glance*, OECD indicators, 2000 edition.
13 TIMSS, Swedish National Agency for Education, report no. 114, 1996.
14 TIMSS, Swedish National Agency for Education, report no. 145.
15 National Agency for Education, report no. 78 (IEA).
16 *Undervisningen i engelska. En jämförelse mellan tre EU-länder: Frankrike, Spanien och Sverige (A comparison between three EU-countries: France, Spain and Sweden)*, National Agency for Education, report no. 154, 1998.
17 *Grunden för fortsatt lärande 96* (IALS), National Agency for Education, p. 265.
18 *Samband mellan resurser och resultat (Teacher resources and school achievment–any*

connection?) National Agency for Education, report no. 170, 1999.

19 In Shavit & Blossfeld, 1989, ibid.

20 *Barnomsorg och skola i siffror, 2000: 1 (Child care and school statistics 2000: 1 Grades and Education Results)*, report no. 181, 2000.

21 An IEA study on literacy, carried out in 1990–91, showed that 90 percent of the variation in achievement was found within schools in the Nordic countries. For another group of OECD countries, variation was found between, as well as within, schools. See also results from TIMSS, showing relatively low variation in student achievement in Sweden.

22 *Konkurrens för stimulans*, internal report (1996).

23 *Välfärd vid vägskäl. Delbetänkande från Kommittén Välfärdsbokslut 3*, SOU, 2000.

24 Lindensjö B., *Från jämlikhet till likvärdighet(From equality to equivalence)*.

25 Government remit, *Utvecklingsplan för förskola, skola och vuxenutbildning—kvalitet och likvärdighet 112 (Development plan for preschool, school and adult education—quality and equivalence). A development plan describes the general direction of government policy for the coming three years*, 1996/97.

26 *Vad menar vi? dnr 99, p. 382 (What do we mean?)*, Internal PM, 1999.

27 Government remit, *Utvecklingsplan för förskola, skola och vuxenutbildning—kvalitet och likvärdighet 112 (Development plan for preschool, school and adult education—quality and equivalence)*, 1996/97.

28 Johnsson J., in Shavit, Blossfield (eds.), 1989, ibid. *(+ ytterligare referenser).*

29 The grades for the academic year 1998–99 indicated that the number of children who did not reach the national goals increased. Of all students in compulsory school, 22, 7 percent did not receive a grade in one or more subjects. Resources in terms of teachers and spending vary, as the level of financing now is a decision at the municipal level (Swedish National Agency for Education).

30 See, for example, the IEA or IALS studies. There seems to be a relatively low variation in study achievement in Sweden.

31 See, for instance, the homepage of the British government, for the action plan for education (www.dfee.gov.uk) .

References

Eriksson R., Jan O., "Social Mobility, and Social Reproduction in Sweden: Patterns and Changes," in Hansen J. (ed.), *Welfare trends in the Scandinavian countries*, 1993.

Eriksson R., Jonsson J., *Ursprung och utbildning,Social snedrekrytering till högre studier, 85*, SOU, Utbildningsdepartementet, 1993.

Frykman J., *Ljusnande framtid! Skola, social mobilitet och kulturell identitet (School, social mobility and cultural identity)*, Historiska media, 1998.

Government remit, *Utvecklingsplan för förskola, skola och vuxenutbildning—kvalitet och likvärdighet (Development plan for preschool, school and adult education—quality and equivalence), 112*, 1996/97.

Jonsson J., "Persisting Inequalities in Sweden," in Shavit, Blossfeld (eds.), *Persisting Inequalities*, Westview Press, Boulder (Colo.), 1993.

Lindensjö B., *Från jämlikhet till likvärdighet* (not yet published).

Nordic Council of Ministers, *Nordisk Utbildning i fokus—indikatorer, 13*, 1999.

OECD, *Education at a Glance*, 2000 Edition.

OECD, *Early Childhood Education and Care Policy in Sweden*, Country Note, revised December 1999.

Shavit, Muller, *From School to work—a Comparative Study of Educational Qualifications and Occupational Destinations*, Clarendon Press, 1998.

SOU, *Välfärd vid vägskäl, 3*, Delbetänkande från Kommittén Välfärdsbokslut, 2000.

SOU, *Långtidsutredningen, 7,* Finansdepartementet, Stockholm, 1999/2000.

Swedish National Agency for Education, *Barnomsorg och skola i siffror 2000: 1, (Child care and school statistics 2000: 1 Grades and Education Results)*, report no. 181, 2000.

Swedish National Agency for Education, *Barnomsorg och skola i siffror 2000: 2, (Child care and school statistics 2000: 2 Children, Staff, Pupils and Teachers)*, report no. 185, 2000.

Swedish National Agency for Education, *Läroplanerna i praktiken—utvärdering av skolan 1998 avseende läroplanernas mål*, report no. 175, 1999.

Swedish National Agency for Education, *Barnomsorg och skola i siffror 1999:3, (Child care and school statistics 1999:3 Costs)*, report no. 171, 1999.

Swedish National Agency for Education, "Gymnasieskolans kursprov vårterminen 1999 (National examinations in upper secondary school, spring 1999)," *Liber beställningnr, 99,* p. 493, 1999.

Swedish National Agency for Education, "Ämnesproven skolår 9, 1999 (National examinations in school year nine, 1999)," *Liber beställningnr, 99,* p. 502, 1999.

Swedish National Agency for Education, "Vad menar vi?" *Internt pm dnr, 99,* p. 382, 1999.

Swedish National Agency for Education, *Undervisningen i engelska. En jämförelse mellan tre EU-länder: Frankrike, Spanien och Sverige (A comparison between three EU-countries: France, Spain and Sweden)*, report no. 154, 1998.

Swedish National Agency for Education, *Third International Mathematics and Science Study TIMSS Svenska 13-åringars kunskaper i matematik och naturvetenskap i ett internationellt perpektiv*, report no. 114, 1996.

Swedish National Agency for Education, *Likvärdighet—ett delat ansvar (Equity—a shared responsibility)*, report no. 110, 1996.

Swedish National Agency for Education, *Valfrihet, likvärdighet och segregation* (summary in english), report no. 109, 1996.

Swedish National Agency for Education, "Grunden för fortsatt lärande," (IALS), *Liber beställningsnr, 96,* p. 265, 1996.

Swedish National Agency for Education, *Utblick—svensk skola i internationellt perspektiv*, report no. 82, 1995.

Swedish National Agency for Education, *Val av skola. Rapport om valfrihet inom skolpliktens ram läsåret 1992/93*, report no. 40, 1993.

Swedish National Agency for Education, *Konkurrens för stimulans*, intern rapport, 1993.

Teacher resources and school achievement—any connection? An analysis of the importance of the volume of resources in relation to the importance of socio-cultural preconditions in Swedish compulsory schools, paper to the Twelfth International Congress for School Effectiveness and Improvement, San Antonio, January 3–6, 1999, Samband mellan resurser och resultat, Skolverkets rapport nr. 170, December 1998.

Chapter 14

Narrowing the Gap
Educational equity policy in Flanders

Kurt Dewitt
University of Antwerp, Belgium

Peter Van Petegem
University of Antwerp, Belgium

In education, inequalities occur on the basis of differences that from an equity point of view should not play a role in scholastic success or failure; for example, differences in gender, socioeconomic status (SES) or ethnic background. During the past decades, attempts have been made by governments in different countries to tackle this persistent phenomenon. Equity in education is important for policy-makers because the legitimacy of a policy depends on the perception of (in)justice by the citizens (Meuret, Chapter 3).

Also in Flemish educational policies, inequity has been an ongoing concern. This chapter aims to describe the education policy initiatives on equity taken by the Flemish Community in the last three decades. It will focus on what Meuret calls "educational inequalities between categories," and mainly addresses issues related to ethnic background, SES and gender. More specifically, three major policies pursued in Flanders will be discussed: the educational priority policy for immigrant children in primary and secondary education, the democratization of secondary education and the opening of higher education to the masses. For each policy, we will describe the context in which it emerged, clarify its objectives and content, and indicate whether or not the policy has reached its objectives in terms of equity. But first, for those who are not familiar with education in Flanders, we point out some basic characteristics of the Flemish education system.

1.   The Flemish education system[1]

In Flanders, children can enter *nursery education* when they are two and a half years old. Nurseries prepare children for *primary education*, which normally starts in September of the year in which the child reaches the age of six. This is also the start of a 12-year period of compulsory education. Primary education is composed of six school years and three grades. Classes are formed on the basis of school years or grades.

In general, pupils are 12 years old when they enter *secondary education*. This consists of three grades of two school years each. The first grade has a common curriculum for all pupils. The second and third grades offer four types of education: general, technical, vocational and artistic education. In theory, students are grouped on the basis of school years. In the third grade, pupils can pursue part-time vocational secondary education (from age 16, compulsory education is only half-time). At the end of the third grade, or after a special seventh year in the vocational strand, pupils are awarded an official secondary education diploma, granting them access to higher education.

Higher education in Flanders consists of universities and colleges. Universities offer two-cycle courses (in general, four or five years), possibly followed by a doctoral cycle. They provide "academic education;" that is, education based on scientific research. Colleges offer courses of one cycle (three years) or two cycles (four or sometimes five years). In general, a college education is less academic and more vocationally oriented, but these distinctions are not always rigid.[2]

Outside the regular education system, *special education* provides education for children and young people, 3 to 21 years of age, with handicaps, severe learning difficulties, or behavioral or emotional problems. The range of possibilities for integration of special and ordinary education has, however, increased over the years.

Two principles governing the Flemish education system have to be pointed out. First, the Constitution upholds the principle of freedom of education; that is, the right to establish schools not connected in any way to the official authorities. The State is authorized to establish schools to guarantee freedom of choice to parents, but it also has to subsidize schools organized by other entities when they meet the legal and statutory requirements.

Second, the principle of free access to education guarantees that no entrance requirements are imposed and that until the end of compulsory education (at age 18), education is free of charge to pupils and their parents. Nor is access restricted at the higher education level, except for courses in civil engineering, medicine and dentistry.

As education is compulsory until age 18, the level of participation[3] approximates 96 percent in the period of full-time compulsory education (ages 6 to 16), and exceeds the OECD-mean after age 16 (see Table 1, page 325).

A major problem in the Flemish education system, however, is the number of young people falling behind (see Table 2, page 325), and also, as a consequence, the number of young people leaving the education system without proper qualifications for further study or employment.

Table 1. The level of participation in the Flemish education system (in %) (1994–1995)

	ages 5–29	age 18	age 19	age 20
Flanders	63.6	81.8	67.5	60.9
OECD countries—mean	61.3	63.6	47.2	39.4
Sweden	67.1	87.9	35.3	30.6
Netherlands	65.0	82.5	70.1	59.6

Source: Ministry of the Flemish Community, Department of Education, 1998, pp. 26, 38.

Table 2. Falling behind in the Flemish education system

Education level		% of pupils fallen behind
Regular primary education[1]		13.90
Regular secondary education[2]	1st year	19.85
	6th year	38.06
	7th year[3]	60.07

Source: Ministry of the Flemish Community, Department of Education, 1998, pp. 187, 200.
[1] School year 1994–1995.
[2] School year 1995–1996.
[3] Only a small number of pupils enters a 7th vocational year.

It is important to note that boys fall behind more than girls (in the sixth year of regular secondary education, the percentages of boys and girls falling behind are 45.35 percent and 30.97 percent, respectively). In addition, the percentage of non-Belgian pupils falling behind is much higher than that of Belgian pupils: currently, 61 percent in the first year of regular secondary education and up to 73 percent in the sixth year (Ministry of the Flemish Community, 1998, p. 201).

2. The educational priority policy for immigrant children

The figures on falling behind in the Flemish education system clearly indicate the existence of educational inequality between pupils of non-Belgian and Flemish origin. The Flemish government developed an educational priority policy for immigrant children to combat this inequality. This policy is a coherent and structural program of support for primary and secondary schools having certain percentages of immigrant pupils. Drawing on past experience, it seeks to tackle problems of both social integration of immigrant pupils and the educational gap at school by focusing on many domains at once. The effects of this educational priority policy for immigrant children are not yet clear, but it is an important step with respect to equity.

2.1.   Background

The specific problems of ethnic-cultural minorities and their integration into Flemish society became a priority policy issue only at the end of the 1980s. The disadvantaged position of immigrant children in Flemish education also garnered attention about that time. However, the problem was not entirely new. As a result of the recruitment of foreign workers; family unification and natural growth; and, more recently, refugees from other countries seeking political asylum, the immigrant population in Belgium (Flanders) had steadily increased over the years. Immigrant children confronted the Belgian schools with specific problems. Several pilot projects were established by the government in an effort to solve these problems.

The government provided additional resources enabling schools to establish a *course for adaptation to the language of instruction*, i.e., instruction in the Dutch language (three hours per week) for children of foreign origin with unsatisfactory knowledge of Dutch. The so-called *30-percent measure* enabled nursery and primary schools with at least 30 percent of immigrant children among their pupils to appoint an additional teacher, to create smaller classes. Finally, *education by mutual encounter* encompassed initiatives making lessons in the language of the immigrants part of the curriculum (for both foreign and Flemish pupils).

An assessment of these governmental policies showed that these measures did not improve the position of immigrant pupils due to the vague, inconsistent and temporary nature of those policies and because of lower-than-expected participation by eligible schools (Verlot, 1990).

The results of this assessment were published in a period of growing attention to the problems of ethnic-cultural minorities (as a result of, among other things, the growing electoral success of the extreme-right). The Flemish Community then developed a new educational project: the *educational priority policy for immigrant children*.

2.2.   Objectives of the new policy

In contrast to previous governmental projects, the educational priority policy for immigrant children (*onderwijsvoorrangsbeleid*, abbreviated as OVB) is meant to provide an integrated and all-encompassing approach, combining educational stimulation activities (school-based activities designed to directly influence pupils in the target group) with activation activities (addressing the overall school environment). Thus, it is based on concepts of equity to which Benadusi (Chapter 1) refers to as "equality of opportunity" and "fair respect for differences."

The OVB consists of several fields of action (see section 2.3) to be carried out in both primary and (more recently) in secondary schools. Related measures are a reception policy for non-Dutch-speaking newcomers (providing, among other things, extra Dutch instruction for pupils who have not yet completed a full year of Dutch-speaking education) and a non-discrimination policy (a voluntary agreement between the educational networks to stimulate the proportional presence of the target group pupils among the schools of a municipality, and to develop and implement a non-discrimination policy within schools).

The goals of the OVB are defined as:

- preventing, countering or removing educational disadvantages;
- promoting positive interaction among Flemish and foreign pupils, on the basis of mutual respect and in view of the multi-ethnic and multi-cultural composition of society;
- providing immigrant pupils the possibility to develop an understanding and appreciation of their unique cultural heritage; and
- receiving and guiding newcomers in a way that facilitates their transfer to the regular education system.

Soon after its establishment in 1991–92, the OVB was placed within the framework of a more general welfare policy for the underprivileged, reflecting the view that immigrants are not only socially deprived in a structural way—as are other people—but have problems on top of this because they are culturally and ethnically different. In this way, the OVB has been turned into an extension of the special-needs provision, meaning that specific characteristics of pupils (the social, economic and cultural conditions in which they grow up) are taken into account. Since 1993–94, within the framework of special-needs projects, the Flemish government has granted extra course hours to primary schools to support children who belong in mainstream education, but cannot yet derive sufficient benefit from the usual teaching methods.

2.3. Content of the priority policy

The OVB is the core of the educational policy towards ethnic-cultural minorities. Its target group includes third-generation immigrant children who already have Belgian nationality.[4] A school can obtain additional financial resources (under certain conditions; for example, by justifying the uses to which they will be put and by requiring refresher courses for teachers) in relation to the proportion of immigrant children in the school. When a school has a minimum percentage of pupils who are eligible for the OVB, but no more than 50 percent, it receives additional support in proportion to their number. Between 50 and 80 percent, the increase in support decreases to zero. In this way, the government tries to combat segregation and concentration in schools.

The main idea supporting the OVB is that the learning difficulties of immigrant children are the result of a combination of structural, social and cultural factors. It is therefore focused in several fields of action at a time to facilitate both the integration of the target group and members' transition within the secondary system to general and some technical courses. The fields of action of the OVB are the following:

- First, *intercultural education* is aimed at teaching both Flemish and immigrant pupils the necessary skills and attitudes to cope with cultural and social diversity.
- Second, *Dutch language education* tries to systematically build up pupils' language proficiency, to help them understand the educational content of their courses and enable them to participate in education and society in the best possible way.
- Third, *pupil guidance* provides at-risk pupils with assistance in their course work, and in their choice of study, to prevent or remedy possible learning and developmental problems related to their socio-cultural and ethnic backgrounds.
- Fourth, *involvement of parents* implies attempts by the school to bring educators, immigrant pupils and their parents closer together (through active involvement in the school and insight into the educational structure).
- Fifth, *minority-language and cultural instruction*—teaching part of the regular curriculum in the language of the country of origin, or teaching the language or culture of that country—is optional, requiring the permission of all parents of pupils in the minority group.

Because all these actions can be successful only when they are implemented by teachers, some supportive measures were taken by the Flemish government: An additional guidance team was appointed, two support services were established (one for intercultural education and one for language education) and in-service initiatives were taken to retrain teachers.

2.4.   Evaluation of the priority policy for immigrant children

The educational priority policy for immigrant children is an elaborate program consisting of many activities for which schools can receive additional resources. An evaluation of this program is not straightforward, especially because no indicators are readily available. In this section, we present the results of two qualitative studies of the OVB and some general data on the position of immigrants in the Flemish education system. Finally, we take a look at the Third International Mathematics and Science Study (TIMSS) to put the findings in an international perspective.

Evaluative studies of the implementation of the OVB (VLOR, 1995; Verhoeven & Doms, 1998) have concluded that both the government and the schools had ambiguous attitudes towards it. In the beginning of the implementation period, the government relied too heavily on a top-down approach. Moreover, it took insufficient structural measures, i.e., it did not guarantee long-term financial support. At the school level, the studies criticize a lack of resources, resulting in a very unsatisfactory implementation of OVB components not related to language education, and attitudes of school leaders, who often assigned the extra hours authorized by the government to the youngest or least experienced teachers. Those teachers did not always have sufficient authority to introduce the OVB to the entire teaching staff.

These two studies point out the problems encountered in the implementation of the OVB. They do not, however, provide us with information about the effects of the OVB on the position of target group pupils in Flemish education. Because no scientific research is yet available that assesses these effects, we can only present general data on the position of immigrants in the system, without specific reference to pupils in OVB schools.

Figures of the Department of Education of the Ministry of the Flemish Community show a decreasing share of immigrant children[5] as the level of education becomes higher. For example, in the 1998–99 school year, 6.04 percent of the pupils in primary education were of foreign origin, but they totalled only 4.32 percent in secondary education. On the other hand, immigrant children were overrepresented in special education (7.39 percent in special primary education and 8.88 percent in special secondary education). This situation has not changed much during the period of implementation of the OVB. In the 1991–92 school year, the percentages of immigrant children were 6.00 percent in primary education, 4.74 percent in secondary education, 8.15 percent in special primary education and 8.95 percent in special secondary education.

When they do participate, immigrant children fall behind more than Belgian pupils, notwithstanding the fact that the number of Belgian pupils who are not performing at grade level is already high. This is apparent from the first year of primary education onwards, as is shown in Table 3. Again, we note that the situation has not really changed since the 1991–92 school year.

In short, the position of immigrant children in Flemish education (in terms of participation and falling behind) does not seem to be improving. This does not

Table 3. Belgian and non-Belgian pupils falling behind in primary education, as a percentage of the total number of Belgian and non-Belgian pupils

Nationality	Belgian	Foreign	Belgian	Foreign	Belgian	Foreign
Falling behind	*1 year*	*1 year*	*2 years*	*2 years*	*3 years*	*3 years*
			1991–92			
1st study year	9.26	27.24	0.22	3.27	0.02	0.53
6th study year	11.01	36.81	0.45	7.99	0.02	0.51
			1998–99			
1st study year	9.37	26.86	0.26	3.51	0.02	0.47
6th study year	11.95	34.84	0.44	8.51	0.02	0.44

Source: Ministry of the Flemish Community, Department of Education, 1998.

mean that the realization of a coherent and substantial priority policy was pointless. We have to await the results of an effect study that is currently being carried out[6] to get a clear picture of the consequences of the OVB. But in the meantime, some results of the TIMSS[7] math tests shed a more optimistic light on the position of immigrant pupils in Flemish education. Table 4 compares the average scores on mathematics tests in several countries, for different language, education and ethnic categories.

On the basis of Table 4, two conclusions can be drawn with regard to immigrant pupils in Flanders. On the one hand, the differences between Flemish and foreign pupils are confirmed, to the disadvantage of the latter (on average, foreign pupils score 14 points less than Flemish pupils). On the other hand, when compared internationally, the foreign pupils in Flanders score very well in the TIMSS test, even higher than non-immigrant children in other countries. Their score of 561 is well above the international average of 513 (Beaton, et al., 1996, p. 24). Of course, we cannot relate this result directly to the educational

Table 4. Average results on the TIMSS math tests in four countries, broken down by language, educational level of the father and ethnic background[1]

	Flanders		USA		The Netherlands		Sweden	
	Mean	*Signif.*	*Mean*	*Signif.*	*Mean*	*Signif.*	*Mean*	*Signif.*
Overall mean	574.77		480.93		536.09		513.55	
Language: frequency of use of language of the country		0.010		0.000		0.007		0.000
Always	578.01		522.65		539.83		522.26	
Sometimes	564.26		481.28		505.59		470.92	
Never	575.64		514.93		552.57		482.23	
Educational level of the father		0.000		0.000		0.003		0.000
Primary	550.66		484.61		494.32		−	
Secondary	572.54		511.52		532.45		516.98	
Vocational	−[2]		512.17		557.44		−	
University	599.66		534.60		563.10		542.60	
Unknown	559.37		514.05		524.65		517.58	
Immigrant position: born or not in the country concerned		0.009		0.055[3]		0.003		0.000
Yes	575.42		483.22		538.51		517.47	
No	561.44		464.29		500.31		470.10	

Source: TIMSS data; calculations by Sven De Mayer (University of Antwerp, Belgium).
[1] The results of the test are shown with an average of 500 and a standard deviation of 100.
[2] Does not apply
[3] The results do not differ significantly.

priority policy of the Flemish government. But the sustained attention to problems encountered by schools with immigrant children does seem to be important for equity in terms of the consequences of ethnic background on scholastic success. A definitive assertion, however, can only be made when more indicators become available, giving a more detailed view on the educational position of immigrant pupils over time.

3. The democratization of secondary education

The second Flemish policy to be discussed relative to equity in education is the democratization of secondary education. Evidence of the continued effect of social background on pupils' enrollment in "heavy" or "light" courses persuaded the Belgian government to introduce a program of "renewed secondary education." The Flemish government, responsible for the Dutch education sector in Belgium since 1989, established the "general framework for secondary education" in 1989. However, indicators of pupils' school careers in secondary education show that the effect of socioeconomic background has not yet been ruled out.

3.1. Historical perspective: Increasing, but unequal, participation

After the Second World War, the hierarchical and categorical secondary education system was opened up to all children. The government imposed new and mutually comparable structures on general, technical and vocational education. It removed some financial and material barriers to secondary education and in 1954 established a system of student grants. The principle of tuition-free education was agreed upon in 1958. The so-called Omnivalence Law (1964) granted equal status to the different forms of secondary education—at least in principle—in terms of eligibility for higher education.

As a result of these measures, the number of students in secondary education tripled from 1950 to 1970 (Vandekerckhove & Huyse, 1976). But the democratization process was not complete. Children from inferior social backgrounds, although participating more than before, chose those options that were the least appreciated and offered the poorest career prospects.

Pursuant to a growing belief in education as a lever for social change, there was more interest in the idea of adapting the structure of secondary education itself. State secondary education experiments, carried out since 1967, led to the introduction of an "observation" and "orientation" cycle (see below) in all state schools. But the democratization of secondary education was an issue in all of Europe. Great Britain and Sweden had already introduced "comprehensive" (i.e., more democratic) education. The Council of Europe adopted a resolution in 1968 elaborating the structure of comprehensive secondary education, which became the basis for reform in France, Germany, Italy and also Belgium.

3.2.   Renewed secondary education

The positive climate for comprehensive education and the assessment of the incomplete democratization process led to experimentation with what was called "renewed secondary education" (*Vernieuwd Secundair Onderwijs*, abbreviated as VSO). It was legally established in 1971, but was not made compulsory.

The goal of the reform was to make the secondary school less socially discriminating and more democratic. The old structure, consisting of two cycles of three years each, was replaced by three two-year cycles. In the first of these cycles, the "observation" cycle, pupils received a common curriculum. Pupils with learning problems could (temporarily) enter the B-structure, a class providing more individualized guidance. In the second or "orientation" cycle, pupils had to choose a certain option, but changes were still possible. From this cycle on, the VSO was divided into two streams: "transition" (preparation for higher education) and "qualification"(preparation for working life). In the final or "determination" cycle, the choice of the pupil became definitive, and the number of shared courses was greatly reduced. In the qualification stream, pupils could opt to leave education or follow an additional year after the orientation or determination cycle.

In other words, the definitive choice of study was postponed as long as possible to lessen the influence of the pupil's social background. Moreover, classes were composed of pupils from different social backgrounds, and remedial instruction was arranged for the disadvantaged. Other principles of the VSO were to broaden basic education (not only with respect to knowledge, but also with respect to skills and attitudes), provide ongoing guidance and evaluation by the teacher and the teaching staff as a whole, and promote a democratic school environment.

These goals seem clear, but there were challenges; from the beginning, little political clarity existed regarding the VSO. The original aim was to make the VSO mandatory for all schools, but no obligation was introduced to adopt the new structures. In time, the goals became even less clear, as each minister of education sought to put his/her own stamp on the program. In 1975, the VSO was suddenly made compulsory in state-run schools without consulting the teachers, which caused a lot of resistance. The Catholic network opted for "guided graduality," leading to discord between schools that favored or rejected the VSO approach (after 1976, they were referred to as type I schools and type II schools, respectively). This division also led to administrative problems and an unhealthy competition between schools. Type I schools also reflected an unequal distribution of financial resources (the VSO was a costly structure, as the government was forced to acknowledge during the economic crisis of the 1970s).

Given this political lack of clarity and resistance in the field, it is not surprising that evaluation of the VSO has been problematic. Not only was scant research carried out, but on top of this it tended to be politically motivated, and was often used to defend or attack the VSO.

Nevertheless, the research made clear that the VSO did not succeed in eradicating inequality in secondary education. Although the results of the VSO were better than those of traditional schools in this respect, socioeconomic variables also influenced patterns of participation and choice in the VSO.

Children from inferior social backgrounds (defined in terms of the education level and labor-market position of the parents) participated less in secondary education and left school sooner, at least until 1983, when compulsory education was extended from age 14 to age 18. They were less likely to choose studies preparing them for higher education and more likely to choose vocational studies, even after 1983, regardless of the type of school they attended. The hierarchy separating general, technical and vocational education also existed in the VSO (from the second year onwards), as did the hierarchy within each form of education—meaning, for example, that pupils with parents from the lower social strata in general education opted more for social studies than for Latin.

3.3. The general framework for secondary education

The Flemish government tried to solve the (mainly political) problems attached to the VSO by introducing the *general framework for secondary education* progressively from 1989–90 on in all secondary schools. Although reducing inequality was only a secondary goal of this reform, the compromise between the traditional and the reformed structure maintained elements of the comprehensive system.

For instance, the first year is almost exactly the same for all pupils and the second year is very similar as well. In this way, the choice of study is—in theory—postponed until after the first cycle. Pupils with learning difficulties enter a class that provides them more individualized guidance (the B-structure), then they can either proceed to the second pre-vocational year or start the first year again but in the general strand (A-structure). Further comprehensive elements are: the heterogeneous composition of classes by social background; the compulsory nature of less knowledge-oriented courses, such as physical education, religious education and moral philosophy; pupil-centered teaching; and broad-based evaluations.

On the other hand, the comprehensiveness of the general framework compared to the VSO has decreased. There are four clearly divided forms of education starting from the second cycle: general, technical, artistic and vocational secondary education. Transition between them is very difficult in an "upward" direction (that is, from vocational to technical or from technical to general education). Even in the first year, there is a division between an A- and a B-structure. The courses important in the traditional structure (for example, math and Latin) still have greater weight than courses aimed at a broader basic education.

3.4.   Evaluation of the general framework in terms of equity

The democratization of secondary education was meant to diminish inequalities related to the socioeconomic background of pupils. It mainly concerned specific opportunities offered by the school system; in other words, scholastic conditions that influence the attainment of results (Benadusi, Chapter 1). We cannot evaluate the democratization as such because its principles were only partially implemented in Flanders. Nevertheless, the question remains relevant whether the general framework for secondary education has reduced inequalities. To answer this question, we will again refer to TIMSS data on pupils' entrance into different strands of secondary education, as well as data about the position of immigrant children in secondary education.

First, we turn back to Table 4 regarding TIMSS results in Flanders. The second case in this table relates to the educational level of the father, which can be taken as an indicator of SES. On average, pupils in the first two years of secondary education score less than others on the TIMSS mathematics test when the educational level of their father is lower. Pupils whose fathers had completed university educations on average scored 49 points more than pupils whose fathers had completed only primary education (599.66 compared to 550.66). Flanders follows an international trend in this respect: The point gap is, for instance, 50 in the USA and 69 in the Netherlands. Again, we can see that the lowest scoring group in Flanders (father completed primary education) is still among the best results internationally (550.66 compared to 484.61 in the USA and 494.32 in the Netherlands), as was the case for immigrant pupils in Flemish education.

Other research (Van de Velde, Van Brusselen & Douterlungne, 1996) shows the continued effect of socioeconomic background on students' school careers, in particular with respect to their choice of general, technical or vocational educations. Table 5 (page 335) clearly indicates the preference among pupils of low SES for "light" courses.

Moreover, this choice appears to be decisive for later schooling. Only a limited number of pupils go from the B-structure to the A-structure; transitions

Table 5. Educational level of the parents compared to the type of education of their children, 1992 (in %)

	General	Technical	Vocational
Educational level of the head of the family			
Higher education	*41.3*	19.7	11.2
General secondary education	*23.8*	12.7	10.3
Technical secondary education	18.0	*35.7*	23.0
Vocational secondary education	9.0	10.8	*10.8*
Primary education	5.6	17.2	*32.2*
Educational level of the partner			
Higher education	*29.4*	17.9	8.3
General secondary education	*26.3*	15.2	11.1
Technical secondary education	17.5	16.5	15.1
Vocational secondary education	12.1	*22.0*	*22.2*
Primary education	9.6	*24.8*	*38.9*

Source: Van de Velde et al., 1996, p. 111 (bold and italics added).

to a "higher" type of education are also rare in the later years. On the reverse side, going "down" from general to technical education, or from general or technical to vocational education, occurs often.

What about immigrant pupils in Flanders who already face an educational gap as compared to Flemish pupils at the end of primary education? Their situation in secondary education is very similar to that of pupils of low SES. They are clearly overrepresented in the vocational strands of secondary education. Expressed as a percentage of the total number of pupils, immigrant pupils make up 2.2 percent in general secondary education, 3.4 percent in technical education, 3.5 percent in art education and 10.1 percent in vocational education (Jennes, 1997, p. 57).

4. The opening of higher education to the masses

Finally, we turn to higher education in Flanders. We will discuss the effects of gender and socioeconomic background on participation in higher education.[8]

The number of students in higher education increased dramatically in recent decades as a result of the democratization of higher education. However, the proportion of students from certain categories remained low. Nowadays, participation in higher education is high in Flanders in comparison with that of other countries. The participation of boys and girls has become balanced; however, with respect to socioeconomic background (indicators regarding the socio-professional category and the level of education of the father), inequalities remain.

4.1.   The democratization of access to higher education

Belgian student organizations and labor movements in the 1950s complained about the imbalance between the demographic majority of the working class in the total population and the small minority of students from the working class in universities, which was about 5 percent at that time (Vandekerckhove & Huyse, 1976). Because of the demographic growth and increasing school attendance of this class, among other things, demands for the democratization of higher education soon received broad attention, especially from the government. To improve access to higher education, a number of measures were taken to remove financial and material barriers.

Since 1954, indigent students have been able to apply for study grants—as in secondary education—in the form of government loans or payments. Another important measure is the above-mentioned Omnivalence Law of 1964, which gave every secondary education graduate the right to enter higher education. Finally, the geographical spread of universities in the second half of the 1960s should be noted. Although this was also the result of ideological and language-policy struggles, the argument used initially to justify this spread was enhancing access to higher education, especially for the lower socioeconomic strata. Afterwards, findings showed that this goal was only partially reached (see also the following paragraphs).

4.2.   Increasing participation and persistent inequality

As a result of these measures and growing participation in secondary education, the number of students in higher education increased dramatically. However, it became clear that unequal participation in higher education by socioeconomic background remained. Vandekerckhove and Huyse (1976), for example, found that in decisions regarding study at the university, choice of study and choice of occupation, a tendency of status congruency was in force. This tendency discouraged children of the working classes from going to the university, from choosing courses that would have prepared them for prestigious occupations and from choosing those occupations.

In the 1970s, the phrase "democratization of higher education" acquired another meaning. Emphasis was placed on rendering decision-making more open and participatory. The number of colleges and courses at universities had increased, in particular in the 1960s. But because of the economic crisis that struck the whole of Western Europe in the 1970s, this growing sector became unaffordable for the Belgian government. At the end of the 1970s, but especially in the 1980s, cost-cutting was the key word in higher education. No other real policies were pursued.

Nevertheless, higher education evolved into mass education. Since 1960–

61, the number of students has increased more than fivefold in university education and more than fourfold in college education. In the 1994–95 academic year, 9.7 percent of the Flemish population participated in higher education, compared to an average in the OECD of 9.4 percent (VRIND, 1998, p. 236). The proportion of higher education graduates in the Flemish population is also high. Among 25- to 34-year-olds, 32 percent have higher education diplomas, while the average in the OECD is 23 percent (Ministry of the Flemish Community, 1998, p. 324).

The increase in the number of higher education students is caused not only by demographic and social factors, but also by a number of characteristics of the educational system as such, which make access to higher education in Flanders very liberal (and which Benadusi (Chapter 1) would place in a conception of equity that relates to "simple equality of opportunity").

Most pupils in secondary education choose a general education course: In the 1997–98 school year, 40.2 percent of the pupils in the second and third cycle were enrolled in general education (ASO). The most logical step for these pupils is to enroll in higher education. All secondary education graduates can—in theory—do so, along with graduates of technical and vocational secondary education.

In higher education, there are no entrance exams, with a few exceptions. At universities, entrance exams are provided for civil engineering and, since 1997, medicine and dentistry. Colleges provide an artistic entrance exam for courses in audio-visual and fine arts, music and drama, and an ability test for the course in nautical sciences.

No central limit is placed on the number of student enrollments in higher education institutions. Moreover, these institutions are financed partly on the basis of student numbers. On the financial level, students can use the student grant system, and on top of this, the entrance and exam fees are limited by decree (and lowered for students who receive grants).

4.3.   The current situation: Gender equality

The growth in the number of higher education students is caused in large part by an increase in the number of female students. In the colleges, girls have made up the majority since the 1960s; in the universities, this only happened in the 1990s. The gender-inequality gap in higher education therefore seems to have been closed.

Nevertheless, two remarks must be made. First, a difference remains in the choice of studies. Girls are strongly overrepresented in health care, education, psychology and pedagogy, but are clearly underrepresented in industrial science, economics, science and applied science. Second, young women participate less in advanced training compared to the male participation in Flanders, but not in international comparisons. The complementary courses at universities[9] have 40.5 percent women; specialized courses at universities, 44.3 percent; doctoral training, 39.2 percent; and doctorates, 37.2 percent. The only exception is the teacher training course, in which women are a majority (62.9 percent).

4.4. The current situation: Socioeconomic inequality

A recent study (Tan, 1998) shows that in Flemish higher education a clear social hierarchy according to the socio-professional category and educational level of the parents still exists. The study shows that participation by social category more or less followed the general student trend, meaning that their ratio remained the same. In other words, in terms of the socio-professional category of the head of the family, the underrepresentation of working-class children continues (see Table 6).

The data with regard to educational levels of parents indicate a similar underrepresentation of children of parents with low educational levels. Children of highly educated fathers and mothers participate about four times more in higher education than children of poorly educated mothers and fathers (Tan, 1998, p. 9). The inequality according to social background can be seen in both universities and colleges, although somewhat less in the latter (Lammertyn & Brijs, 1992).

Finally, when we look at gender differences in terms of socioeconomic background, these differences seem to have been eliminated, at least that is what an analysis of the student population of the University of Leuven from 1964 to 1995 shows (Smedts, 1998). In 1964, the composition of the female student population was much less democratic than the male population (see Table 7, page 339). About 17 percent of girls had fathers with low socio-professional levels compared to 30 percent of the boys. For the higher socio-professional level, the situation was reversed. In 1994, the distribution of both groups with regard to socio-professional level was almost the same for all socio-professional categories.

Table 6. Participation in higher education of 18- to 25-year-olds, broken down by socio-professional category of the head of the family, Flanders, 1976–1985–1992

Socio-professional category	Participation-indices			Share in the total group of 18- to 25-year-olds		
	1976	*1985*	*1992*	*1976*	*1985*	*1992*
Workers	8	9	14	47%	40%	35%
Employees	32	27	41	29%	43%	43%
Other occupation	22	21	28	24%	17%	22%
Total participation	17	18	29	100%	100%	100%
				N = 1553	N = 1188	N = 1146

Source: Tan, 1998, p. 6.

Table 7. Evolution of the student population of the University of Leuven (Belgium), broken down by socio-professional level of the father (in %, with regard to 100% girls and 100% boys, respectively)

	Socio-professional level							
	Higher		**Middle-higher**		**Middle-lower**		**Lower**	
Year	*Girls*	*Boys*	*Girls*	*Boys*	*Girls*	*Boys*	*Girls*	*Boys*
1964	29.69	17.26	22.91	18.37	30.07	34.55	17.33	29.82
1969	24.33	16.38	22.15	17.73	34.52	36.65	19.00	29.24
1974	22.16	17.57	20.17	16.69	38.15	39.80	19.52	25.94
1979	22.92	19.85	18.31	16.17	37.37	39.57	21.40	24.41
1984	25.11	23.30	20.46	19.30	36.44	36.85	17.99	20.55
1989	27.19	27.20	24.69	23.01	32.83	33.37	15.30	16.42
1994	29.65	30.58	26.91	25.86	27.75	26.70	15.69	16.86

Source: Smedts, 1998, pp. 52–53.

Conclusion

Equity issues have been and still are an important topic in Flemish education policy. In the last three decades, numerous policy measures have been taken to guarantee equality of educational opportunities regardless of the socioeconomic background, ethnic origin or gender of students. To provide an idea of the wide scope of these measures, we have highlighted three major policies concerning different levels of the education system.

First, we described the "educational priority policy for immigrant children" in primary and secondary education. This was the first substantial and coherent program for tackling the various problems that immigrant children encounter in education. It was an important step in eliminating educational arrears and in fighting social discrimination.

Second, we turned to the democratization of secondary education; in particular the structural changes that followed the introduction of "renewed secondary education" and later the "general framework for secondary education." Providing equal opportunities for all socioeconomic groups was the aim of both reforms. In comparison with traditional education, comprehensive education has succeeded in offering more opportunities to children from lower socioeconomic backgrounds (which is also the case at international level).

Finally, we discussed the long-standing tradition of free access to higher education in Flanders. Restrictions in enrollment are almost completely absent, and financial and material obstacles that might restrain people from going on to higher education are in large part removed. This has led to a high degree of participation in higher education in Flanders.

However, although important in many respects, these policies have not reached their objectives entirely. At all levels of the Flemish education system, educational inequalities between categories remain. Indicators—though of limited availability in Flanders—show that certain socioeconomic groups in particular, with relation to ethnic background, are still in a disadvantaged position. Already in primary education, immigrant pupils tend to drop out of school early, fall behind more often and to be overrepresented in special education services. These negative trends continue in secondary education, in fact for the whole group of children from families of low SES. They can be found more in technical and especially vocational secondary education, where they often end up after having tried general and/or technical education. Throughout their school careers, these pupils get lower results and fall behind more. When they reach the end of secondary education, their opportunities to pursue higher education are significantly diminished. Notwithstanding the overall growth of participation in higher education, the relative proportion of enrollees from low socioeconomic backgrounds has not increased over the years.

The sources of exclusion that continue to inhibit the fair distribution of opportunities (in Flanders as elsewhere) apparently cannot be relieved by focusing policy only on education as such. Equity should be a broader concern of policy-makers in such diverse fields as economy and welfare, as well as a continuous concern for all actors in the educational field.

Notes

1 For more background information, see, for instance, the Eurydice database at http://www.eurydice.org

2 The Flemish laws define college education of four or five years as "of an academic level," meaning that it is based on scientific knowledge. Moreover, the laws specify the equivalence between the college degree "Commercial Sciences"and the university degree "Applied Economic Sciences."

3 The level of participation is defined as the number of young people in education as a percentage of the reference age group in the total population.

4 The target group is defined as pupils whose maternal grandmothers were not born in Belgium, who were lacking Belgian or Dutch nationality at birth, and whose mothers were not educated past age 18.

5 The participation of immigrant pupils in education is measured here as the proportion of immigrant pupils in the total pupil population.

6 As this book went to press, an effect study was being carried out by the Higher Institute of Labour Studies (Leuven, Belgium).

7 TIMSS is an international study, carried out by the IEA in 1995, consisting of several mathematics and science tests taken by 13-year-old pupils.

8 Because of the large number of non-Belgian students in Flemish higher education who are not resident in Flanders, an analysis in terms of ethnic background is more complicated and surpasses the possibilities of this chapter.

9 Advanced training at universities in Flanders consists of one-year complementary courses (an addition to or broadening of a basic academic course) and specialist courses (a specialization in a certain discipline) of one or two years.

References

Beaton A.E., et al., *Mathematics Achievement in the Middle School Years. IEA's Third International Mathematics and Science Study*, IEA–TIMSS International Study Center, Chestnut Hill (Mass.), 1996.

Benadusi L., "Equity and Education," Chapter 1, in this volume.

Jennes A., *Analyse van de beroepsopleiding in Vlaanderen. Implementatie en impact van het Europese Leonardo-da-Vinci-programma op Vlaams niveau,* HIVA, Leuven, Belgium, 1997.

Lammertyn F., Brijs R., *De democratisering van het hoger onderwijs buiten de universiteit,* KU Leuven, Departement Sociologie, Leuven, Belgium, 1992.

Meuret D., "A System of Equity Indicators for Educational Systems," in this volume.

Ministerie van de Vlaamse Gemeenschap, *Vlaamse Regionale INDicatoren 1998,* Administratie Planning en Statistiek, Brussels, 1999.

Ministry of the Flemish Community, *Flemish Educational Indicators in an International Perspective, Edition 1998,* Department of Education, Brussels, 1998.

Smedts D., *Evolutie sociale herkomst studentenpopulatie KU Leuven 1964–1995,* KU Leuven, Studentendiensten, Leuven, Belgium, 1998.

Tan B., *Blijvende sociale ongelijkheden in het Vlaamse onderwijs,* CSB, Antwerpen, Belgium, 1998.

Vandekerckhove L., Huyse L., *In de buitenbaan*, Standaard Wetenschappelijke Uitgeverij, Antwerpen/Amsterdam, 1976.

Van de Velde V., Van Brusselen B., Douterlungne M., *Gezin en school. Een onderzoek over het gezin als indicator voor de schoolloopbaan in het se cundair onderwijs,* HIVA, Leuven, Belgium, 1996.

Verhoeven J.C., Doms K., *Evaluatieonderzoek extra-begeleiding onderwijsvoorrangs-beleid,* KU Leuven, Departement Sociologie, Leuven, Belgium, 1998.

Verlot M., *Migranten in het basisonderwijs. Analyse van beleidsmaatregelen en experimenten. Deel 1: Sleutelen aan de marge,* HIVA, Leuven, Belgium, 1990.

VLOR, *Cahier 8. Onderwijsvoorrangsbeleid voor migranten,* VLOR, Brussels, 1995.

VRIND 1998 (Vlaamse Regionale Indicatoren 1998), p. 236, Administratie Planning en Statistiek, Brussels, 1999.

Chapter 15

Economics and Demographics in Metropolitan Communities
An argument for international equity indicators

Douglas Cochrane
American Institutes for Research/Education Statistics Services Institute, Washington, D.C.

Central-city, suburban and rural-metro or outer-fringe communities are spatial or geographic components of cities that affect the cities' social and economic evolution and that of surrounding schools. This social and economic evolution may be distinctive to a city, nation or region of the world. In the United States, for example, central cities have high concentrations of poverty and high proportions of minorities, while the middle class and wealthy tend to live in the suburbs. In some European and Latin-American cities, however, it is the suburbs surrounding the central city where there are high concentrations of poverty.

Immigration has also changed the socioeconomic mixes in many countries, not just of specific communities, but of schools—bringing a flood of language and cultural diversity, amid often egalitarian expectations and public demands for continuing access to tertiary as well as basic education (Costa-Lascoux, 1989). In this regard, the American metropolitan experience provides some opportunity for comparative study.

Resources necessary to provide successful educational outcomes for students are influenced by these geographical patterns—producing hard-to-resolve disparities in both productive human capacity developed by education (human capital) and strong social bonds that provide, among other things, valuable networks (social capital).[1] These disparities are reflected in the classroom. Patterns of racial and/or ethnic population migration, and related residential segregation, are associated with both the type and economic experience of the metro school district,[2] and demographic, economic and density mixes challenge our ability to provide equitable per-pupil revenues across school districts.

There are a wide variety of concepts of educational equity across countries and a range of tolerance associated with disparities. These raise questions about the impact of disparities on education outcomes within countries. Also, many OECD (Organisation for Economic Co-operation and Development) countries invest in the development of internationally competitive outcomes, with specific strategies for math, science and literacy. Questions exist, however, about providing specific curricular strategies for successful outcomes to the disenfranchised. Whether to address inequities, or to better understand and improve strategies for math, science and literacy education, we need to develop international indicators that measure the demographics, economic experiences and density of a community and its educational environment.

1.   Background

The residential neighborhoods in which students live are largely understudied as environments that influence educational outcomes. Much has been said, however, about the high correlation of other environmental factors with educational outcomes. Several well-documented factors (see Cochrane, "Why Education Matters," Chapter 4) are the income and education level of parents (Nöel & de Broucker, Chapter 12; Coleman, 1966), income and education of students' peers (Coleman, 1966), and school finance and educational resources (Coleman & Hoffer, 1987).

Work by Coleman (1966) and others on these well-known social and economic environmental factors [socioeconomic status (SES)] and their influence on student outcomes has led to equity research on the degree of SES heterogeneity within individual schools, school districts and national school systems (see Cochrane, Chapter 4). This research is done to evaluate achievement in relation to SES. For students with disadvantaged backgrounds, as exposure to students of upper- and middle-class backgrounds and their resources increases, educational achievement improves. The greater the SES diversity, the greater the educational opportunities for disadvantaged students. Communities provide financial, human and social-capital resources that have a bearing on the quality of schools and teachers, the learning environment (including the SES mix of students in the community) and parental support. Community networks can also give students direction and help in the transition from school to work or to further education or training.

Therefore, studying the economic and demographic experience of communities and regions is important because it:
* helps us to assess the degree of educational disparity among communities, the reasons for the disparities and the resources on which governments can draw to address them. In contrast, much current analysis blurs educational disparities by averaging the resources of wealthier and poorer communities, and by failing to consider the impact of economic and demographic change on school and government resources.
* helps us to understand where and why residential segregation is intensifying

or decreasing. It also helps policy-makers spot, in a timely fashion, the demographic and economic trends that contribute to at-risk school districts. Residential segregation is the main source of concentration of at-risk students in schools, posing an obstacle to the creation of SES heterogeneity. It also significantly determines the human, social and financial resources that a community and its governmental entities can provide to schools.

- for those nations, states and/or communities with the will and political capacity, allows policy-makers to use various strategies to increase communal resources, especially by promoting more SES-diverse neighborhoods and school districts.

This chapter focuses on metropolitan areas because these are often where:
a) the greatest educational disparities exist between very affluent and very poor neighborhoods and;
b) there are more opportunities to address such disparities through integration and resource distribution, and;
c) the size and nature of urban populations are growing in importance.

This chapter also proposes a set of geographic and demographic indicators for studying educational resource disparities in metropolitan areas (internationally as well as in the United States). While limited here to metropolitan communities, the development of geographically based indicators is important for non-metropolitan communities as well.

School districts in the U.S. are good representations of communities, and are characterized as such in this chapter. Much of the chapter is focused on demonstrating the value of these suggested indicators using American metropolitan school district data. However comparisons can and have been made between American states and EU nations in relation to education, for example, "Education in States and Nations," (Phelps, Smith & Alsalam, 1996; Salganik, et al., 1993). A rationale for considering the American community data here as relevant to federal and non-federal nations is presented in section 2. International comparisons and implications are taken up again briefly in section 3.2 and continued from section 4 through the conclusion.

2. Resources and links to outcomes

Whatever the type of metropolitan school district, if there are a disproportionate or growing number of disenfranchised residents, there are related human and social capital costs. With respect to educational outcomes of at-risk or disenfranchised children, these costs refer in part to parents' ability to support students in their education and/or transition to work or higher education—an ability related in large part to parents' own educational shortcomings or lack of knowledge of what may help. Parents or caregivers may not understand or trust the educational system. Some families may also be unable to provide adequate health, nutrition, housing, safety and other basic human needs—all necessary if children are to be expected to self-actualize as learners on a day-to-day basis (Maslow, 1970). To the degree that these unhappy realities are a component of the home and community environment, they will reflect on students' abilities and readiness to learn in school.

School communities, states and countries that want to improve the educational outcomes of the disenfranchised need to provide additional programs and resources to overcome these environmental costs. It is not enough to equalize educational resources among communities; in the United States, some schools have become centers for community development—providing health, nutrition, social services, counseling, job training, day care and other resources to improve the home and community environment of their students. These schools do this to improve the likelihood that their students are able to arrive at school ready to learn (see Maslow, 1970; Goals 2000, Maslow in Cochrane, ch. 4).

Some may argue that the American data presented here is from a federal governance and finance structure, and does not relate well to non-federal governance and finance structures (for example France). However, the U.S. has the most decentralized education system. States are responsible for their education systems and are largely responsible for attracting and maintaining their economic base. The federal government provides only 6-9 percent of educational funding for public schools (Digest of Education, 1997). States must provide the financial and political resources to acquire the best teachers and educational programs.

The finance data in this chapter is limited to state and local revenues. Each state then can be viewed as one of many in a loose federation, or as individual, self-reliant "nations" in a loose confederation, not that dissimilar to the nations within the European Union. As a result, in this chapter, variations in economics and demographics between and within individual self-reliant states and across all of the states are considered and the conclusions expanded and related to "nations."

Great disparities in resources and school outcomes among communities are products of specific types of variations in metropolitan communities. When a community has a combination of low and/or declining property values, low and/or declining per-capita income, and high and/or rising proportions of persons living in poverty, there is a distinct limitation on its ability to fund and/or support the education of its children. In communities with high and/or rising property values, high and/or rising per-capita income, and low and/or declining proportions of persons living in poverty, funding and support for education of their children is possible with little stress on community budgets. It also happens in the United States that central-city communities tend towards the first, more negative experience of property values, income and poverty, while the suburbs tend to be overrepresented in the latter. The state's ability to bridge the difference in community resources is limited in part by the sum of state and/or national community resources, and shaped by the will (and political capacity) of these very different types of communities.

It is the disparity between metropolitan communities and the concentration of people in them that provides the focus of this chapter. Data from two-thirds of the metropolitan areas in the United States are included, representing approximately 60 percent of public school students. In Latin America, Gilbert (1998) notes that 72 percent of Latin Americans live in metropolitan areas.

The United States and, to a growing extent, other industrialized nations are experiencing a growth of the disenfranchised in cities. Cities in the United States are the sites of much inequality in education. Although there is a growing minority middle class, poverty and race/ethnicity are closely correlated. A recent report[3] found that in the largest U.S. cities, 15 percent of children were living in extremely poor neighborhoods, three times the nation's average. Of those children living in extremely poor neighborhoods in these cities, 86 percent were minorities, either African American or Hispanic/Latino (in relation to the United States, these two groups are the minorities referenced throughout this chapter).

Approximately a third of the children in these 75 largest cities live in poverty, almost twice the U.S. average. Additionally, minority children reside in these cities at approximately twice the national average and represent more than half the cities' children.

There has been and continues to be a minority-white test score gap. In most states, children in urban districts (not just the 75 city districts referenced above) performed much worse than non-urban children on reading, math and science tests. From these findings, it is clear that a disproportionate number of minority children who live in poverty and/or have poor educational outcomes reside in urban communities.

What should be no surprise is that the disparity in school outcomes associated with these communities is mirrored in community resources (i.e., human and social capital, public financing) and vice versa. The following section will highlight some of these community-based resource disparities.

Community-based human/social capital. As demonstrated in Tables 1 through 3 and Figures 1 through 3 and 7, and discussed more fully below, there is a relationship between schools and community resources. Communities with low and/or declining property values and per-capita income, and high and/or rising proportions of people living in poverty, have less per-pupil financing of schools and human or social capital in the community than those with good economies. Also, individually and within groupings of economic status, central-city and rural communities receive fewer resources than suburban districts.

And these disparities are compounded by the influence of neighborhoods which, through concentrated housing patterns of the poor and minorities, create school environments that demand additional, not fewer, resources if they are to be conducive to learning. This pattern is also exacerbated when not adequately addressed, as the middle classes tend to abandon poor schools and communities with little educational success.

Figures 1 and 2 provide a useful community indicator of potential school outcome problems. These figures reflect the proportion of at-risk students by metro community type. At-risk students are those exposed by several environmental factors to higher school failure rates. These factors include having only one parent, living in poverty and being a member of a racial or ethnic minority group.

Central-city communities have twice the proportion of at-risk students (or

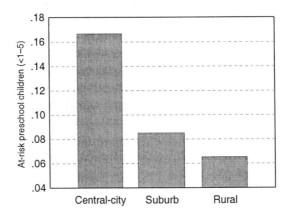

Figure 1. Proportion of preschool students at risk by metro type (ages less than 1 to 5) (Data source: Cochrane, combined 1980 & 1990 Census and NCES F33 (school finance) data)

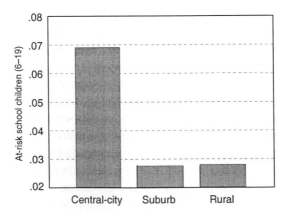

Figure 2. Proportion of school students at risk by metro type (ages 6–19) (Data source: Cochrane, combined 1980 & 1990 Census and NCES F33 (school finance) data)

preschoolers) than either rural or suburban communities (Figures 1 and 2). Figure 7 (page 357) and the associated discussion provides evidence of the tendency of central cities, which experienced poor economic times in 1980, to have negative economic experiences during the entire decade.

Of some interest is that there were proportionally twice as many preschool

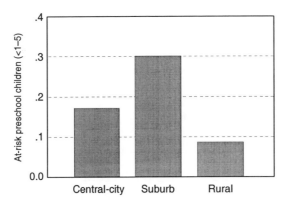

Figure 3. Proportion of preschool students at risk (1990) by metro type with negative economic experience (Data source: Cochrane, combined 1980 & 1990 Census and NCES F33 (school finance) data)

students at risk (Figure 1) as there were school-age students (Figure 2). Of more interest is that suburban districts with negative economic experiences during the 1980s also had almost twice as many preschool students at risk (Figure 3) as central-city districts, and almost four times the rural rate. In particular, Orfield and Yun (1999) noted the high birth rates of both African Americans and Hispanic/Latinos in comparison to whites. These suburban communities with negative economic experiences had evidence of significant human and social capital resource deficits in the 1980s and 1990s. The expectation was that with high birth rates, the percentages of at-risk students would grow, in both the preschool and school populations.

Parental as well as peer education levels and incomes are clearly associated with educational outcomes (see Coleman, 1966; Noël & de Broucker, Chapter 13). Community residents' incomes and their growth are reflected in the 1980s economic indicators. Table 1 (page 350) reflects the differences in education among metropolitan community types, which includes variations in economic change.

School-finance resources. Table 3 (page 360) demonstrates the combined influence of economics and density on per-pupil revenue increases in metropolitan communities during the 1980s. Those districts with the most economic progress received substantially more than those districts with economic declines. There were also substantial differences based on density. In

Table 1. Proportion of college graduates by metropolitan district density and economic change (1980–90)

Metro status	1980–90 economic change	Mean
Central-city	Negative	.18
	Mixed	.2
	Positive	.30
	Total	.20
Suburb	Negative	.13
	Mixed	.23
	Positive	.29
	Total	.23
Rural-metro	Negative	.10
	Mixed	.14
	Positive	.26
	Total	.14

combination, these two characteristics produced a $2,164 per-student gap between the district with the strongest economy/suburban density and the district with the most declining economy/central-city density, and a $2,194 per-student gap between the district with the strongest economy/suburban density and the district with the most declining economy/rural-metro density.

A regression analysis (Cochrane, 1999) identifies communities distinguished by their density and economics and regions as having different per-pupil revenue increases or decreases. A similar analysis also finds the economics of states and regional differences in funding reflected in the changes in per-pupil revenues during the 1980s. States and regions with varying economic changes had corresponding and substantially different per-pupil revenue increases or decreases.

3.   Assessing educational disparities among communities

In the United States, the author's study of metropolitan areas confirms that density, economics and population migration (increases of minorities and decreases of whites in central cities[5] and suburbs[6] with the least economic improvement, as well as the reverse for rural-metro districts with good economic change) together influenced state and local education funding choices in the 1980s. Table 2 (page 358) relates proportional changes in specific populations to community variations in density and economic change. Table 3 (page 360) then provides the per pupil revenue changes for communities based on these variations in density and economics. The regression analysis previously mentioned finds a significant relationship during the 1980s between combined state and local per-pupil revenue increases and economic change, density or metro type, proportional change in population, change in the Hispanic/Latino proportion of the total population and state economic capacity.[7]

3.1.   The reasons for the disparities

Residential segregation is a growing concern of city schools and the populations they serve; for one thing, there are not enough white children in many cities to create well-balanced schools for large minority populations. Orfield and Yun (1999) have found that minorities who have moved to the suburbs or rural areas have tended to move together. So, even in the suburbs where there may be less density than in extreme-poverty city neighborhoods, there are still high concentrations of both minorities and poverty in some non-central city districts, [8] and unequal educational outcomes.

Several circumstances combined to allow for the continuation, and worsening in some cases, of disparities discussed in this chapter. In the United States, there has been historic segregation of African-American and Hispanic/Latino populations. Federally enforced *de jure* school desegregation in the South was directed against the legally imposed racial segregation that prevailed prior to the U.S. Supreme Court's ruling in *Brown v. Board of Education* (1954). It was imposed in all Southern school districts. The *de facto* desegregation of both African-American and Hispanic/Latino schools in the rest of the country, was enacted, defined and adjudicated—primarily in central cities—school district by school district. The basis for a finding of *de facto* desegregation was evidence of a community's institutional involvement in the development or preservation of residential segregation, combined with school-boundary definitions that maintained that segregation.

Jonathan Barnett (1995), a noted urban designer, describes the process of urban expansion in the United States after World War II, supported by federal mortgage insurance. This included the movement of the middle and upper classes to the suburbs in growing numbers. Jeanne Anjon (1997) outlines the federal role in maintaining residential segregation in the cities during this period; buyers in African-American neighborhoods were not provided mortgages, making suburban home ownership more desirable to mortgage seekers, but difficult for African Americans. Once the historic segregation was furthered by the movement of white populations to the suburbs, several things took place that assured the continued shift away from central cities: Some companies moved to the suburbs, creating jobs outside the cities, and new transportation networks were developed to enable suburban dwellers to commute to the cities. Before long, these transportation systems linked suburban residents to suburban employment (Barnett, 1995). As noted above, such shifts rarely left enough middle-class white, African-American or Hispanic/Latino students to provide good racial or socioeconomic balance in many city schools.

This chapter also documents the migration of minorities and whites to communities with quite different characteristics. As noted earlier, there was a proportional increase of minorities and a decrease of whites in communities with declining economies and higher density. The opposite was true in communities with growing economies and lower density. This migration and demographic change exacerbated existing residential segregation pressures and their attendant effects.

These effects include the resource disparities cited earlier. The large sums of money invested in education in this country during the 1980s were generally distributed differently, depending on the quality of economic experiences of a district and/or state and the density of the community. This has led to a growing school-revenue gap that disproportionately affects minorities and declining communities.

There is evidence of a similar trend in the metropolitan areas surrounding some of Europe's world cities (Kunzmann, 1998; Veld, 1992). There are also, since the 1970s, rapidly growing populations of minorities (Eldering & Klopprogge, 1989) representing diverse ethnic, language and religious (Berque, 1991) backgrounds.

The most significant U.S. finding for Europeans may be the demographic changes in the 1980s of suburban districts that experienced declining economic change. These poor and newly poor American suburban districts experienced proportional increases in minority populations. Shockingly, in these poor suburban districts, almost one in three preschool children are at risk for school failure (Figure 3). This is almost twice the rate of city districts with negative economic experiences and four times the rate of rural-metro districts with negative economic experiences. The at-risk population of preschool children is twice the size of the population of at-risk school-age children across all metropolitan school-district types, and there continues to be rapid growth of this vulnerable preschool population.

3.2. The significance of local-education outcome disparities for states and nations

The issue of response to inequities can be reframed, in part, for states and nations as one of economic capacity. Baldi et al. (2000); Phelps, Smith and Alsalam (1996); and Salganik et al., (1993) all note the association between gross domestic product (GDP) and education resources. A variable (STECON) in the regression analysis identifies the state proxy for change in GDP to be significantly related to changes in per-pupil revenues. That is, a percentage increase in the state proxy for GDP has a positive ($660) effect on changes in state and local per-pupil revenue.

Fiscal effort in school finance is an expression of the resources funded and the capacity to provide resources. A district or state with poor economic conditions, which provides the same level of funding as a district or state with mixed or good economic conditions, demonstrates more fiscal effort. Likewise, a district or state with good economic conditions or a high capacity to provide resources, which does not match the funding of a district or state with poor or mixed economic conditions or capacity, demonstrates poor fiscal effort.

Several American studies suggest there has been some effort at the state level in the United States to invest in education in such a way as to provide more resources for the disadvantaged (GAO, 1998; Cochrane, 1999). However, Alexander (1997) and Orland and Cohen (1996) suggest there is an issue of economic capacity at the state level. States with positive economic experiences and large populations have greater ability to provide educational resources than states with negative economic experiences and smaller populations.

Figure 4 gives us a visual image of the geography of metropolitan economic capacity within American states; Figure 5 (page 354) shows changes in metropolitan per-pupil revenues within states. We can see that the Northeastern and Southeastern coastal states, with high economic capacity, have provided greater resources. Smaller and interior states, some of which rely more on agriculture and natural resources, have both negative economics and smaller populations, and provide fewer per-pupil revenue resources.

In the regression analysis summarized by region, the Northeast (REG1)—which was seen in Figure 4 to have a high economic capacity and in Figure 5 to have effected a strong increase in per-pupil revenues—has fewer per-pupil revenue changes than any of the other regions, after taking changes in state GDP into account. This would suggest poor fiscal effort, given its positive

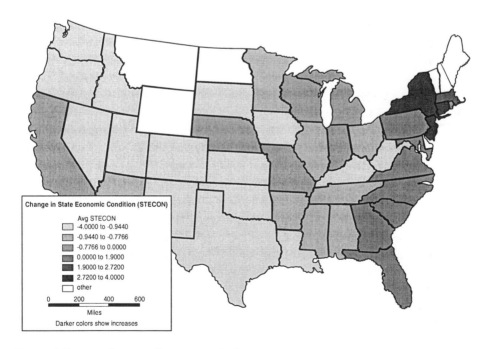

Figure 4. States and metropolitan economic change

economic change, compared to other regions. However, as all of the resources have been equalized with a district-based cost-of-education index, these states with improved GDP provided the greatest real increases in per-pupil revenue. It is reasonable to suggest that they have been able to do so because educational expenses create less pressure on their total budget than in other states.

This suggests that there are structural problems within states (and we suggest also within nations) that limit their ability to either equalize resources across districts or provide the resources necessary to compete with states (or countries) with better economic conditions—an issue of some import in an age of global competition.

3.3.   The value of defining both suburban and rural-metro communities

"Suburb" has been defined in a variety of spatial and sociocultural ways (Sharpe & Wallock, 1994). Suburban district definitions have an impact on comparisons with central-city districts, as education researchers have tended to use a single "suburban" category for districts outside central cities but within a metropolitan area, or to categorize suburban towns and villages not as suburban but rather as cities or small-city school districts. As shown below, using definitions for two types of districts outside the central city but within the metropolitan area, as well as for central-city districts, provides subtler results than the typical

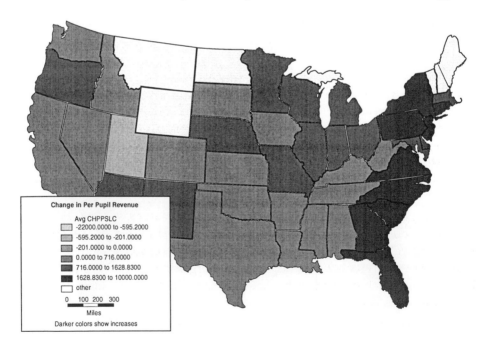

Figure 5. States and change in per-pupil revenue (1980–90)

dual typology.

Within metropolitan areas, when census-classified urban/non-central city (suburban) and rural-metro districts are combined into larger "suburban" districts, the relatively poorer rural-metro districts dampen the effects of relatively wealthier (suburban) ones. Also, by using rural-metro and suburban as two distinct district types, we find that rural-metro districts had the most negative economic conditions in 1980 but, in comparison to central cities, enjoyed greater economic gains over the course of the 1980s (Cochrane, 1998b). Thus, being able to identify more distinct district types helps us to understand some of the significant changes in economics and school-district revenues that had not previously been captured by available data. Thus, in this study, we consider three metropolitan district types: central-city districts (which will be called central city), and the two types of urban/non-central city districts (which will be called suburban and rural-metro). Suburban school districts have higher density than rural-metro districts; rural-metro districts are low in density, yet within commuting distance of the central city.

Variations in density. Philadelphia represents a Northeastern metropolitan area with a not-uncommon history and development. It is presented here in Figure 6 (page 356) to visually illustrate district density in a metropolitan area. Density is not unrelated to issues of economics. When a denser population is functioning well economically, it can be efficient at dispersing and utilizing resources. However, should economic conditions not be good, it is much harder to coordinate, for the purposes of economic development, the investment in and activities of a larger, denser population than those of a more dispersed group.

The opposite effect is that areas that are less dense can respond more quickly to well-funded development investment. After federal transportation infrastructure investment for the metro area was used to create access to rural-metro communities, Myron Orfield (1997) documented the rapid economic development of and migration to rural-metro communities, by upper- and middle-class residence, in the twin cities of Minneapolis and St. Paul, Minnesota, during the 1980s. These were previously relatively poor rural-metro areas.

The Philadelphia School District, a central-city district, is shown below what is initially a ring of suburban school districts. Population is represented by dots. Each dot represents an equal number of people. The closer together the dots, the denser the population. As the districts extend farther from the city, there are fewer of them, and there are fewer towns and other geographic/political entities. These rural-metro school districts are much larger in geographic size than the inner-suburban school districts, but not necessarily in student enrollment.

In Figure 6, the lighter the color of the district, the fewer the resources. Note that the central city and several inner suburbs provide fewer per-pupil resources than outlying suburban districts. The geographically larger rural districts also provide fewer per-pupil revenue changes; only a couple of rural-metro districts on the outer edges of the metropolitan community are darker, representing greater increases in education resources.

The experience of variations in economics and density. The indicators developed to capture the economic condition and changing nature of school districts classify them based on per-capita income, housing values and the percentage of people living in poverty. To be characterized as having a poor or declining economy, a district would have had to be in approximately the bottom third of this group of metropolitan school districts on all three of these measures in 1980 (the lowest per-capita income, the lowest property values and the highest percentage of people living in poverty). Measures are also proportional, so that increases can be captured even if a district had a poor rating initially. To be shown to have had a negative economic change during the 1980s, school districts would have had to demonstrate the least proportional gain in per-capita income, the lowest proportional increase in property values and the highest proportional increase in people living in poverty.

Figure 6. Density and resource variation in central-city, suburban and rural-metro school districts: Metropolitan Philadelphia, Penn.

Both rural-metro and central-city districts are overrepresented among districts with poor economic conditions, but central cities demonstrate even less flexibility in moving from poor economic conditions to mixed or positive economic change and are less inclined to sustain healthy economies. As a result, central cities were also overrepresented in negative economic change during the 1980s. As suggested by observation of extreme economic changes during the 1980s (Figure 7 and Table 2, below and page 384) and by a previous study (Cochrane, 1998b), rural-metro districts, while remaining as a group poor, demonstrated the most economic flexibility and gained economic strength during the 1980s. Suburban districts, while not as flexible as rural-metro districts, maintained and increased their overrepresentation in positive economies during the 1980s.

However, these findings are blurred when non-central city communities are not disaggregated; thus, there is a need to distinguish urban-fringe or suburban

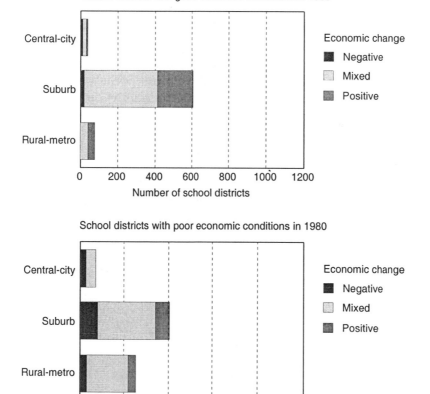

Figure 7. Community density and economic flexibility: the experience of economic change based on economic condition (1980) and metro type (Data source: Cochrane, 1999)

districts from rural-metro districts.

3.4. The value of studying change

Economics and demographics. The movement or proportional change of specific populations between and among these three types of metropolitan school districts, by economic experiences during the 1980s, is also illustrative. As has been much discussed in the United States, from the early 1980s, there was, and continues to be, a general decrease in the white population as a percentage of the total population of these districts (Table 2). This is a result of the low birth rates of whites compared to African-American and Hispanic/Latino minority populations, and the immigration of Hispanic/Latino and other non-native populations.

There is one noted exception to the decrease of the white population as a proportion of the population of rural-metro areas with positive economic change (Table 2): Whites decreased less as a percentage of the total population as density decreased and the quality of the economic experience improved during the 1980s. This held true for cities that experienced negative economic change, where the white population decreased the most as a percentage of the total, through rural-metro areas that experienced positive economic change. These rural-metro districts with positive economic change actually had proportional increases in the white population in relation to the total.

Table 2. Proportional change in population by metropolitan district density and economic change (1980–90)

1980–90 economic change	Metro status	African American change in % of total population	Hispanic/ Latino change in % of total population	White change in % of total population
Negative	City	.019	.029	-.057
	Suburb	.021	.020	-.048
	Rural-metro	-.001	.026	-.029
	Total	.015	.024	-.045
Mixed	City	.013	.028	-.058
	Suburb	.010	.017	-.042
	Rural-metro	-.004	.014	-.012
	Total	.005	.017	-.033
Positive	City	.015	.018	-.059
	Suburb	.006	.012	-.032
	Rural-metro	-.004	-.002	.005
	Total	.004	.009	-.025
Total	City	.015	.028	-.058
	Suburb	.010	.016	-.041
	Rural-metro	-.003	.014	-.013
	Total	.007	.017	-.034

Data source: Cochrane, combined 1980 & 1990 Census and NCES F33 (school finance) data

Table 2 demonstrates the growth of minority populations in districts with negative economic experiences and the flight of whites from those communities. African-American and Hispanic/Latino minorities experienced a demographic change that is the reverse of the white experience in this three-by-three district matrix of density and economics. These two minority populations increased proportionally as density increased (i.e., from rural-metro to central city) and as the quality of economic change decreased (i.e., from positive to negative). For example, the rural-metro school districts had the least proportional gain in Hispanic/Latinos as a percentage of the total population; those with positive economic change had not the lowest increase, but actually a proportional decrease in the Hispanic/Latino population. For Hispanic/Latinos, the one exception to this demographic—dynamic related to density and quality of economic experiences—was that among districts with negative economic change, rural-metro districts had a higher mean proportional increase in Hispanic/Latinos than suburban districts.

The changes in African-American proportions are very similar to Hispanic/Latino changes. Density increases and economic decreases to some extent dictate the flow of demographic change in these school districts for African Americans. This also meant a decrease in the mean proportion of African Americans in the population of rural-metro districts, regardless of economic experience. Like the Hispanic/Latino population, there was one telling exception: In districts with negative economic experiences, the suburbs, rather than the predicted central city, had the greatest increases of African Americans as a proportion of the total population.

Table 3 (page 360) gives us some perception as to what happened to the change in total population and combined state and local per-pupil revenue changes during the 1980s. First, there was a mean increase in population in each of these nine district types, with one exception: central cities with positive economic change, where there was a decrease in population. From Table 2, we can see that this loss was driven by a mean white proportional loss in the population of city districts with positive economies. That exception did not affect the fact that mean proportional increases in population followed from high density to low density, with cities having the greatest gain and rural-metro districts the smallest. By the economic experience of districts, the mean population increased most in districts that experienced a mixed economy and least in districts with a positive economic experience. Notably different than cities with positive economies, city districts with mixed economies had the greatest mean proportional gains in population across the nine district types.

The challenge to funding successful educational outcomes for all. The migration patterns outlined above demonstrate an increase in the isolation of minority students in school districts with high density and negative economics. There are higher costs associated with providing poor students in poor schools

Table 3. Change in population and combined state and local per-pupil revenue, by metropolitan district density and economic change (1980–90)

1980–90 economic change	Metro status	1990 total population/ 1980 total population	Change in state and local per-pupil revenue 1980–90
Negative	City	1.15	$544
	Suburb	1.12	$519
	Rural-metro	1.18	$512
	Total	1.14	$522
Mixed	City	1.32	$1130
	Suburb	1.28	$1346
	Rural-metro	1.18	$855
	Total	1.25	$1151
Positive	City	.99	$2373
	Suburb	1.05	$2706
	Rural-metro	1.14	$2454
	Total	1.06	$2647
Total	City	1.25	$998
	Suburb	1.20	$1534
	Rural-metro	1.18	$975
	Total	1.20	$1302

with basic reading and math skills, and these costs increase where—as in the case of Hispanic/Latino students—the primary language of instruction is a second language (Orfield, 1994). On the other hand, we find whites—the group with the highest cultural capital—having fewer reductions in their proportion of the population in districts with less density (suburban and rural-metro) and better economics. As a result, these suburban and rural-metro districts with positive economic change and lower density have fewer costs in providing, for example, basic reading and math skills.

Financial resources. Using per-pupil revenue changes as a measure of resources, demographic and economic changes are exacerbated by the fact that one can expect fewer local resources to be available in districts with negative economic change compared to those with mixed economic change, or in districts with mixed economic change as opposed to those experiencing positive change. Of course, central cities also have fewer resources than suburban districts[10] (Cochrane, 1998a, 1998b, 1999). The role of the state is, in part, to equalize the differences.

Mean gap in local community resources. The question of some importance then is whether, across districts, states are indeed able to leverage or supplement local school-district revenues so as to equalize changes in revenues regardless of density and economic experiences. This is also an important equity question internationally.

Table 3 demonstrates that, in spite of what we can expect to have been some reasonable effort, states have not been able to equalize disparities among districts. There are very large differences in combined state and local per-pupil revenues as economic experience improves: a $600 per-pupil gap between districts experiencing negative vs. mixed economic change, and a $900 per-pupil difference between those experiencing mixed vs. positive economic change. Within the three categories of metropolitan school-district density, the suburbs received the largest per-pupil revenue increase, and rural-metro and central-city districts the least—a per-pupil revenue disparity of approximately $550. The combination of density and economics, contextualized by the demographic trends noted above, results in a $2,100 to $2,200 per-pupil revenue difference for central-city districts or rural-metro districts with negative economic experiences, relative to suburban districts with positive economic change.

That rural-metro districts so closely match city increases in per-pupil revenues is unusual. Most prevalent throughout the world is a pattern in which rural districts are generally the least affluent and the least dense, rarely having the political ability to greatly influence state or national budgets. However, the rural-metro districts in this study are rural districts within commuting distance of a central city. The migration to rural-metro districts of the majority white population, as the economic experience of the rural-metro district improves, suggests less density is valued over greater density. This increased value appears to be captured in the comparative increase in combined state and local revenues between city and rural-metro districts.

The following demonstration of the human/social capital differences for the disenfranchised in the United States, based on density, is also a demonstration of spatially based indicators that can be used with international data. The growth in the United States throughout the 1980s in the populations of African Americans and Hispanic/Latinos, most specifically in central cities—regardless of their economic conditions—was demonstrated in Table 2. As noted, African Americans and Hispanic/Latinos are also disproportionately associated with poverty in the United States, specifically in the large central cities. This same combination of minority demographics and central-city geography was also correlated to significantly lower academic performance.

3.5. Understanding where and why residential segregation is intensifying or decreasing

The data presented previously in this chapter as an assessment of the disparities between communities also provide us with an opportunity to understand the location and nature of variations in residential segregation. What we have learned is that communities with different economic experiences over time have difficulty maintaining a balanced and diverse population. In the United

States, central cities were particularly vulnerable to the negative economic forces that intensified residential segregation for minorities. Rural-metro communities demonstrated a lot of flexibility in turning around previously poor economic conditions and, where they were successful, became the only ones to experience increases in the proportion of whites. Of course, they typically created more segregated white communities in the process.

This information allows us to understand economics, or economic change, and the density of population as variables that interact to create conditions conducive to residential segregation.

This is, of course, the contemporary American experience. However, some of the large cities in Europe and Latin America also experience high poverty/ minority residential segregation in their suburbs. We also now understand that there are growing numbers of American suburban communities with comparable conditions. Tracking economic change and population demographics, in conjunction with variations in metropolitan density, enables us to anticipate where conditions conducive to residential segregation occur.

4.   The economic and demographic experience of communities and regions

Mega-cities and world cities. The residential segregation found in U.S. metropolitan areas is not exclusive to North America. Internationally, two groups of cities, mega-cities and world cities, demonstrate similar patterns of residential density combined with social and economic disparity. The largest cities in the world, classified as "mega-cities"[4] can also be world cities if they provide essential goods and services to markets in other countries; several American cities—New York and Los Angeles, for example—are both mega-cities and world cities. Mega-cities in other countries are often close to the proportion of minority-majority populations and poverty levels reflected in the American experience. However, world cities have a tendency to experience very rapid social and economic change; even in Europe, world cities that had not previously experienced these trends have started to demonstrate similar patterns of dense poverty and growing minority populations.

Two trends—increased globalization and reliance on information technology— have created a recent phenomenon of city centers that control national and international services. These global urban areas consciously harness resources and strategic commitments to develop an infrastructure of services and information that meets a particular global demand. Fu-chen Lo and Yue-man Yeung (1998) observed that social and economic polarization develops rapidly as a result of globalization in world cities. These world cities/regions have had the greatest dedicated development in the Pacific Rim, but development is also occurring in large European centers such as London, Paris, Rhine-Main, Rhine-Ruhr and Randstad.

Until recently, the American pattern of central-city density and growing rings of suburban and rural-metro development, with geographically preferential areas attracting disparate wealth and densely segregated inner-city pockets of high poverty, has not been a European problem. There is now, however, growing evidence of a similar trend emerging in some of Europe's world-city metropolitan areas (Kunzmann, 1998; Veld, 1992). Although there has been a reduction in the immigration of workers since the mid-1970s in Europe, there has been a growing population of immigrants or minorities (Extra, 1990) representing diverse ethnic, language and religious backgrounds. The increase in this diverse immigrant/minority population has been due to both the social migration of families and the additions of sons and daughters born in the new country (Berques, 1991). Extra (1990) noted that a third of the population in Europe under the age of 35 was predicted to be minority by the year 2000.

New Asian world cities, such as Bangkok, Taipei, Manila, Kuala Lumpur and Jakarta—as well as Tokyo, Seoul and Hong Kong—are experiencing "sharpened social inequalities and tensions" (Yueng & Lo, 1998). Related to heightened social tensions is ongoing population growth, stemming from combined migration (internal and international) and natural increases. Rural areas remain the poorest sections of many Asian countries, but these large developing urban centers have created communities with disparate resources. How effective are these Asian mega-cities, urban corridors and newly developing world-city centers at providing educational services for poor communities? The poorest metropolitan communities are the most likely to be comprised of combinations of language, ethnic and religious minorities.

The rapid social and economic polarization of world cities has been seen most prominently in Rio de Janeiro, although Gilbert (1998) suggests that in Latin America there are no global or world cities, simply large mega-cities. Mega-cities are cities expected to have 4 to 10 million inhabitants or more by the year 2000. There are questions as to whether the large cities in Latin America provide essential services to foreign markets outside of Latin America, a qualification for world-city status. Mega-cities have less economic viability then world cities and as such have potentially greater gaps between the wealthy and the poor. The middle classes are often of smaller proportion. Gilbert characterizes Latin-American cities as currently inequitable and unstable. What seems clear to Gilbert is that at a time when 72 percent of Latin Americans live in urban areas, the only sure thing that can be said about globalization is that it will increase their inequity and instability.

For cities in Europe and elsewhere, with inequities exacerbated by rapid change and where metropolitan economic disparity and residential segregation are relatively new and/or not of the proportion found in North America, there is a need to monitor patterns of migration, economics and density to identify potentially vulnerable groups and areas. Given the poverty and social tensions in mega-cities and assuming a desire to provide more options for these urban citizens and their countries, there is a need to collect better education and associated background data.

4.1. Helping policy-makers spot early economic and demographic trends that contribute to at-risk school districts

The resource disparities associated with residential segregation outlined earlier in this chapter, including the contribution to higher proportions of at-risk student populations, identify negative economics and increasing minority proportions as indicators of schools that may need increased resources. Once these data on metropolitan communities are collected and maintained, policy-makers can monitor demographic and economic trends that will help identify potential at-risk communities and their schools.

Once at-risk communities and their schools are identified, it is possible to make policy decisions about appropriate interventions. Cochrane (Chapter 4) reports on a variety of early childhood, school and regional interventions that have proved effective at improving educational outcomes. Of particular interest is the development of regional or metropolitan-wide schools. Given the condition of negative economics and changing minority populations, it is also possible to consider regional economic development and other diversity-supportive political and legal strategies as means to forestall further erosion of SES diversity within communities.

4.2. Residential segregation is the main source of concentrations of at-risk students in schools and poses a key obstacle to creating greater SES heterogeneity

Orfield (Chapter 6) clearly describes residential segregation of minorities as correlating closely with concentrations of at-risk students in American schools. Poor minority students are 11 times more likely to go to schools with high concentrations of other at-risk students than are poor white students. Tomlinson (1989) notes minority-population concentrations in urban areas with poor housing in England. She also reports that efforts in the 1960s to keep minority children to no more than 30 percent in any given school were unsuccessful due to increased immigration to urban areas.

Demeuse, Crahay and Monseur (Chapter 2) describe SES community differences and poorer educational outcomes for French-speaking Belgian students compared to Flemish-speaking Belgian students. Various TIMSS studies have also reported significant educational differences between the Flemish and the French students in Belgium.

Eldering (1989) also describes ethnic minorities in Holland as being heavily concentrated in large urban areas. Half of the students in the largest cities (Amsterdam, Rotterdam and The Hague) were projected in 2000 to be children of immigrants.

In France, Costa-Lascoux (1989) noted several reports of malaise in the French education system attributed to immigrant pupils or pupils of foreign ancestry. At the provincial level, but most emphatically at the district level in large cities, there was a clear indication of a "strong geographical concentration of immigrant communities." Some schools in large cities in France had enrollments in which more than 80 percent of the students were not French.

With this language and cultural complexity, immigration has had an effect on the SES mixes of communities and schools. In spite of often egalitarian standards, education systems have not surprisingly been strained. Thus, this examination of the American metropolitan experience has broad international implications.

The human, social and financial resource costs. All of the above-mentioned authors associate the residential segregation of minorities with poorer communities. This American analysis introduces some interesting concerns. Earlier, we outlined some of the human and social resource costs for communities with indicators of at-risk schools. These included fewer college graduates, more at-risk children and higher concentrations of minorities.

The regression analysis and an HLM analysis provide convincing evidence, along with the descriptive data referenced earlier, of the large differences in changes in per-pupil revenues over the 1980s being associated with the economic capacities of states and the differences between regions and communities. The negative associations of Hispanic/Latino migration with changes in per-pupil revenue, city districts with less money than either rural-metro or suburban districts and the additional differences related to economic experience all confirm the following observation. Communities, states and, by extension, nations are affected in their ability to invest in education in such a way as to provide comparable educational opportunities to all children, by the density, economic experience and social context of the places where students live.

What is also clear is that the residential segregation in metropolitan areas (the primary reason for the concentration of at-risk students in schools) is a hindrance to creating the SES diversity that improves educational outcomes. Thus, studying or implementing interventions that create opportunities for greater SES diversity in a region is of international import, particularly if they can be developed by countries and/or regions where resources are scarce. The promotion and development of metropolitan-wide schools—an intervention mentioned elsewhere in this book (Cochrane, Chapter 4)—meets these criteria.

5.   Findings

A variety of descriptive data presented here demonstrate patterns of density, economics and demographics that are related to substantially different per-pupil revenues and/or human/social capital resources for students in metropolitan school districts. Supported by a regression and HLM analysis the disparity in resources related to economic experience and density is substantial: $1,150 per pupil between states with positive economic capacity and those with negative economic capacity, an additional $400 to $500 per pupil within states between city districts and either rural or suburban districts and as much as $300 more per pupil based on the economic experience of the district. Taken together, the regression and HLM analyses suggest per-pupil gaps ranging from $1,600 to $1,900. In a classroom of 25 students, this represents $40,000 to almost $48,000 per year. While some might suggest that this is not relevant to the educational outcomes of these two classrooms, the National Research Council (NRC) in its 1999 publication "Making Money Matter," notes: "Not only is the committee convinced that money can matter, but we are also convinced that it can and should be made to matter more."

> In terms of competitiveness, how may we define the costs of these increased disparities? In the U.S. an additional $1,000 per pupil, per year can be used to: divide three classes, with 30 students apiece, into four classes with 22.5 students per class—leaving $2,500 per teacher annually for professional development, and $20,000 per year for classroom construction. (Cochrane, 1999)[11]

Alternatively, the NRC (1999a) also suggests that hiring better teachers—a challenge in schools with high numbers of disadvantaged students—can be a good investment. Again, schools and districts with high proportions of disadvantaged students will have to invest substantially in higher teacher salaries to attract more qualified teachers.

The NRC (1999b) found that when technology was used appropriately it could be very helpful to students and teachers interested in developing the competencies needed for the 21st century. This is relevant to poor communities.

> Low-income school districts are likely to face the greatest funding challenge, not only because their sources of funding may be limited, but also because the cost of deploying technology in their schools may be high for various reasons, including having more older buildings and greater security problems. (Pelavin/AIR, 1997)

On an annual basis, an additional $500 per pupil can put half a dozen computers in each classroom, wire them to the Internet and provide schools with the human resources to integrate them successfully into the curriculum.

Of more relevance from an equity perspective is that the classroom with $40,000 to $48,000 less funding is most likely to be found in a geographically denser neighborhood, prone to negative economic experiences, and to have a high and growing proportion of minority students. This suggests that it would cost more to provide basic reading and math skills for students in districts with the fewest resources. It should also be noted that the classroom with $40,000 to $48,000 more to spend per year will almost surely have a preponderance of majority students who go home to much more conducive learning environments.

Clune (1994), attempting to replace equity financing of schools with an adequacy formula that would provide some accountability for school performance, listed eight spending categories necessary to provide some level of comparable education for disadvantaged students. After referencing a mean per-pupil per-year expense of $5,000 in the United States, he made an educated guess that an additional $5,000 per pupil per year would be needed. Of that sum, $2,000 would be used to improve performance in one subject area; the remainder would provide such enhancements as social services, enriched academic programs and facilities, and higher salaries.

With Clune's (1994) estimate of the approximately $3,000 per-pupil per-year cost for poor schools to respond to the human and social capital deficits of their community, we now have some notion of the scale of the difficulties they face. The $1,600 per-pupil disparity noted earlier in this chapter for school districts with negative economic change adds considerably to the cost of providing comparable education for poor minority children.

The state-level HLM analysis provides verification that there are large per-pupil resource differences based on the economic capacity of a state. Regardless of the effort (education spending by economic capacity) that has not been measured here, but that is assumed to be varied and often substantial, states are substantially limited, on average, in their education funding choices by their economic capacity. At the extremes of economic capacity, that represents in this analysis a $1,150 per-pupil or $27,500 per-classroom difference between states.

This finding supports a concern that within the United States there are growing educational disparities. This would be particularly relevant for those with the greatest needs, but also suggests that some states will, on their own, be unable to provide a competitive education to their students. This discussion — relevant at the level of nations—may in turn affect the location or relocation of businesses and organizations that need well-educated employees to compete nationally or globally, perpetuating cycles of poor economic capacity and inadequate education funding.

Conclusion

This chapter successfully argues, in part, that the American metropolitan data presented here, with the help of the indicator system, has comparative value for developed OECD nations, such as those in Western Europe, and for developing and less developed countries and regions throughout the world. The pace of economic change, even in the world class cities of Europe has increased disparities. There are community based patterns of density and economic and demographic change that are related to substantially different per-pupil revenues and/or human/ social capital resources for students in metropolitan communities. While this pattern may vary by metropolitan area, country or even region of the world, a robust indicator system, such as the one demonstrated here, accomodates differences and provides valuable insight into significant school related resource issues.

For example, while the density of a community (central-city, suburb, rural-metro) was associated with substantial resource differences and resource differences were also based on the economic change of a district, the greatest per pupil revenue differences between communities were related to the economic change of the state. And, while the American education equity case is often identified as centered in the central-city and to a lesser degree in rural communities, this system also found negative economic change and associated educational resource differences to have occurred in all three metro community types, something an international system must be able to capture.

Density proved particularly valuable, in combination with economic change, in identifying types of communities with demographic patterns that need different amounts and types of resources if comparable educational outcomes are to be expected. Communities with needs for additional resources to assist with children whose native language is not the primary language of instruction, or for growing numbers of children with a variety of other educational risk factors, such as having only one parent, living in poverty or being a minority. Should some other form of education equity be the norm, the above information captures important issues. Issues that must be at least identified if equitable, equitable and efficient (Demeuse, Crahay, & Monsuer, Chapter 2, and; Vandenberghe, Dupray, & Zachary, Chapter 9) or equivalent (Wildt-Persson & Rosengren, Chapter 13) education outcomes are to be achieved. This is true whether equity is defined by justice (Meuret, Chapter 3) or ethics (Demeuse, Crahay, & Monsuer, Chapter 2, and, Crahay, 2000).

Recommendations: A need then has been demonstrated for a system of international education indicators similar to the one used in this chapter. It should, as this does, define the density/geography and economic experiences of a community in conjunction with reporting its demographics and resources. A time frame should be captured, at least five years. And schools and their outcomes must be associated with specific communities.

This suggests a group of geographic/community linked census or census like data, most specifically community based economic and demographic variables. Economic variables would include changes in housing values, per capita income, rent, people in poverty and unemployment rates. These would be converted into index and or categorical variables that capture the range of possible economic conditions and economic change of a community.

Demographic variables that define minority groups and changes in their proportion of the general population include: nationality, race and ethnicity. Given the complexity of determining a minority/majority status based on nationality, race/ethnicity in Europe, the number of immigrants and the change in the number of immigrants in a community may be important. This can be done, perhaps, in conjunction with nationality, race and/or ethnicity. The effort is to identify a 'minority' or 'minorities'.

The indicators associated with human resource and social capital referenced in this chapter are only suggestive. Other demographic variables related to community resources can also be used to determine human resource and social capital and are not limited to: levels of education in a community; or the proportion of at-risk children, and; the occupation of residents. For example, this chapter shows, the proportion of people in a community over a specific age who are college graduates in a community; or how many in a specific age range are without a high school degree. The number of at-risk children is a computed variable based on, for example, the number of children with more than one of the following characteristics: being a non-primary language speaker, a child in poverty, a child with a single parent, a minority child. School drop-outs are also becoming an important measure, particularly in association with test scores and graduation rates. The predominant occupation type of individuals within a community would also allow for interesting determinations of community SES.

Additionally school finance variables linked to communities are very important for equity work or studies of disparity. These can be expense and/or revenue variables. However, these finance data are best when variations in value over time, currency, cost of living, and if possible cost of education, are incorporated. Revenue variables are very helpful in determining funding policies, as long as they are collected and reported at various political levels, such as the local community, state and or nation.

A system like this can be very effective associated with education outcomes such as test scores and graduation rates. Or perhaps most appropriately education outcomes are only fairly understood when presented in the context a good community indicator system can provide. There were no test score outcomes associated with this system, as it is only very recently that national test scores (National Assessment of Educational Progress, NAEP) could be aggregated to a district level. However, trials indicate that, when "peer" districts are created based on similar combinations of urbanicity, minority status and or economics as are being outlined here, they demonstrate significant educational test score differences. There are also regional differences in test scores for these "peers." Additional background data, very much like the indicators presented here, also provide important context to these scores.

This system of indicators allows us to create community based assessments of economic status and economic change, and, as demonstrated here, are very useful in comparing community financial, human and social capital resources. All of these are vitally related to the quality of schools and the education they deliver. Of some interest perhaps, given the inclusion of 'justice' as a theoretic framework for education equity (Demeuse, Chapters 3 & 5) and because of the possible range and diversity of communities that can be captured with this system, are social justice indicators that would allow for interesting comparisons between, for example, the elite, the middle class, the working class and the poor.

Notes

1 Traub, J., "What No School Can Do, The New York Times," 1/16/00.
2 See "The reasons for the disparities," p. 347.
3 *Education Week's* Quality Counts '98 issue was entitled "The Urban Challenge: Public Education in the 50 States."
4 Mega-city has also been synonymous with "super-city," "giant-city," "megalopolis," which have been variously defined. Size definitions for mega-cities range from 4 to 10 million (Gilbert, 1998).
5 Central cities have the denser populations and tend to have more difficult economics.
6 Suburban districts are denser than rural-metro districts and when combined with less favorable economic change experience population migrations and school funding changes similar to central city districts.
7 See discussion on "state capacity" in the Background section of this chapter.
8 See Table 3, this chapter.
9 The economic change of metropolitan school districts is a good proxy for the district level contribution to GDP. The variable (STECON) is the aggregate of this school district proxy for GDP and is itself a good proxy for state domestic product or a state's contribution to GDP.
10 Unless both the city and the suburban communities have experienced declining economies.
11 Reduced class size has been found to significantly improve student outcomes and the results are most dramatic for minority students. See Cochrane, Chapter 4, in this volume.

References

Alexander N., "The Growth of Education Revenues from 1981–82 to 1991–92: What Accounts for Differences Among States?" *Journal of Education Finance, 22*, pp. 435–63, Spring 1997.
Anjon J., *Ghetto Schooling: A political economy of urban educational reform*, Teachers College Press, New York, 1997.
Baldi S., et al., *International Education Indicators: A time series perspective 1985–1995*, National Center for Education Statistics, Washington, DC, 2000.

Berques J., "New Minority Groups in the Citadel of Europe," *General Report of a Multidisciplinary Conference on the Educational and Cultural Aspects of Community Relations*, Council for Cultural Cooperation, Strasbourg, France, 1991.

Boos-Nunning U., Hohmann M., "The educational situation of migrant workers' children in the Federal Republic of Germany," in Eldering L., Kloprogge J. (eds.), *Different Cultures Same Schools: Ethnic minority children in Europe*, Swets & Zeitlinger, Amsterdam, 1989.

Clune W., "The Shift from Equity to Adequacy in School Finance," *Educational Policy*, *4*, pp. 376–394, December 1994.

Cochrane D., "Power and Place: Metropolitan resource struggles in the U.S.: 1980–90," *International Journal of Education Reform*, April 1999.

Cochrane D., "Metropolitan School District Revenues during the 1980s: Did central cities get more?" Education Finance and Governance SIG conference papers, AERA, San Diego (Calif.), Spring 1998a.

Cochrane D., " Metropolitan School District Revenues: 1980–90," conference papers, AEFA, Mobile (Ala.), Spring 1998b.

Cochrane D., *American School Desegregation: 1980, A Comparative Regional Investigation of Outcomes,* dissertation, University of Buffalo, 1995.

Coleman J., et al., *Equality of Educational Opportunity*, U.S. Government Printing Office, Washington, DC, 1966.

Coleman J., Hoffer T., Kilgore S., *Public, Catholic and Private High Schools Compared*, Basic Books, New York, 1982.

Coleman J., Hoffer T., *Public and Private Schools: The impact of community*, Basic Books, New York, 1987.

Costa-Lascoux J., "Immigrant Children in French Schools: Equality or discrimination," in Eldering L., Kloprogge J. (eds.), *Different Cultures Same Schools: Ethnic minority children in Europe*, Swets & Zeitlinger, Amsterdam, 1989.

Eldering L., "Ethnic Minority Children in Dutch Schools: Underachievement and its explanations," in Eldering L., Kloprogge J. (eds.), *Different Cultures Same Schools: Ethnic minority children in Europe*, Swets & Zeitlinger, Amsterdam, 1989.

Extra G., "Ethnic Minorities, Language Diversity, and Educational Implications: A case study on the Netherlands*," Toegepaste Taalwetenschap in Artikelen* (Applied Linguistics in Articles), *35*, pp. 45–71, 1990.

Gilbert A., "World Cities and the Urban Future: The view from Latin America," in Lo F., Yeung Y. (eds.), *Globalization and the World of Large Cities*, United Nations University Press, Tokyo, New York, Paris, 1998.

Kunzmann K., "World City Regions in Europe: Structural change and future challenges," in Lo F., Yeung Y. (eds.), *Globalization and the World of Large Cities*, United Nations University Press, Tokyo, New York, Paris, 1998.

Lo F., Yeung Y., "Introduction" in Lo F., Yeung Y. (eds.), *Globalization and the World of Large Cities*, United Nations University Press, Tokyo, New York, Paris, 1998.

Maslow A., *Motivation and Personality* (2nd ed.), Harper & Row, New York, 1970.

National Research Council, *Making Money Matter: Financing America's schools,* Committee on Education Finance, Ladd H., Hansen J. (eds.), Commission on Behavioral and Social Sciences and Education, National Academy Press, Washington, DC, 1999a.

National Research Council, *How People Learn: Brain, Mind Experience, and School,* Committee on Developments in the Science of Learning, Bransford J., Brown A., Cocking R. (eds.), Commission on Behavioral and Social Sciences and Education, National Academy Press, Washington, DC, 1999b.

Orfield, G. "Asking the Right Question," *Educational Policy*, *8*, pp. 404–413, 1994.

Orfield, G., Yunn., *Resegregation in American Schools*, The Civil Rights Project, Harvard, 1999.

Orfield M. *Metropolitics: A Regional Agenda for Community Stability*, Brookings Institution, Washington, DC, 1997.

Orland M., Cohen, C., "Meeting the Challenges of Devolution. How Changing Demographics and Fiscal Contexts Affect State Investments in Education," *Advances in Educational Productivity*, 6, pp. 101–125, 1996.

Pelavin Research Institute and American Institutes of Research, *Investing in School Technology: Strategies to meet the funding challenge,* Office of Educational Technology, U.S. Department of Education, Washington, DC, 1997.

Phelps R., Smith T., Alsalam A., *Education in States and Nations: Indicators comparing U.S. states with other industrialized countries in 1991*, National Center for Education Statistics, Washington, DC, 1996.

Roosens E., "Cultural Ecology and Achievement Motivation: Ethnic minority youngsters in the Belgian system," in Eldering L., Kloprogge J. (eds.), *Different Cultures Same Schools: Ethnic minority children in Europe*, Swets & Zeitlinger, Amsterdam, 1989.

Salganik L., et al., *Education in States and Nations: Indicators comparing U.S. states with the OECD countries in 1988*, National Center for Education Statistics, Washington, DC, 1993.

Sharpe W., Wallock L., "Bold New City or Built-Up Burb?: Redefining contemporary suburbia," *American Quarterly*, March 1994.

Tomlinson S., " Ethnicity and Educational Achievement in Britain," in Eldering L., Kloprogge J. (eds.), *Different Cultures Same Schools: Ethnic minority children in Europe*, Swets & Zeitlinger. Amsterdam, 1989.

Veld T., " Urban Education Issues in the Netherlands," in Coulby C. et al. (eds.), *Urban Education: World Yearbook of Education*, *1999*, Kogan Page, London, 1992.

Yueng Y., Lo F., "Globalization and World City Formation in Pacific Asia," in Lo F., Yueng Y. (eds.), *Globalization and the World of Large Cities*, United Nations University Press, Tokyo, New York, Paris, 1998.

United States General Accounting Office, *State and Federal Efforts to Target Poor Students: A report to congressional requesters*, Health Education and Human Services Division, Washington, DC, January 1998.

Index